Flamboyant Fictions

The Failed Art of Passing

Ian Fleishman

NORTHWESTERN UNIVERSITY PRESS
EVANSTON, ILLINOIS

Northwestern University Press
www.nupress.northwestern.edu

Printed in the United States of America

10 9 8 7 6 5 4 3 2 1

Library of Congress Cataloging-in-Publication Data

Names: Fleishman, Ian Thomas, author.
Title: Flamboyant fictions : the failed art of passing / Ian Fleishman.
Description: Evanston, Illinois : Northwestern University Press, 2024. | Includes bibliographical references and index.
Identifiers: LCCN 2024031407 | ISBN 9780810148031 (paperback) | ISBN 9780810148048 (cloth) | ISBN 9780810148055 (ebook)
Subjects: LCSH: Passing (Identity) in motion pictures. | Passing (Identity) in literature. | Gay men in motion pictures. | Gay men in literature. | Gay men—Identity. | Motion pictures—20th century—History and criticism. | Motion pictures—21st century—History and criticism. | French literature—20th century—History and criticism.
Classification: LCC PN1995.9.H55 F57 2024 | DDC 791.436552—dc23/eng/20240812
LC record available at https://lccn.loc.gov/2024031407

for Rumur

Flamboyant Fictions

CONTENTS

ACKNOWLEDGMENTS

It was Robert Deam Tobin, a colleague of unparalleled generosity and good spirit, who first emboldened me, at an embarrassingly late date in my academic trajectory, to engage with queer studies—modeling what it might look like to be out as an academic, not only personally but professionally. (Not that anyone would have mistaken me for closeted before.) I liked the look: confident and informed, serious and playful, daring, often mischievous, often flippant, kind and unapologetic. I can't claim to embody too many of these qualities myself with any regularity, but I remain acutely grateful for the goal.

An early draft of chapter 3 was delivered at Bob's invitation at Clark University in October of 2019, and I was fortunate to have the opportunity to workshop that material further in a lecture at Brown University a few days later. My thanks especially to Zachary Sng, Dominik Zechner, Kristina Mendicino, and Thomas Schestag for an enjoyable and incisive conversation afterward. A first draft toward this chapter had been authored a year prior for a panel on queer failure organized by Ervin Malakaj and Javier Samper Vendrell, providing important context and bringing contour to a still just nascent book project. Coteaching that semester with Naomi Waltham-Smith provided additional ear training in sound studies and deconstructive thought.

Other conference panels on body beautification and the anatomy of injury—one virtually during the pandemic, another in-person in the Netherlands—allowed me to test out aspects of chapter 4 in dialogue with Rosemarie Brucher, Adrian Daub, Sabine Doran, Simone Stirner, Lauren Stone, Nicole Sütterlin, Kaliane Ung, and others. Chapter 6 was developed in part as guest lectures, and enriched by the ensuing discussions, for classes at Ohio University and Wagner College at the invitation of Erin Schlumpf and Katica Urbanc. Dominik Zechner was, as always, also a keen interlocutor at a workshop at Princeton University organized by Paul Babinski, Benjamin Bernard, and Emily Rutherford, where I presented a sketch of portions of chapter 1. Exchanges with Ian Beacock, Daniel Hoffmann-Schwartz, Carlos Kong, and Barbara Nagel on that occasion are surely reflected here. In the final stages of writing, I was particularly honored to share the whole of chapter 4 as the keynote for a conference at New York University organized by Aviv Hilbig-Bokaer and Francesco Mercuri. I am indebted to all who attended for a weekend of intense and fruitful dialogue, to Aviv for his flattering faith and ongoing encouragement, and to Francesco for an illuminating discussion about Georgette Dee.

This monograph was made possible by two semester-long research leaves, one in 2019 and another in 2023, both spent between Berlin and Paris. In Germany I was hosted each time by the Institute for Cultural Inquiry, and I have been touched by the hospitality, curiosity, and enthusiasm of the staff and fellows there, especially Claudia Peppel, Lele Gragnolati, and Christoph Holzhey. Thanks also to Gerrit Thies for his assistance in consulting various materials surrounding Rainer Werner Fassbinder's *Querelle* at the Deutsche Kinemathek.

Memorable moments during various European sojourns include an exhibition on Elfi Mikesch, Rosa von Praunheim, and Werner Schroeter at the Akademie der Künste, which I had the pleasure of attending with Simon Richter, and another at the Haus der Kulturen der Welt on Ulrike Ottinger's Parisian period, where Larry Rickels introduced me briefly to Ottinger herself as well as to Mikesch in passing. An enlightening chat with Riccardo Antoniani on a Belleville balcony during final revisions brought the coda and the question of accident into alignment. A Prenzlauerberg dinner discussion with Erica Weitzman on writerly bluster and bravado helped further hone my understanding of flamboyance as intentionally self-deflating overinsistence.

A faculty fellowship to participate in the Wolf Humanities Center's forum on the topic choice in 2020 and 2021 allowed me to research and refine my thinking on queer agency, and I am grateful to the participants in that yearlong seminar for their erudition, acumen, and, more than anything, patient feedback on an onerous early draft of my introduction. Additional commendations are owed to Sophia Rosenfeld and Karen Redrobe for so expertly facilitating these discussions. And my most heartfelt thanks go to Karen, in particular, for her continued mentorship and unflagging support of both this project and myself.

Generously braving this same unwieldly methodological introduction, CJ Jones instantly homed in on and helped me to identify the notion of *failed passing* as the study's central concern and most operable concept— although it took many months for that insight fully to register. Scholarship itself, CJ suggested, and not only queer scholarship, can be a form of failed passing: we emulate the same influences from whom we seek to distinguish ourselves, marking the novelty of our own projects and approaches in contradistinction to those whose successes we most desire to replicate and to rival. A Hershey Humanities Development Workshop in the fall of 2021 aided me in finally overcoming—at least enough, apparently, to see the book to completion—my own fears of failing to pass as a queer theorist. I am grateful to Sara Varney and Jamal Elias for coordinating and hosting at the Wolf Humanities Center and deeply indebted to the participants in that workshop for a rich, critical, and bolstering colloquy: Julia Alekseyeva, Hamit Arvas, Tim Corrigan, André Dombrowski, Kathryn Hellerstein, Jonathan Katz, Heather Love, Meta Mazaj, Rahul Mukherjee, Kevin Platt, Melissa Sanchez, Filippo Trentin, Liliane Weissberg, Dag Woubshet, and Chenshu Zhou, to list just those not mentioned elsewhere. Michael Lucey, our invited respondent, lent a magisterial presence and encyclopedic knowledge to the whole affair; it was a true pleasure to get to know a scholar whose work I have long admired and whose influence is palpable especially in this volume's early chapters.

Additional thanks are owed to Iggy Cortez, who debated and helped define many aspects of my thinking; to Adam Sax for providing orientation as I explored new disciplinary directions; to Marco Abel, Nora Alter, Martina Bale, Gwendolyn Beetham, Siarhei Biareishyk, Pearl Brilmyer, Scott Burkhardt, Vance Byrd, Anna Corrigan, Peter Decherney, Kathy DeMarco Van Cleve, David Eng, Jennifer Fay, Jaimey Fisher, Nicola Gentili, Andrea Goulet, Corine Labridy, Jules O'Dwyer, Shannon Mattern, Philippe Met, Maria Murphy, Gerry Prince, Eric Rentschler, Jonas Rosenbrück, and many others for reasons too myriad to enumerate. Kyle Stevens was the last fresh set of eyes to read the manuscript before it went off to the publisher and provided some helpful thoughts on camp as well as the final boost of confidence required.

Cat Dawson is deserving of distinctive mention for their generative comments on different drafts of the revised introduction and for cheerfully entertaining endless variations on the title. Faith Wilson Stein's exemplary contributions as an editor go far beyond finding the final necessary tweak to the phrasing of the subtitle; she has been a joy to work with—forthright, diplomatic, personally invested, wise—and Maia Rigas, she, and everyone at Northwestern, including and especially the anonymous readers, have my gratitude.

Portions of chapter 1 previously appeared, in somewhat different form, in *French Forum* 45, no. 2 (2020): 155–69. I am grateful to the editors and to the University of Pennsylvania Press for permission to republish those passages here.

Introduction

✦

Agency as Failed Passing

The first time I can recall hearing the word *gay*, it was set to the adagietto of Mahler's Fifth Symphony. My father, my brother, and I had just finished watching Visconti's *Death in Venice* and, as the credits rolled, my father idly wondered aloud, bewildered by what we had just seen, if my piano teacher, who had suggested the film, was gay. In retrospect, I'm somewhat surprised that the response was so mild. My father proceeded to list, by way of speculation, other acquaintances who were, or might be, gay. At no point in this conversation, or in any conversation, was it explained to me what gay meant. Or rather, I understood from this composite sketch *exactly* what it meant: to be a loner, to be artistic, to play the organ at a local church, to have halitosis and a taste in foreign films that made me deeply, uncannily uncomfortable. It meant to be, like Dirk Bogarde's Gustav von Aschenbach, ridiculously made up as a fop, feverish and sickly, perpetually overdressed for the weather, black hair dye dripping down your cheek (fig. 1). It would never have occurred to me that it had anything to do with desire. I'm a slow learner.

There is another aspect to this film that surely must have bothered me: its disembodied voices. *Death in Venice* is awash with sound, lushy layered with incomprehensibly faint dialogue in various languages, its actors dubbed by detached speech, making almost no attempt, it seems, to match the movements of their mouths—tough viewing for a child of ten at most. As the camera alternates between exceedingly long takes and impossible points of view, the dissonance of acousmatic conversations and decontextualized voice-overs makes Aschenbach appear at once continuously out of step with his own story, oddly independent from its trajectory, and yet ineluctably fated to its abject end.

✦

This book posits narrative flamboyance as an index for evolving expressions of male homosexuality from the advent of literary modernism to the present day.[1] Mapping queer strategies of storytelling onto queer subjectivities' practices of self-invention, *Flamboyant Fictions: The Failed Art of*

Fig. 1. Gustav von Aschenbach (Dirk Bogarde) failing to pass as a younger man. From *Morte a Venezia* (*Death in Venice*, dir. Luchino Visconti, 1971).

Passing exposes a form of authorial counterfeiting in gay film and literature continuing forward from roughly around the same historical moment that homosexuality in its contemporary form begins to emerge as a recognizable identity category. I wager that it is precisely in instances of conflict between these authors and their inventions that narrative becomes a laboratory for testing the sovereignty and self-determination of queer identity.

In their various depictions of homosexuality, the novelists and film directors discussed in this volume repeatedly problematize questions of creative restriction or stylistic restraint, and frequently with pyrotechnic flair—highlighting their own failure to tell more persuasive tales, to give more plausible accounts. More often than not it is precisely those authors and auteurs who resist linear narrative and work to *de*form established forms to whom we turn in our search for historically queer identity formations-in-(un)becoming. Refusing seamless diegesis, the narrative tradition excavated by this book is perpetually losing track of its own inventions, relinquishing control over its characters, gleefully renouncing any mastery over the (re)imagined subjectivities and sexualities it has set in motion. This book thus exposes a tradition of flamingly *failed passing* that is itself a surreptitious mode of passing: the flaunting of queer style as an intentionally unconvincing cover for queer content.

Flamboyant Fictions constitutes an unexpected continuum ranging from the literary modernism of André Gide and Jean Genet to the German New Wave represented by Werner Schroeter and Rainer Werner Fassbinder, onward to the New French Extremity but also the comedic registers of François Ozon, as well as, finally, the more millennial zeitgeist symptomatized by Quebec's Xavier Dolan. Correlating these authors' and filmmakers' frequent emphasis on the arbitrariness of their narrative choices to the purported eccentricity of their sexualities, my project seeks to demonstrate the continued pertinence of gay modernist paradigms of subjectivity to the critical study of postmodern and contemporary minoritarian politics and aesthetics.

This book explores, then, how gay novelists and filmmakers historically negotiate between contingency and control—alternating between, on the one hand, uncommon admissions of narrative accident or constraint and, on the other, an insistence on the arbitrariness of authorial interventions into their plots. Correlating this double gesture to the willful self-fashioning of queer identities, to an explicit program of self-forgery within these texts, I theorize a mode of obstinately failed passing through which male homosexuality is offered as an insoluble contradiction, as an inconsistent and intentionally unconvincing imposture.

At stake in this paradigm of failed passing is an underlying conviction, shared to some degree by all of the figures treated here, that queer authenticity requires of the artwork that it remain rough around the edges: unpersuasive, hyperbolic, tactless, out of measure. Proffering the queer self as a spontaneous and subversive coinage, these texts struggle, over the course of a century or so, from modernist literature to contemporary cinema, with the risk of that identity's eventual devaluation into a codified and widely circulated currency—nothing but a token of the novelty that once was. What this anxiety reveals is that, despite its denaturalizing impulse, such self-counterfeiting never entirely succeeds in sidestepping essentializing epistemologies: at once embodied and abstracted, these counterfeit identities distill themselves into mere mannerism while at the same time insisting that there is nothing truer or more real than such self-fabrication. They occupy the interstices between the self and its performance, between affect and affectation. Failed passing of this sort asserts a prerogative to sexuality—but sometimes at the price of its direct display. It demands rather to be seen, and to be seen as deviation, while at once diverting the gaze from an implied and purportedly more secret self.

✦

What struck me, even as a child, about Visconti, for example, was a kind of spectacular self-effacement: for all of that film's ostentatious outness, I couldn't crack the code. Or rather I only had the code itself without knowing what it meant. I was conscripted into a language I didn't understand, condemned to be a cypher to and of myself.

The bourgeois pretentions of this particular queer origin story are not lost on me and imply, I think, a somewhat different model of disidentification than the one so influentially outlined by José Esteban Muñoz in his book on the subject.[2] As I will discuss more thoroughly in chapter 2, for Muñoz, disidentifying is a means by which queers of color recycle racist, phobic stereotypes, redirecting them into more affirming avenues of self-realization. But in my case there was also a profound *de*realization in being identified with such a visibly invisible cliché:[3] the relative privilege of Visconti so publicly airing his sexual fantasies under the auspices of art relies on an open conceit of plausible nondetection, on the mythic possibility of passing.

I'm not saying that self-abstraction (into the template of established identity categories) isn't part of disidentification for *all* minoritarian subjects—I think it is—but rather that being otherwise unmarked might help Visconti, like most of the figures treated in this book, to vanish in this way, if always precariously, to hide out in the open—a dynamic Eve Kosofsky Sedgwick might describe as an open secret.[4] As I remember someone once cheekily describing a now-defunct line of homoerotic or queer coming-of-age films dubbed into English for American home distribution: "It's not gay, it's European!"[5] My interpellation into counterculture had managed to market itself as an entrance into art cinema and, by arrogant extension, into supposed high culture tout court. Visconti somehow passed as polite company—not by attenuating his film's oddities, its decadence and morbid romanticism, but instead precisely by playing up the weirdness of his work. Rather than attempting to remain unmarked as gay or even as grotesque, he had redirected attention elsewhere through a filmic sleight of hand, a fabulous swish of the auteurist wrist.

✦

I employ the term *passing* here in its conventional—and colloquial—sense: to pass as straight, for instance, as white, as nondisabled, as cisgendered. While queer theoretical work on passing is surprisingly scant, it is, as Linda Schlossberg puts it in the introduction to *Passing: Identity and Interpretation in Sexuality, Race, and Religion* (2001), nevertheless a question at the very origins of the discipline, "a critical conversation on queer identity, structured by the twin issues of the closet (Eve Sedgwick) and performativity (Judith Butler)."[6] Over the past decades, scholarly discourse has frequently come to celebrate passing as a potential form of queer resistance and self-determination.[7] In her introduction to a volume on *Passing and the Fictions of Identity* (1996), for example, Elaine Ginsberg praises its de-essentializing implications: "Both the process and the discourse of passing interrogate the ontology of identity categories and their construction."[8] Or, to quote Pamela Caughie, who goes so far as to assert that all subjectivity is passing, "Contemporary critics have come to reconceive of passing as a performative practice. . . . The conception of passing as dishonesty, deception or betrayal is produced by the very problem of identity to which the practice of passing is the solution."[9] Which is to say that the autofictional quality of passing reveals identity itself to be a performative and potentially pernicious fiction.[10] More recently, in an insightful examination of the self-presentation of bisexual women, Jessa Lingel explores the "conception of passing as freedom via deliberate self-displacement" and proposes passing, although not unambivalently, as a possible form of queer agency—a view I intend to build upon, but also to complicate, in what follows.[11]

After all, passing is not always volitional or even entirely conscious, nor is it always successful. In an autoethnographic account of his self-described experience as a black, non-operative, no-hormone transsexual, C. Riley Snorton pushes back against the traditional view of passing as "a deceitful practice" in order to demonstrate how the "psychic act of passing is an essential part of what it means to know myself."[12] Challenging the interdiction against passing at the core of Sandy Stone's foundational "Posttranssexual Manifesto,"[13] and arguing instead for an attention to passing cognizant of its frequent disappointments, Snorton cautions that

> for the vast majority of transsexuals who are not able to "pass" all the time, passing is not simply a question of how one is read but includes an agential power of affirming one's own reading of self. Definitions of passing therefore must also include its psychological function, that is, that it brings one's "self" into view. Through the experiences of psychic dissonance, affirmation, disavowal, and recognition, we engage in the process of passing off our daily experiences of embodiment as identifications—creating "fragile fictions" of personhood. Therefore passing is not simply the essence of transsexualism; it is the way we make identity.[14]

It is especially important to acknowledge the fragility and instability of the experience Snorton outlines here—the "identifications . . . formed by passing through identity and passing back into it."[15] As (un)persuasive as its execution may be in any given case or context, the very possibility of passing ultimately and invariably plays into the same fictions of identity it troubles.

For Snorton such dissonances and disavowals are part and parcel of "the person I know myself to be: a black body, misread, spectacularized, and often confusing to others. . . . As a trans man often read as a little boy or a butch lesbian, I . . . confront the 'failure' of my masculinity—one that I understand as both queer and male."[16] And it is here that the psychological focus of his argument becomes important: if we regard passing not solely as an attempt to manage the perception of one's self by others but rather also as a form of *self*-presentation, indeed as the very basis of selfhood, then such apparent failures come into view not as the antonym of passing but as themselves *a form of passing*, if not even as its ur-form. "On the numerous occasions where I am read as a cisgender woman," he continues, "passing becomes a necessary mechanism to understand these situations as not simply a failure to present as the gender I recognize myself to be, but also as instances of passing. These moments of passing (of visibility and misrecognition) for a woman become the substance (a process of dissonance and disidentification) of my own psychic recognition as a trans man."[17] Difference here precedes identity: it is within this gap between self-perception and perception-by-others that the self must assert itself. The theory of failed passing offered by this volume similarly understands such infelicitous occurrences not in opposition to paradigms of passing but instead as within their purview—indeed even as the requisite structuring precondition for the forms of self-determination that the practice of passing might make possible.[18]

For what if agency were born not of freedom but rather of constraint, as Judith Butler suggests as early as the inaugural issue of *GLQ: A Journal of Lesbian and Gay Studies* (where Snorton currently serves as an editor) and again, in an expanded version of the same essay, toward the conclusion of *Bodies That Matter: On the Discursive Limits of Sex* (1993). Assessing—at this (self-)defining moment in the history of queer inquiry—the efficacy and political potential of the then still fairly recent reclamation of the appellation *queer*, Butler rejects "the conceit of autonomy implied by self-naming" and instead seeks to excavate the discursive history "through which a queer and queering agency is forged and reworked." As Butler has it, "To recast queer agency in this chain of historicity is thus to avow a set of constraints . . . that mark at once the *limits* of agency and its most *enabling conditions*."[19] If this passage scans, given the context, almost as a manifesto on the possibilities and restrictions governing the self-invention of contemporary queer studies, the writers and filmmakers treated throughout the present volume will all participate in this conceit of self-creation ex nihilo while at once, and perhaps not unparadoxically, emphasizing the limitations of such autogenesis. As flamboyant as their narratological and stylistic innovations may be, after all, this book submits that these also serve as a coping mechanism—sometimes rebellious, sometimes playfully resigned—for the inhibitions placed on self-invention.

This apparent paradox requires us to take a different view toward what we might call queer free will: one that locates agency not in an originary act but rather in the discrepancies between iterations of a socially prescribed role and in the (sometimes slight, sometimes more pronounced) aberrations that haunt citations of an assigned or chosen identity category. *Bodies That Matter* offers a few such caveats regarding the view of drag that emerged from readings and critiques of Butler's earlier *Gender Trouble: Feminism and the Subversion of Identity* (1990), marking boundaries to the perceived voluntarism of that account.[20] It is not, Butler now more vigorously clarifies, that the gendered subject creates itself by virtue of sheer neologism but rather that it defines itself through contestation of the existing terms of discourse.

As the disorderly narratives and disobedient literary characters treated in *Flamboyant Fictions* will demonstrate, this process is no more equivalent to pure self-sovereignty than it is tantamount to absolute predetermination. This is a needle Butler tries to thread by attending to how established tropes—in the sense of gender norms—are resignified in practice through their adoption and adaptation and by thus exposing "the workings of an agency" reducible neither to voluntarism nor to social or biological determinism.[21] Arguing that sexual identities emerge as imperfect citations of received tropes (recognizable rhetorical patterns, recurring motifs), Butler's early work suggests that individual autonomy is at most a form of catachresis: a misuse or strained usage of an established figure of speech. It is not that we invent ourselves out of nothing nor that our identifications are fully compulsory. Instead, we find ourselves—or engender ourselves—in this margin of error.

If free will or freedom of choice emerges first as an inaccurate, distorted, or unconvincing citation, then it makes sense to understand agency itself, queer or otherwise, not as passing per se but rather as a form of *failed* passing, as willful or involuntary as this failure might be.[22] Butler's rhetorical description of this process of miscitation of an imposed or expected norm as catachresis invites us further to consider the stylistic innovations of the authors and auteurs under consideration in the chapters to follow as themselves identity-performative deviations governed by but not entirely beholden to established narrative convention: queer style itself as an instance of failed passing and as a matter of identity.[23]

Flamboyant Fictions will therefore explore what Eve Kosofsky Sedgwick once optimistically described as the undertheorized "middle ranges of agency"—which she hoped might carve out space between the reproduction of existing ideologies and their potential revision.[24] Ellen Samuels notes in the context of disability that "condemnations of passing often conflate two dynamics: passing deliberately (as implied by the term *hidden*) and passing by default, as it were."[25] Or, as Caughie specifies, "while . . . passing happens because of the choices we make, it is not itself a choice." And this is in part due to the plasticity of the term, with its various semantic associations:[26] "The distinction between passing as a conscious practice and passing as an inevitable condition of subjectivity in postmodernity is never sure; for to fix that distinction would be to insist on a kind of control and certainty that my reconceptualization of 'passing' is meant to call into question. There is a constant slippage between conscious and unconscious passing and between passing as a deliberate practice and passing as the experience of subjectivity."[27] Attributing full lucidity to the practice of passing suggests a stable subject to be presented with varying degrees of authenticity, whereas recognizing its frequently unconscious nature reveals passing itself as the very site of the subject's emergence. To my mind the notion of *failed* passing better problematizes such questions of self-determination by revealing surprising and sometimes discomfiting continuities between involuntary affect and deliberate affectation, between automatism and apparent autonomy.

These are tensions that will characterize not only the literary and filmic works treated throughout this study but also the theoretical discourses in which it hopes to intervene. To feel interpellated by a term like *queer* is inevitably also to perform, to imitate, and to embody it—and always to ambivalent ends.[28] If the revaluation of such stigmatizing designations wrests them from their original connotations to potentially subversive effect, it also remains fundamentally dependent on and to some extent problematically derivative of the sense of abjection it repurposes. Such self-hatred is the flipside of the fantasy of self-determination through nonconformity: the idea that we might not be in control of ourselves or our projected selves, that we might give ourselves away.

Not only does citational performativity, in Butler's sense, necessarily flirt with the confirmation of uncomfortable clichés by echoing the very interpellative terms it seeks to contest, but—ever alert to the perils and the promise of failed passing—it also ineluctably invites speculations of insincerity and inauthenticity that plague both the historical emergence of male homosexuality as a legible identity category (as I'll explore especially in chapters 1 and 2) and, more surprisingly, certain strands of recent queer theory (as I intend to demonstrate at the outset of chapter 3). This is in part because it is difficult to imagine any earnest convergence of essence and expression if identity is always dependent on the possibility of parody: the gap between citation and resignification entails a fissure in the subject. Beyond revealing queer agency to be responsive to and always already anticipatory of homophobic disdain, the origin of this agency in such worries and feelings of failure complicates the deontologizing task attributed to passing by so much of the extant scholarship: its self-displacements continue to imply the absent presence of a preexisting self to be displaced.

Counterfeit Identities

Historically, after all, the phenomenon of passing, be it sexual or racial, has been viewed mistrustfully, with predictable panic over the doubt it casts on the ostensibly immutable, bedrock ontology of selfhood. As Schlossberg has it, "The passing subject's ability to transcend or abandon his or her 'authentic' identity calls into question the very notion of authenticity itself. Passing, it seems, threatens to call attention to the performative and contingent nature of all seemingly 'natural' or 'obvious' identities."[29] Testifying to the persistence of such anxieties surrounding passing, the editors of a more recent volume on the subject still find it indispensable, for example, to distinguish "accidental traits that can change over time without affecting the person's identity" from purportedly "essential properties."[30] But this is precisely the kind of distinction undermined by the ontology of accident to be documented in *Flamboyant Fictions*—where an idea, once imagined, becomes *true*.

Building on the work of Cheryl Wall and many others to expand discussions of passing beyond initial associations with race to gender, sexuality, and other identity markers, Anna Camaiti Hostert helpfully sums up such lingering suspicions of inauthenticity in language resonant with the title above: "The institutionalized view has been to see passing as a negation of subjectivity, read as the denial of one's essential racial self. . . . Passing is to present oneself as something that one is not; it is a matter of violating the laws of identity and sameness. In so viewing passing as deception, as an individual assuming a *counterfeit identity*, the tendency has been to understand passing as racial self-hatred."[31] On this account passing would be of a piece with tropes of fakery and artifice closely tied to phobic insecurities emerging early on with regard to male homosexuality, as I will begin to explore in my opening chapters on novels by André Gide and Jean Genet. As Camaiti Hostert continues, "There is a certain language or semantic of passing: passing as being an impostor, as being a fake, as being an infiltrator, as being opportunistic, as pretending, as concealing and as simulating. This semantic of passing operates in accordance with a logic grounded in a reality and appearance distinction. Hence, passing is a matter of taking the appearance for reality."[32] It is, initially, just this conflation of appearance and reality—or, more pointedly, the refusal to privilege the latter over the former—that is celebrated by the authors and filmmakers treated in this book. The self is not a given, they implicitly insist, but an artwork, a performance, although no less *real* because of it.

Taking Gide's *Les faux-monnayeurs* (*The Counterfeiters*, 1927) as its point of departure, chapter 1, "Counterfeit Narratives: André Gide's Queer Coinages," demonstrates how the novel's rival narrating voices negotiate conflicting modes of literary modernism as they relate to the representation of male homosexuality. Though on the surface something else entirely, Gide's *Faux-monnayeurs* is, I will argue, at base a frustrated pornographic fantasy—a quality it shares with most of the works treated in this study. Variously transparent in terms of narrative disguise, it is sometimes more acutely in this sense of erotic dissimulation than as overt plots about uncloseting that these flamboyant fictions thematize passing and its failures: the narratological novelty of Gide's text, for instance, consists in its capricious and surprisingly tacit approach to insinuating same-sex desire, which serves as the book's not-so-secret but nonetheless unspoken center. Paying particular attention to Gide's reputedly unimportant passing comments and affectedly offhand remarks will expose this strategy as a *poetics of failed passing*—revealing as it conceals, insistently and conflictingly remaining at once marked and unmarked, visible and invisible. What I will theorize as a form of narrative forgery in Gide suggests that both identity and art are a matter of make-believe made real: self-determination is figured as a narrative whim granted ontological weight not despite but rather precisely because of its arbitrariness. This paradigm sets a precedent, I will argue at the conclusion of the chapter, for queer studies' continued commitment to perpetual self-reinvention.

If homosexuality in Gide is sometimes a game of hide-and-seek, for Jean Genet, it is almost always explicit, and more often than not obscenely so. While Genet insisted throughout his life that sexuality itself is not a choice, sexual identity in his work is nevertheless a matter of willful and provocative performance. Chapter 2, "Counterfeit Sexualities: Performativity in Jean

Genet," treats the author's debut novel, *Notre-Dame-des-Fleurs* (*Our Lady of the Flowers*, 1943), in which Genet fantasizes the theatrical self-reinvention of Divine, a drag queen of the Parisian demimonde, as a foil for his own fictionalized autobiography. An excavation of formal caprice in Genet further exposes how the elasticity and lability of what we have come to understand as queer has been historically constituted by a modernist gambit of narrative forgery.

Metaleptic tensions in Genet's text between the narrator and his inventions—including implicit disputes between the author and Divine regarding her gender identity—point up both the arbitrary but also and especially the constrained aspects of artistic invention, elaborating a mode of queer self-creation that is perhaps more autonomic than autonomous. Despite the gratuitously and graphically masturbatory impulse of his fiction, Genet repeatedly confesses to his dissatisfaction with this erotic fantasy, to his inability to get it right. The failed passings of Genet's characters in this novel, I argue, are paradigmatic for his narrative approach to the limited invention of the ever-imperfected self, which haunts the text as a specter and which can only be unified through the impossible fantasies and implausible contrivances of fiction. Counterfeit identities of the kind explored here turn out, then, to be essentializing on both ends: at once in the ostensible ontology insistently assumed by forged identities but also by the inherent restrictions of the apparently inalterable autobiographical self—which is to say, both through passing and its failures.[33]

Embodied Abstraction

If passing is, as Jessa Lingel rightly emphasizes, "inextricably tied to the physicality of the body,"[34] it is also true, as Elaine Ginsberg has it, that "passing forces reconsideration of the cultural logic that the physical body is the site of identic intelligibility."[35] But beginning with Sedgwick's *Touching Feeling: Affect, Pedagogy, Performativity* (2002, collecting work from the previous decade), and in what Heather Love identifies as a field-shifting "campaign to seize queer studies by the root," the discipline has taken a decisive turn "away from the strategy of denaturalization to an emphasis on affect and embodiment."[36] Dwelling on the peculiar form of incarnation implied by the self-dissonance of failed passing, I will expose—especially in the second section of this book, but continuing into the third—how such a conceptual return to the body is paradoxically concomitant with a redefinition of queerness divorced from sexuality. The result is both an insistent embodiment and a strange sublimation: a self-contradiction paradigmatic not only for queer studies as a discipline but also for the narratives on which it draws.

Sedgwick herself announces the new attention to affect as a "distinct step to the side of the deconstructive project of analyzing apparently nonlinguistic phenomena in rigorously linguistic terms, as when Butler analyzes a particular gestural style as a variety of performative utterance."[37] In plain English: it's not always about language. Rather there is also the *body* to consider, its rhythms and its movements, its involuntary tics and spasms, its affective expressions—without instantly subsuming these into discourse, elaborating them into a universal grammar, or reducing them to rhetoric.[38]

This in turn, says Sedgwick, "requires a step to the side of antiessentialism, a relative lightening of the epistemological demand on essential truth."[39] And zooming in on this repeated vocabulary of sidestepping brings to the fore the consequences of her decision toward the end of her career to uncouple queerness from sexuality: "The thing I least want to be heard as offering here is a 'theory of homosexuality.' I have none and want none."[40] Pivoting from the question of homosexuality to one of "queerness, or queer performativity" is part of Sedgwick's further insistence that this investigation is by no means intended to provide any sort of taxonomic rubric to determine who might count as queer: "Least of all does it pretend to define the relation between queerness and same-sex love and desire."[41] Or, as Love again summarizes, "*Queer* sidesteps traditional identity categories such as gay, lesbian, and bisexual in favor of a more general category of social marginality."[42] In the introduction to her enormously impactful collection of essays, Sedgwick even expresses an amused ambivalence about this fairly desexualized contribution to the study of sexuality: "I'm rather abashed that *Touching Feeling* includes so little sex."[43] For Sedgwick, as in my first encounter with the word *gay*, queerness need not be defined has having anything to do with sex at all.

The queer mode of *camp*, as I will be arguing at the outset of chapter 3, "Camp/Abject: Queer Failure in Rainer Werner Fassbinder," is similarly desexualizing: historically it refers primarily to mannerisms and outward markers of effeminacy without necessarily referring these back to an underlying sexual preference—and only by association suggests homosexuality as such. Sexuality, in the abstract sense of an identity, has come to supplant the sexual, as pertains to identification or desire, as its own determinant parameter. With this in mind, chapter 3 posits that Fassbinder's Genet adaptation invites us to reconsider and reconfigure queer as a narrative function of self-erasure: the biographical author's disappearance into the work that bears his name.

Ever the provocateur, Fassbinder plays up the grotesquery of his source text, the quasi-pornographic *Querelle de Brest* (*Querelle of Brest*, 1947), but by further contorting Genet's already jumbled plot, the filmmaker loyally follows an instinct of narrative caprice unmistakably inscribed in the novel itself. If *Querelle* (1983) is to be considered camp, it is because it embodies the quality of failed seriousness Susan Sontag ascribes to the sensibility.[44] The film would thus also seem aptly to exemplify the titular concept of Jack Halberstam's *Queer Art of Failure* (2011), though the later theorist expresses explicit reservations about the camp tradition to which these texts (both novel and film) belong. Adapting Halberstam's understanding of queer failure to this paragon of incongruously eroticized camp will lay bare how such affected performativity, despite his hesitations, crafts itself out of abjection and as abject.

This is just part of an implicit demand of the heteronormative regime, which relies on the rejection of a constitutive border against which to define itself. In the case of the identity category treated in this book, the result is a societal requirement for gay men to occupy a dual position in the cultural imaginary: to be at once camp (desexualized, unthreatening, even sophisticated) and abject (promiscuous, predatory, dangerous, diseased)—at once the favorite fabulous gay uncle and the pervy potential pedophile. On the one hand, this affords certain gay men, arguably at the expense of their queerness, a privileged visibility and a certain measure of acceptance. But it seems to me that the uncoupling of the descriptor *queer* from questions of sex risks occluding the obverse of the coin and downplaying the difficulty of this demand and of the ever-evolving metrics of taste (which must always remain unmarked, passing) as they relate to camp as a cultural currency. If gay men get to count as cultivated it is often only at the price of undercutting this refinement through sufficiently gaudy over-the-top-ness so as to mark it plainly as new money—as the flamboyant aspect of the queer eye and its hypertrophic, histrionically exaggerated aesthetic judgment.

Such perpetually failed posturing is at once indirectly acknowledged and, I suspect, fundamentally misunderstood by Sedgwick when she asserts that a conceptual framework grounded in stigma "may get us a lot further with the cluster of phenomena generally called 'camp' than the notion of parody will."[45] While a more sensitive reader of Butler than most, Sedgwick nevertheless takes *Gender Trouble* and its "programmatic argument in favor of demystification" to be paradigmatic of the kind of "paranoid" reading practices that her own late work seeks to overcome.[46] And her reflections on shame and performativity—which first appeared in dialogue with Butler as the flagship article of the maiden issue of *GLQ* and which, alongside the essay on paranoia, come to constitute some of the major conceptual axes of Sedgwick's late work—culminate ("if parenthetically") in the curiously apophatic suggestion that

> the queer-identified practice of camp . . . may be seriously misrecognized when it is viewed, as Butler and others view it, through paranoid lenses. As we've seen, camp is most often understood as uniquely appropriate to the projects of parody, denaturalization, demystification, and mocking exposure of the elements and assumptions of a dominant culture. And the degree to which camping is motivated by love seems often to be understood mainly as the degree of its self-hating complicity with an oppressive status quo.[47]

The gesture to reclaim camp in particular as a lovingly accretive mode—rather than one complicit, by dint of parodic repetition, in the abjection that engendered it—is a privileged illustration of the kind of "reparative reading" Sedgwick comes to champion.

But if the pivotal shift of attention to affect seeks to ground the thinking of identity not in language but rather in the body, Sedgwick's repeated sidestepping of sexuality as the defining aspect of queerness and her nonessentialist view of queer identity ultimately make of it, if anything, and more than she might have recognized, an *abstraction*. Or perhaps even a euphemism, as she herself seems to suggest in another parenthetical: "('Remember the fifties?' Lily Tomlin used to ask. 'No one was gay in the fifties; they were just shy')."[48] In this manner, the sublimation of a queerness determined by sex and sexuality into one defined by social stigma corresponds to the formal abstraction of the queer subject discussed in chapter 1 and throughout this book. It gestures toward the site of a queer self but only as a cypher—one that skirts eroticism, in the contranymic sense of avoiding while remaining adjacent.

Indeed, the result of such a generalized queerness, with its sexual component placed between brackets, is at once an embodiment by way of abstraction and an abstraction by way of embodiment.[49] Chapter 4, "The Wound in Bloom: Werner Schroeter's Gay Stigmata," probes a persistent association between wounds and blossoming flowers from Genet's *Miracle de la Rose* (*Miracle of the Rose*, 1946) into Schroeter's *Der Rosenkönig* (*The Rose King*, 1986) and onward. Part of what is at stake, as framed by Rosa von Praunheim's public attack on Schroeter, is a question of the latter's purported closetedness and of mere kitsch versus what might be characterized as more oppositionally out-and-out camp filmmaking. Genet's repeated project is to transmute the body of a beautiful young man into an aesthetic and erotic object by debasing the most sanctified of iconographic traditions, namely, stigmata, through an association with anal sex; Schroeter then radicalizes but also further aestheticizes this approach. (In this sense the body horror of *Der Rosenkönig* anticipates the recourse to the corporeal, and its legacy of queer abjection, which will be at issue in the following chapter on François Ozon.) Across these texts, and despite its promise of brutal authenticity, the spectacularly wounded and pornological body ends up a locus of derealization and a surprising site of a new codification of a recognizably queer aesthetic.

Chapter 4 then continues by further examining the legacy of this injurious aesthetic in Monika Treut's *Verführung: Die grausame Frau* (*Seduction: The Cruel Woman*, 1985), codirected by Elfi Mikesch, who also served as cinematographer for Schroeter's *Rosenkönig*, and Todd Haynes's *Poison* (1991), one of the formative films of New Queer Cinema. Whereas Treut and Mikesch seem to offer a subtle critique of the notion that filmic violence might penetrate through to the real, Haynes's loose adaptation of vignettes from Genet's *Miracle de la Rose* sublimates and, to a certain extent, desexualizes this violence into its aesthetic expression: the erotic wound is gone and we are left with only flowers. Haynes expressly aspires for his early film to wed oppositional politics to avant-garde aesthetic form, even at the risk of celebrating and thus confirming a cliché of homosexual abjection at the height of the American AIDS epidemic. But by the time of Haynes's appropriation, the strategy has, if anything, become too successful, gaining currency as a standardized rhetorical token, as a recognizably homosexual style. The scale and type of circulation are probably as significant in this regard as the works themselves, and this chapter concludes by surveying the traces of this queer style in music videos by gay pop star Troye Sivan and his straight contemporary Shawn Mendes.

Collapsed in the figure of the exquisitely and erotically injured young man are the two poles of the pornographic—where the body is at its most ontologizing but also at its most imaginary. This revered form is, then, at once a sacred, spectral icon and its disavowed libidinal idolatry. Within the literary and cinematic corpus treated in this book, the universalizing tendency of such ambivalently embodied abstraction is made particularly apparent by a recurring erotic ideal: a figure I am identifying as the *off-straight twink*. At once ethereal and corporeal, exhibiting and overcoming the self-differences inherent to paradigms of passing, the romanticized trope of the off-straight pretty boy transcends contradiction in general—but most especially this specific contradiction: he can engage in homosexual activity without, through this activity, becoming gay. He is the fantasy of a self so pure it requires no uncovering, a subjectivity so absolute, so clean, it cannot be tarnished by the politics or particulars of identity. He is a metaphor brought to life: he gives substance and unity to the fiction of identity itself.

Gay slang for an attractive, slender young man, a twink is generally coded white—and this detail is hardly incidental here. Snorton and others have rightly emphasized the similarly tacit whiteness of Sedgwick's epistemologically foundational understanding of the closet for the structuring of gay-straight binaries more globally: "When Sedgwick gestures toward a universalizing (as opposed to minoritizing) view of sexuality as constitutive of ways of knowing in Western culture, her methods and objects constrain her closet theory from thinking about the axiomatic conjunctures of race and sexuality, thereby fixing whiteness as a universal condition."[50] This ethnically unmarked queerness occurs, as Sedgwick herself acknowledges, because, whereas race is (mis)taken to be visibly apparent, sexuality is not necessarily so.[51]

Ginsberg has noted that "passing is about specularity: the visible and the invisible, the seen and the unseen."[52] And the visual register of embodiment will become increasingly important as this book turns its focus to cinema—demonstrating, as Amy Robinson puts it, that the "'problem' of identity, a problem to which passing owes the very possibility of its practice, is predicated on the false promise of the visible as an epistemological guarantee."[53] It is through the sexual fantasy of the off-straight twink that the narratives discussed in the present volume arbitrate the visibility and visualization of difference and desire. We might, mutatis mutandis, situate failed passing's peculiar strategies of making itself (in)visible somewhere in between—or rather at both extremes of—what Snorton calls "the glass closet" of black sexuality (a space "marked by hypervisibility and confinement, spectacle, and speculation") and what Nicholas de Villiers proposes to term the "queer opacity" of certain prominent gay white men ("an alternative queer strategy or tactic that is not linked to an interpretation of hidden depths, concealed meanings, or a neat opposition between silence and speech").[54]

There is no paucity of racially fetishized black and brown bodies across the authors and directors under consideration: from André Gide's sex tourism in North Africa to Jean Genet's highly eroticized engagement with Palestinian refugees and the Black Panthers; from Rainer Werner Fassbinder's fraught relationships with his racialized male leads, Günther Kaufmann and El Hedi ben Salem, to the interrogation of this dynamic in François Ozon's most recent filmic tribute to the earlier director, *Peter von Kant* (2022). As this last example makes particularly apparent, these figures can and frequently do share many qualities with the youthful idols in question here. But the often otherworldly whiteness of certain of the off-straight icons observed throughout this corpus persistently fetishizes and consequently racializes them *as white*: it backhandedly makes a spectacle of the purportedly invisible, of an identity so entirely unmarked, a self ostensibly so self-consistent, a passing therefore so pure that it hardly warrants the name.

Which is to say that the fantasy of unadulterated identification bootstraps and sustains the very *dis*identification that—conversely and recursively—makes it visible to begin with: all but vanishing into his own iconicity, this figure remains, by the optical logic of transparent overinsistence, perpetually just *off*-white, still visible only as a trace against the pure blankness that he fails to be. Whiteness, in this tradition, becomes the mechanism through which cis male gay identity negotiates its own minoritarian status. As in the "aesthetics of failure" described by Svetlana Boym's notion of the *off-modern*, though decidedly more insidious than what she has in mind, perhaps the off-white, off-straight twink "takes us away from postmodernism and its discontents towards a broader consideration of modernities in the plural and over a long duration of time," a space somewhere to the side of "the modern with all its prefixes and suffixes."[55] He is the imagined authentic other of a modernist mode of unpersuasive forgery, the projection of authenticity itself, the limit case against which these authors' and auteurs' own counterfeit identities define themselves.

It is unsurprising, then, that a desire for material substantiation is invested in this trope: the off-straight twink reflects at once a fetish for reality and its aesthetic sublimation, both an onanistic fantasy and its repeated pragmatic frustrations. He marks the impossible convergence of accident and essence, of the incidental and the inevitable, the particular and the general, the minoritarian and the universal. He is the vanishing point of pure ipseity and the site at which the queer and queering agency of failed passing might emerge in the absence of the subject.

Token Subversion

If the literary and filmic characters treated in this book repeatedly attempt to exert agency by absenting themselves from the text, so too do their creators tend toward spectacular narrative vanishing acts. Parenthetical bracketings and lateral evasions of this sort in fact have a habit of embodying precisely the personal experience they disincarnate. In defining queerness by an attunement to stigma rather than by same-sex desire, in fact at moments rather insistently divorcing queerness from homosexuality, queer thought after Sedgwick perhaps also intimates the degree to which the queered subject is required to fill in the blanks of the interpellative process. As I intended to illustrate with my own prefatory anecdote about first learning the word *gay*, to be called a sissy or a fag, to be called camp, is to become aware of one's appearance to others, but the perlocutionary leap to a sense of actual gayness as an internal disposition is in no way assured by the signifier. It must be intuited—and through this intuition, in some measure imitated and affirmed—by the subject so baptized. The affirmation is inevitable to the degree that it is safer, in a very real, existential sense, to assume this implication: arguably less symptomatic of the "faith in exposure"[56] exposed by Sedgwick than of a *fear of exposure*, for queer subjects' paranoia can operate as a survival mechanism, an unwillingness to allow oneself to be duped or to succumb to the danger of self-deception—to assume, that is, that one is passing only to be unpleasantly surprised.

What a poetics of failed passing abhors more than anything, then, is the charge of taking itself too seriously. It doesn't mind being the butt of the joke, but it does insist on being *in on* the joke.[57] The desexualizing refusal of earnest identification is an escape hatch: by sublimating sexuality into mere performativity (all artifice, no essence) it allows an out from the fear of being outed, it keeps the closet door perpetually and comfortingly ajar. Ever poised to disavow what it avers, camp irony is dissonant not only in the habitual sense that it stages self-contradiction but also through its readiness to self-erasure. The result, in the later works under consideration here, is an increasing tendency to polish away imperfections while simultaneously playing up bad taste as a trope—no longer "a seriousness that fails," as Sontag describes "naïve, or pure, Camp," but rather a seriousness that succeeds.[58]

Distancing herself slightly—in a gesture of catachrestic revision—from Butler's vocabulary, Pamela Caughie confesses to preferring the rubric of passing to one of performativity because, for her, "passing brings out the historical emergence of this concept in actual social practices (not linguistic or philosophical theories) within a specific historical context."[59] This is a history

Caughie relates as a movement from modernism into what she designates as a more postmodern moment: "I use passing to name those practices by which we try to refuse the identities that have been historically offered to us, and that continue to structure our responses even as we seek to disavow them. . . . If for modernists, writing was a matter of effacing—not expressing—the self, today self-disclosure seems far more pressing. Getting personal, breaking silence, coming out—these are the moral imperatives of our present age."[60] Similarly, Camaiti Hostert explicitly aligns herself with theorists like Ginsberg, who, as she phrases it, "seek to link passing with postmodernist sentiments."[61] As Lisa Walker begins her book on "what it means to look like a lesbian, and what it means to be a lesbian but not look like one": "Demanding visibility has been one of the principles of late-twentieth-century identity politics, and flaunting visibility has become one of its tactics."[62] If the texts and discourses under consideration in this book define themselves through the kind of resignifications discussed above, viewed from a literary or film historical angle they also trace this movement from modernist self-effacement to postmodern self-display, from the germinal beginnings that first give contour to the domain of male homosexuality through its various iterations and historical revisions in later, purportedly more confessional, cultural moments.

Caughie identifies the problem with passing in our own era as a convergence of philosophical and epistemological developments that increasingly deconstruct the notion of selfhood, the celebrated death of the subject, with a converse resurgence, within the contemporary cultural landscape, of identity politics.[63] At this meeting point, she writes: "Passing is an appropriate figure for the anxiety of having no secure position."[64] As gay male identity, once quintessentially countercultural, becomes more recognizable, more socially acceptable, and arguably more mainstream over the course of the twentieth and into the present century, contradictory reactions are provoked. Among the phenomena *Flamboyant Fictions* documents is an ongoing anxiety over the loss of queer credentials.

While some of the personalities appearing in my later chapters (Werner Schroeter, Todd Haynes) seek to reassert or resuscitate the subversiveness of homosexuality, others (Rainer Werner Fassbinder, François Ozon, Xavier Dolan) sometimes seem to regard that association as silly or passé. (I am speaking here specifically of these filmmakers' programmatic assertions; whether their aesthetic practice corresponds to these intentions is another matter altogether.) But what I will describe in this book's third and final section as subversive tokenism does not so much seek to preserve the cultural specificity of a certain kind of homosexual experience (cis, male, white) as it on occasion unwittingly appears, even despite itself, to universalize this experience as representative of queerness in general. Passing, in this sense, accrues its additional associations of exchange and fungibility.[65]

As the literary, cinematic, and, indeed, theoretical histories discussed in this volume waver between subversion and institution, subversion itself becomes institutionalizing: a certain normativity comes into view as a residual history of sedimented agitations. The novels and films treated here, from André Gide to Xavier Dolan, do not merely reappropriate and parody received notions of homosexuality but rather inaugurate and over time increasingly *reify* these formulae into recognizable forms or even, as I'll be arguing in my later chapters, into stylistic queer commodities. There is no more refuge from such copycatism than there is any hope for recourse to an autonomous originality.

Loosely associated with the explicit sexuality and graphic violence of what was, at the turn of the twenty-first century, dubbed the New French Extremity, François Ozon's work vacillates wildly between films befitting this description and campy (musical) comedies—thus providing an apt corpus to test the heritage of camp abjection: here a mode of ludic and nostalgic identification with queer historicities and icons is seemingly dissociated from another mode that desires once again to locate the authenticity of queer subjecthood in the ontology of the abject body. Chapter 5, "New Camp Extremity: Adaptation and Experimentation in François Ozon," examines his *Gouttes d'eau sur pierres brûlantes* (*Water Drops on Burning Rocks*, 2000), itself an adaptation of an early play of Fassbinder's, to probe the later filmmaker's negotiation of this heritage of gay cinema and its tendency to tokenize subversion.

If agency can be defined, as I am arguing, as failed passing, for Ozon this includes the distortions and permutations his work brings to Fassbinder's legacy. Tracing the trope of the trans feminine—with its problematic tendency to allegorize gay male identity—from Genet's Divine through Fassbinder's Elvira, the protagonist of *In einem Jahr mit 13 Monden* (*In a Year of 13 Moons*, 1978), and finally to the figure of Véra in *Gouttes d'eau* will suggest that Ozon is unable to overcome strategies of corporeal verification and that his play between artifice and abjection instead ends up derealizing the body itself—a sublimation that (dis)embodies the queer subject in order to render it culturally intelligible.

Sensitive to the consequences of such dissociations and disappearances, in my final chapter, "Not Nothing: Xavier Dolan's Vanishing Gay Aesthetic," I will propose that Dolan's work thematizes homosexuality even, if not especially, where it appears not to, suggesting that the filmmaker's depiction of motherhood in his directorial debut, *J'ai tué ma mère* (*I Killed My Mother*, 2009), and in his most widely praised film, *Mommy* (2014), reflects an evolving attitude toward homosexuality, gay style, and his own disputed status as a queer filmmaker. Examining how Dolan self-consciously mobilizes maternal kitsch, I will argue that his deployment of an avowedly camp aesthetic enacts an unexpected form of closeting: allowing queer content to vanish behind an arguably commodified queer style.

While Ozon sometimes seems to want to divorce playfulness from negativity, in Dolan visceral dramatic tension is prone at any moment to transform itself into an overly stylized music video. Dolan's depiction of gay, and in one instance trans, protagonists is complicated by the fact that his narrative fragmentation and formal pyrotechnics no longer constitute a modernist oppositional aesthetic but are instead often seen as symptomatic of a postmodern embrace of artifice, hybridity, and pastiche—as if to confirm Halberstam's misgivings about camp style. That is to say that while his films often feel delightfully contrived, little in Dolan seems arbitrary or whimsical. The original promise of Gide's narrative forgery, the capricious falsification of queer subjectivities, has finally been fulfilled—a matter of style granted the full force of reality—and thus, potentially, betrayed. The narcissism and apparent incapacity for self-irony some critics claim to diagnose in Dolan seem to have diminished the dissonance fundamental to failed passing and constitutive of its subversive power.

It is not, then, that postmodern derealization deprives gay sexualities of their substance (which was always illusory to begin with) but rather that their self-legitimation has become, if anything, too self-evident. Through this insight, I also hope to shed some light on queer theory's own insistent efforts at self-reinvention within a discursive field committed to the problematic, if often unspoken, assumption that nonnormative sexualities should somehow inherently correspond to both progressive politics and an avant-garde aesthetic.

✦

While a number these names are familiar from previous studies of queer subjectivity, *Flamboyant Fictions* assembles this series of gay authors and film directors into a corpus that explodes conventional canonical thinking and expands it into popular culture and the present day. Interloping into what might otherwise seem a hagiographic roster of only the most established antiestablishment queer auteurs are upstarts like Ozon and Dolan, not to mention the brief intrusion of the pop star Troye Sivan, whose public gayness is considered, as already noted, in an epilogue to chapter 4. The tropes I am discussing are not unique to the figures treated here, and for this reason I have tended to favor direct borrowings and allusions in my selection of texts. The archive suggests itself, in a manner of speaking, though these are in many cases connections that as yet have never been remarked upon.

Though I focus here primarily on white cis male auteurs and writers, I hope this work's theory of failed passing will have some relevance to the various disciplines on which it draws conceptually—trans studies, for instance, or black studies. Even within the limited scope of the present emphasis there are, to be sure, any number of chapters that could be added here. The most obvious omissions are Jean Cocteau, who was André Gide's chief rival and Jean Genet's protector, and Rosa von Praunheim, Werner Schroeter's onetime lover and later frenemy. It is possible, though, that these figures are *too* flamboyant for a theory of failed passing to have much traction. Oscar Wilde, whom Gide credits for having introduced him to his own homosexuality, might, at a glance, also seem to belong to this category, but his literary work and program of aestheticism toy with disclosure and displacement in ways that make his personal and public self-stylization as a dandy legible as a willful distraction from the sexuality it would seem so extravagantly to express. Marcel Proust's closeted gay characters, on the other hand, and his narrative approach to insinuating fictionalized autobiography make his work on the whole interpretable as an extended treatise on a slyly suggestive passing.

Although he may draw less attention to flamboyant narrativity than someone like Genet, there are moments in James Baldwin where an author figure loses control over his characters.[66] And there are plenty of his own characters who pass as straight or remain ambivalently so despite gay sexual encounters.[67] Indeed, Valerie Rohy has read the author's work as an illustration of how "agency and self-consciousness are never fully ours," revealed by the fact that "the logics of homophobia and racism . . . are each rooted in the nostalgia of an impossible essentialism whose desire for coherent identity is barred by an ineluctable passing."[68] I would be pleased if future interpretations of any of these individuals or of the countless others—Pier Paolo Pasolini, Yukio Mishima, Pedro Almodóvar, to name just a few—who appear in passing or on the margins of the present inquiry were to be rewarded by whatever insights it may have to offer.

Throughout this study I will be using the term *auteur* to describe both writers and filmmakers, not only for the sake of efficiency but also because the question of authorship or auteurism (art as self-expression) is important to my investigation. Similarly, I tend to use the labels *gay* or *homosexual* as a general heuristic of comparison while remaining fully aware that they may not always capture a given historical nuance. While Gide, for instance, favors the designation *pédéraste* (pederast) over *inverti* (invert, a term he associates with passivity and femininity) to describe himself, the notion of *inversion* will nevertheless provide the primary vocabulary for much of Jean Genet's depiction of homosexuality, treated throughout chapters 2–4 of this book. Part of my indolence on this point involves the near impossibility of charting these terms with total accuracy as they navigate not only historical but also transnational and translinguistic contexts.[69] When, in order to establish general comparability, I opt for more recent umbrella terms such as *queer* (the meaning of which will, as the word itself mandates, be perpetually refined and redefined over the course of the study), I do so not because I find precision to be undesirable but precisely because I want to avoid being overly categorical in my assumptions or conclusions.[70] While most, if not all, of the figures centrally discussed here would readily describe themselves as gay—using one word or another—most, from Fassbinder onward, would also bristle at having their work reduced to this label. If I persist in reading them through the lens of homosexuality it is because I am curious about what this perceived reduction or all-too-easy intelligibility signifies.

In a sense I am still trying to answer my childhood question: What makes an artwork, or a person for that matter, gay? To those versed in the history of queer studies, beginning with Gide and Genet might seem like a throwback, but I do so because this questionable canonization is precisely the point: I am interested in the elaboration and evolution of male homosexuality as a culturally legible identity and aesthetic category as its once-subversive edge becomes a token coinage of refinement or even of market(ing) value.[71] I began this study with the suspicion that as the modes of queer narrative it investigates ceased over time to insist on the contingent, feigned, or forged nature of their depictions, the political potential of their aesthetic paradigm would also gradually decay. I fully anticipated marking the emergence and eventual canonization (or perhaps, more problematically, domestication) of a distinctly gay avant-garde by observing how what Leo Bersani once famously identified as the outlaw mentality of Gide and Genet gives way to the lush, melodramatic sensibilities of Fassbinder and Schroeter, becomes diluted through the polar oscillation between graphic brutality and campy comedy in Ozon, and finally disappears into the glossy histrionics of Dolan.[72] But I have come to recognize such vanishing as a defining trait of this tradition, which draws attention to the very stigma it unsuccessfully conceals—finding its freedom in this failure. In the end it is perhaps not so much that male homosexuality is naturalized, even in its most unmarked iterations, as that it is asserted as stylistic choice and reaffirmed, beyond the imposition of identity, as sexual preference.

Part 1

Counterfeit Identities

Chapter 1

✦

Counterfeit Narratives

André Gide's Queer Coinages

Queer studies, argues Kadji Amin in the methodological epilogue to *Disturbing Attachments: Genet, Modern Pederasty, and Queer History* (2017), has, since its inception, sought "to preserve the convergence of same-sex-sexuality, political urgency and radical transgression."[1] Committed to this Holy Trinity of revolutionary sex, politics, and aesthetics, the notoriously capacious category of *queer* thus inevitably discovers familiar sentiments "such as shame, camp irony or radical opposition" wherever it turns its gaze—paradoxically upholding queerness as a political alignment independent of any specific sexual orientation while at the same time reaffirming the inalienably transgressive force of these sexualities.[2] This perhaps accounts, in part, for the extraordinary, and not unproblematic, lability of the term *queer*, which has long since come to constitute not only a blanket designation for various nonnormative sexual practices or gender identities but also a mode of reading or, indeed, even an epistemological orientation to the world.

Since the very birth of the field, then, queer theory has been reinventing itself, and seemingly at an ever-accelerating pace. It has become a trope bordering on the commonplace for each new study to proclaim a fresh methodology, turn, or queering not only of the textual objects under consideration but also of the investigative approach itself—highlighting a perennial tension between *queer* as an adjective or noun (marking an identity category) and as a verb (signaling an approach or disposition). As a recent iteration of this tradition, the publication of *Disturbing Attachments* has itself occasioned reconceptualization of and in queer thought. Amin's impassioned argument for a "deidealization" of the ideological foundations of queer studies seeks to bring "unsavory, complicit, and politically problematic modes of queer relation to bear on queer theory. The result is an interrogation of the political imperative of *queer* and the disavowed historical imaginaries that inform the term's contemporary use, and a reorientation of *queer* toward unsavory and historically dated modes of attachment."[3] Amin describes his method as one of "attachment genealogy" aiming to exhume the often uncomfortable historical foundations of identities and forms of relation now recognized as queer.

Specifically of interest is the obsolete custom of pederasty found in authors like Jean Genet or André Gide: a mode of attachment that "becomes all but illegible once pederasty—in the reproved form of pedophilia—is cast out of the definitional orbit of homosexuality altogether."[4] What Amin chooses to call *modern pederasty* thus "names a genealogical overlap between the seemingly incompatible notions of pederasty as a nonreciprocal act of sexual subordination that does *not* confer a sexual identity and homosexuality *as* a sexual identity."[5] Precisely this "curious overlap," argues Amin, "and the distinctive temporalities, relationship forms, and politics to which it gave rise, have been all but ignored by queer theory."[6] As a means of examining the historical constitution of queer theory's disciplinary formations, in what follows I propose to investigate this historical interval—in which an outdated episteme of sexual *activity* imperfectly passes into more contemporary conceptions of sexual *identity*—on the example of André Gide's 1925 novel *Les faux-monnayeurs* (*The Counterfeiters*). Mindful of the ludic and willfully artificial aspects of such identity, I will argue, through Gide, for an understanding of queerness neither primarily as a sexual orientation nor as a perpetually unsettling worldview but rather as a distinctly narrative mode of playful, and playfully contrived, identity formation insistent on internal dissonance and self-abstraction.

At its core, Gide's *Faux-monnayeurs* might be described as a double narrative of parallel instructional failures. While the author's initial intent and continual preoccupation throughout the book appear to be to imagine an erotic encounter between his two young protagonists, the desired scene of seduction never takes place and the boys end up, instead, in an unfortunate chiasmus, under the tutelage of rival older authors, each of whom would have been better suited to the other's pupil. Understood as a bildungsroman, a novel of education or, more properly, a novel of *formation*, it brings into view Gide's contributions to the formulation of queer identities.

In a scene of instruction central to the book's narrative, Gide stages an extended debate on narrative itself, tracing a genealogy from French literary realism into his own modernism and perhaps implicitly suggesting, if read carefully, that this shift might in some sense be a function of historically evolving conceptions of sexual identity. Through my reading of the novel, I hope to reveal how the work's dueling narrative voices (these parodied author figures *within* the text and a meddlesome external narrator who repeatedly intrudes into the action) negotiate competing forms of modernist storytelling corresponding to different modes of representing male homosexuality. The narrative innovation of Gide's novel seems born, almost accidentally, of a surprisingly semicloseted approach to depicting same-sex desire, which is simultaneously revealed and concealed through a willfully failed passing.

Ultimately, I intend to expose a form of forgery in Gide: a strategy by which self-determination, be it textual or sexual, gains quasi-ontological currency precisely for its arbitrariness—affirming queerness not as an essential or innate attribute but rather as stylistic-sexual preference. In rereading Gide's *Faux-monnayeurs* by the light of Amin, and thus rereading Amin by contours of the shadow Gide casts, my aim is to reveal Gide's particular form of "modern pederasty" as a precursor to queer studies' own insistence on the kind of *coinages* (deidealization, attachment genealogy, modern pederasty, or the perpetual renegotiation of the very notion of queerness) by which the discourse stubbornly redefines itself at the precise pace dictated by the news cycle of the academic monograph.[7]

Pass/Fail Pedagogy

While the various interlacing plotlines of Gide's meandering novel would be difficult to summarize succinctly, the central story concerns two adolescent boys, Olivier and Bernard, and the adult author figures competing especially for Olivier's affection: his uncle Édouard and Édouard's adversary, the Comte de Passavant. (If Édouard is generally regarded as a stand-in for Gide himself, Passavant is modeled primarily on Gide's professional rival, Jean Cocteau.[8]) Through a series of narrative accidents, the devious Bernard usurps Olivier's obvious place as secretary to benevolent Édouard while innocent Olivier ends up serving as secretary to the conniving Passavant. At the conclusion to the novel's second part, not too long before setting aright this mismatched pair of couplings, the unembodied but (as I'll demonstrate) not entirely extradiegetic narrator laments of Bernard: "I cannot console myself for the whim [*passade*] that made him take Olivier's place beside Édouard. These events turned out all wrong. Olivier is the one that Édouard loved. With what care he would have helped him to mature. With what loving respect he would have guided and supported him, brought him to his true self. Passavant will ruin him, that's certain."[9] Subtly contrasted in this passage, perhaps, are an exclusively erotic mode of intergenerational attachment (*passade*, beyond its initial assonance with *Passavant*, can, among other things, imply a romantic fling) and another grounded in a pedagogical goodwill that seeks to help the student *become himself*, forming the beloved object into a subject. The book, in this pivotal moment, definitively reconfirms its focus on the cultivation of homosexual desire, on the education and formation of the nascent queer self—a project shared, it would seem, by Édouard and the novel's narrator.

But although it is often considered Gide's masterpiece, and despite its chronological proximity to the publication of other works in which Gide overtly and clamorously discusses (his) homosexuality,[10] scholarship on *Les faux-monnayeurs* long rather neglected the centrality of its insinuations of same-sex desire. Only in the 1990s were these elements first brought to the fore by studies like Michael Lucey's *Gide's Bent: Sexuality, Politics, Writing* (1995) and Naomi Segal's *André Gide: Pederasty and Pedagogy* (1998).[11] Lucey's monograph expressly seeks to correct what he sees as a "phobic distanciation from questions of sexuality"[12] that plagued earlier treatments of the novel, revealing a homophobic undercurrent to "an opposition of sincerity and inauthenticity" that previous interpretations took up on the apparent suggestion of the novel's title. Implicit in the critical insistence on authenticity, Lucey compellingly argues, are "certain phobic cultural discourses [which] paint homosexuality as a depravity given to masquerade, mimicry, deception."[13] This "sincerity game" thus devolves into what Lucey calls a "'find the good fag' game, where Édouard usually wins and Passavant usually loses."[14] For Segal, while she doesn't phrase it quite this way, the game Gide is playing would be closer to finding the good *pederast* (a word that surprisingly does not appear in Lucey's reading of the novel), since it is only by contrast with Passavant that Édouard can appear exonerated: "The goodness of the good pederast . . . has to be overdetermined by a series of moral binaries, chief of which is the contrast with Passavant. . . . The bad gay writer must get in first if the good gay writer is not to be a corruptor."[15] The pederast that Gide, on Segal's reading, wishes to see as good must initially remain "ignorant and therefore innocent of his own desire"—the story told time and again throughout the oeuvre is of *his* sexual awakening through the influence of seductive youth.[16]

This claim is perhaps somewhat overstated in the case of *Les faux-monnayeurs*, which is arguably more concerned with the education or aware of the exploitation of its younger protagonists than certain others of Gide's works and where even the well-meaning Édouard is less than entirely guileless. But it is nonetheless here at the intersection of the depiction of youth and the disclosure of homosexual desire that we witness the birth of queer subjectivity in and *through* narrative—be it the narrative of the young apprentice's sexual maturation or that of the pederast's. Édouard appears acutely, if only tacitly, aware of his attraction to teenage boys: throughout the novel he plays a fairly passive role in scenes of seduction, profiting more from chance and dumb luck than from exploited opportunity.

After an early scene in which he is rather unwittingly cruised by an even younger nephew, Georges, and following a suspicious ellipsis that leaves unsaid what may have transpired between the two, Édouard begins to develop what I would like to identify as a queer poetics of failed passing, itself pedagogical in nature:

> This episode must be very much shortened. Precision in the reader's imagination should be obtained not by accumulating details but by two or three touches put in exactly the right places. I expect for that matter that it would be a better plan to make the boy tell the story himself; his point of view is of more signification than mine. But the

> weight of my look makes him deviate a little from his own real direction [*fausse un peu sa direction*]. A personality which is over tender and still too young to be conscious of itself, takes shelter behind an attitude [*se defend et dérobe derrière une attitude*]. Nothing is more difficult to observe than creatures in the period of formation [*les êtres en formation*]. One ought to look at them only sideways—in profile.[17]

Drawing attention to his own narrative caprice—another passing fancy or *passade*, mentioned, as it were, merely *en passant*, in passing—Édouard passes off the erotic impetus of his writing as incidental. But that there may well be an evasive and ulterior motive to this misdirection, an avoidance of self-incrimination, is an inference the author does not simply skirt but rather seems to court. As the criminal Jean Genet avows in the novel treated in my next chapter: "This is an old trick, the trick of partial confessions. Spontaneously I confess a little, the better to keep more serious things hidden."[18] The implication is a self more secret, and more salacious, than the one put on display: with "two or three touches" marking the points of an ellipsis, Gide invites his reader to supply precisely the kind of otherwise foiled erotic fantasy he has omitted from his novel. Meanwhile, his own authorial foil, Édouard, lays himself bare precisely through suppression and disguise, just as the child "se . . . dérobe derrière une attitude" (vanishes into a pose): *dérober* implying, at once, flight (as in to steal away), theft (Édouard has just caught Georges stealing a book), and dissimulation—but also, etymologically, undressing (as in the English *disrobe*).[19]

The didactic thrust of this narrative method consists as much in its engagement with its imagined audience as it does in its treatment of the young boy whose perspective it seeks to imitate or to invent. Just as the reader, according to Édouard, must not be too pedantically instructed as to what might have just occurred in the text and instead be allowed instead to intuit the action from carefully and efficiently placed cues, so too is Georges's viewpoint to be described only obliquely—so that he, like Olivier under his uncle's imagined tutelage, can be gently guided to himself without damage done along the way. Gide's published notes on the novel counsel a similar approach: "The poor novelist constructs his characters; he controls them and makes them speak. The true novelist listens to them and watches them function; he eavesdrops on them even before he knows them. It is only according to what he hears them say that he begins to understand *who* they are."[20] As if acknowledging an onanistic impetus to his work, the novelist as a kind of Peeping Tom, Gide advocates a laissez-faire approach to pedagogy that has as its analogue a writerly embrace of the aleatoric.

What interests the pederast, after all, is *youth*: the fragile being-in-becoming (être en formation), the not-yet-fully-formed. As Lucey has it, "The discourse of sexuality does not always produce itself with intention. It is Gide's ability to live with and write out of that fact, sous le coup de la sexualité, that gives his work its insistent presence. Gide's novel might well convey something other than the discourse mentioned in its title."[21] Such a temperament, however, is elusive, and describing it in prose inevitably risks *de*forming, distorting, falsifying, or counterfeiting it—the various associations of the verb *fausser*. My argument here runs parallel to but also radicalizes Lucey's: of interest to me is how Gide, as I'm about to show, affirms the spontaneous onset of sexuality (le coup de la sexualité) *as if it were* a conscious and even arbitrary decision—transforming a discourse of authenticity into one of willful counterfeiting. Thus, to an even greater extent than Lucey perhaps recognizes, the "novel offers a peremptory challenge to its own cult of sincerity, its own title,"[22] upsetting the standard of authenticity that would otherwise appear to contrast Édouard, the good pederast, with Passavant, the bad.

Fiendish Forgery

At the very core of *Les faux-monnayeurs*, midway through its central section, is a scene of failed instruction. Having proven himself a rather clumsy educator to stubborn Bernard, Édouard reluctantly gets carried away in a self-indulgent lecture, discoursing on his project for a sort of antinovel, itself entitled *Les faux-monnayeurs*, drafts and sketches of which have been interspersed throughout Gide's book of the same name. The ensuing debate between Édouard and Bernard—who advocate competing strategies of storytelling correlated, I'll argue, to differing conceptions of sexual identity and of sexual substance—can be read rather transparently as staging Gide's critique of literary realism in favor of a more modernist mode of narrative. Read obliquely, from the angle of a failed passing, the manner in which this debate is itself staged and narrativized suggests a more nuanced but also more drastic literary program of narrative forgery implicitly affirming sexual identity, as well, as willfully arbitrary.

"Le difficile dans la vie," reflects Bernard early in the novel, "c'est de prendre au sérieux longtemps de suite la même chose" ("The difficulty in life is to take the same thing seriously for long at a time").[23] Recalling Édouard's comment about the challenge of observing beings in formation, Bernard's maxim could stand as an epigraph for the work on the whole: *Les faux-monnayeurs* flits flirtatiously between different characters, scenarios, styles, and narrative voices, never settling on a single plotline or point of view. Within the diegesis as well, Édouard elevates inconstancy to a poetic principle, while Passavant, true to form, conversely counsels *against* aleatory approaches: "L'important, dans la vie, c'est de ne pas se laisser entraîner. Une chose en amène une autre et puis on ne sait plus où l'on va" ("The important thing in life is not to get carried away. One thing leads to another and suddenly one doesn't know where one is going").[24] It is not immediately clear how one might reconcile Édouard's fickle whims or Passavant's self-controlled rigidity to what Lucey sees as phobic readings of surface versus depth, of the arch posturing of a Passavant versus the apparent authenticity of an Édouard; perhaps the chiasmus between the two figures has crossed itself a second time.

If we nonetheless persist, for the time being, and I see no good reason not to, in casting Édouard as the soi-disant good pederast and Passavant as a bad influence, then these *partis pris* (or *not*, in the case of Édouard), while not explicitly referring to sexuality, would already call into question Jonathan Dollimore's influential identification of Gide's ostensible essentialism.[25] As Édouard's character is at one point described, "He is never the same for long. . . . He is perpetually forming, unforming, re-forming himself. One thinks one has grasped him . . . Proteus! He takes the shape of what he loves."[26] Édouard's is a peculiar form of narcissism in which the self is formed, but always only provisionally, as a reflection of the desired other.[27] At issue in Édouard's pedagogy or pederasty, then, would be not just the education of his pupil but also a self-creation on the basis of the delicately malleable nature of the adolescent in his charge.

Gide, in his journal, will outline a literary program of self-invention echoing this (auto)didactic model: "To know oneself: this is the last thing to which the artist should aspire; and it can only happen through his works, only through creating them. . . . The best way to learn to know oneself is to try and understand others."[28] At stake, in either event, is a kind of *Bildung* tasked first with forming its younger characters and then the author-educator in their image. And if there is any evidence of Édouard's *Faux-monnayeurs* being framed through Olivier's perspective, as its author would seem to imply, it is this self-producing narcissism as well as the childlike caprice with which his would-be novel-within-the-novel aspires to a kind of formlessness, a "*lawless*"[29] nonstructure promiscuously liberated from the precedent of any (single) given reality: "My novel hasn't got a subject. [Or,] if you prefer, it hasn't got *one* subject."[30] Instead, his book, he concludes at a later moment, will take for its subject precisely "the rivalry between the real world and the representation of it which we make to ourselves. The manner in which the world of appearances imposes itself upon us, and the manner in which we try to impose on the outside world our own interpretation—this is the drama of our lives."[31] The facts of life, for Édouard, are an inconvenience to literary representation, ontology a nuisance for epistemology and aesthetics; and it is just this bother that his novel should aspire to depict.

Bernard, by contrast, Édouard surmises, would have his writing grow organically from the soil of the factual: "Realists start from facts—fit their ideas to suit the facts. Bernard is a realist. I am afraid we shall never understand each other."[32] If, for Bernard, authenticity and integrity are the most revered of values, Édouard admits, in a Nietzschean vein, to preferring style even at the expense of taking distance from the truth—one could be forgiven for suspecting, although it would seem to run counter to the sincerity game central to the novel's earlier reception, that he prefers style over substance.

Édouard insists, however, that an aestheticized version of reality isn't the ultimate aim: "And even that isn't what I want to do. What I want is to represent reality on the one hand, and on the other that effort to stylize it into art."[33] And it is here that the novel reaches its apogee of mise en abyme and where Édouard achieves his most self-conscious instance of self-invention: "In order to arrive at this effect . . . I invent the character of a novelist, whom I make my central figure; and the subject of the book, if you must have one, is just that very struggle between what reality offers him and what he himself desires to make of it."[34] While it is tempting to think of this as an indication that Édouard is more or less identical to his creator, André Gide, it is more accurate to read this doubling as an instance of (self-)difference—a tension between autobiography and fiction, another struggle between reality and its representation.[35]

More importantly, it is critical to distinguish yet *another* narrative voice in the background, who points out that Édouard is acting involuntarily, even against his own will: "Edouard knew it; he said so to himself over and over again; but in spite of all his resolutions, as soon as he was in Bernard's company, he behaved quite differently from what he wished, and spoke in a manner which immediately appeared absurd to him (and which indeed was so). This might almost make one suppose that he loved Bernard? . . . No; I think not."[36] If Édouard is a stand-in for the author, it is to no small extent as winking self-parody. There is a kind of reverse free indirect discourse at work here, as the focalization on Édouard's self-doubt dissipates for a moment into the metareflections of a higher authorial agency, as if the narrative perspective had suddenly zoomed out. It is the voice of this parenthesis that concerns me here: the *other* first-person narrator, who provides both ontological confirmation of Édouard's absurdity and raises, under erasure, suspicions of his (romantic) attachment to Bernard—outing Édouard, as it were.

This is, after all, also the instant at which the novel's title is introduced—not by Édouard, but by Bernard, who has indiscreetly read the drafts in Édouard's journals. This title, it is revealed, is grounded not in any narrative events to be recounted but rather in an abstractly metaphorical literary critique: "In reality, Edouard had in the first place been thinking of certain of his fellow novelists when he began to think of counterfeiters, and in particular of the Comte de Passavant."[37] Pressed to explain this, Édouard again rather helplessly begins with *ideas* rather than with plot points: "Well, imagine a false ten-franc gold piece [*une pièce d'or de dix francs qui soit fausse*]. In reality it's not worth two sous. But it will be worth ten francs as long as no one recognizes it to be false [*qu'elle est fausse*]. So if I start from the idea that . . ."[38] But Bernard interrupts: "But why start from an idea? . . . If you were to start from a fact and make a good exposition of it, the idea would come of its own accord to inhabit it. If I were writing *The Counterfeiters* I should begin by showing the counterfeit coin—the little ten-franc piece you were speaking of just now . . . *this* one here."[39] And at this moment, Bernard produces from his pocket, as if by magic, through a curious deus (or, rather, as I will demonstrate momentarily, diabolus) ex machina, an actual counterfeit coin not previously alluded to in the novel.

It is my contention that this coin is metaleptically provided (inserted from *beyond* the work's recounted reality) by the not entirely extradiegetic narrator, who mischievously interferes from time to time in the action of the novel.[40] Nor is this the first surprise currency he has supplied. The plot of the book—the exchange, a passing between hands, of Bernard for Olivier, and vice versa, which occupies the first half of the narrative—is occasioned by an act of petty theft, as Bernard absconds with Édouard's suitcase from the train station. In the pages preceding this act, Gide had meticulously detailed how Bernard spends the very last of his cash, his final fourteen sous: ten for coffee and a croissant, two as a gratuity and the final two given to a beggar.[41] But when he suddenly needs another ten cents to redeem Édouard's surreptitiously acquired luggage claim ticket and set the story in motion, some force of fate intervenes: "But the demon [*le démon*] is watching over him; he slips between Bernard's anxious fingers, as they go searching from pocket to pocket with a pretence of feigned despair, a fifty-centime bit, which had lain forgotten since goodness knows when in his waistcoat pocket."[42] This demon is present, even intrusive, from the very first page of the book, where it voyeuristically observes as Bernard, instead of preparing for his *baccalauréat*, rummages through his parents' drawers: "La famille respectait sa solitude; le démon pas!" ("His family respected his solitude—not so the demon!").[43] Itself groping around in the boy's clothing and spying on him in a moment of solitary mischief, the demon, in such instances, fulfills the pederastic and masturbatory impulses left otherwise unsatisfied by the rather sexless narrative.

Hovering precariously between the idiomatic and the literal, Gide's evocations of *le démon* connote whim, caprice, gratuity, chance, risk, contingency, or curiosity (as in the not uncommon personification *le démon de la curiosité*) and recur at decisive points in the action.[44] As Susan Ringler has it, this demon "roguishly springs into sight at key moments to assist the characters, but succeeds only in making the plot seem thoroughly contrived."[45] It is, in fact, the very signal of contrivance itself, a refusal of the feint of realism and a foregrounding of the arbitrariness of narration. It is, to name one key example, "a devil [*un diable*]" on whom the *passade* of swapping Bernard and Olivier is blamed.[46]

It is worth recalling, in this context, that Henri Massis, in a series of vitriolic pieces for the *Revue universelle* from 1914 to 1934, repeatedly attacked Gide himself as devilish—for instance, three short years before the publication of *Les faux-monnayeurs,* he wrote, "There is only one word to define such a man, a word of rare and reserved usage . . . the word demonic [*celui de démoniaque*]."[47] This was not an uncommon view. As Catharine Savage Brosman has summarized, "More than one reader of André Gide concluded his character to be diabolical [*diabolique*]. Claudel proclaims, 'He's a demon

[*C'est un démon*]'; Julien Green describes him as 'Lucifer disguised as a tourist.' "[48] Gide, himself, moreover, famously contends of Dostoyevsky that "il n'est point de véritable œuvre d'art où n'entre la collaboration du demon" (there is no veritable work of art without the collaboration of the demon).[49] Perhaps, then, beyond an understanding of Gide's work as merely animated by the demonic, we are invited to consider the author himself as an impish intruder into his own texts, or at least as this figure's willing coconspirator—to read repeated mentions of *le démon* in Gide as a sly *clin d'œil* from the extratextual author himself.

While Gide's narrator in *Les faux-monnayeurs* and this mischievous daemon[50] appear sometimes to be working at cross-purposes, they are most often in cahoots, and it seems appropriate, in any event, to situate Gide's authorial presence on this quasi-extradiegetic level rather than identifying him strictly with the intradiegetic Édouard. If Édouard's original discourse of forgery is a critique aimed at the insincerity of Passavant, the *novel's* narrator participates in an explicit act of counterfeiting, conspiring with Bernard to contravene Édouard's aesthetic platform. But beyond Bernard's position (the realist authenticity of facts) and Édouard's (an advocacy of abstraction), we must recognize another—the author's own: a narrative procedure by which a notion, once imagined, *becomes* fact.

This is the reason that Gide can treat his characters as if, once set in motion, they existed independently of his authorship. It is also the status of Bernard's counterfeit coin: a metaphor made real, the *very* coin of which Édouard had been speaking, although hitherto ignorant of its existence. It is as if this were the consummation of a passage from Gide's notes on the novel, where he asserts, "I stick to Wilde's paradox: nature copies art. The artist's rule should be never to restrict himself to what nature proposes, but to propose nothing to nature but what nature can and should shortly imitate."[51] Gide's world is meant to be of the author's own making, and this includes the discourses on same-sex attraction his work can be said to inaugurate.

Fabulous Ontology

Bernard, with his reality fetish, is the first in a series of seductively off-straight twinks to be cataloged by this study. Like his predecessor Lafcadio, the central figure of *Les caves du Vatican* (*Lafcadio's Adventures*, 1914), whose name Bernard bore in early drafts of *Les faux-monnayeurs*, he is what Naomi Segal has aptly described as Gide's bad boy: eternally youthful, eminently desirable, "simultaneously erotically polymorphous and . . . sexually sophisticated."[52] He can be perverted—indeed is always already puerilely perverse—without risk of compromising his innocence: "The bad boy is almost universally good . . . because his very badness makes him sexy."[53] He seems, and most often is, sexually available but nonetheless remains forever out of reach.

Édouard's avowed preference for Olivier notwithstanding, it is, I would argue, Bernard who is idealized in *Les faux-monnayeurs*. Quoting from earlier notes, with which he will himself immediately disagree, the narrator laments: "Without a doubt not one of my heroes has disappointed me more than he, for perhaps there was not one who had given me greater hopes. Perhaps he gave way too early to his own bent [*Peut-être s'est-il laissé aller à lui-même trop tôt*]."[54] While clever, Dorothy Bussy's standard translation of this sentence is unfortunately somewhat misleading. Which is to say that it is not Bernard but rather Olivier who is implied to have an innate homosexual disposition. Reviewing his characters here at the end of the book's second section, the narrator attributes to Olivier tellingly fickle and effeminate qualities: "His is a tender nature and sensitive to flattery. Everything goes to his head. Moreover I seem to gather . . . that he is a little vain. Sensuality, pique, vanity—to what does not all this lay him open?"[55] Bernard, on the other hand, demonstrates, upon further narratorial reflection, "virility and strength," and, despite acknowledged change and growth, follows a much *straighter* path. The reason for both the disappointment and its retraction can be read—against the grain but perhaps not contrary to authorial intention—as a failing not of Bernard's but of a narrator who confides, "I mistrust feelings that find their expression too quickly."[56] Like his coin, Bernard exists at the point of pure coincidence between the thing in itself and its expression. He is, as it turns out, perfectly sincere: "He enjoys hearing himself talk a little too much; but it's a fact that he talks well. . . . He has already read too much, remembered too much, and learnt a great deal more from books than from life."[57] Our narrator ultimately appears to share Bernard's fetish for reality: the only critique that sticks is that he is still too literary, is not just yet quite real enough.

"Peut-être s'est-il laissé aller à lui-même trop tôt." An alternate translation might read: "Perhaps he lost himself to himself too early." Letting himself go (*se laisser aller*), losing his way through this alliteratively stuttering sentence, Bernard discovers only his own being. Bernard's bent, as I see it, is not homosexuality per se—although it's not *not* homosexuality either. The trope of the off-straight twink, in my reading, does not so much embody as transcend such contradictions. He is himself a metaphor made real, wholly pleasure principle passing flawlessly for an unadulterated realism.

This eroticized veracity, like the insistent reality of Bernard's coin—an indexical referent exceeding the text's immediate diegesis—causes some issues for an ontology of pure caprice: Gide's counterfeiting turns out to be, despite itself, an *essentializing* gesture after all. This is mirrored formally by the fact that the most arbitrary of narrative details repeatedly turn out to be precisely the most requisite. In this manner *Les faux-monnayeurs* will also test the limits of authorial omnipotence and of the autonomy of literature from life in revealing ways, partly through an insistence on a homosexual tropism toward suicide as a model for (and itself modeled on) a sense of narrative inevitability.

The novel ends with Édouard's greatest pedagogical failure, the spectacular suicide of the troubled young Boris, who is coerced and manipulated by a group of schoolmates—through what are tellingly described as "*diable*ries d'écolier" ("schoolboy be*devil*ments")[58]—into shooting himself in front of the class and their instructor, his grandfather, La Pérouse. However, the book also unwrites this ending, ripped from the headlines, supplementing it with Édouard's decision *not* to include this detail in his own fictionalized version of events:

> Without exactly pretending to explain anything, I should not like to put forward any fact which was not accounted for by sufficiency of motive. And for that reason I shall not make use of little Boris's suicide for my *Counterfeiters*; I have too much difficulty in understanding it. And then, I dislike police court items [*faits divers*]. There is something peremptory, irrefutable, brutal, outrageously real about them. . . . I accept reality coming as a proof in support of my thought, but not as preceding it. It displeases me to be surprised. Boris's suicide seems to me an *indecency*, for I was not expecting it.[59]

It can no longer be a question of Édouard's uncomplicated identification with his creator: through his refusal to depict precisely the kind of "outrageously real" arbitrary action, the *acte gratuit*, that is the very hallmark of Gidean fiction up until this point, Édouard definitively distinguishes the novel he is writing from the one in which he finds himself. The two novels—and the two authors—emphatically fail to pass for one another while at the same moment continuously hinting at their shared identity.

This is all the more astounding from an author who, from his early satire *Paludes* (1895) through his *soties* (as Gide called his book-length narratives before *Les faux-monnayeurs*), and most specifically in *Les caves du Vatican*, ruminates obsessively on the apparently unmotivated *acte gratuit* as a model for human freedom of will. Gide's own inclusion of this *fait divers* signals a self-contradictory text, foregrounding the conflict between reality and (its) representation Édouard had sought to dramatize. (Taken literally, as a fact or deed that differs from itself, the very phrase *fait divers* inherently implies non-self-identity; the singular noun is a back-formation from the plural.) What is more, the ultimate presence in the actual novel of this concluding suicide would seem to constitute an exact converse to Wilde's prescription that life imitate literature (paraphrased here by Édouard's sentiment that reality ought to serve as a proof of but not a model for the artwork) and thus to run counter to the kind of free narrative forgery I have just described.

As an appendix to his own notebook for this novel, Gide in fact reproduces a sampling of the salacious news items that inspired it, supplementing the story with the real-life antecedents it aestheticizes. It is in these very *faits divers* that Gide identifies the template for the teenage prostitution ring, mentioned merely in passing early in the book, presumably responsible for the counterfeit coins that later furnish its most paradigmatic plot point. It is all the more perplexing, then, that Édouard in this instance would resist the authorial temptation to draw on the factuality of the *fait divers* whereas *his* author manages to sneak it into the book *sous rature*—especially considering that Gide, in his published notes on the novel, explicitly foregrounds the origin of this fictionalized event in an actual newspaper account of a teen suicide from 1909, another of the *fait divers* he later had republished in the *Nouvelle revue française*.[60] Including this retouched incident in his novel while banishing it from Édouard's, Gide smuggles in its outrageous ontology, but as an irritant, a foreign element to the realism it might otherwise underwrite. It's the same showy coin trick, or *tour de passe-passe*, as it would be called in French, he had had Bernard play earlier. But like that counterfeit currency, the reality of the kind of *fait divers* it draws on is suspect, scandalous, unpersuasive—and insistently so, even after it has been fictionalized. At once garish and instructive, straining against the limits of credulity for pedagogical purposes, it is, in a word, fabulous.

That his only book Gide is willing to designate a novel would be so self-consciously oriented around a *fait divers* implies that a certain narrativity was always at stake in the earlier formulations and explorations of the *acte gratuit*—yielding, as Emily Apter has argued, "a definition of narratological perversity" and a "paradigm of devious narrativity (in which characters, having pitched their intellects against the global wit of plot structure, lose out)."[61] As Gide complains in a letter on the subject,

> I feel that psychology . . . of the sort that "has currency" [*a cours*] is based on commonplaces and poorly controlled data, and its conclusions are often skewed [*faussés*]. I perceive a great deal of laziness and scant critical spirit. Unfortunately, most novelists and playwrights are satisfied with banal and dubious data that authorizes facile effects and guarantees public approval. It is a paper currency with a daily rate [*une monnaie de papier, qui a cours*], whose true cash reserves do not guarantee its value; it's a merely conventional value.
>
> I am interested in news items that jar any too easily accepted ideas, forcing us to think.[62]

There is an evident anxiety, in this passage, over the potential devaluation that comes with fungibility, perhaps partially explaining Gide's desire to emphasize the counterfeit nature of his own literary coinages. What passes for psychological realism, according to Gide, is in fact itself a form of narratological or dramaturgical forgery—although one persuasive to its public and thus subject to inflation.

As antidote to this approach, which lazily adjusts the facts to fit its desired findings, Gide proposes another: the perversity of the psychologically *in*explicable, of the fundamentally implausible. Gide's abiding interest in such titillating human interest stories as those one finds represented in the tabloid genre of the *fait divers*—clippings of which he collected for decades—opens this narrative climax onto a larger nexus of concerns. Responding to nothing in particular in his correspondent's missive, an earlier public letter on the subject, in the years following the publication of his *Faux-monnayeurs*, suddenly dismisses the possibility of the *acte gratuit* so central philosophically to the author's narrative work: "A gratuitous act. . . . Let's be clear. Personally I don't believe in gratuitous acts, an act without any motivation. That is fundamentally out of the question. There are no effects without causes. The words 'gratuitous act' [*acte gratuit*] are a temporary label that seems convenient to describe acts that transcend ordinary psychological explanations, gestures that do not result in simple personal advantage."[63] The inexplicable but indisputable reality of the morbidly surprising news item (recalling the etymology of *nouvelle*, novella, novel) provides a formal corollary for gratuitous action while by the same gesture grounding it, if only provisionally, in precisely the kind of causal and psychological realism Gide otherwise so adamantly resists. It is in fact all the more realistic for its perplexing nature. More rigorously conceptualized, what the author celebrates in the *acte gratuit* turns out to transcend the psychological not because it constitutes a pure expression of unhampered human volition but rather because it is a recognition of the *accidental*, of an action exceeding agency. If anything, this would seem to amount to a refutation of free will as such, with the psychologically coherent subject emerging only postfactually as an abstraction, as a gloss on the free play of libidinal drives and their observable effects.

Still, reassuring himself and his reader that there is more at stake than mere self-interest, Gide aims to distinguish the *acte gratuit* from simple self-gratification, to attest to a reality principle more profound than idly abstract onanism. Gide's fascination with the *fait divers* reposes on an affinity for the kind of narrative that resists easy narrativity, for the constraints of the factual even and especially where they disrupt its recounting. His other pronouncements on the matter notwithstanding, Gide seems to subscribe to a gold standard of literary authenticity for which the apparently motiveless crime of the truly surprising (and surprisingly true) *fait divers* serves as the guarantor.

In chapter 4, especially, I will examine how such assurances of (extratextual) veracity are increasingly attached to the exquisitely wounded queer body, making the body itself into an aesthetic and narrative abstraction; in the final chapters, this will more often than not pertain to the corpse of a suicide. In Gide, too, the *fait divers* inspiring Boris's death is both the site of the breakdown of narrativity and its ultimate overcoming through (new forms of) narrative. There are in fact a series of discussions or depictions of self-harm throughout the text: most notably Olivier's attempted suicide (under the influence of Bernard's theory that one might commit suicide out of excessive enthusiasm) after his first night spent with Édouard. Often linked to homosexuality, such instances can be recognized in retrospect, perhaps, as so many deferrals of the story's only conceivable conclusion—as gratuitous as it is predictable. This dynamic attaches not only to the *fait divers* on which Gide models Boris's calamity but also, biographically, to Gide's working through of the loss of his friend Émile Ambresin in this and other fictionalized accounts of suicide, including that of Alexis in *Corydon*, who kills himself over unrequited love—connecting this preoccupation again to manifest reflections on homosexuality.[64] Boris's compulsive masturbation is explicitly linked, moreover, to Gide's autobiographical accounts of his own childhood in *Si le grain ne meurt . . .* (*If it Die . . .*, 1924), further intensifying the game of hide-and-seek through which Gide highlights the tension between (erotic) experience and its literary depiction.

The inclusion of this suicide turns out, then, to be pornographic in its logic. Its appeal reposes on the irrefutable if obscene existence of the cadaver promised by the *fait divers* as does a pornographic image on the absent presence of the profilmic body. The gunshot substitutes a cumshot, providing necessary narrative satisfaction and cathartic release to what would—to remain within pornological vocabulary—otherwise amount to nonejaculative edging. At the same time, its simultaneous exclusion from the novel serves as a sublimation. Gide's "outrageously real" *fait divers* exists at the intersection where the inextricability of life from literature appears most inevitable: Gide cannot resist, it seems, the intrusion of an external, preexisting reality into his text any more than that reality can resist succumbing to the very narrativity and psychology whose failings it had been intended to emblematize. This is certainly true of the concluding demonic intrusion, the *diableries d'écoliers*, of *Les faux-monnayeurs* and of the narratological motivation of a deed that appears diegetically unmotivated. Boris's action is perplexing to Édouard and the other characters because it seems so puzzlingly arbitrary. The reader, however, recognizes it to be governed (as Gide's repeated insistence, in this context, on the impossibility of a truly motiveless deed would suggest) by both erotic-psychological and, especially, narratological necessity. Boris's obligatory suicide, apparently extraneous to the plot of *Les faux-monnayeurs*, proves indispensable to whatever minimal degree of narrative closure the would-be novel deigns to deliver.[65]

Autonomy, Authenticity, Performativity, Passing

Gide has a soft spot for the kind of figures who rage against the narrativity he imposes, a conflict of wills between character and creator staged most dramatically in *Les faux-monnayeurs* not by Édouard's arguments with his author but by La Pérouse, who asserts more than once that God "plays with us like a cat, tormenting a mouse" and meditates at length on the question of free will.[66] Having contemplated but abandoned his own plans for suicide, he compares himself to a marionette:

> In reality, the reason I didn't kill myself is that I wasn't free. I say now that I was afraid; but no; it wasn't that. Something completely foreign to my will held me back. As if God didn't want to let me go. Imagine a marionette who should want to leave the stage before the end of the play. . . . Halt! You're wanted for the *finale*. Ah! Ah! you thought you would be able to go off whenever you liked! . . . I understood that what we call our will is merely the threads which work the marionette, and which God pulls. Don't you see? Well, I'll explain. For instance, I say to myself: "Now I'm going to raise my right arm"; and I raise it. (And he did raise it.) But it's because the string had already been pulled which made me think and say: "I'm going to raise my right arm." . . . And the proof that I'm not free is that if it had been my left arm that I had had to raise, I should have said to you: "Now I'm going to raise my left arm." . . . No; I see you don't understand. . . . You are not free to understand. . . . Oh! I realize now that God is playing with us. It amuses him to let us think that what he makes us do is what we wanted to do. That's his horrible game [*vilain jeu*].[67]

This is an evident example of Gide's penchant for allowing his characters moments of meta-awareness where they become conscious of their role in a larger plot beyond their control. La Pérouse's purported proof of his theory and his dismissal of human motivation as an explanation only postfactually applied also reinforces Gide's critique of easy psychology in his thinking on the *fait divers*. If this *vilain jeu* indirectly invokes Gide's demon, La Pérouse's ultimate understanding—advanced "confusedly" at the conclusion of the novel—that "the devil and God are one and the same" ought also to be understood as a kind of misappropriative and demonic simulation: "I have often thought that the word of God was the whole of creation. But the devil seized hold of it. His noise drowns the voice of God."[68] Here Gide's demon acts as a sort of *souffleur*, providing La Pérouse with lines of dialogue to repeat aloud.

That the demonic deity referred to is an author figure, in this case apparently a playwright, is further emphasized by the dramaturgical language employed both by La Pérouse and by Édouard, his interlocutor here and the source of the parenthetical stage direction regarding the raised arm in his recounting of their conversation.[69] Describing "cette triste comédie" ("this melancholy piece of acting"), Édouard relates that La Pérouse takes on "a declamatory tone, unspeakably affected, to which I was unaccustomed in my old master—so natural with me, as a rule—so confiding."[70] The role of unconvincing drama queen is one that La Pérouse readopts ("the words brought back to him the remembrance of the part he was playing") and ultimately drops ("at last consenting to abandon his role") over the course of the conversation.[71]

But if Édouard dismisses La Pérouse's paranoia, Gide, the puppet master, will by the end of the novel insinuate its accuracy. It is La Pérouse, after all, who prepares the Chekovian gun that, thought to be unloaded by most of the players involved, Boris later tragically fires. In this light, and by this stage logic, Boris's death, executed with the same firearm La Pérouse had intended for his own suicide, comes into view as the consummation of the earlier inaction, with undeniable echoes of La Pérouse's discourse:

> So Boris stepped forward to the appointed place; he walked slowly, like an automaton—or rather like a somnambulist. *His right hand* had seized the pistol but kept it hidden in the pocket of his coat; he took it out only at the last moment. The fatal place [*la place fatale*] was, as I have said, in the recess made by a disused door [*la porte condamnée*] on the right of the master's desk, so that the master could only see it by leaning forward.[72]

As if controlled by unseen stage machinery, operating entirely of its own accord, the right hand—the same one La Pérouse lifted in his demonstration of the fallacy of free will—raises and the child moves mechanically in the direction of his destiny: *la place fatale*, *la porte condamnée*. This is perhaps the closest we come to actual gratuity in Gide: an almost-Nietzschean *amor fati*, a full affirmation of the inevitable.

La Pérouse's impotence to react in the face of this event seems to confirm his earlier suspicion of the nonexistence of human agency but is placed in immediate contrast to Boris's execution of the very act of which his grandfather discovered himself incapable:

> La Pérouse leant forward. And at first he did not understand what his grandson was doing, though the strange solemnity of his actions was of a nature to alarm him. Speaking as loudly and as authoritatively as he could, he began:
>
> "Master Boris, kindly return at once to your . . ."
>
> But he suddenly recognized the pistol: Boris had just raised it to his temple. La Pérouse understood and immediately turned icy cold as if the blood were freezing in his veins. He tried to rise and run towards Boris—stop him—call to him. . . . A kind of hoarse rattle came from his throat; he remained rooted to the spot, paralytic, shaken by a violent trembling.
>
> The shot went off. Boris did not drop at once. The body stayed upright for a moment, as though caught in the corner of the recess; then the head, falling on to the shoulder, bore it down; it collapsed.[73]

Surprisingly, then, it is not La Pérouse's inability to commit suicide that demonstrates the lack of free will in *Les faux-monnayeurs*, but rather the narrative *inevitability* of this suicide within the context of the novel. (Boris, for his part, had recognized even before signing "la feuille maudite" ["accursed paper"] that sealed his fate that the game was rigged: "C'était couru" ["It was bound to happen."][74]) The completion of the gesture La Pérouse had found impossible anticipates Édouard's interdiction against including this *fait divers* in his novel and the ultimate suspension of that interdiction by a higher authorial power. It highlights the hiatus between the trope and its iteration.

This returns us to Judith Butler's redefinition, in *Bodies That Matter*, of agency as a function of constraint: "Agency is the hiatus in iterability, the compulsion to install an identity through repetition, which requires the very contingency, that undetermined interval, that identity insistently seeks to foreclose."[75] Or, as the central character of *Les caves du Vatican* remarks on his own apparent destiny, despite his guiding pursuit of gratuity: "One imagines *what would happen if*, but there's always a little hiatus [*laps*] through which the unexpected creeps in. Nothing ever happens exactly as one thinks it's going to. . . . That's what makes me want to act."[76] It is not that either La Pérouse or Boris exercises agency in the sense of a pure freedom of choice but rather that the potential for such liberty materializes in a lapse, an accident, a slipping up. It comes to be precisely as the nonidentity across these generations of the trope in question, just as the explicit difference between Édouard and Gide on the subject of the *fait divers* creates an aperture for contingency, for the ever-present could-be-otherwiseness of the text.

This oxymoronically inevitable contingency is linked directly, as I have already noted, to the question of specifically queer agency. Leonid Livak has compellingly argued that "homosexuality and suicide are inseparable in *Les Faux-monnayeurs*" and that Boris's suicide is "laden with homoeroticism."[77] The act is indeed preceded by "two hearty, childish kisses" on the cheek shared between Boris and his classmate Phiphi, but it might be more accurate to say that the situation is laden with homophobia; Boris is condemned to die in large part because his perceived effeminacy irks his classmate Ghéridanisol: "His musical voice, his grace, his girlish look—everything about him exasperates him. The very sight of Boris seems to inspire him with that instinctive aversion which, in a herd, makes the strong fall ruthlessly upon the weak."[78] Victoria Reid has contended more generally that "Gide makes Édouard and his pederasty complicit in, or at least touched by, the suicide attempts or the contemplated suicide of others in the text."[79] But while Édouard undoubtedly bears part of the blame for this turn of events, he does have some help.

Of the young coconspirators involved in what is meant to be merely a simulated suicide, only the diabolical Ghéridanisol recognizes that the chamber of the pistol has a bullet in it, seeming to understand that this dramaturgical device has a fated function: "Ghéridanisol . . . began to insinuate that old La Pérouse's pistol would come in handy [*trouver ici son emploi*]."[80] The French here is more revealing in that the pistol idiomatically has *its* purpose, *son emploi*, as if it lay in wait all along for its usage to arrive. Notably, and this point is crucial,

Ghéridanisol is also responsible for the traffic of counterfeit coins that must be presumed the diegetic source of Bernard's—Bernard eventually reveals that he has it from a local grocer in Saas-Fée. And like Bernard's prop, seemingly cut from the whole cloth of Édouard's errant idea, it illustrates and makes real with fatal force a thought experiment that had previously been, for La Pérouse, purely heuristic. If the coin and bullet share the same not entirely diegetic but not entirely metaleptic origin, the devilish undertones of the *vilain jeu* evoked by La Pérouse shortly after the gun is loaded also hint that the wickedness of Ghéridanisol and his classmates is of a piece with the demonic mischief that characterizes Gide's plotting as these figures' sometimes cruel creator.

That Gide identifies with this narrative agency but also externalizes it, projecting it onto demonic forces, suggests that the simultaneous interdiction against and ultimate inclusion of this coerced suicide is also characteristic of the boundaries of authorial control as Gide imagines them. In his not infrequent disagreements with his own characters, Gide does not, as we have seen, always prevail. This is a matter both of narratological preference and of Gide's quest for sincerity in his writing, as Anna-Louise Milne has noted in a summary of Gide's critique of Cocteau, the model for Passavant in *Les faux-monnayeurs*: "Gide was pulling the notion of sincerity away from self-possession, since it was precisely the appearance of self-possession or self-consciousness that he disliked in Cocteau. So while contemporary rereadings of modernism value Cocteau's work for its sensitivity to the way mechanical forms of reproduction break down the ideal of natural, authentic and unified expression of the self, Gide objected to the all-consuming ego that set himself up as the master behind the machine."[81] For Susan Sontag, the reason that Cocteau is to be counted as camp—as I think is indisputable—but Gide should not be is a question of quality and literary-historical significance: "There is a sense in which it is correct to say: 'It's too good to be Camp.' Or 'too important,' not marginal enough. . . . Thus, the personality and many of the works of Jean Cocteau are Camp, but not those of André Gide."[82] But one might, guided by Gide's objection to the seamlessness of Cocteau's self-mythologization, see it instead as connected to this question of self-possession and the pretension to sovereign self-coherence. Throughout his writing, autobiographical and fictional alike, Gide focuses on his avowed self-contradictions and failed passings, underscoring both his authorial machinations and the moments at which they get away from him.

Milne has excavated how true sincerity, for Gide, involves a loosening of the self and inherently exceeds the meaning the subject is conscious of giving—a new "open, porous sense of authenticity" to counter Cocteau's composure.[83] Sincerity is redefined as a constant effort toward self-transformation rather than one of revelation: "The movement of understanding here is not about peeling away the layers of social hypocrisy, uncovering some deep-rooted, natural truth, but rather about the projection of a unified life, which is both 'fictive' because not yet realized, yet true because unified and 'naturel.' "[84]

This helps connect Gide's obsession with the *fait divers* to his evolving representation of homosexuality by way of what Milne has described as his "long struggle to be sincere, which resulted in a multiplicity of fictional personas but also the publication of his private diary."[85] The fabulation of these various selves, some more self-consciously fictionalized than others, represents for Milne Gide's realization "that writing only releases counterfeit tokens into circulation" but also his "undeterred will to anchor the sign in the truth of personal experience."[86] Gide gradually develops a view of authenticity not as an expression of anything innate but rather as an adopted, fictive-narrative essence of the kind afforded to the counterfeit coin or demonic bullet in *Les faux-monnayeurs*.[87] Its aesthetic coherence supplements its ontological insufficiency but without ever completely papering over the cracks.

Such a poetics of failed passing or of failed posturing reveals that Gide can subscribe to subjectivity only as narrative abstraction, and only with the caveat of irreconcilable self-discrepancy. This queer embrace of dissonance ("Very well . . . then I contradict myself"[88]) is perhaps epitomized by the concluding gesture of *Les faux-monnayeurs*: a scene of suicide that both is and isn't in the novel, that at once represents reality and the refusal to do so and that depicts a gratuitous act that was ineluctably fated to occur. The perverse narratology that dictates that *Les faux-monnayeurs* repose on the reality of the *fait divers* and autobiographical detail turns out to be an even more radical *mise-en-pratique* of Wilde's dictum that life imitate art. It implies not only, to paraphrase Stéphane Mallarmé, that everything in the world exists in order to end up in a book but also that a certain self-contradictory narrativity is always already at work in life experience itself.

It is precisely this aestheticist impulse that Paul de Man, for one, finds so troubling in Gide's work, identifying it as the result of a narcissistic "autoeroticism" that "reintroduces, somewhat surreptitiously, the antisocial, inhumane element present in aestheticism, the negative side of a coin whose positive side is Mallarmé's self-reflection. Under the guise of rebellion, Gide in fact urges us to rediscover our authentic inner self in an erotic fervor even more intensely inward than Mallarmé's concentration on the poetic resources of language."[89] Ahead of its time, de Man's discussion of the antisocial aestheticism of Gide's textually masturbatory practices is illustrative and worth pondering. Implicitly correlating homosexuality to artifice and aestheticism as well as to a deceptive inwardness of which he is critical, de Man's take is in some ways reminiscent of the phobic discourse of sincerity excavated earlier. But de Man's evident homophobia in this instance is especially interesting for its generic alignment, which does not oppose autobiography to fiction, but rather (tacitly, as de Man never mentions homosexuality by name) sets Gide's more open treatment of sexuality in *Corydon* against the rest of the oeuvre.

Initially praising the author, de Man ultimately asserts that Gide "offers little opportunity for . . . self-deceptions" precisely because his various apologiae for pederasty are so unconvincing:

> Whenever he was tempted to make uncritical assertions, he pulled the rug out from under them. On the one occasion, in *Corydon*, where he rationalizes his personal aberrations into self-justifying generalities, his bad faith is so blatant that he can hardly be taken seriously. Most of the time, his irony and self-criticism remain fully operative. The constant self-analysis that underlies the autobiographical works, the *Journal*, and most of the novels, is always aimed at dispelling false constructs of the self that would allow him to strike seductive but artificial poses.[90]

Gide is redeemed, in this view, by a campy kind of failed passing: a bad faith so blatant that its seriousness fails. But what de Man appears not to recognize is that the author's undoing of the false constructs of the self emanate precisely, even by the implications of his own analysis, from the poses persistently fictionalized in the autobiographical and narrative writings. If Gide succeeds in deconstructing the myth of inwardness and of the secure and stable subject, it is by dint of an artificial posturing and an aestheticist sublimation.[91]

With this in mind, and by way of wrapping up, I'd like to dwell a moment longer on what becomes of such pathologizing discourses and the cult of sincerity against which Michael Lucey's first book on Gide had argued. Bringing Gide's two dominant narrative modes—confessional and metafictional—to bear on one another, Scott Branson concludes that, when writing in the first person, Gide undertakes "a formal abstraction that empties out the autobiographical instance."[92] In so doing, he builds on a later monograph by Lucey, *Never Say I* (the title refers to an injunction made independently to Gide by Wilde and Marcel Proust), which demonstrates how authors like Gide perform this "work of abstraction on the relation between first-person utterance and same-sex sexualities for practical reasons: in order to find the means to say new things."[93] Which is to say that the first-person pronoun, especially in proto-queer authors such as Gide, does not have a fixed referent but rather invites "interpretive attention to be paid to the work of abstraction itself."[94] In short, Gide's literary representation is always also unavoidably an expository deconstruction of what is being represented and of the process of figuration itself.

Thus, as Branson summarizes, Lucey "resituates Gide's contribution against the grain of narcissistic formalization that accompanies the pathologizing of homosexuality as a recognizable identity at the turn of the century. In other words, Gide's queer 'I' is not an avatar for stable identity, but rather a vanishing point for competing and ever-shifting expressions of desire."[95] Gide's work proves definitional for, while also resisting, the codification of homosexual identity—recalling in advance the later pathologization of pederasty as pedophilia: the historical endpoint to the discomfiting genealogical gray zone designated by Amin's notion of "modern" pederasty. And it is worth noting that *pédéraste*, in its shortened form *pédé*, remains among the most common designations for a male homosexual in idiomatic French even today—testifying to the uncomfortably continued legacy of an earlier definition of intergenerational male same-sex attachment that has clearly failed to pass away entirely. In the chapters to come, I will repeatedly observe its echoes in a daddy-twink dynamic that figures centrally across the core texts treated in this study.

Pederasty, in *Les faux-monnayeurs*, is envisioned as a practice of allowing youthful subjectivities to develop freely, unencumbered by pedagogical or narrative restraint, so that the educator might awaken to himself in the image of his desired changelings or the author as the reflection of his oeuvre.[96] Recognizing the formal, narratological implications of this approach can shed light on both Gide's modernism and the ideological formations of contemporary queer theory and queer identities.

Conclusion: Gide's Queer Coinages

Édouard's hands-off approach to education and Gide's correspondingly voyeuristic, sometimes noninterventionist attitude to the development of his young characters would seem, at first blush, intrinsically at odds with the kind of demonic counterfeiting by which life imitates art, just as Gide's recourse to the *fait divers* and to evident autobiographical inspiration appears incompatible with an avowed practice of willful narrative forgery. But, taken seriously, our encounter with Gide might encourage an overcoming of the hierarchies of substance and style, being and becoming. At once noun and nominalized verb, the space of *Bildung* in this *roman d'apprentissage*, the twilight between formation and form, is the unsteady interval of *queer* itself. As Cocteau describes the author of *Les faux-monnayeurs*, "Gide was fraud incarnate. . . . False coin [*Faux jeton*] is redundant. Gide was a real coin [*un vrai jeton*]. A casino token. This token was worth a veritable fortune. . . . But you needed to submit to the conditions of exchange. You didn't exactly have this fortune in hand but rather a precious disk which represented it."[97] A *faux jeton*, in idiomatic French, is a hypocrite, a sneak or a cheat, but Cocteau's literalization of the expression seems to intimate, however critically, that all currencies are aspirational just as all selfhoods are perpetually forged. Gide heuristically commits to the identities, sexual or otherwise, represented in his texts, while nonetheless never ceasing to recognize their contingency—just as queer theory commits to its newly minted formulations and coinages, allowing them to gain currency, while at the same time perpetually negotiating the rate of exchange and anticipating their revision.

There has been, as I've noted, from the very moment in the early 1990s that queer studies began to replace an older disciplinary designation of lesbian and gay studies, a continuous contestation of the term *queer* itself. An important aspect of this ongoing debate has been the persistent worry that conclusively defining queer might deprive it of its characteristic elasticity and lead to its codification. Lee Edelman, already in the midnineties, cautioned that there was a tension between the contingency and open possibility of queer and the foreclosure of the same by its gradual tokenization as a legible coinage: "Though 'queer' as the endlessly mutating token of non-assimilation (and hence as the utopian badge of a would-be 'authentic' position of resistance) may reflect a certain bourgeois aspiration to be always *au courant*, its vigorous and unmethodical dislocations of 'identity' create, at the risk, to be sure, of producing a version of identity politics as postmodern commodity fetishism, a zone of possibilities in which the embodiment of the subject might be experienced otherwise."[98] Only a few years later, David Halperin, whose work on Jean Genet will be important for the chapters to come, will complain that this fetishization of a sexy, nonspecific queer identity divorced from any particular sexuality had already occurred and that, taking its place among other disciplines, queer studies had now become an intellectual commodity deprived of its radical potential.[99] According to this thinking, as the token of subversion gains currency, it loses both its verbal-epistemological power to reframe experience and its nominal diffusiveness, coming instead to constitute an ill-defined postmodern identity category all its own.

Flamboyant Fictions will observe a similar legacy in literature and narrative film extending from Gide onward, demonstrating how his queer counterfeiting, over the course of the last century or so, has slowly taken on discernible exchange value as a standardized rhetorical tender: as a recognizably homosexual style. In so doing, this token arguably succumbs first to inflation (insofar as its subversiveness is slowly diminished) and then to reification (in the sense that becomes naturalized and concretized). Or, to borrow a Nietzschean metaphor for how accepted truths are born from epistemological error, these sexualities are reduced to "coins which have lost their image and now can be used only as metal, and no longer as coins."[100] Noting, in their introduction to a special issue of *differences* on "Queer Theory without Antinormativity"—and perhaps not without a hint of schadenfreude—that "Halperin's lament that 'queer theory was simply too lucrative to give up' has not been widely adopted," Robyn Wiegman and Elizabeth A. Wilson, remind us that "while 'queer' has etymological connections to movements that transverse and twist, its most frequent deployment has been in the service of defiance and reprimand. The allure of moving against appears to have had greater critical currency than the more intimate and complicit gesture of moving athwart."[101] I am neither suggesting that queer theory has sold out nor am I arguing for a resuscitation of an older oppositional antinormativity. But perhaps a paradigm of failed passing, by forcing us to countenance internal alterity, might also lead to freer forms of self-invention less beholden to externally or self-imposed identity politics, might make possible varieties of self-affirmation less restricted by self-commodifying subjectivity.

Chapter 2

✦

Counterfeit Sexualities

Performativity in Jean Genet

Introducing the homosexual transvestite Divine, the central character of his first novel, *Notre-Dame-des-Fleurs* (*Our Lady of the Flowers*, 1943), to Paris and at the same moment to the reader, Jean Genet confesses that this is not, or at least not entirely, the book he wishes he were writing:

> Divine was full of grace, and yet was like all those prowlers at country fairs on the lookout for rare sights and artistic visions, good sports who trail behind them all the inevitable hodge-podge of side shows. At the slightest movement—if they knot their tie, if they flick the ash of their cigarette—they set slot machines [*des appareils à sous*] in motion. Divine knotted, garroted arteries. Her seductiveness will be implacable. If it were only up to me, I would make her the kind of fatal hero I like [*un héros fatal comme je les aime*]. Fatal, that is, determining the fate of those who gaze at them, spellbound [*médusés*]. I would make her with hips of stone, flat and polished cheeks, heavy eyelids, pagan [*païens*] knees so lovely that they reflected the desperate intelligence of the faces of mystics. I would strip her of all sentimental trappings. Let her consent to be the frozen statue. But I know that the poor Demiurge is forced to make his creature in his own image and that he did not invent Lucifer. In my cell, little by little, I shall have to give my thrills to the granite. I shall remain alone with it for a long time, and I shall make it live with my breath and the smell of my farts, both the solemn and the mild ones. It will take me an entire book to draw her from her petrification and gradually impart my suffering to her, gradually deliver her from evil, and, holding her by the hand lead her to saintliness.[1]

The Divine Genet would prefer to imagine, if left to his own devices, would be, true to her name, godlike: spellbinding, determining the fate of those who cross her path. Instead, as we're about to see, she is an object of scorn and derision in the Montmartre brasserie where she has come to make her first public appearance in drag. Her failure to be as Genet had purportedly intended stems from his own status as an incompetent or at least not-entirely-omnipotent creator, limited to the raw materials of the self and unable, at least in this case, to fashion a character not in some way reflecting his own image. Genet's reference to the demiurge and the devil recalls the metaleptic contingencies governing Gide's narrative writing, but if Divine fails to turn to stone those who gaze upon her (for we ought not overlook the etymology of *médusé*), it is in part because Genet, like Daedalus, can't get his statues to stand still. Instead, the granite—of his sculpture, of his cell walls—trembles with the thrill of unrealized desire.

At once abjectly deflating and ornately overinsisting on the solemnity of his tone, Genet's is a prose style characterized by failed passing, by an intentionally ever-inelegant eloquence. The same can be said of both his narratives and of his characters. It would, for instance, be uncommon—unheard of, in fact—to find such desirous description of a female physique in Genet's work, but still, admittedly, the traits Genet claims he would prefer to ascribe to his imagined hero are rather gender ambiguous: strong hips, flat cheeks, heavy eyelids, "pagan" knees. That he retains the feminine pronoun even while describing "*un* héros . . . comme je les aime [the kind of . . . hero I like]" points, then, to a potential conflict of wills between Genet and his creation: alone in his prison cell, the quasi-autobiographical narrator would apparently prefer to indulge here, as he does throughout the book, in masturbatory fantasy, but it is possible that Divine's self-determination and gender expression get in the way. Genet's failure to imagine Divine as he would like becomes a moment where invention and identity collide.

Or where *self*-invention and *self*-identity collide: conscious of her own studied grace, it is, perhaps, Divine's self-awareness, her distance from herself, that makes it impossible to be beautiful with quite the same enviable naïveté her author would seemingly favor. Genet is hardly incapable, after all, of imagining his heroes as he'd like. Describing Divine's first love, for instance, he proclaims: "He was good-looking—as are all the males in this book, powerful and lithe, and unaware of their grace."[2] But Divine, unlike her lovers, is not what she or Genet would call a *mâle*, a term more commonly used to refer to the male organism of a given species—suggesting an almost taxonomic impulse to the novel, a desire to enumerate and scrutinize "les tantes-filles et tantes-gars, tapettes, pédales, tantouzes, dont je vous parle" ("the girl-queens and boy-queens, the aunties, fags, and nellies of whom I am speaking").[3] And Divine's poise could hardly be more different than the unadorned and unreflected grace of these *mâles*: hers Genet describes as counterfeit, as a relatively transparent con, comparing her to a carnival huckster whose seductions surreptitiously put into motion coin machines (*appareils à sous*).

If we take seriously the author's repeated assertions that Divine is his primary surrogate within the story, then these coinages might be read as a reflection of his own poetics—restricted in its authenticity, as he confesses early on, by the narrator's limited knowledge: "I'm sorry to say I know too little (nothing) about the secret relations between those beings who are beautiful and know it [*des êtres qui sont beaux et savent qu'ils le sont*], and nothing about the seemingly friendly but perhaps hostile contacts between handsome boys. If they smile [*S'ils se sourient*] at each other over a trifle, is there, unknown to them, some tenderness in their smile, and do they feel its influence in some obscure way?"[4] The mirroring imagined here—the reflexive *ils se sourient*—involves a love-hate mutual (mis)recognition. Even when attempting to depict beings perfectly at peace with their own beauty, Genet's narrator cannot, it seems, conceive of a narcissism unfettered by disappointment, a tenderness or amity untinged by aversion. He cannot, in other words, conceive of an identification that is not at the same time a distancing and *dis*identification.

Already in the first pages of *Bodies That Matter*, and central to that book's investigation, Judith Butler speculates:

> Although the political discourses that mobilize identity categories tend to cultivate identifications in the service of a political goal, it may be that the persistence of *dis*identification is equally crucial to the rearticulation of democratic contestation. Indeed, it may be precisely through practices which underscore disidentification with those regulatory norms by which sexual difference is materialized that . . . queer politics are mobilized. Such collective disidentifications can facilitate a reconceptualization of which bodies matter, and which bodies are yet to emerge as critical matters of concern.[5]

Or, to phrase this in terms familiar from my introduction: troping on received identity categories, individuals also warp these received patterns, push them to their limits and redefine them through a kind of catachresis—a forced figure of speech, a usage inappropriate to its context.[6] That this is fundamental to the oppositional politics of queerness is reflected in the ongoing contestation over the term *queer* itself.

It was, most notably, José Esteban Muñoz who furthered this line of inquiry into disidentification as a social survival strategy, celebrating the potential of a "disidentification that enables politics" and asserting that

> disidentification is about recycling and rethinking encoded meaning. The process of disidentification scrambles and reconstructs the encoded message of a cultural text in a fashion that both exposes the encoded message's universalizing and exclusionary machinations and

> recircuits its workings to account for, include, and empower minority identities and identifications. Thus, disidentification is a step further than cracking open the code of the majority; it proceeds to use this code as raw material for representing a disempowered politics or positionality that has been rendered unthinkable by the dominant culture.[7]

In this chapter and those to come I will be examining various disidentificatory strategies depicted and enacted by Genet and by a range of filmmakers working under his influence. Narrative self-invention—relying, as it does, on both continuity and difference between writing and written selves—always involves a degree of dissonance. What Muñoz describes as identity-in-difference is a "version of identity politics . . . imagin[ing] a reconstructed narrative of identity formation that locates the enacting of self at precisely the point where the discourses of essentialism and constructivism short-circuit."[8] Negotiating similarly between these poles, as well as between voluntarist and determinist paradigms, this chapter will remain attuned not only to the political potential of the kinds of resignifying strategies Muñoz describes as disidentifications but also critically highlight their often involuntary and sometimes disconcertingly derivative aspects.

If Divine's identity, for example, is determined by the avowed impotence of her author, by the limits of the writing self, it is also conditioned by an encounter with alterity. Returning to her coming out where we left off, in the Montmartre café Graff, we can see how lonely the same cheeky smile depicted above can be for the abjected:

> The waiter who served her felt very much like snickering, but out of decency he did not dare in front of her. As for the manager, he approached her table and decided that as soon as she finished her tea, he would ask her to leave, to make sure she would not turn up again some other evening.
>
> Finally, she patted her snowy forehead with a flowered handkerchief. Then she crossed her legs; on her ankle could be seen [*l'on vit*] a chain fastened by a locket which *we* [*nous*] know contained a few hairs. She smiled all around, and everyone answered only by turning away, but that was a way of answering. The café was so quiet that you could hear everything clearly [*l'on y entendait distinctement tous les bruits*]. The whole café thought that the smile of (for the colonel: the invert; for the shopkeepers: the fairy; for the banker and the waiters: the fag; for the gigolos: 'that one"; etc. [*pour le colonel: l'inverti; pour les commerçants: la chochotte; pour le banquier et les garçons: la proutt; pour les gigolos: « celle-ci », etc.*]) was abject. Divine did not press the point. From a tiny black purse she took a few coins which she laid noiselessly on the marble table. The café disappeared

> [*le café disparut*], and Divine was metamorphosed into one of those monsters that are painted on walls—chimeras or griffins—for a customer, in spite of himself [*malgré lui*], murmured a magic word as he thought of her:
>
> "Homoseckshual [*Pédérasque*]."[9]

My concern in this book is with the literary and filmic treatment of male homosexuality as a trope that is returned to and thus re*turned* throughout the twentieth century and into the twenty-first. In this passage the concatenation of soliloquized slurs, beginning with the colonel's *inverti* (invert), with its explicit resonances of turning,[10] already trope, as if by acoustic association, on a common theme—as the lisping *chochotte* (sissy, possibly a feminized affectation of *chouchou*, for darling) leads into the bawdier and more bodily *proutt* (connoting sodomy with an onomatopoeic approximation of the sound of a fart, recalling the material out of which Divine is fashioned). If these various appellations operate almost as revisions each of the last, the obscurely euphemistic *celle-ci* (translated as "*that* one" but more acutely gendered feminine in the original French) initially dilutes the description but also distills it into the common element tacitly unifying these various designations: namely, social stigma.

"One of the consequences of insult," writes Didier Eribon, "is to shape the relation one has to others and to the world and thereby to shape the personality, the subjectivity, the very being of the individual in question."[11] The narrative perspective of the passage is uncertain or unstable: while we are largely left to discern Divine's motivations and emotions from her actions—regarding her from the exterior as she crosses her legs, smiles, and pays—we are privy to the unspoken intentions and the silent thoughts of the others in the café. We thus view Divine filtered through the lens of the crowd's disdain and, indeed, embarrassment. Still, Genet distinguishes between the impersonal pronoun *on* to describe the crowd and a rather more intimate *nous* (we), which apparently includes the reader—not so much alerting us to the trivial detail of the locket's contents but assuming and assuring this shared knowledge. (The apparently superfluous gratuity of the inclusion of this prop, never again mentioned in the book, speaks to a reality fetish resembling the role of the coin discussed in the previous chapter.) While Divine and the others in the café find themselves in a standoff of mutual mockery, the reader is, from both angles, *in* on the joke, deprived of any stable identification precisely by a surfeit of possible identifications—and thus given a privileged view of how Divine's ostensibly inner identity is contested and affected in response to the innuendo of imagined invective.

Divine's public presentation, at least, is, to some degree, a selfhood with its origin in insult, as Eribon would argue: variously interpellated, as we've just seen, hers is "an identity without identity, or better, an identity without an essence—an identity to be created."[12] Properly grotesque, cobbled together from the various (mis)perceptions of others, like these stuttering collective drafts of a description of Divine, the magic word for her identity—uttered mistakenly and involuntarily ("malgré lui")—turns out to be the fantastically chimeric coinage *pédérasque*. (The customer means to say *pédéraste* but unwittingly affixes an alternate ending.) This is not so much homosexuality itself as a near-miss catachrestically approaching it. Accruing a rich but coherent nexus of resonances beyond its intended denotation, the solecism means not quite what it means to mean but rather *more*. An incongruous word at odds with itself, moreover, the imperfect portmanteau reveals the origin of the self in the kind of non-self-identity Jacques Derrida early on theorizes as *différance*: a noncoincidence of the self with the self.[13] Better described by an errant neologism, an idiomatic accident, than the more stable and more legible identity categories that precede it, Divine becomes herself at the very moment she ceases to be (herself) and dissolves into an artwork: fading into one of the outlandish creatures of the café walls, which (given their concomitant vanishing act: "le café disparut" ["the café disappeared"]) themselves also ultimately evaporate into the literary text.

Genet's (Dis)identifications

Elaborating the view of the queer self as vanishing point or formal abstraction, discussed at the conclusion to the previous chapter, my interpretation of *Notre-Dame-des-Fleurs* will attend to such repeated disappearances. It will focus on the work's three central characters: Divine, Mignon Les-Petits-Pieds (the camped-up mobster feel of the name is aptly rendered in Bernard Frechtman's translation as Darling Daintyfoot), and the titular Notre-Dame-des-Fleurs (Our Lady of the Flowers). Observed closely, Genet's approach to these figures does not, on the whole, amount to the composition of stable identity categories for queer subjectivities. Instead, it consists of a perpetual undoing of selves that remain irremediably and insistently at odds with themselves. Moreover, while not the focus here, Genet's theater—the labile roleplaying of *Les bonnes* (*The Maids*, 1947), the pornological simulacra of *Le balcon* (*The Balcony*, 1956), the whiteface of *Les nègres* (*The Blacks*, 1948)—would seem to constitute an extended, even obsessive, rumination on the subject of failed passing. In the theatrical corpus such reflections are most often taken as dramaturgical metacommentary, but such dissonances also have profound consequences for Genet's quasi-autobiographical *narrative* endeavor of representing the writing self through its fictionalized projections.

If (dis)identification between the author and his characters is part and parcel of Genet's peculiar approach to fictionalized autobiography, these identity conflicts apply equally to the reader's relationship to the author and his inventions. Notably, Leo Bersani influentially makes the Genetian embrace of abjection the basis of a revolutionary gay antirelationality, the repercussions of which are still being felt in queer studies nearly three decades on.[14] Some years later, James Creech, in an essay titled "Outing Jean Genet," admits initially to finding this view too optimistic—but then, ultimately, through a not entirely convincing readerly sleight of hand, attempts to out Genet's celebration of stigma instead as a gesture of closeted gay pride.[15] For Eribon, not dissimilarly, writing at the beginning of the present century, Genet's work is emblematic of a tradition in which minoritarian populations affirm imposed abjection in order to produce new forms of subjectivity.[16] Following Eribon, and paying careful attention to the initial circulation of Genet's texts to assess whether they participate in an avant-garde, Michael Lucey makes a compelling case for how the author knowingly negotiates an address to but also contributes to the formation of sexually marginal counterpublics.[17] For Claire Boyle, on the other hand, Genet not only presumes a heterosexual audience but in fact resolutely "straightens his reader," in order to rebuff any complicity, community, or collective elaboration of identity.[18]

Genet thus becomes the poster boy both for queer community *and* antirelationality, for a community predicated precisely on shared antirelationality. His often undeniably contradictory depictions of homosexuality, when taken together, come to constitute a worldview in which sexual identity cannot be neatly correlated to either sexual desire or sexual activity. One can begin to observe such deconstruction of sexual identity, as well as Genet's stubbornly oppositional stance at the time, in an oft-quoted passage from the novel explaining how unceremoniously even the most stable-seeming of homosexual unions can be dissolved; there Genet forcefully asserts: "Nos ménages, la loi de nos Maisons, ne ressemblent pas à vos Maisons. On s'aime sans amour. Ils n'ont pas le caractère sacramentel. Les tantes sont les grandes immorales" ("Our domestic life and the law of our Homes do not resemble your Homes. We love each other without love. Our homes do not have the sacramental character. Fags are the great immoralists").[19] Even within this brief excerpt, the narrative position wanders from identification into a subtle disidentification through its precariously shifting pronouns: at first part of the collective description *nous*, then the somewhat less personal *on*, it passes over the vague catchall *ils* (here obscurely attached to *ménages*, perhaps then also to *lois* and *maisons*, if he means all three) before finally turning its focalization to an implied and almost ethnographic *elles*: namely, *les tantes*. (This is the taxonomic counter-category to the *mâles* discussed above.) Genet may, then, be offering a new view of homosexual subjectivity, but it is certainly not with the aim of celebrating the sociability of homosexual community, let alone of finding solidarity with an imagined reader. It is less that he offers a comprehensive theory of homosexuality (or even theories in the plural) than that he develops a narrative mode through which its elaboration might be possible.

Which is to say that *Notre-Dame-des-Fleurs* begins to give distinct narrative form to the kind of counterfeiting discussed in the previous chapter—hinted at, perhaps, by Genet's mention in the very first pages of the novel that he shares his prison with "des faussaires mes voisins" ("my forger neighbors") and "des faux monnayeurs" ("counterfeiters").[20] Past scholarship on *Notre-Dame-des-Fleurs* has tended to celebrate what has most often been perceived as its radical narrative freedom, offering art as a refuge and aestheticism as an antidote to real-world suffering. Noting that Genet's oneiric and onanistic "fantasy originates in the dreamer-author's desire to possess his characters,"[21] Jerry Aline Flieger has argued, for instance, that "by dreaming the text, the author may violate diurnal constraints at his whim, creating a game where he alone determines the rules." Flieger emphasizes how "Genet confesses that he delights in shattering, decomposing, and reassembling his characters, affixing their images on the prison wall, celebrating and re-celebrating his control over these beloved figments of his imagination. Genet's use of dream technique, then, seems ultimately to coincide with a maniacal manifestation of erotic will."[22] For Pierre Laforgue, too, Genet's masturbatory fiction offers an imaginary escape from his carceral reality, made possible precisely because fantasy has become indistinguishable from reality."[23] Nadia Louar further connects this apparent freedom of invention more specifically to identarian issues within the text: "The author of *Our Lady* thus stages his ludic talent in language itself and ironically represents it as it is: a clever ruse figuring, according to the narrator's whim, the different identity postures taken up by his characters."[24] Reducing sexuality to a language game,[25] or perhaps revealing it as such, *Notre-Dame-des-Fleurs* would be of a piece, as Claire Boyle has it, with the author's tendency to "highlight the ubiquity of artifice and performance, and the absence of essence."[26] Just like that, it seems, the written word has played a dirty little trick on what it would otherwise represent, allowing Genet freely to create his characters and their sexualities following only the dictates of his own whim.

As we've already seen, however, it isn't entirely the case, even according to the internal logic of the text, that Genet performs a (self-)invention unbeholden to preexisting reality or absent any constraint. Even Genet's first serious reader, Jean-Paul Sartre, for all of the flaws of his interpretation, had recognized this: "We can be sure that our 'dreamer' never leaves reality; he *arranges* it. . . . He weaves a dream around his experiences, and that means, most of the time, that he simply changes their sign. . . . All of these traits will finally compose a fleeting and inimitable figure that will have the contingency and truth of life and that will be the obverse of the fake coin of which Genet himself is the reverse."[27] Introducing Genet to a wider readership, Sartre acknowledges the novelist's celebration of his feelings of abjection as a merely cosmetic revaluation of values and as an act of counterfeiting: the author does not change reality; he merely changes its meaning. Genet himself is already a forgery, his fiction only the flipside of the same coin.

Elsewhere, in what remains one of the most insightful readings of the novel to date, Michael Lucey therefore chooses to highlight the limits of the narrator's imagination, that is, which of and to what degree his (day)dreams can find full representation within the novel: "Even though this is the narrator's fantasy, he apparently cannot just produce any scenario he wants. . . . *Notre-Dame-des-Fleurs* is thus evidently not a novel about the *freedom* of fantasy even within a prison. Fantasy itself proves to have a frustratingly complex relation to constraint. *Notre-Dame-des-Fleurs* in its form explicitly investigates the nature of fantasy: the conditions of its production, the space of its elaboration, the temporalities it engages, the work it does on identity structures."[28] As Lucey begins to suggest here, this vexed (and often vexing) relationship between fantasy and constraint also conditions the various sexualities made possible within Genet's work—sexualities that count as queer perhaps especially in the sense of their lability: "an experience of sexual identity built upon the unstable ground of a fantasy that never achieves permanence."[29] More than merely a document of gay male subjectivities at a specific historical moment, Genet's novel offers us a view of competing or complementary nonnormative sexual identities and how they are perpetually negotiated.

Narrative compromise is performative and, indeed, paradigmatic of how these identities are contested in Genet; my aim in this chapter is to demonstrate both the liberatory potential and the limitations of queer self-invention and world-making in this mode. Inventorying these possibilities and restrictions, Genet's first novel provides not only an introduction to but even an ethnography of sorts of the author's contemporary queer milieu. Taking his own categories as a cue, we might observe both the differences and the surprising commonalities of queer self-invention represented by the three main characters: Divine (a feminized *tante*), Darling (a manly top), and Our Lady of the Flowers (more fluid in his sexual identity and, tellingly, the only character to bear a drag name but a male pronoun). If Darling and Divine embody strategies of disidentification related, respectively, to relative passing and failed passing, Our Lady represents at once an erotic fantasy of unified self-identity and the impossibility of its fulfillment. Modeling Genet's at-once conflictual and complicit—in a word: disidentificatory—rapport with a queer audience and with his queer subjects, it is, as I will insist throughout, precisely at moments when the narrator grapples with his characters for control of their destinies that the peculiar agency of their resignifying practices is revealed.

Failed Passing

Despite its being named for another character, at the core of Genet's first novel is the story of how a rural boy named Louis Culafroy moves to Paris and becomes the drag queen Divine. As tempting as it might be to see Culafroy's evolution as a freely spontaneous self-invention, as a flourishing of the queer self and celebration of the transformative power of camp performance, Genet takes care to note that the metamorphosis is preconditioned by a *fault* in the raw material: "The sitting posture of Michelangelo's *Moses* is said to have been necessitated by the compact form of the block of marble he had to work with. Divine is always being presented with odd-shaped marbles that make her achieve masterpieces."[30] Nor is this a process of self-creation that is ever truly completed: Divine persistently makes her masterpieces out of awkward and imperfect stone, as it is such imperfection that makes the task possible, and indeed *necessary*, to begin with. And this, Genet continues in the next sentence, is how Divine is born:

> Culafroy, in the public park, the time he ran away, had had the same good luck. He had been strolling through the lanes; when he reached the end of one of them, he saw that he would have to turn around so as not to walk on the lawn. As he watched himself moving, he thought: "'He spun about," and the word "spun," immediately caught on the wing, made him about-face smartly. He was about to begin a dance with restrained, barely indicated gesticulations, everything to be merely suggested, but the sole of his yawning shoe dragged over the sand and made such a shamefully vulgar sound (for this also should be noted: that Culafroy or Divine, they of the delicate, that is, finical, in short, civil tastes—for in imaginations our heroes are attracted, as girls are, by monsters—have always found themselves in situations that repel them). He heard the sound of the sole. This reminder made him lower his head. He assumed with utter naturalness a meditative posture and sauntered back slowly. The strollers in the park watched him go by. Culafroy saw that they noticed his paleness, his thinness, his lowered eyelids, which were as round and heavy as marbles. He bowed his head more deeply, his pace grew even slower, so much so that all of him was the very image of vocative fervor and that he—not thought—but whispered aloud a cry:
>
> "Lord, I am among Thy elect."
>
> For a few steps, God carried him off toward His throne.[31]

At a moment of narcissistic self-realization, both in the sense of recognition and creation, Culafroy is transformed through a pirouette no less involuntary for its agility.

We know from earlier in the novel that Culafroy has an innate penchant, coded as a homosexual disposition, for the ballet—that he cannot *help* but dance through daily chores—and that this is a furtive affinity tied to a sense of embarrassment.[32] The young boy's inherent gracefulness is itself stigmatizing insofar as it introduces an inevitable artifice and effeminacy to his every gesture—rendering his movements mincing and preventing Culafroy from behaving unreflectedly. It is precisely his innate grace that prevents him from being graceful and that will require him, with a *new* naturalness, to adopt a different pose.

The campiness of Culafroy's demeanor is not initially the self-affirmative performance Divine will attempt to make of it but rather an inborn performat*ivity*—a proclivity for embellishment and an incapacity for naïvely earnest, self-ignorant action. This lends a deeper and more multifarious sense to the failed seriousness Sontag associates with camp: not only does Culafroy's love of ballet read as ludicrously aspirational given his circumstances, but, concealing the seriousness of his ambition, Culafroy fails, in a sense, to take it seriously—to take *himself* seriously.

Turning back on himself, Culafroy sees himself, as it were, from the outside; in fact, he even describes himself, in the unspoken start to his soliloquy, in the third person. Necessary for Culafroy's self-creation is self-difference—a fault also in the sense of a crack or fissure—confirming the Derridean suspicion that the experience of the self is never immediate or fully self-present. (Derrida's deconstruction on this point focuses on Edmund Husserl's investigation of soliloquy, or internal monologue, as a purportedly privileged phenomenological experience of selfhood.) This queer context makes especially apparent that auto-affection—self-presentation or, more precisely, the self's creation of the self—is always an encounter with, or rather invention of, the self as ineluctably unattainable other.[33] It is from and *as* a noncoincidence with himself/herself that Culafroy/Divine is forged. If the sound of Culafroy's dragging shoe sole causes the dance to be aborted before it begins, it is not because this noise is inherently so abhorrent, but rather because Culafroy is too delicate—because he is, as Eve Kosofsky Sedgwick would have it, among those "whose sense of identity is for some reason tuned most durably to the note of shame."[34] Lowering his head and his eyelids in the habitual embodiment of this affect, the trope of disgrace, Culafroy now speaks aloud, to God, and in the first person. Reborn in this moment as a subject, it is out of a sense and performance of stigma that Culafroy becomes, quite literally, Divine.

Accordingly, Genet transitions without pause into a moment Divine is given her name:

> Divine—let us get back to her—was leaning against a tree on the boulevard. All the youngsters knew her. Three of these hooligans approached her. First, they came up laughing about something or other, perhaps about Divine; then they said hello and asked how the grind was going. Divine was holding a pencil, the pencil played mechanically over her fingernails and drew an irregular piece of lace and then, more consciously, a diamond shape, a rosette, a holly leaf. The little tramps started teasing her. They said that pricks must hurt, that old men . . . that women had more charm . . . that they themselves were pimps . . . and other things, which they no doubt say without meaning any harm but which hurt Divine. She feels more and

> more uncomfortable. They're just young little hoodlums, whereas she's thirty. She could shut them up with the back of her hand. But *they* are males. Still very young, but tough-looking and with tough muscles. And all three of them there, dreadfully inflexible, like the Fates. Divine's cheeks are burning. She pretends to be seriously occupied with the drawings on her nails and occupied with that only. "Here's what I might say," she thought, "to make them think I'm not upset." And holding out her hands to the children, with the nails up, she smiles and says:
>
> "I'm going to start a fashion. Yes, yes, a new fashion. You see, it's pretty, the we-women [*les femmes-nous*] and the they-women [*les femmes-autres*] will have lace drawn on their nails. We'll send for artists from Persia. They'll paint miniatures that you'll have to look at with a magnifying glass! Oh God!"
>
> The three hoodlums felt foolish, and one of them, speaking for the others as well, said:
>
> "Jesus, she's the limit [*Sacrée Divine*]."
>
> They left.
>
> The fashion of decorating fingernails with Persian miniatures dates from this episode.[35]

It is precisely such "disidentificatory desire for [a] once toxic representation" that José Esteban Muñoz celebrates: "The phobic object, through a campy over-the-top performance, is recognized as sexy and glamorous, and not as the pathetic and abject spectacle that it appears to be in the dominant eyes of heteronormative culture."[36] Coupled here with a redundant insult, the very name Divine is no different from the derogatory labels applied to her in the brasserie. Like the incantatory *pédérasque*, it is a self-fulfilling prophecy, an unironic affirmation of what had been intended to be tongue-in-cheek. Divine's subversion consists in taking the word at face value, as *monnaie comptant*, making a mockery of the insult by appropriating it as an identity. At the same time, Genet's odd insistence that the youths mean no harm with their ridicule situates the shame squarely with Divine, as if it originated with her in the involuntary affect of blushing. Feigning indifference and drawing attention instead to her initially unconscious doodling, which she increasingly affirms as an exaggerated performance of femininity, Divine replaces a spontaneous self-expression with another, more deliberate one.

Famously, in Judith Butler's view, by "imitating gender, drag implicitly reveals the imitative structure of gender itself—as well as its contingency."[37] Divine's ostentatious accoutrements so thoroughly denaturalize gender that it is cis-gendered women who are othered as *les femmes-autres* (a resonance rather lost in the English translation as "they-women"), who, as Divine's own fantasy bleeds into the diegesis in which she finds herself, ultimately come to signal their femininity through the same fad of painted fingernails Divine is fabled to have inaugurated. That gender is constituted as a whim without underlying essence has been Genet's implicit view since the first pages of the book, where already he declares: "I shall speak to you of Divine, mixing masculine and feminine as my mood dictates, and if, in the course of the tale, I shall have to refer to a woman, I shall manage, I shall find an angle [*un biais*], a good device [*un bon tour*], to avoid any confusion."[38] This statement amounts to more than simply a misogynistic dismissal of women within the homoerotic imaginary of Genet's textual world, where gender is more likely to be figured as something internal to gay male relationships: tops and bottoms, *mâles* and *femelles*, manly *macs* (translated by Frechtman as *pimps*) and effeminate *tantes*. It also initially imagines gender identity as primarily a matter of narrative whimsy—"mixing masculine and feminine as my mood dictates"—where the ostensible essence of "a woman" can only be hinted at indirectly, from an angle. (Genet's *biais* recalls the likely etymology of *queer* in the German *quer*, meaning oblique or transverse.) It is achieved here only through a narrative ruse or stylistic flourish: "un bon *tour*." The kind of sidestepping of sexual difference discussed in my introduction to this book turns out to be a turning, a troping.

Emma Heaney has recently argued that Genet's first novel opens up a space for a progressive representation of the trans feminine *avant la lettre*, contrary to the sexological models of gender inversion still in vogue at the time of Genet's writing, by emphasizing Divine's experience of womanhood *through* (rather than despite) her embodiment. Which is to say, on Heaney's account, that Divine does not suffer from what today one might characterize as gender dysphoria, since she perceives no inherent contradiction between her assigned sex and her gender identity. There is much to recommend this reading, and Heaney's notion of the "feminine remainder" as the unwanted effeminacy from which male homosexuality has so often sought to insulate itself speaks to the theory of failed passing being sketched here.[39]

Admittedly, I do hesitate somewhat to regard Divine and her fellow *tantes* as trans or even proto-trans not only because of the potential presentism this entails but also because, as I'll explore in my final chapters, a reverse occlusion of the genuinely trans feminine inheres in certain representations of male homosexuality—which is very much Heaney's larger point. More immediately, however, there is, undeniably, a fundamental dissonance to Divine's camp performativity. An incongruity Genet takes care to stress: "Si elle sentait 'femme', elle pensait 'homme' " ("though she felt as a 'woman,' she thought as a 'man' ").[40] This caveat is interesting not only for its scare-quoting of gender: impossible to translate adequately into English, Genet employs *sentir* (to feel) in this instance not in the pronominal, reflexive construction one might expect, but rather as a transitive verb: it is not exactly that Divine feels herself to be a woman but rather that she feels (in) woman as if feeling "woman" (*sentir « femme »*) and thinking "man" (*penser « homme »*) were opposing musical modes or linguistic idioms. This impression is reinforced by Genet's subsequent clarification that it is not that masculinity is Divine's native language, so to speak, an accent that becomes perceptible at certain moments, nor that her femininity is merely learned, acquired, or imitated: "One might think that, in . . . reverting spontaneously to her true nature [*sa véritable nature*], Divine was a male wearing make-up, disheveled by false gestures [*de gestes postiches*] but this is not a case of the phenomenon of recourse to the mother tongue in times of stress. In order to think with precision, Divine must never formulate her thoughts aloud, for herself."[41] Which is to say that Divine's camp trappings are not cosmetic, not sham ornamentation, not make-believe (as the abandoned adjective *postiche*, also missing from Frechtman's translation, would imply), not an adulteration of an underlying masculine essence: "Sa féminité n'était pas *qu'une* mascarade" ("Her femininity was not *only* a masquerade").[42]

Still, her uncharacteristic inhibition on this point—her incapacity or unwillingness truly to think as a woman—highlights both the persistence and also the constraints of gender performativity through language: the free play of pronouns Genet celebrates above finds its precedent but also its limitation in Divine's linguistic practice. She feels comfortable taking on feminine declensions, but, oddly, can do so only at the expense of *feeling* feminine: "Doubtless there had been times when she had said to herself aloud: 'I'm just a foolish girl,' but having felt this, she felt it no longer, and, in saying it, she no longer thought it."[43] Precisely the kind of soliloquy that should ideally, from Husserl's phenomenological perspective, constitute successful auto-affection of the self as the self—the perfect coincidence of thought, speech, and experience—instead, as Derrida suspects, institutes difference and self-alienation: the feeling and even the abstract thought of being female evaporate with their expression.

Contrary to Heaney's perhaps too-generous interpretation of Genet's progressive thinking on the subject, Divine *does* explicitly experience gender dysphoria, although at a cognitive as much as at a corporeal level: "Elle arrivait à penser 'femme' à propos de choses graves mais jamais essentielles. . . . Mais pour penser 'femme' en plein, ses organes la *gênaient*" ("She managed to think "woman" with regard to serious but never essential things. . . . But as for thinking "woman" completely, her organs hindered her").[44] That this impediment bears orthographic and phonetic resonances with the author's name (coming even closer, *Genet* was sometimes written as *Genêt* in early editions of and commentaries on his work) perhaps signals another rift between the character and her creator, a quarrel between Divine and Genet over her gender. If this is true, then there may be something subtly thorny about Genet's distinction here between serious and *essential* matters—an atypical evocation of essence that seems to serve as an irritating authorial reminder of Divine's genitalia and the discomfort (*gêne*) they cause.

But, aside from such possibly barbed comments, Genet's treatment of Divine is, on the whole, sympathetic and generally complicit. Divine's hyperbolic femininity, the narrator insists, goes beyond mere masquerade but seems not quite to constitute action: "Penser, c'est faire un acte" ("To think is to perform an act").[45] (The French *acte* does not imply theatricality as directly as its English cognate, although the proximity is fortuitous.) The passage is even more misogynist than it seems at first blush; the sticking point is maybe less that Divine's genitalia keep her from thinking woman than it is that women, as Divine sees it, can't quite think: "To think is to perform an act. In order to act, you have to discard frivolity and set your idea on a solid base. So she was aided by the idea of solidity, which she associated with the idea of virility, and it was in grammar that she found it near at hand."[46] Despite the apparent rejection of language as a grounding for gender, it is through a chain of semantic associations that Divine is masculinized: thought suggests action, action solidity, solidity, in turn, virility, and in the instances where virility is required, Divine apparently takes recourse to masculine pronouns. Though we are given no example of this, there are plenty of moments in the novel where Divine thinks back on her days as Culafroy tenderly—not without dissonance, but without any perceptible bitterness.

At this point, however, Genet himself effectuates a sudden and surprising volte-face, though one masked by the conjunction *and*, as if the thought followed without any apparent contradiction: "And all the 'woman' judgments she made were, in reality [*en réalité*], poetic conclusions. Hence, only then was Divine true [*Divine n'était vraie qu'alors*]. It would be curious to know what women corresponded to in Divine's mind, and particularly, in her life. No doubt, she herself was not a woman (that is, a female in a skirt [*femelle à jupe*]); she was womanly only through her submission to the imperious male."[47] Divine, in this floating, free-indirect rendering of her errant thoughts, distills gender into a discursive principle of relationality, the male who commands and the female who obeys, confirming Butler's suspicion that "the gendered body is performative [and] has no ontological status apart from the various acts which constitute its reality."[48] Fittingly, here cis-gendered women are distinguished from Divine and her fellow queens only by their clothing: *femelles à jupe*. While the rather zoological *femelle* would seem to hint at a corporeal definition of gender, this impression is immediately undone by the seeming redundancy of what follows, considering that Divine also dresses as a woman. Adding this implicit qualification and proviso to what could otherwise be presumed to be self-evident, Genet de-essentializes gender identity and the stability of identity as such.

Divine's femininity is not *only* a masquerade, but that it *is*, among other things, an act and an impersonation is the point of Genet's italics: "pas *qu'une* mascarade." In the French this might indicate degree, as the English translation emphasizes, but it also attests to multiplicity: not just *one*, or not at one with herself. Through her flamboyant costuming and affected self-staging Divine points up the performativity and dissonance of identity. Concealed in plain sight as an idiomatic aside ("en réalité"), reality here comes into conflict with the surreptitious allusion to essence a few sentences earlier: Divine's very *real* femininity (note the feminine declension of *vraie*) is truest when it is least essential. As in Gide, her true, authentic self resides not in the unmasking of a core being but in the performance of an adopted identity. As Heaney eloquently phrases it, "Everything that is lovely about Divine is not revealed but rather expressed. The feminine remainder roosts in pigeon sips, rises with her pinky, walks with a mincing step that is revealed as dancing."[49] Similarly, Divine's womanly judgments are not thoughts, strictly speaking, but rather *poetic conclusions*—more aesthetic than ontological, form instead of content. Divine's femininity is not *mere* masquerade but rather much more: poetry. Creating an artwork out of herself, she shares in Genet's own narrative poetics, revealing this aesthetic strategy, in turn, to constitute an implicit theory of (sexual) identity.

Divine's failed seriousness does not contradict or call into question her femininity but rather reveals the mode of willful self-contradiction by which it operates—what Genet calls a "seconde nature" ("second nature") and "la duplicité du sexe des tantes" ("duplicity of the sex of fags").[50] And if Divine never fully comes to identify as a woman, she is nevertheless far less convincing as a man. When Our Lady of the Flowers comes on the scene, Divine finds herself attracted to his twinky charm, although she has habitually only gone in for manly tops. This novel configuration of desire provides her with another block of marble from which to sculpt a new self: "Something different, a kind of feeling of power, sprang up (in the vegetal, germinative sense) in Divine. She thought she had been virilified. A wild hope made her strong and husky and vigorous. She felt muscles growing, and felt herself emerging from rock carved by Michelangelo in the form of a slave."[51] (Michelangelo already makes his second appearance here as a proto-gay forefather. He'll have another cameo in my final chapter.) If again this feeling of virility—as implied by the metaphors Genet uses to describe it—is involuntary, vegetal, even slavish, it will be put in practice by an effort no less strenuous and sustained for its clumsiness:

> She tried for male gestures, which are rarely the gestures of males. She whistled, put her hands into her pockets, and this whole performance was carried out so unskillfully that in the course of a single evening she seemed to be four or five characters at the same time. She thereby acquired the richness of a multiple personality. She ran from boy to girl, and the transitions from one to the other—because the attitude was a new one—were made stumblingly.[52]

Bringing masquerade to masculinity, Divine undermines the assumption of maleness as universal default.[53] Attempting to *perform* the presumed universal neutrality of masculinity, Divine overdoes it. Genet elsewhere expresses a poignant appreciation for this kind of failure: "I still wonder what is the significance of the emotion that rises up within me when I hear some silly song just as it does when I am in the presence of a recognized masterpiece."[54] Accordingly, the depiction of Divine's attempt to imitate a male is equal parts tender and mocking: the camp quality of Divine's public persona(e) results not only from her exaggerated approach to femininity but also—and perhaps more profoundly—from the sincerity with which she fails to be otherwise.

As a final effort to effectuate her newly masculine personality, Divine imagines for herself a manly double, Marchetti, complicit in this pursuit: "Finally, to crown her metamorphosis from female into tough male, she imagined a man-to-man friendship which would link her with one of those faultless pimps whose gestures could not be regarded as ambiguous [*qui la lierait à quelqu'un de ces macs sans défaut, de qui l'on ne puisse dire que leurs gestes sont ambigus*]. And to be on the safe side, she invented Marchetti."[55] Given the purely relational nature of gender as configured within Genet's textual economy and Divine's habitual position in the submissive, feminine role, such an imagined fraternal amity serves as a necessary initiation into the position of a top: she must first pass as a man among men, Divine implicitly reasons, before attempting to dominate Our Lady. Masculinity, filtered through Divine's perspective, is again associated with a stability she does not usually possess: a state of being without fault (*défaut*), ambiguity, or uncertainty. There is, to the modern ear, at least a double sense to this *défaut*, as this passage superficially confirms a view of masculinity as a presumed default from which the feminine is mere deviation while at the same time fundamentally subverting this assumption both through the demonstration of the contortions necessary for the performance of masculinity and through the verb tenses the narrator employs to render Divine's thoughts: the conditional *lierait* and the subjunctive *puisse* undermine the doubtlessness she so desires to achieve.

Though she will never manage to pass as convincingly as Marchetti, Divine quite readily pieces together an image for him from a private collection of masturbatory fantasies: "It was a simple matter to choose a physique for him, for she possessed in her secret, lonely-girl's imagination, for her nights' pleasure, a stock of thighs, arms, torsos, faces, hair, teeth, necks, and knees, and she knew how to assemble them so as to make of them a live man to whom she loaned a soul—which was always the same one for each of these constructions: the one she would have liked to have herself."[56] This Frankensteinian process of bricolage by which Marchetti is assembled is something Divine has in common with her author, who speaks throughout the novel of how its dreamscape is populated by clippings from newspapers and magazines and the attributes of heroes of cheap romance novels:

> I continue my reading of cheap novels. It satisfies my love of hoodlums dressed up as gentlemen. Also my taste for imposture, my taste for the sham, which could very well make me write on my visiting

> cards: "Jean Genet, bogus Count of Tillancourt." Amidst the pages of these thick books, in flattened type, marvels appeared. Like straight lilies there surge up young men, who are, thanks in part to me, both princes and beggars. If from myself I make Divine, from them I make her lovers: Our Lady, Darling, Gabriel, Alberto, lads who whistle through their teeth and on whose heads you can, if you look closely, see, in the form of an aureole, a royal crown.[57]

At a certain moment in Gide's *Caves du Vatican*, Lafcadio, upon discovering that he is the bastard son of a count, has visiting cards made up adopting the name of his father. If the irony of these forged *cartes de visite* is that Lafcadio is a pretender to a legacy not entirely illegitimate, it is precisely the illegitimacy of impersonation that attracts Genet—the (dis)guise of identity, just as Divine is a mask donned by her author.[58] This chiasmus offers insight into the surprising *truth value* of such imposture, which operates not so much according to a mode opposing essence and appearance as one embracing this dissonance to grant appearance unexpected essence.

The mise en abyme of Divine's artistry and narratological approach casts light on the odd ontology of the kind of forgery Genet shares with Gide. Like her own author, Divine negotiates with her creation and ultimately grants him an uncustomary degree of independence: "Then, one night, she told him that she was tired of Our Lady of the Flowers and that she was willing to let Marchetti have him. The agreement was sealed with a male handshake."[59] While Divine ultimately abandons the project of *becoming* Marchetti, her narrative invention thus mirrors and ultimately even contaminates Genet's, as the reality of Marchetti becomes at moments nearly indistinguishable from that of the text's other equally phantasmatic figures.[60] It is precisely the *failure* of Divine's willful adoption of an invented identity that permits this identity to gain its independence and ultimately to outlive her.

As Genet's representative and fictionalized double within the text, and as an author figure similarly frustrated with her impotence over her fantasies, Divine is ultimately more than merely a character; she is a narrative principle—the embodiment of contingency itself: "Here we must perhaps recognize Divine's influence. She is present wherever the inexplicable arises. She, the Giddy One [*la Folle*], strews traps in her wake, artful pitfalls, deep dungeon cells, even at the risk of being caught in them herself if she does an about-face, and because of her the minds of Darling, Our Lady, and their cronies bristle with ridiculous gestures. With their heads high, they take falls that doom them to the worst of fates."[61] Even this revelation of Divine's influence, very near the end of the novel, is advanced as an unconfirmed hypothesis signaling once again that her doings are not necessarily always aligned with her author's desires. But like Gide's demon, which intrudes on the action only and wherever serendipity is necessary to advance the plot, Divine's spontaneous tricks and traps (like the whims of Genet's own *bons tours*) have a

divided against itself and can therefore never be depicted independently of its fictional reflections. The narrator's purported reality has been rendered every bit as fictitious as his autoerotic inventions. For no sooner has Darling's story come into direct contact with the narrator's than these once-distinct plotlines become not only entangled but indeed unsettlingly exchangeable: "A guard opens the door and pushes a newcomer into the cell. Is it I or Darling who will receive him?"[69] The playful narrative uncertainty of the novel, the uncustomary freedom Genet affords to his characters and the contingency he allows their circumstances, has called the writing self itself into question, as it risks being supplanted (if not even effaced) by its invention, Darling.

Accordingly, it is at this moment of conflation of fiction and reality that both modes—the confessional and the metafictional—attain their acme, with Genet abandoning his project of a more stripped-down style at the very instant he would appear to have achieved it. Christening this new arrival to the prison Jean, Genet wonders: "And after all, is it necessary for me to talk about myself so directly? I much prefer to describe myself in the caresses I reserve for my lovers. The new Jean came very close to becoming Darling. What did he lack?"[70] Darling's facility to adopt other, desired personalities turns out to correspond to the revelation expressed in Genet's Rembrandt fragments—where the author feels himself, with a profound sense of nausea, vanishing into a stranger on a train—"que tout homme *en vaut* un autre" ("that every man *is worth as much* as every other").[71] Darling operates as a narrative manifestation of the principle expressed there of utter exchangeability of ostensibly autonomous individuals. Put in different terms, he manifests the uncanny discomfort of a porous self, the inability to isolate subject from object, described, as I'll outline in the next chapter, by Julia Kristeva's theory of abjection.

If the metaleptic confusion of diegetic registers (Darling's and the narrator's) in *Notre-Dame-des-Fleurs* should signal a point of coincidence between the two, it instead results in an infinite refraction. As this new Jean becomes the narrator's cellmate, it ceases to be clear which self is the reflection of the other:

> It is another Jean, here, who is telling me his story. I am no longer alone, but I am thereby more alone than ever. I mean that the solitude of prison gave me the freedom to be with my hundred Jean Genets glimpsed in a hundred passers-by, for I am quite like Darling, who also stole the Darlings whom a thoughtless gesture let escape from all the strangers he had brushed against; but the new Jean brings into me—as a folding fan draws in the designs on the gauze—brings in I know not what.[72]

Both the narrator and Darling audition many possible selves, which are taken from contact with alterity by an act of theft—or caught as if by contagion.

The author is simultaneously attracted to and repulsed by the anchoring of identity occasioned by his doppelgänger: a feeling of uncanniness (*das Unheimliche* in Sigmund Freud's sense) or of abjection (in Julia Kristeva's). It is as if this new Jean reveals an unwanted through line—the imprint, shadow, or projection of a stable self through the many poses or identities adopted—and with it the threat of a loss of the illusion that self-making was a free endeavor. Genet is dogged and dragged down by the autobiographical: too much self, not enough fiction. The disgust Genet feels in his Rembrandt fragments that he might disappear into another man seems also to be a disgust that he might vanish within himself.

Darling's prompting of this metaleptic moment reveals him to be not only a quilting point between metafictional and autobiographical modes of self-presentation but also an apparently paradoxical coincidence between the self-as-other and the self-as-self, between identification and disidentification. What distinguishes Darling from a figure like Divine, importantly, is his ability to *pass*. He passes as masculine, as macho, virile, in a word, as we're reminded on occasion throughout the novel, as *straight*. In fact, in Genetian terms, as we'll see in the following chapter on *Querelle de Brest* (*Querelle of Brest*, 1947), he might even be considered heterosexual despite his predominantly homosexual attachments. It is crucial to remember here that passing and its failures are not opposing paradigms but rather inextricably ouroboric: it is precisely *failed* passing and *dis*identification, the difference of the self from alterity, that makes identification (of the self with another) possible to begin with. Passing itself is enabled by its very potential for failure; conversely, it is only the prospect of passing that makes this failure imaginable in the first place.

For Darling, passing is also a form of counterfeit currency in more than one sense. After agreeing to become a police informant, for instance, Darling revels in the false value of the self he projects:

> He was thrilled by a prankishness that was born from within: "I'm a double crosser [*faux jeton*]." As he walked down the rue Dankour, drunk with the hidden splendor (as of a treasure) of his abjection (for it really must intoxicate us if we are not to be killed by its intensity), he glanced at the mirror in a shop window where he saw a Darling luminous with extinguished pride. He saw this Darling wearing a glen plaid suit, a felt hat over one eye, his shoulders stiff, and when he walks he holds them like that to resemble Sebastopol Pete, and Pete holds them like that to resemble Pauley the Rat, and Pauley to resemble Teewee, and so on; a procession of pure, irreproachable pimps leads to Darling Daintyfoot, the double crosser [*faux jeton*], and it seems that as a result of having rubbed against them and stolen their bearing, he has, you might say, soiled them with his own abjection: that's how I want him to be, for my delight.[73]

This mirror scene—or house of mirrors—reveals Darling's masculine identity to be every bit as constructed, accreted onto the body, as Divine's femininity. Like Divine's associative slippage into masculinity through stability and virility, Darling's physical comportment is adopted from elsewhere in a metonymic chain of signifiers from Pete (Pierrot) to Pauley (Polo) to Teewee (Tioui) to Darling—reaching from one to the next in a repeated performance of machismo. This echoes in advance Butler's later account: "If the inner truth of gender is a fabrication and if true gender is a fantasy instituted and inscribed on the surface of bodies, then it seems that genders can be neither true nor false, but are only produced as the truth effects of a discourse of primary or stable identity."[74] Troubling this discourse, Darling is, by the same token, like Gide in Cocteau's description, a *faux jeton*, a false coin, a forgery: his celebration of abjection, embodying the virtue of betrayal Genet holds so sacred, is also exposed as a not-entirely-unambivalent strategy of distilling pride from stigma (*griser* can mean, as in Frechtman's translation, to intoxicate, but also to gray, as in to age or weather), but Darling's abjection is a hidden treasure, a secret of betrayal to which only he is privy.

And if Darling's approach to auto-affection is distinct from Divine's, it is perhaps because, while her masquerade is always obviously double, Darling needn't worry about being caught in the *act*, as it were, of being exposed as the fake he is. At the same time, just as he is associated narratively with the surprising concurrence of the candidly confessional and the convolutedly fabricated, his promiscuous passing (here also in the sense of relay) has an expositional aspect: rubbing off on the similarly performed masculinities with which he comes into contact, Darling wears away at their faces, exposing them, as well, as counterfeit coins. But Darling is also exhausted, in more than one sense, by this effort: "Darling is a fake pimp. The schemes he devises suddenly peter out in poetical meanderings."[75] Used up, burnt out, through its own performance, this poetics once again succeeds in failure, through a kind of sublation. "For a long time I thought," confesses Genet at just this moment, "that the poetic work posed conflicts: it cancels them."[76] It is a failure that unifies the self—which can only ever phantasmatically and aesthetically resolve its contradictions by poetic sleight of hand.

Pure Passing

The eponym of *Notre-Dame-des-Fleurs* is neither *mac* nor *tante* but somehow something more: "Our Lady was coyer than a queen [*coquette plus qu'une tante*]. He was as whorish as a gigolo [*putain comme un gigolo*]."[77] He embodies both Divine's artifice and Darling's capacity to commit. He is the only figure in the text to have a campy drag name but a predominantly masculine identity and masculine pronouns. He is, in the terms established by my previous chapter and introduction, *off-straight*.

Inspired, we are told, by Genet's worshipful lust for the real-life murderer Maurice Pilorge, Our Lady acquires his name not from any femininity but instead by virtue of the murder he has committed: "He knows that his destiny is being fulfilled, and although he knows (Our Lady knows or seems to know it better than anyone) that his destiny is being fulfilled at every moment, he has the pure mystic feeling that this murder is going to turn him, by virtue of the baptism of blood, into Our Lady of the Flowers."[78] It is telling that Our Lady's acceptance of his predestination is alluded to in the same breath as a double reminder of his autonomy from his author: Genet first states as fact that Our Lady understands his fate, before wondering *if* he knows his every moment to be fated and then confirming parenthetically that he at least *appears* to. It is by exercising free will, or rather by transcending it in an ecstatic suspension of the ego, that Our Lady realizes his predetermined fate.

Unlike Divine, who must recreate herself saintly out of Culafroy, Our Lady's election is unreflected. He is consecrated by a crime committed entirely unthinkingly, far more aimlessly than any of Gide's supposedly unmotivated *actes gratuits*. And it is precisely this lack of introspection that makes Our Lady so graceful in a way Divine could never be: "As always, he answered as one answers from the depth of thought. Our Lady never thought of anything, and that was what gave him the air of knowing everything straight away, as by a kind of grace. Was he the favorite of the Creator? Perhaps God had let him in on things."[79] More than any of the other characters, Our Lady is chosen, sanctified, and most favored by his creator—certainly to be equated here on some level with Genet, who has seemingly let Our Lady in on this secret. Our Lady achieves an earnestness of being (himself being one of those beings who are beautiful and know it ["des êtres qui sont beaux et savent qu'ils le sont"]) unattainable for either Divine or Darling, who must make do with self-dissonance.

What makes Our Lady so beautiful, it seems, is his simplicity (in an etymological sense of single foldedness): his ability to be himself, to correspond to himself. In sexual scenarios, he is both active and passive, as in an encounter where he is penetrated by Seck Gorgui—the first of a series of racially fetishized black men in Genet's oeuvre—while simultaneously being fellated by Divine. Embarking for a ball where he will find himself aroused by dressing in drag, Genet notes that Our Lady "se trouve bien" ("rather likes the way he looks").[80] More literally, the French suggests that he *finds* himself this way, as in the old self-help cliché. For Our Lady no help is necessary; his self is easy to find. But even in drag, there is no contradiction to Our Lady: "Our Lady, in his pale-blue faille dress, edged with white Valenciennes lace, was more than himself. He was himself and his complement."[81] Simultaneously himself and his reflection, Our Lady is at once a fantasy of sexual fluidity and wet dream of pure self-coincidence.

Our Lady is not unique (within the story, but also in the sense of being one with himself) because he is in between, neither one thing nor the other, but rather because he is both at once. He is not so much indecipherable as *too* easily interpreted, too beautiful to be believed: "The face of Our Lady of the Flowers is so radiantly pure that the idea immediately occurred to everyone that it was false, that this angel must be two-faced, with flames and smoke, for everyone has had occasion to say at least once in his life: 'You'd have thought he was a true saint,' and wants at all costs to be foxier than destiny."[82] A face too pure and innocent to be taken at face value, Our Lady's revealing tell, the sign of his double nature, is that he has none. Our Lady is, impossibly, exactly as he seems, namely, too good to be true. If Divine is haunted by the perpetual phantoms of other possible selves and Darling only adopts a single personality at a time, Our Lady is only ever singularly himself, as incongruous as that self might appear.

While Our Lady is quite clearly an erotic desideratum, one might also discern in him a perilous temptation. He strikes me less as an ideal of queer indeterminacy than as an idealization of stable ipseity, of the constancy of a secured identity and its specular seductions. (There is, I will be arguing in the chapters to come, an iconic, ideological, and cinematic aspect to this allure.) If a paradigm of passing—failed or felicitous—delights in difference, Our Lady reveals its disavowed imaginary: the fantasy of a unified self.

If Divine embodies contingency, it's only because she affirms necessity as if it were freely chosen: she's campy even as Culafroy, before she starts camping it up as Divine, and the various narrative caprices she strews across the text are mere adornments for narrative necessities required to advance the plot. Our Lady, conversely, represents contingency (narrative whim, one possibility among many) as if it were necessity—marrying the nearly contranymic senses of *contingency* as a dependence on chance and as a condition of possibility. And just as Divine is associated with unpredictability, Our Lady is often the representative in the novel of the inescapability of fate, an avowed must-be-such-ness of the narrative, and the corresponding abdication of authorial control. To put it playfully, Our Lady's self-coincidence (in the sense of self-identity) coincides with coincidence as narrative necessity.

Genet's first novel literalizes the kind of daddy-twink dynamic present in Gide's pederasty with regard to the relationship between Our Lady and Darling, whom the reader knows to be his father, though neither character ever comes to learn this over the course of the book—the implausibility of the coincidence, as so often in Gide, being precisely the point. But here Genet, quite uncharacteristically, observes an incest taboo exactly where we might otherwise expect him to indulge in forbidden fantasy:

> Darling drew Our Lady toward him, and, the better to embrace him, struggled with him briefly. I would like to dream them both in many other positions, if, when I closed my eyes, my dream still obeyed my will. . . . Darling, Divine, and Our Lady flee from me at top speed, taking with them the consolation of their existence, which has its

> being only in me, for they are not content with fleeing, they do away with themselves, dilute themselves in the appalling insubstantiality of my dreams, or rather of my sleep, and become my sleep; they melt into the very stuff of my sleep and compose it.[83]

What should have been a structuring conceit has been reduced to mere happenstance. Envisaging a struggle between his characters to mirror his own internal conflict, the author confesses to having lost his grasp on his oneiric-onanistic projections precisely when it comes to Our Lady: the perfect, exquisite, off-straight twink who, more than any other figure in the book, is meant to constitute an unadulterated sexual fantasy at the very core of the artwork.

Especially considering that the whole story—and perhaps foremost the gratuitous narrative implausibility of Darling's paternity—seems constructed to achieve the desired end of coupling these characters, there is no reason for Genet suddenly to avoid the provocation of depicting incest. (His work elatedly depicts far worse.) But the author acts as if the choice were unavoidable. This capitulation occurs, in part, because Genet inevitably realizes that his creations have no substance beyond his self; this unconscious knowledge seems metaleptically to inform even those characters' actions:

> They knew they were characters in a movie. And so, mingling their gestures in this dream, Darling and Our Lady of the Flowers quietly wove a brotherly friendship. How hard it is for me not to mate the two of them better, not to arrange it so that Darling, with a thrust of the hips—rock of unconsciousness and innocence, desperate with love—deeply sinks his smooth, heavy prick, as polished and warm as a column in the sun, into the waiting mouth of the adolescent murderer who is pulverized with gratitude.
>
> That too might be, but will not. Darling and Our Lady, however rigorous the destiny I plot for you, it will never cease to be—oh, in the very faintest way, tormented by what it might also have been but will not be because of me.[84]

What *could* occur will not: Our Lady forecloses the variety of contingencies that Divine, with her perpetual queerings and resignifications, opens up. An impossible fantasy of self-unity, of passing so pure it isn't even feigned, Our Lady occasions a kind of textual coitus interruptus: the erotic desire for identity and the disappointment of this same longing. The stone-carving metaphor subtly associated, at moments throughout the book that I have been highlighting here, at once with Genet's artistic aptitude as well as with the material limitations of his forging of fictional selves attaches in this instance both to Darling's physique (his sculptural member) and his psychology (the rock-like self-ignorance he unfortunately lacks). But it is as if the author's own awareness comes to contaminate his creations': Darling's and Our Lady's desires are, seemingly inexplicably, restrained by the intransigencies of a destiny to which they remain knowingly enslaved. Genet laments this restriction, while, in the same breath, nonetheless concluding that abiding by it is his own fully arbitrary decision.

This is not so much, perhaps, because the choice itself was inevitable as it is a recognition of the inevitability of *choosing*—an acknowledgement that any given narrative decision rules out other, competing possibilities. Instead, Genet leaves it to his reader to imagine these parallel abandoned plotlines haunting the one he has pursued, as well as to supply the psychological motivation he has refused to provide, instead insisting on his own sovereign authorial agency:

> I leave you free to imagine any dialogue you please. Choose whatever may charm you. Have it, if you like, that they hear the voice of the blood, or that they fall in love at first sight, or that Darling, by indisputable signs invisible to the vulgar eye, betrays the fact that he is a thief . . . Conceive of the wildest improbabilities [*les plus folles invraisemblances*]. Have it that the depths of their being are thrilled at accosting each other in slang. Tangle them suddenly in a swift embrace or a brotherly kiss. Do whatever you like.[85]

Leaving the implication of incest up to the imagination of his reader, Genet invites camp folly: *les plus folles invraisemblances*. The text suggests vulgar improbabilities and virtualities that are only activated through the process of reading, a sort of choose-your-own-adventure pornographic fantasy.

At once eliciting and rebuffing identification by his audience, queer or otherwise, Genet does not undo hegemonic and heteronormative characterizations, nor do his transgressions suspend the laws they violate: instead, he foregrounds the narrativity, in both its accidents and its necessities, of the identity formations explored within his texts, as well as the undoing of such narratives. Ultimately, the greatest challenge he issues to his readers is not to project themselves onto his characters, discovering themselves in these figures as they are, but instead to reimagine them as they might otherwise be.

Conclusion: Beyond Authenticity

Genet alternately insists that his novel is pure fiction and apologizes that it is not. At the beginning of the book, the author confesses, for instance, that there are limits to the fantasy and absolute inauthenticity he would seemingly prefer: "This story may not always seem artificial, and in spite of me you may recognize in it the call of the blood: the reason is that within my night I shall have happened to strike my forehead at some door, freeing an anguished memory that had been haunting me since the world began. Forgive me for it. This book aims to be only a small fragment of my inner life."[86] Like his characters, whose attempts at self-invention are ultimately restricted not only by the society in which they find themselves but also by their inner life, so too is Genet's narrative subject to the constraints of the writing self.

Read attentively, the insistent and intrusive authorial metareflections that punctuate the novel reveal it to be a project aimed precisely at liberating the author from these constraints—and, more radically, from the truth value of his writing. Introducing one of the narrative's final episodes, for instance, he cautions his reader:

> Don't complain about improbability. What's going to follow is false, *and no one has to accept it at face value* [*pour argent comptant*]. Truth is not my strong point. But "one must lie in order to be true." And even go beyond. What truth do I want to talk about? If it is really true [*S'il est bien vrai*] that I am a prisoner who plays (who plays for himself [*qui se joue*]) scenes of the inner life, you will require nothing other than a game.[87]

Insisting that his narrative is counterfeit and without legitimate currency, Genet begins to transform his life into an artwork, into an aesthetic game—derealizing it in the process: *s'il est bien vrai* (if it really is true). This parenthetical (*qui se joue*) has a double sense, at once reminding the reader, as Frechtman's translation opts to emphasize, that *Notre-Dame-des-Fleurs* projects the inner cinema of its incarcerated author and, more subtly, that the author is also playing a role, playing *himself* in this mental motion picture. This roleplaying reposes on identification but also insists on disidentification: Genet is both an actor and the role he plays, just as he is both the author of the novel and a character in it.

His double, Divine, although hallowed in death, remains equally self-conscious: "Unlike most saints, Divine had knowledge of it."[88] As she approaches her passing, her gradual canonization will therefore necessarily entail a "detachment from the world," a fading away from color and from corporeal form: "Now that she no longer has a body (or she has so little left, a little that is whitish, pale, bony, and at the same time very flabby), she slips off to heaven."[89] Effecting such spectralization in parenthetical asides, as if this whispered vanishing were itself under erasure, Genet describes her "pale, celestial voice (a voice I would like to imagine being that of movie actors, a voice of an image)."[90] And in this cinematic whiteness she finally comes to resemble the murderers upon whom Our Lady has been modeled and to whom her author pays homage in the novel's opening pages—where they are imagined as angels: "white, filmy, and frightening, like the translucent bodies of ghosts."[91] On this same note, that Our Lady occupies so few pages, compared to Divine or Darling, in the book that bears his name, and that he comes to stand for the impossibility of the very sexual fantasy he had been intended to constitute, seems to demonstrate a growing awareness on the author's part of the impossibility of the unfractured selfhood Our Lady embodies. If Genetian autofiction responds to this predicament by progressively freeing its creator from the imprisonment of the self, it does so only by hollowing out the autobiographical instance, by effacing the author in favor of his fiction. This queer self-erasure will be the subject of the following chapter.

Part 2

Embodied Abstraction

Chapter 3

✦

Camp/Abject

Queer Failure in Rainer Werner Fassbinder

Rainer Werner Fassbinder's swan song *Querelle*, released in August 1982, in the wake of the director's death by drug overdose, is marked both thematically and stylistically by a self-destructive narcissism and an embrace of abjection. The depiction of dueling near-identical brothers (a failed passing accentuated by the film where they are played by different actors bearing very little resemblance to one another) and sadomasochistic sexual encounters indulges in willful and willfully awkward anachronism, alienatingly unconvincing postdubbing, shoddy sets in garish colors, and tacky costuming that *Die Zeit* considered, in its review of the film, befitting the "the wardrobe of a glamorous gay carnival."[1] According to Edmund White, Fassbinder's version deliberately mangled the narrative progression of a script—itself, of course, an adaptation of Jean Genet's *Querelle de Brest* (1947)—coauthored by Fassbinder's contemporary, Werner Schroeter, who, as he recounts in a chapter of his autobiography titled "Misserfolg macht menschlich" ("Failure Makes You Human") was unable to raise the funds to make the film himself and was ultimately ousted from the project.[2] In a review he later called "a passionate farewell to Fassbinder," queer film critic Thomas Waugh describes *Querelle* as "a dramatic exit if I ever saw one."[3] It was this seemingly camp sensibility that earned the film two nominations at the Golden Raspberries—a mock award for bad cinema.[4]

With all of this in mind, the manifesto-like final lines of Jack Halberstam's *Queer Art of Failure* read almost as if they were a film review of *Querelle*: "To live is to fail, to bungle, to disappoint, and ultimately to die; rather than searching for ways around death and disappointment, the queer art of failure involves the acceptance of the finite, the embrace of the absurd, the silly, and the hopelessly goofy. Rather than resisting endings and limits, let us instead revel in and cleave to all of our own inevitable fantastic failures."[5] Despite this overarching celebration of silliness, however, Halberstam, takes care to distance himself from the "narrow range of affective responses [including] fatigue, ennui, boredom, indifference, ironic distancing, indirectness, arch dismissal, insincerity, and *camp*" that constitute the "camp archive" to which this text, which revels in its own bad taste, would presumably belong.[6]

Attempting more radically to politicize an older antirelational turn in queer studies, Halberstam takes especially Leo Bersani and Lee Edelman to task for their overreliance on an "excessively small . . . gay male archive" in which Gide and Genet are privileged points of reference and which "coincides with the canonical archive [but] narrows that archive down to a select group of antisocial queer aesthetes and camp icons and texts."[7] This is, in itself, a point well taken. But I am less convinced of what Halberstam makes of this reduction—deducing a historical overemphasis on affective and aesthetic(ist) sensibilities privileging fluffy, ironic distance rather than a darker, more earnest queer despair presumably better aligned with the variety of self-shattering the antisocial thesis had originally sought.

"If we want to make the antisocial turn in queer theory," Halberstam eloquently advises, "we must be willing to turn away from the comfort zone of polite exchange in order to embrace a truly *political* negativity, one that promises, this time, to fail, to make a mess, to fuck shit up, to be loud, unruly, impolite, to breed resentment, to bash back, to speak up and out, to disrupt, assassinate, shock, and annihilate."[8] The implication that Fassbinder, let alone Genet, could belong to a sphere of public decency might initially appear laughable—but Halberstam again has a point: this is precisely the effect of queer acculturation I described in my introduction with regard to Luchino Visconti. Which is to say it is another form of willfully failed passing as a backhanded approach to effective passing. In the introduction to his book on Genet, Kadji Amin has described this as particularly camp process of canonization: "Like many minoritarian subjects, Genet had to learn to perform other people's exotic fantasies about him in order to achieve recognition and success. . . . Writing during a moment in which transgression, marginality, and the destruction of bourgeois social values [had] been claimed as the tenets of high modernism, Genet issues a dare: 'Canonize me. I'm so bad I'm good.' "[9] The literary establishment responds with enthusiasm, Amin points out, awarding Genet the oxymoronic laurels of an officially sanctioned abject.

At the risk of speaking reductively, we might distill Halberstam's schema into an implied opposition between camp irony, on the one hand, and a deeper, more earnest sense of abjection, on the other. But, putting pressure on this distinction and pushing back somewhat against Halberstam's declawing of camp's subversive potential, this chapter seeks an updated definition of camp *as* abject in the repeated and evolving failure of *Querelle* in its various iterations. After all, as disquieting as it is to admit, and despite Halberstam's explicit goal of "exploring alternatives [to] the usual traps and impasses of binary formations," one might infer an implicitly gendered inversion from his critique. Namely, it seems to betray a desire to supplant the effeminate aspects of camp's purported "repertoire of formalized and often formulaic responses to the banality of straight culture" through the more manly attributes of "dyke anger, anticolonial despair, racial rage, counterhegemonic violence, punk pugilism"—as if the gay male archive of camp is simply too girly, catty, bitchy when considered beside a gritty, muscular, butch embrace of abjection.[10]

The reasons for Halberstam's resistance to camp are made clearer, perhaps, by earlier work, especially *Female Masculinity* (1998), where camp is seen to parody femininity as a social construct but to leave masculinity largely untroubled and unchallenged as an ostensibly natural given: "Because camp is predicated on exposing and exploiting the theatricality of gender, it tends to be the genre of an outrageous performance of femininity (by men or women) rather than outrageous performances of masculinity. . . . It is difficult to make masculinity the target of camp precisely because . . . masculinity tends to manifest as non-performative."[11] Surveying the theories of camp and gender performativity available at the time—Esther Newton's *Mother Camp* (1979) and Judith Butler's *Gender Trouble* (1990)—Halberstam persuasively concludes that "camp is always about femininity."[12] More specifically, we might see it as a practice of "male femininity, which fulfills a kind of ritual function in male homosocial cultures,"[13] as described by Halberstam in the introduction to *Female Masculinity*.

To camp female impersonation, Halberstam thus opposes what is called drag "kinging" (predominantly female-identifying artists parodying male stereotypes)—performances that "are noticeably sincere, or, to use a Wildean term that tends to typify the very opposite of camp, 'earnest.'"[14] The critique that camp is too often prone to slipping into misogynistic stereotype (discussed in greater detail below) is common enough and fair enough. It is important to remain vigilant in addressing how camp practices flirt disconcertingly not only with internalized homophobia and misogyny but also at times with racialized tropes—acknowledging camp both as a privileged discourse within queer culture and itself sometimes a discourse of privilege and appropriation.[15] But there is, conversely, an uncomfortable and, I think, undeniable echo in Halberstam's take on camp of the homophobic critical discourses discussed in chapter 1, which oppose the earnestness he associates with kinging to the perceived insincerity and superficial histrionics of gay men. (Which is not even to enter into the complications of parsing the significance and value of earnestness in Oscar Wilde.) I might even submit that, while not crossing gender lines, the clichéd depictions of butchness and machismo in Fassbinder's *Querelle*—leather daddies, sailors, construction workers, and the fetishization of Günther Kaufmann as a black stud—might themselves be understood as something similar to kinging in their undermining of masculinity's implicit claim to nonperformativity.[16]

That these depictions are denaturalizing does not, however, suspend the sincerity of the obvious erotic investment underlying them. Indeed, they might be better described as the kind of "camping . . . motivated by love" and *over*attachment that causes Eve Kosofsky Sedgwick to align camp with her call for reparative reading practices (as opposed to a paranoid viewpoint that would see camp as exclusively parodic).[17] More light cast on Halberstam's surprisingly chiaroscuro view might reveal some shades of gray, elucidating both camp and the abject as affective responses to the same fear of femininity or of being feminized, illuminating a shadow of heartfelt abjection in camp's feigned haughtiness. More pointedly, I intend to argue for a view of camp performativity as *precisely* a politically ambivalent expression and embodiment of perceived abjection: camp articulates abjection as a reflection of an already distorted reflection, taking what is abjected as effeminate and elevating it into queer style.[18]

In this chapter I'll very briefly sketch an intellectual genealogy of camp and the abject before examining how Fassbinder weds them in *Querelle* by infusing the irony of the former with the deeply felt sincerity of the latter. Theories and practices of both modes, as I'll show, have too often tended to reduce them to stable subject positions, an identification as camp or as abject, concretizing these into recognizable homosexual (stereo)types. The tortured playfulness of Fassbinder's *Querelle* flirts with such typecasting while at the same time repurposing and perverting it. Bringing to the screen the narratological self-dismantling that already characterized Genet's novel, the film deconstructs the very possibility not only of stable identity categories but of ipseity itself, working toward an aesthetic of self-erasure.

Camp/Abject

Queer studies in the wake of the so-called affective turn has remained particularly mindful of the transformative capacity of shame. A slew of scholarly monographs and edited collections since then—Heather Love's *Feeling Backward: Loss and the Politics of Queer History* (2007), David Halperin's *What Do Gay Men Want? An Essay on Sex, Risk, and Subjectivity* (2007), Halperin and Valerie Traub's edited collection on *Gay Shame* (2009), to name only a very few—testifies to the enduring intellectual interest in queer abjection. Corollary to this field of inquiry, but until recently seldom recognized as such, is a revitalized celebration of the camp sensibility and its subversive potential. To give a culturally visible example: pushing back, as have many others, against Susan Sontag's well-known designation of camp as apolitical, Karen Van Godtsenhoven, associate curator of the Met Costume Institute's much-discussed recent exhibition Camp: Notes on Fashion, triumphs camp style's capacity "to flaunt oppression, as it addresses the artificiality of notions such as gender, race, sexuality, class, and taste."[19] Beyond camp's habitual associations primarily with (white) gay male culture, the Met exhibition, timed to coincide with the fiftieth anniversary of the Stonewall Uprising and World-Pride NYC, thus sought to introduce visitors to "designers and personalities who use camp to overcome their roles as the marginalized Other."[20] By insisting on the metamorphic and cathartic qualities of camp, however, this perspective subtly casts it not as a token of queer pride, per se, but rather as rooted in an experience of one's own abjection.

In keeping with queer studies' abiding investment in shame and negativity, here I will similarly insist not only on the playfully ironic, volitional aspects of camp but also on its foundational disavowals: something closer to an unwitting limp-wristedness than to the ostentatious contrapposto known as the camp pose, less the flamboyant strut originally designated by the seventeenth-century French *se camper* than the stigmatized lisp of a falsely pronounced shibboleth. Attention to these more homophobic associations often overlooked in the scholarly discourse on camp reveals the affectation as an endeavored revaluation of values originating in feelings of *ressentiment*. Crucially, this complicates Sedgwick's perhaps too generous distinction between kitsch-attribution (the bad taste we project onto others) and camp-recognition (the kind we feel secretly speaks to and welcomes us), since the in-crowd to whom the camp code addresses itself is not self-selecting but rather constituted by abjection from a social field whose habitus (or, more specifically, hexis) it cannot always convincingly imitate.[21] Avowing by exaggeration precisely the disavowed attributes of stereotypical effeminacy habitually imputed to the male homosexual, camp cloaks abjection in hyperbole, passing off failed passing as a conscious choice.

In what follows I will attempt to account for the alchemy through which shame is meant to be transmuted into pride by theorizing *camp abjection* as a simultaneous mode of interpellation and performativity: a form of failed passing issuing from an identity formation first imposed and then affirmed—and thus aspirationally, ambivalently transformed. In so doing, I respond to recent approaches in queer studies that rightly insist on abjection as the underside of an often deceptively glamorous camp affect and attempt to exhume what a camp aesthetic works to occlude. Kathryn Bond Stockton has, for instance, maintained that "shame and camp have important, entangled relations with each other" and called for "someone to write a 'pocket history' of dark camp" to complement Sontag's seminal "Notes" on the genre's seemingly more frivolous manifestations.[22] Providing such a history in a volume on *The Dark Side of Camp Aesthetics*, Ingrid Hotz-Davies recognizes camp as "a discursive mode that seeks to *incorporate* the inacceptable, shameful, ingloriously abject, rather than splitting it off and casting it elsewhere, a technique (and a desire) bound up with the origins of camp in the management of stigma."[23] Both camp and abjection involve an identification *as* disidentification, but whereas the latter attempts unsuccessfully to jettison the undesirable element, the former aspires to reclaim it as a sign of taste and sophistication.

Attempting a critical definition of the reputedly homosexual sensibility of camp remains a daunting task. Already, Susan Sontag's still foundational

1964 "Notes" popularizing the notion declare camp's very indefinability as one of its many, sometimes seemingly contradictory, defining characteristics. "To talk about Camp," says Sontag, "is to betray it."[24] And this is, in part, because "the *essence* of Camp is its love of the unnatural: of artifice and exaggeration."[25] If camp is, as Sontag claims, all about style at the expense of content, though, putting into ironic scare quotes everything that it encounters,[26] then this would also apply to the sentiment itself: camp is the very act of scare-quoting, the calling into question of appearance's subjugation to essence, and thus involves a skepticism toward essences altogether, even, if not especially, its own.

The question has been further complicated by the very hegemony of Sontag's essay and the profusion of scholarly discourse it has since inspired: the impression given is, inevitably, that the camp sensibility (already associated by Sontag largely with snobby, winking elitism) is a matter only for the loftiest of intellectual debates and most exclusive of Met Gala red carpet costume parties. But all of this is worlds away from the mode's arguably more organic habitat in seedy drag bars, the grittiness of a John Waters film, or the orgiastic public atmosphere of a gay pride parade. Camp is, after all, in Sontag's description, a good taste of *bad* taste.

Another part of the difficulty involves deciding whether camp is fundamentally a matter of taste at all or rather a question of *style*—an aesthetic preference or a code of comportment. Mark Booth and others have insisted, and I would be inclined to agree, that "camp is primarily a mode of behavior and only secondarily a sensibility"—first a bearing and only afterward an appreciation of the same.[27] But this doesn't mean that camp is entirely a product of conscious control.[28] For Harald and David Galef, camp is always to an extent involuntary: "What the camper projects . . . is a pose, a behavior that, no matter how blatant, has a largely unconscious component."[29] That some aspect of camp behavior would be unconscious seems to indicate an internal tension with its love of appearance at the expense of essence, perhaps even pointing to what might, with homophobic resonances, imply a fixed disposition.

If shrewd camp *perception* tends to have a wisp of tender irony to it, camp *production* is perhaps seldom so self-aware. Sontag, for one, prefers her camp innocent and unintentional: "One must distinguish between naïve and deliberate Camp. Pure Camp is always naïve. Camp which knows itself to be camp ('camping') is usually less satisfying. . . . Probably," she concludes, "intending to be camp is always harmful."[30] This preference for artlessness points, unnervingly, to more phobic possible associations. But, in any event, the codification of camp as recognizably homosexual style marks the emergence of sexual identity unmoored from same-sex desire.

Thus camp can paradoxically be counted as *queer* but not necessarily *homosexual* in the sense of any given object choice—recalling Sedgwick's suggestion that the affect of shame might be a better index of what it means to be queer than sexuality itself. As she puts it in another often-quoted passage:

> Queer, I'd suggest, might usefully be thought of as referring in the first place to . . . an overlapping group . . . whose sense of identity is for some reason tuned most durably to the note of shame. . . . Everyone knows that there are some lesbians and gay men who could never count as queer and other people who vibrate to the chord of queer without having much same-sex eroticism, or without routing their same-sex eroticism through the identity labels lesbian or gay.[31]

Perhaps not unproblematically, this deprives queerness of a stable referent beyond or prior to social exclusion: the queen camping it up has to at first recognize at least the risk of being perceived by others as effeminate before embracing this affect or developing it into an epistemological disposition.[32] Even as an aesthetic sensibility or mode of perception, then, camp progresses from a misrecognition, or what I describe in chapter 2 as disidentification, through which one comes unsteadily to identify with an unflattering image of oneself supplied by alterity.[33]

Philip Core describes it as "a disguise that fails"[34]—an evocation of failure (recalling Sontag's failed seriousness) to which we should remain attentive in the current context, as it seems to imply at once a homosexual tropism toward masquerade and, even more problematically, an abjected homosexual disposition that this attempts to conceal. Both structurally and tonally, camp thus occupies an unsettling position for queer thought, and not only by dint of this potentially misogynistic parody of femininity, since it is not truly a wholly affirmative performance of any allegedly sovereign selfhood nor, on the surface, does its ludic, even chipper tenor always tend to match the more lugubrious antisocial affects—to give Heather Love's list—of "nostalgia, regret, shame, despair, *ressentiment*, passivity, escapism, self-hatred, withdrawal, bitterness, defeatism and loneliness" emphasized by a still-burgeoning discursive field within queer studies opposed to what it sees as the redoubled stigmatization occasioned by models of gay pride.[35] To argue in favor of camp necessarily flirts with uncomfortable cliché; to argue against it seems to disclose an internalized homophobia embodied in a preference for passing.

As this apparent aporia would suggest, part of the difficulty of theorizing gay identity is reconciling camp's willful embrace of surface and exaggerated artifice and its pretension to autonomous self-invention with a depth model of abjection predicated on social rejection and a *lack* of agency. And if a celebration of camp performativity risks casting doubt on the authenticity of queer subjectivity altogether, an intellectual engagement with abjection as damaged personhood hazards perpetuating an impression of homosexuality as a psychic defect. This chiasmus perhaps accounts, in part, for the often evident mutual antipathy between psychoanalytic discourses and those that theorize camp: the psychoanalytic description of abjection as a crisis within the subject would seem fundamentally antithetical to camp self-affirmation.[36]

Perhaps in part in order to avoid any impression of an inherent homosexual perversion, recent approaches have tended to emphasize the origins of psychological abjection in *social* rejection. As queer theorist David Halperin points out, for instance, the discussion of abjection, applied to Jean Genet specifically, reaches much farther back: to Jean-Paul Sartre's biography of the author and to Genet's own use of the word, influenced—as Didier Eribon had earlier revealed—by Marcel Jouhandeau's treatise on the subject.[37] Without becoming distracted by unnecessary detail, what is important, for Halperin, in excavating this forgotten genealogy, is an understanding of abjection not as a psychological but rather as a social phenomenon, a casting out by society of its unassimilated and unwanted homosexual element.

If Halperin is right in his suspicions, and I suspect he largely is, then Genetian hagiography—a celebration and consecration of abjection—implies a social survival strategy more than a belief in one's own inherent perversion. As Genet writes, comparing himself to Divine in the novel treated in the previous chapter,

> I might . . . confide that if I take contempt with a smile or a burst of laughter, it is not yet—and will it someday be?—out of contempt for contempt, but rather in order not to be ridiculous, not to be reviled, by anything or anyone, that I have placed myself lower than dirt. I could not do otherwise. If I declare that I am an old whore, no one can better that, I discourage insult. People can't even spit in my face any more.[38]

Despite divergent appearances, Genetian abjection, on this account, attempts to manage stigma much as Divine's camping it up does—although, in this case, at least, merely by affirming rather than by necessarily thereby transforming it.

This does not, however, discount psychoanalytic insight into abjection to the extent Halperin—who goes so far as to insist that Julia Kristeva never so much as mentions homosexuality in her landmark study of abjection—sometimes seems to want to imply.[39] In fact, Kristeva alludes to homosexuality on at least half a dozen occasions and states more than once in the opening chapters of her study, and not without perpetuating pernicious stereotypes, that the primary narcissism and autoeroticism bound up in abjection relate it to "homosexual symptoms."[40] And even Halperin has to admit (although again transposing Kristeva's model onto the social body) that

> Gay men after all are "abjected," in Kristeva's sense, by straight society. More to the point, homosexuality itself can be a perennial source of abjection for some gay men, a source of horror and revulsion, because it is universally abominated, considered abnormal and perverted, and some gay men take those judgments against homosexuality to heart from a young age. Indeed, even to recognize oneself as

> being named, described, and summed up by the clinical term *homosexual* (or *faggot* or *queer*) is to come to self-awareness and to a recognition of social condemnation at the very same instant.[41]

All of which points up the political ambivalence of camp posturing.[42] Abjection, as Halperin theorizes it, hovers, much like camp, precariously between the involuntary and the intentional: it's not initially chosen, but its affirmation does require effort. This makes sense if we admit that camp isn't merely a mode of imitation but rather of self-mimicry—an imitation of the broken queer self as it had always already been perceived by others.

This is why, for Eribon, in an existentialist phrasing, homosexual existence precedes essence. Or, to quote from Andrew Britton's astute and very similar commentary:

> The very term "a homosexual" (of which "a gay person" is only the recuperation, albeit a progressive one) defines not an object-choice of which any individual is capable, but a type with characteristic modes of behavior and response. Sartre has analysed, in relation to Genet, the process by which a determinate social imperative ("I have been placed in such-and-such a role") can be transformed into existential choice ("Therefore I will take the initiative of adopting it"); and that process describes the fundamental complicity of what may appear to be an act of self-determination. Camp is collaborative in that sense.

Arguing specifically against what he sees as Sontag's and Jack Babuscio's earlier implications that camp might be an *innately* gay sensibility,[43] Britton's reading *should* align nicely, it seems to me, with Halperin's attempt, also on the basis of Genet, to depsychologize and depathologize our understanding of the abject by distinguishing it from masochism. But whereas Britton is consequently quite critical of camp, Halperin understands the Genetian embrace of abjection, if not unambivalently or without reservation, as an overall successful social strategy, indeed as the very "invent[ion] of the homosocial subject" and the birthplace of "gay subjectivity."[44] This divergence is telling in its implications for how queer criticism tends to speak differently about camp versus the abject.

While I am generally receptive to critiques of psychoanalysis and its persistent hegemony in intellectual discourse, what I find preferable about a more strictly Kristevan account of abjection, and the reason I have chosen to retain this term here, is that it locates the phenomenon even further back in the development of the individual: abjection is precisely the simultaneous attraction and revulsion to that which is neither self nor other, neither fully subject nor object. Preobjectival and, in fact, constitutive of the symbolic (and therefore also of the social sphere), abjection responds to an *internal* dissonance rather than to an external alterity—and seems, for this reason, potentially more promising as a model for self-making unbounded by the restrictions of majoritarian ideology. In short, I find that the term *abjection* captures the social sense intended by Genet while at the same moment retaining a necessary emphasis on semiotic and psychic self-difference.

Attention to the intersecting discursive histories of camp and queer abjection, more commonly treated independently of one another, provides new perspective on the cultural concretization of gay male identity as it takes on associations over time. After all, Halberstam's critique of camp is that it is *not* as protean or flexible—in a word, as *queer*—as it might be; instead, if we follow Halberstam, camp is rigidly formulaic in its expressive grammar. And I share this concern that for all of the celebration of camp as a strategy of disidentification, as an affirmational revaluation and resignification of toxic stereotypes, it must also operate—this being in the very nature of disidentification—as an *identification*. By this I mean not only that it recognizes, affirms, and reproduces an initially unwanted interpellation (as effeminate, for instance) but that it over time codifies, reifies, and even tokenizes such identification.

This is, after all, how a legible homosexual typology becomes uncoupled, as Britton points out, from object choice. Queer theory's Borromean rings—sex, politics, aesthetics—have lost a link. Conversely, but relatedly, when an uncomplicated affirmation of abjection becomes, as Halperin has it, the origin of gay subjectivity, it insists on an apparently innate political subversiveness to the homosexual subject without any clear sense of the transformational practice or resignifying form that that subversion might take. In this chapter I will explore how Fassbinder resists camp's desexualizing tendencies by reinserting abjection; in the next, largely on the body abject in queer cinema, I will begin to show how queer aesthetics also risk succumbing to tokenism.

I am distinguishing, then, relatively naïve practices of camping and abjection from a more critical variety. If vulgar, everyday camp purports to purge stigma while näive abjection straightforwardly affirms it, what I propose to theorize—in what, by this point, will be recognizable as an intentionally oxymoronic formula—as the more robust amalgam of camp abjection is a specific mode of performativity or self-(re)invention that resists reification inasmuch as it does not attempt to transmute shame into pride without remainder but instead chooses to retain and even foreground traces of the origins of camp playfulness in a sense of one's own abjection. The camp abject playfully and ambivalently highlights—even exaggerates by caricature—the stigmatized facets of queer experience without seeking to deprive them of their perceived repugnance. Phrased conversely, it is a mode that, as Kathryn Bond Stockton would have it, insistently "link[s] shame to camp. And yet to a dark camp that keeps the violent edge of debasement visibly wedded to camp caprice."[45] The camp abject performs stigma without endeavoring to domesticate it, although also never without the risk of vanishing into this performance—or simply vanishing.

Accidental Identity

We can observe such self-fashioning subjectivity in the mode of the camp abject, as well as its implications for the political stakes of Halberstam's celebration of queer failure, in the various versions of *Querelle*: novel, scripts and screenplays, film. After all, Halberstam's aversion toward or hesitation with regard to camp's purported insincerity is shared by many, if not most, commentators on Fassbinder's last picture. Most recently, Roy Grundmann interrogates how *Querelle* models an "ideal of queer abjection [that], notwithstanding queer theory's recourse to Genet, remains difficult to negotiate for contemporary queer reality," worrying that "Fassinder's campy *mise-en-scène* undermines the serious implications of this point."[46] Ultimately, though, he concludes that the film nevertheless "preserves the meaning of abjection in radical form."[47] Steven Shaviro has noted that "many critics have complained that Fassbinder's campy, kitschy rendering constitutes a betrayal of Genet's novel" but admonishes that "they have forgotten that the inevitability of betrayal is already one of Genet's main preoccupations."[48] On either account, Fassbinder's film would be successful: either *despite* its camp sensibility or precisely by virtue of the appropriately irreverent, even sacrilegious *failure* such a sensibility would represent vis-à-vis the source text.

Indeed, if the various versions of *Querelle* are to be counted as camp, it is because their all-too-apparent failures are so clearly *intended*, even if not necessarily for that reason tongue-in-cheek: it is not the kind of failed seriousness that eschews or prohibits overinvestment that is at issue here but rather the serious—indeed, even earnest—pathos of emotional investment in the principle of aesthetic failure. (Sontag alludes to both varieties.[49]) Fassbinder himself publicly declared the plot of his source text for *Querelle* to be uninspiring: "The plot alone . . . is an uninteresting, rather third-rate police story that would hardly be worth filming."[50] Instead, as in Édouard's account of his undertaking in *Les faux-monnayeurs*, it is the conflict between the story and *how* it is told that makes the project interesting: "What is, however, worth engaging with is Jean Genet's method of narration, the confrontation with an unusual imagination that brings into being an at-first seemingly strange world with its own laws bound to an astonishing mythology."[51] Further recalling Gide on the foundational literary conflict between reality and its representation, Fassbinder goes so far as to declare Genet's *Querelle* to be "perhaps the most radical novel of world literature in terms of the discrepancy between its objective plot and its subjective fantasy."[52] This fantasy, Fassbinder implies in his notes, is a collective one, and indeed, we ought to bear in mind Genet's assertion very early on in the book—his only novel to use the rather scholarly-sounding first-person plural as the narrative voice—that it's addressed to an audience of inverts ("s'adresse aux invertis").[53] While the novel lacks little of the oppositional provocation of the earlier endeavors, it is arguably the first and only of Genet's narrative works not to presume a scandalized heterosexual reader but rather to situate itself within an imagined, if amorphous, queer community.

The adaptation has a similar position within Fassbinder's oeuvre. Although the auteur had made numerous films focusing on nonnormative sexualities and gender identities, he nonetheless, as Caryl Flinn rightly reminds us, "consistently minimized the importance of identity politics even while dramatically staging the obstacles experienced by people of those very identities."[54] In various public statements around the time of the film's release, the filmmaker unrelentingly maintained that *Querelle*, specifically, was not about homosexuality at all but rather about someone searching, within and against society, for his own identity—universalizing the specificities of queer experiences of stigma. More pointedly, in his foreword to the published version of the script, Fassbinder describes the film as a quest for *self*-identity, using language uncharacteristically aligned with calls for gay liberation. Discovering similarities between Genet's fantasy world and our own, Fassbinder argues, also means approaching our own identity ("heißt auch: wir nähern uns unserer Identität!"): "And only he is who is identical with himself no longer needs to fear fear. And only he who is unafraid can love without judgment; the highest aim of all human effort: to live one's life!"[55] This utopian aspect to *Querelle* and its status as Fassbinder's final film account for some of its gravity for queer communities. But if *Querelle* seems to occupy a more predominant place in the gay cultural imaginary than Fassbinder's other queer films, discussed more extensively in chapter 5, it is certainly also because of how it draws on, perpetuates, and remobilizes recognizable queer clichés and camp codes. Through its inventory of unpersuasive pornological poses it takes to heart a lesson laid out by Gide and Genet, highlighting identity as a narrative abstraction.

If it is not the content of *Querelle* that makes it interesting as much as its narrative procedure, then bringing Genet's uniquely self-deconstructive narratology to the screen will involve exploding the clichés and codes represented—achieving and by the same gesture undoing, as I intend to show, the very self-identity to which the filmmaker purports to aspire. Placing the work under the sign of a conflict between narrative and narrativity and insisting that his intention was to make a film *about* Genet's novel, rather than an adaptation, Fassbinder emphasizes especially the work's grotesque aspects. But if Fassbinder's reworking even further dismantles Genet's already hackneyed and jumbled narrative, as he seems to intuit, it does so loyally, following an instinct inscribed in the novel itself. To adapt a line from the film's obnoxiously catchy ballad, borrowed from Oscar Wilde, each author kills the text he loves.

As Genet readily admits in a prefatory note to one of the first private printings of *Querelle de Brest* in December of 1947, "A sudden weariness caused us to abandon 'Querelle' which was already beginning to fray." And this is perhaps less a confession than a programmatic statement. Even before

Fassbinder gets his hands on it, *Querelle* is set under the aegis of an unraveling.[56] Increasingly, throughout the book, the narrator complains of fatigue, hastening the pace of the plot to get it over with, lazily glossing over key scenes and details, and concluding, at one point toward the end, "This book goes on for too many pages, and it bores us."[57] But the more the novel loses steam, the more its actors gain in autonomy.

In order to take narrative form and become a fictional character, Genet professes toward the outset, Querelle must display an independence from his creator: "To become visible to you, to become a character in a novel, Querelle must be shown apart from ourselves. Only then will you get to know the apparent, and real, beauty of his body, his attitudes, his exploits, and their slow disintegration."[58] And as the book draws to a close, Querelle would seem to consummate this purpose:

> In trying to follow the movements in our protagonists' souls, we are also trying to illuminate our own. Freely noting that the attitude we would have liked to adopt—with a view to, or perhaps, with a foreknowledge of the desired end of the story—has led us to the discovery of a given psychological world that supports the idea of freedom of choice; but as soon as the progression of the story requires one or the other of its main characters to pronounce a judgement, to take thought, we are immediately confronted by the *arbitrary* [*l'arbitraire*]: the character escapes from its author, becoming its own, singular being. Thus we have to admit that the author is able to reveal certain traits of this character only after the fact.[59]

Seemingly paradoxically, it is precisely the authorial desire for a predictably fixed narrative that introduces uncustomary, eccentric caprice at the level of character psychology. The very word *arbitrary* can, after all, indicate either random chance or erratic impulse—etymologically it is tied to both passive witnessing and to sovereign judgment.[60] Cognizant of and candid about its own narrative contrivances, *Querelle* depicts a psychological world over which its narration, for all its fickle whims, cannot exercise full control. Here I would like to correlate such an emphasis on the arbitrariness of narrative choices to the spectacularly, ecstatically performed deviance and deterioration of the abjected sexualities on display throughout the plot.

For if *Querelle*, especially in Fassbinder's iteration, is unquestionably *camp*, it is nonetheless at best unstably homosexual. Or, to borrow Flinn's phrasing: "For all its homosexual masculinities . . . *Querelle* seems not so much gay as queer, energized by a wide range of sexual and affective energies, desires, and categories."[61] This nebulous masculinized queerness—as opposed to homosexuality as an identity category—is significant for its negotiation between abjection and its camp expression. Querelle himself suspects that, although effeminate, which is to say, although camp, a faggot tries to make his sexual partner into a woman: "Fairies [*les tantouzes*] . . . (even if they act like women) . . . try to make you into a woman."[62] In the introduction to their volume on *The Dark Side of Camp*, Ingrid Hotz-Davies, Georg Vogt, and Franziska Bergmann point out the troubling gender politics of camp, which "tends to draw on and even embrace, much to the dismay of some feminist critics, a grotesquely overstated, officially debased and disavowed version of femininity, thereby drawing attention to femininity's generally troubling status as, on the one hand, the necessary second part of a hierarchical binary, and on the other hand, as that symbolic system's always already abjected or abjectable 'other.' "[63] At base, Kristeva's notion of abjection is grounded, after all, in the rejection of the maternal, and thus of the female body, as I will explore more fully in my final chapter. Hotz-Davies elsewhere notes, however, how camp embraces specifically "that most prohibited and debased version of the feminine, *effeminacy*."[64] If camp is predicated on misogyny, it is a misogyny transposed onto relationships between men—as in *Querelle*, which notoriously has only one central female character, the brothel keeper Lysiane (Jeanne Moreau), whom Fassbinder designated as representing womanhood *an sich*.

Querelle provides an occasion to reconsider the relation between camp and effeminacy and between camp and abjection—representing, as it does, a hypermasculine sexual bottoming that derives its masculinity from being the hypertrophied mirror image of the manly top. The strictly gendered *mac-tante* relations informing Genet's first novel—the rigidity of which is disrupted only by its titular character—have been reconfigured here as a more idiosyncratic top-bottom discourse from which the proverbial bottom has fallen out. In *Querelle*, what is conventionally referred to as passive anal pleasure, and perceived as feminizing, sensually celebrates masculinity but also denaturalizes it in a procedure akin to camp's parody of femininity. Yoking camp to abjection, returning camp identification with femininity to its foundational dissociations and disavowals, Fassbinder's *Querelle* transforms it into a critique of *masculinity*. Demythologizing the ostensible nonperformativity of masculinity, Fassbinder's narrative slowly unravels both homosexual subjectivity as an identity category and the very category of subjectivity as such.

Michael Lucey interprets the novel in part following a guiding question posed by Querelle early on in an attempt to establish the meaning of "l'idée énorme et mal équilibré de pédé" ("the monstrous and ill-defined notion of 'faggot' "). Straining to distinguish a *pédé* (a gay man, which he is not, in his eyes) from an *enculé* (a sodomized man, which he emphatically is), Querelle explicitly asks: "Pédé, qu'est-ce que c'est?" ("But what's a fag?").[65] In a description echoing Fassbinder's, Lucey reads the novel as a reflection on indexicality as it bears "on its relation to the production of oneself as a social subject" and more specifically "as a sexual subject."[66] This anticipates the almost pornographic desire for the indexical—with a fixation on the reality of the referent itself—that will attach to the abject-cum-eroticized body discussed in the coming chapters. In *Querelle*, this observation pertains especially to narrative form.

A distilled, single-sentence plot summary might well choose to focus on the staunchly off-straight titular character's quest to *own* his own abjection—his homicidal criminality—by discovering the pleasure of taking it up the ass from a revolving cast of equally heterosexual tops. (Although, admittedly, there are moments when the emphasis on this aspect begins to scan as closeted overinsistence.) A more precise and more extensive plot summary might distill the story instead into Querelle's gradual discovery of his *dis*interest in topping, perhaps even his feeling of abjection at the idea: "Since for Querelle, a fag is still just a guy who fucks another guy."[67] Bottoming is traditionally associated in the cultural imaginary and in queer theory—and most pertinently in Bersani's account of self-shattering—with a subversive openness of the subject, an often discomfiting penetration if not complete suspension of the boundaries of the coherent self. But, in a sense, it's through this particularly abject sex act that Querelle insulates himself from the abjection of homosexuality: through an anal pleasure divorced from sexual orientation, the off-straight sailor *acts* gay without adopting any concomitant identity category.[68]

Scholarship on theses texts has therefore frequently returned to Edmund White's assertion that *Querelle* is "a novel about homosexuality in which none of the characters is homosexual,"[69] but, while well phrased, this description is not, for Genet's novel at least, entirely accurate. Genet himself insists that "none of the heroes of this book (excepting Lieutenant Seblon, but Seblon is not *in* the book) is a pederast."[70] And it is worth remembering that, in Genet's vocabulary, *pédéraste* still refers to any male homosexual and, by contrast with its colloquial abbreviation *pédé*, lends this particular phrase a neutral and again almost scholarly tone further emphasized by the elevated literary form of negation employed: "aucun des héros de ce livre . . . n'est pédéraste."[71] The only averred homosexual in *Querelle*, Seblon also has a liminal status in the story: he's both a sometimes-surrogate for an already-almost-embodied narrator and, especially in Fassbinder's film, a voyeuristic observer and implied gay reader who at key moments intrudes, as if metaleptically, on the action.[72]

Both Fassbinder's film and the published version of his script will ultimately bring such intrusions to the fore in a flamboyant surfeit of narratorial asides: intertitles quoting lengthy passages by Genet and others are accompanied throughout by an explanatory voice-over, itself redoubled by the intimate thoughts of this central figure dictated into a tape recorder. The reality of Fassbinder's revisions is, in fact, somewhat more complicated than White's abbreviated description of haphazard chronological reordering would imply. Werner Schroeter's collaboration on the script had already begun to rearrange the various narrative events penned by screenwriter Burkhard Driest; a careful comparison of drafts of the script reveals that Fassbinder's key intervention appears to have been to enhance the presence of the source text, emphasizing *narration* over *narrative* itself.[73] Upon first reading Fassbinder's version, the film's producer, Dieter Schidor, admits to finding it "so difficult to tell as a story that I was shocked."[74] But opting, in a sense, to tell, rather than merely to show, Fassbinder, like Genet before him, emphasizes the contrived nature of his story and its characters—and, more pointedly, the constructed nature of their uncertain or unstable sexual identities.

We can observe the implications of this dynamic as early as the ending of the title sequence of Fassbinder's adaptation of *Querelle*. Seblon (Franco Nero) is first depicted speaking into his tape recorder while observing the sailors on his ship, but, while at moments very nearly synchronized, the voice-over is not *his* but rather the narrator's—a role that Fassbinder had originally intended for Genet himself to play. Genet declined, and this will be important, claiming no longer to identify with the author of the text and expressing his certainty that Fassbinder would sympathize with such dissociation.[75] Given the perplexing mix of accents and emphatically sloppy dubbing of the film in its original English-language release, it is likely only later, if at all, that the viewer notices the discrepancy and the extradiegetic origin of this voice-off: "It's difficult to brush past those shoulders, profiles, curls of those strong and supple boys, without imagining them capable of murder." Mary M. Wiles notes that this sentiment initially "seems to be attributable to the lieutenant, due to the shot/reverse shot code (the supposition that the shot which follows the shot of a character who is looking out of the filmic frame becomes the point of view of the character)."[76] After all, Querelle (Brad Davis) is predominantly framed at this moment from an angle that would seem to imply Seblon's perspective. But this impression is unanchored by what follows, as is the desire it expresses: a strange, homoerotic bloodlust is diffused across the viewer's primary and secondary identifications with the vantage points of the camera and the characters, resulting in a universalizing homoeroticism that draws the audience into its orbit without imposing any fixed identity position.

The next shots of Seblon are indeed accompanied by his own voice (marked, for the attentive listener, by Franco Nero's Italian accent), but this time disembodied, issued from an unseen dictaphone, as he peruses images of classical male beauty in a book on Greek sculpture, his lips no longer moving: "Once I've suffered the solitude caused by my peculiarity long enough, it may be that, naked, I will hold these boys, who shatter me with their audacity and strength, against my body. Though I hardly dare believe it. With tears in my eyes, I thank God for granting me this bliss. My tears soften me. I melt with their wetness on my cheeks. I toss. I roll in waves of tenderness for these boys and their hard, shallow cheeks." Lifting the recorder to pause playback, and thereby revealing the mysterious origin of the previous monologue, Seblon finally begins to narrate his reflections on Querelle *viva voce*, as it were: "Querelle's great passion is his own body in repose. It is as if he's reflecting himself in his own image. He's looking at himself as if through a magnifying glass. He's scrutinizing the minute events like an entomologist. But how shining is his body in the glory of his proud movements." This tripartite soliloquy stages Seblon's precarious process of auto-affection as his voice gradually detaches itself from the narrator's and comes to tell the story in his turn: his own story, but also Querelle's—this being, in fact, the first introduction of the eponymic character by name.

Setting the tone for the film to follow, the mood of this prismatic character exposition is utterly undecidable. Seblon's lament over the isolation caused by his homosexual "peculiarity" and the exceedingly earnest, meditatively repetitive, quasi-religious choral music accompanying the scene engender a sentiment of blissful despair: the variety of self-shattering Bersani identifies and celebrates in Genet is evoked here all but verbatim by the playback of the lieutenant's dictaphone—which, in earlier versions of the script, had alternately been a telescope and a camera, as if to emphasize his role as a kind of ersatz auteur. But Fassbinder also breaks palpably with Genet's constant affirmation of sacral abjection, undercutting its sincerity with the antinaturalistic pseudo-Brechtian delivery of the dialogue and a highly artificial stage-like set—only the theatrical suggestion of a ship and preposterously phallic parapets to represent Brest. In short, he sabotages it through ludic camp hyperbole. As in Genet's prose, it is just this volatile amalgam of overstated goofiness and solemn wretchedness that constitutes the willfully failed seriousness of Fassbinder's camp abject: the mercurial peculiarity (in Seblon's queer sense) of this attitude is that it refuses full-on parody every bit as much as it rejects uncomplicated *Einfühlung*.

This ambivalent tonality and unsteady identification pollute the narrative perspective as well. A similar aural ambivalence and visual confusion obtain, for instance, with regard to the sailors' gossip about the brothel, La Féria, which is interspersed between the bits of monologue quoted above. For one thing, Querelle and the two shipmates on whom the camera focuses are suddenly filmed at this moment from an opposite angle—from the shoreline rather than from Seblon's perspective at the center of the ship. Just as confusingly, the dialogue is delivered largely off camera from unidentifiable sources, presumably other, invisibly anonymous sailors. Just after this "raunchiest whorehouse in the world" has been revealed through an eyeline match from one sailor to the shoreline, followed by a slow pan bringing the bar into view, the seamen relate the rules of a game of dice with the bordello's owner, Nono (Günther Kaufmann), a game Querelle will soon enough play—and intentionally lose: "When you win, you get to have your pick. When you lose, you have to let the boss fuck you first." While the origin of some of these comments seems intuitable from the acoustic perspective, the initial naming of the bar and description of the game, as well as, most significantly, a rejoinder insinuating the possibility of anal pleasure—"I'm damn sure there's plenty of guys who kind of like losing!"—would seem to be spoken by Brad Davis, who plays Querelle. If so, these are his first lines in the entire film, although he is shown on screen at just this moment, wordlessly polishing his boots.

One might almost take this, then, as an instance of interior monologue if it weren't for the response of the other sailor, Vic (played by the film's producer and original instigator, Dieter Schidor), who is sitting back-to-back with Querelle and whom Querelle will kill off in a later scene. Instead, the implication is a diegesis where the characters have not only robust, *internal* mental lives but even *extra*diegetic or metaleptic agency: if Seblon at first seems almost ventriloquized by the narrator before eventually liberating and speaking for himself, Querelle initially *refuses* to play his part, to speak the line apparently assigned to him. That the subject of both this discussion and Seblon's soliloquy is sex and sexuality is hardly incidental: at issue here is nothing less than the self-determination of a sexual identity predicated primarily, it appears, on who fucks whom. And some guys, as Querelle will soon discover, like losing, *failing*, getting fucked. That he might well be the source of this insight acoustically but at the same moment visually resists the homophobic disdain attached to it may be a first hint of both his sexual sovereignty *and* his instability—the same sovereignty and instability that will ultimately occasion the artwork's undoing. If his unspoken line is an indication of agency, after all, it is an agency that arises only *accidentally* through an apparent editing error, a mistake left unfixed if not imposed in post. Highlighting abjection and self-dissonance, even in an acutely aural sense, Fassbinder turns camp against itself, coopting and perverting its formulae to undo it as a rigid typology and instead returning it to a perpetual process of revaluation and resignification. Admittedly more a twunk (a portmanteau of twink and hunk) than a twink proper, if anything distinguishes Querelle from the other off-straight idols treated in this book it is perhaps less this comparable manliness, let alone the degree of any ostensible self-identity, than the force of Fassbinder's deconstruction of these tropes through their failure.

Conclusion: Queer Self-Erasure

The ultimate effect of all these winking nods to the film's creators as well as the repeated reverse cuts jarringly violating the 180-degree axis is not only an increasing independence of the characters represented from the restrictions of their representation but, further, a narratological sloppiness tending toward complete disintegration—echoing Genet's comments about the arbitrary progression and decomposition of his characters and plot. As in Genet's novel, what would otherwise aspire to be an omniscient narrative viewpoint struggles against the seeming autonomy of the figures it depicts—their freedom to explore their sexualities and determine their own fate. Forfeiting control, this cinematic universe bears all the characteristics of the "other archive" of "rage, rudeness, anger, spite, impatience, intensity, mania, sincerity, earnestness, overinvestment, incivility, brutal honesty, and disappointment" that Halberstam understands to be occluded by the camp archive, constituting instead a "second archive . . . far more in keeping with the undisciplined kinds of responses that Leo Bersani at least seems to associate with sex and queer culture, and it is here that the promise of self-shattering, loss of mastery and meaning, unregulated speech and desire are unloosed."[77] For, as its title sequence already makes clear, *Querelle* is nothing if not the deregulation of speech and deterritorialization of desire.

Rather than creating coherent, legible filmic space, Fassbinder's jumbled reestablishing shots and eyeline matches abandon the spectator in a hall of mirrors illustrating, perhaps, Seblon's reflections on the mise en abyme of Querelle's self-observation: the sailor is not only portrayed in profile from both sides he is also doubled from behind by his soon-to-be victim, Vic. As Halberstam would describe his archive of queer failure, "these are the bleak and angry territories of the antisocial turn; these are the jagged zones within which not only self-shattering (the opposite of narcissism in a way) but other-shattering occurs."[78] More radically negatively still, what Fassbinder's camp abjection shatters is neither merely self nor other but the very integrity of coherent selfhood in and of itself, alluding to the impossibility of a self unconditioned by alterity.[79] Working in a mode of camp abjection, the various versions of *Querelle* thus reveal, like Gide's counterfeiting, queer subjectivities to be perpetually forged and even fictionalized, recognizing the queer self as a site of ongoing narrativity. Upsetting hierarchies of irony and authenticity, the camp abject recognizes and even celebrates the contingency and volatility of identity: Seblon is only constituted as Querelle's initially unwanted other; despite his attempts at autonomy, Querelle ultimately exists exclusively as a passive, spectral fantasy projection; the nameless sailors are trapped within an echo chamber of disembodied voices of no discernible origin; Genet and Fassbinder, producer Schidor, and screenwriter Burkhardt Driest (who plays the role of Mario, the cop) persist only as filmic phantoms and authorial traces increasingly deprived of textual authority.

The staying power of *Querelle* for queer imaginaries and queer communities is surely also attributable to its willful failures, to the transparent phantasmaticity of its erotic wish fulfillment. Which is to say that its universalizing utopianism comes at the expense of indexicality, at the cost of specificity and difference of experience: despite its dogged insistence on male homosociality, the film's legacy is arguably less gay than coalitionally queer. Embodying such abstraction, the camp abject, despite its sexualizing intent, begins to pull apart the referential and illusory functions of the pornographic. A paradigm of failed passing has begun to tip into a poetics of erasure.

One of the most tender moments in the novel—and, I would submit, in all of Genet—manifests itself, as is not entirely atypical for the author, in an act of abhorrent violence. Inserted toward the end of the book in a narrative flashback, it relates Querelle's thoughts following his first kill, an Armenian named Joachim who wanted, to Querelle's surprise, not to fuck him but to get fucked:

> In the end, if this was what a faggot was like, a being so light, so fragile, so airy, so transparent, so soft, so delicate, so broken, so clear, so talkative, so melodious, so tender, you could kill it, having been made to be killed. . . . If this was what a fag was, it wasn't a man. It doesn't weigh much. It's a little kitten, a bullfinch, a fawn, a glass lizard, a dragonfly, provocative in its very fragility, exaggerated expressly so that it inevitably attracts death. And also, it's called Joachim.[80]

Concluding with this incidental return to the particular, Querelle appears finally (or in advance, since this action occurs before the book begins) to have answered his essential question as to what makes a man gay and what makes a gay man. If it is monstrous, it is only in the chimeric way that Divine resembles the creatures painted on the walls of the café Graff. A fag is something fragile: in this case its camp provocations are an invitation to the homophobic violence to which it is predestined. A fag is meant to disappear.

Both Genet and Fassbinder will oblige. This passage is cut from the retouched version of the text Genet haphazardly trimmed down for Gallimard, seemingly with more attention to his own evolving aesthetic preferences than to the censorship the publisher had intended to impose. The scene plays a prominent role in various drafts of the script for Fassbinder's adaptation and was apparently even filmed at one point but is absent from the final picture.

Fassbinder's film ends enigmatically with the brothel keeper Lysiane declaring, with what seems perhaps an intentionally unconvincing laugh, that Querelle never existed to begin with. While subtle enough to be missed—in fact I have never seen it remarked upon—the subsequent shot of the sailors setting off to sea is played in reverse, again framing the story with its own untelling. The concluding title card then recounts Genet's itinerary from an anonymous birth to an uncertain, fictionalized death and eventual disappearance into the literature that bears his signature:

> His birth certificate states: born on the 19th of December, 1918 at 10 o'clock in the morning. Mother: Gabrielle Genet. Father: unknown. Apart from his books, we know nothing about him, not even the date of his death, which to him seems near.
>
> Jean Genet

Written in Genet's hand in French but read aloud in English by a voice that is neither his nor Fassbinder's, perhaps it reveals *queer* not as a sexual identity but instead as a narrative function of self-erasure. If the adaptation, like the novel, kills the text it loves, in the end the queerest failure of the artwork is its attempted assassination of its author.

Chapter 4

✦

The Wound in Bloom

Werner Schroeter's Gay Stigmata

Werner Schroeter's *Der Rosenkönig* (*The Rose King*, 1986) begins with a perfectly innocuous image of a flower and climaxes in a violent deconstruction of this same cliché.

Behind the opening titles is a time-lapse shot of a red rose blossoming, revealing layer upon layer, over high-pitched, slightly eerie but ethereal music that eventually gives way to Puccini. The brutal narrative consummation of this floral imagery and its erotic promise occurs in the final minutes of the film when blood-red roses are inserted into the copiously bleeding gashes that the director, by means of visual effects, has inflicted on the body of his beloved beauty, Antonio Orlando. The age-old wound of love has become the locus of a self-conscious allegory for an avant-garde queer aesthetic.

That this moment itself would appear implicitly to rework the core motif of Jean Genet's second novel, *Miracle de la Rose* (*Miracle of the Rose*, 1946), invites an interrogation into an insistent association between wounds and flowers as it evolves from French literary modernism into the afterlives of New German Cinema—a movement for which Schroeter is an obscurely central figure. Here I will attend to this trope as it is adapted from Genet by Schroeter before looking for its afterimages in Monika Treut's and Elfi Mikesch's *Verführung oder die grausame Frau* (*Seduction: The Cruel Woman*, 1985) and the scattered sequences of Todd Haynes's "Homo," the third interwoven narrative of his feature directorial debut, *Poison* (1991). In revisiting and revitalizing this familiar trope, these queer auteurs seek to reconfigure, and often violently, established schemata of signification. They do so through a transformative cinematic poetics that works to transubstantiate discourses of abjection into an aesthetic of erotic injury intimately connected to the perceived outness of its authors. In this vein, the rose/wound acts as an emblem of queer authenticity and its visibility. And yet, I will be arguing, such insistence on corporeal verification ultimately makes of this figure an abstraction, occasioning *dis*embodiment and increasing spectacularization.

I take my cue here from Genet himself, who, on the first page of his quasi-autobiographical *Journal du Voleur* (*The Thief's Journal*, 1949), declares in a half-rhyme that in order to describe what has been, to this point in his career, the key erotic object—the criminal, the outsider, the convict, "je le parerai en tant de fleurs que lui-même disparaissant sous elle en deviendra une autre, géante, nouvelle" ("I shall so bedeck him with flowers that, as he disappears beneath them, he will himself become a flower, a gigantic and a new one").[1] If the cultivation of such an aesthetic of ugliness and artifice—in short, of such flowers of evil—continues a tradition that can be traced back to Charles Baudelaire, it is also of a piece with a properly Genetian (and properly cinematic, as I will contend in a moment) aesthetic of injury, which holds, as the author phrases it in a later essay, that "beauty has no other origin than the wound."[2]

Which is to say that, for Genet, as for the filmmakers treated here, this process of transforming the body of the beloved into a flower is itself a kind of wounding consonant with the very real physical violence that Genet admires in the murderers he venerates and eroticizes: "this audacity which dared, by massacring the flesh of adolescents, to destroy a visible, established beauty in order to achieve a beauty—or poetry—resulting from that shattered beauty's encounter with that barbaric gesture."[3] The aesthetic-erotic strategy for which these floral figures serve as an apt case study thus aligns itself with wounding fragmentation, disintegration, and reconstitution: an iconoclasm toward existing representational traditions in order to allow for a new beauty to come into being. Here I will trace the heritage of this injurious aesthetic procedure and its consequences for the construction of gay identities through filmic narrative into and out of New German Cinema and New Queer Cinema before turning, finally, to its surprisingly pop-cultural legacies.

Rose/Wound

This aesthetic of injury is both practiced by the idol of *Miracle de la Rose*, the murderer Harcamone, and, as I intend to show, implied in the violence done to him by Genet in the process of making him meaningful and sacred—of turning Harcamone into a flower of evil. For if Baudelaire's purpose was "to make the best of ugliness itself,"[4] Genet's will be to draw saintliness from abjection: "Harcamone's influence acted truly in accordance with his perfect destination: through him our minds were opened to extreme abjection. I cannot avoid using the figurative terminology that is commonly employed. Do not be surprised if the images that indicate my movement are the opposite of those that indicate the movement of the saints in heaven. You may say that they rose, and that I lowered myself."[5] This metamorphosis will require Genet, as he readily recognizes, to upend the most established, even clichéd, of representational traditions: stigmata, hagiography, and the attendant variety of wound/flower constellation at issue here.

Genet's *Miracle de la Rose*, like most of his fiction, is an unsteady amalgam of romanticized reminiscences of childhood and adult incarceration, masturbatory fantasy, and a few key moments of magical realism generally attached to the narrator's erotic and ethical obsession with the condemned Harcamone, whose uniquely violent and uniquely senseless crimes, as well as his impending death, elevate him within Genet's carceral imaginary to a certain celebrity and qualify him even for quasi-religious worship: "For he was funereal, despite his grace, funereal as are roses, which symbolize both love and death."[6] The rose is chosen by Genet precisely for its overdetermined and ambivalent symbolism—its sometimes contradictory erotic and divine valences. As Richard Dyer describes the use of flowers in Genet's sole film, *Un chant d'amour* (*A Song of Love*, 1950), which itself was shot in the space above a Parisian cabaret called La Rose Rouge: "Two things characteristic of Genet's use of objects as symbols, in all his work, are the way any one object may symbolize many different, often seemingly incompatible things, and the way that they generally symbolize the opposite of what they do elsewhere, in poetry or everyday life."[7] In short, Genet's work operates to queer the symbolic precedents upon which it itself reposes. There is a specifically filmic quality, I would suggest, to this queering, this simultaneous displacement and condensation: whereas a kind of written cinematography (in the strict sense of moving images) allows for the dislocation of a figure's habitual signification, it is a form of montage that permits Genet to superimpose contradictory and competing meanings one upon the other.

We can observe this already in Harcamone's first appearance, which is related in language reminiscent of the cinema: the other convicts face the wall, turning like sunflowers to watch the condemned man walking, and the narrator identifies Harcamone explicitly as a projection, an "exceptional creature whose story was familiar only to the well guarded chamber of my eyeballs."[8] The experience itself, however, is a bodily one, since, as the narrator notes in this immediate context, "flesh is still the most obvious means of certainty. Harcamone 'appeared unto me.' "[9]

> I felt in all my veins that the miracle was under way. But the fervour of our admiration and the burden of saintliness which weighed on the chain that gripped his wrists—his hair had had time to grow and the curls had matted over his forehead with the cunning cruelty of the twists of the crown of thorns—caused the chain to be transformed before our unastonished eyes into a garland of white roses. The transformation began at the left wrist, which it encircled with a bracelet of flowers, and continued along the chain, from link to link, to the right wrist.[10]

A feeling of physical anticipation gives way to a quasi-cinematographic pan along this concatenation from wrist to wrist, from link to link, and ultimately from flower to flower. It is cinematic, even pornographic, contemplation, the desiring gaze, that instigates the metamorphosis of this metonym of bondage: "The fervor of our admiration . . . *caused* the chain to be transformed before our unastonished eyes"—a transformation that takes place as seamlessly as a film dissolve.

Genet thus introduces montage into the image through a cut prefiguring both "the sacred stigmata of decapitation"[11] and the penetration of the "Mystic Rose"[12] of Harcamone's heart with which the novel concludes:

> I was holding the pair of scissors with which, once a month, we were allowed, each in turn, to cut our fingernails and toenails. I was therefore barefooted. I made the same movement that religious fanatics make to seize the hem of a cloak and kiss it. I took two steps, with my body bent forward and the scissors in my hand, and cut off the loveliest rose, which was hanging by a supple stem near his left wrist. The head of the rose fell on my bare foot and rolled on the pavestones among the dirty curls of cut hair. I picked it up and raised my enraptured face, just in time to see the horror stamped on that of Harcamone, whose nervousness had been unable to resist that sure prefiguration of his death.[13]

Edmund White notes the cinematic qualities of much of Genet's literary narrative, revealing how a filmic grammar and vocabulary allow for the kind of narrative caprice I have been focusing on throughout this book: "Close-ups of gestures are also essential to Genet's conception of the novel, since in his ontology accidents determine fate, gestures form character and costume triggers events."[14] Now fetishistically fragmenting the bodies on display into their constituent parts (first fingernails and toenails, bare feet, then the narrator's hand, Harcamone's left wrist, its rose, a bare foot, dirty curls of hair, an enraptured face, a horrified face), Genet choreographs a kind of shot-countershot of close-ups through which Harcamone comes face to face with his creator, exerting in this moment, by his suspension of the established rules of the otherwise plausibly realistic narrative, a form of authorial agency.

His physiognomy is stamped with a stigma and a premonition of his own mortality that exposes Harcamone, like a negative exposed to light, to the advent of his own Genetian saintliness, or what Michael Hardt calls "a certain abjection with respect to the force of things. . . . Exposure actualizes the divinity of the flesh."[15] The very emblem of Genet's erotics, politics, and aesthetics, this "orgasmic moment of severing"—an exposure, outing, or uncloseting situated somewhere between the promise of fellatio and the threat of castration—condenses the libidinal, religious, and mortal associations of the rose. It consists of what John Plotz identifies as a "moment of 'cumming/cutting' [that] marks the collapse and the reintegration of the sign."[16] As in Walter Benjamin's description of the operation of the allegorical, here the process of becoming significant first requires coming apart.[17]

Frequently in Genet, most notably in the typographical fragmentation of "Ce qui est resté d'un Rembrandt déchiré en petits carrés bien réguliers, et foutu aux chiottes" ("What Remains of a Rembrandt Torn into Four Equal Pieces and Flushed Down the Toilet," 1967), itself the model for Jacques Derrida's study of Genet and Hegel, *Glas* (recently retranslated as *Clang*, 1974), reflections on aesthetics are also the site of textual disintegration and productive dismemberment. White insists that Genet was interested in cinema throughout his career and in fact "wrote more pages of film scenarios than he did any other literary genre."[18] But Genet, it should be noted, would most likely have been more inclined to classify the entirety of his writing under the rubric of poetry and, as Pascal Caron reminds us, described *Le funambule* (*The Tightrope Walker*, 1958)—perhaps his most significant of many meditations on injury, aesthetics, and the aesthetics of injury—as a poem, although it is rarely designated as such by Genet scholars.[19] More pointedly, it is in such texts that Genet works out a programmatic, if elusive, choreography of the wound, what Caron calls a poetics of movement or what we can understand more broadly as a poetics of the body.[20] But for White, and I would agree, if Genet cannot, despite the graphic nature of his depictions of the male form, including full frontal nudity, be called pornographic, it is because the male figure in his work is also always the site of an abstraction.[21]

Indeed, if there is a coherence and a consistency to Genet's heteroclite oeuvre, it is the fundamentally aestheticizing impulse underlying the whole. In the next chapter, which situates filmmaker François Ozon with regard to what has often been described as the New French Extremity, we will see how, in another mode, the evidentiary body makes an implicit claim to an ontology beyond figuration. But there is a different, indeed opposite, kind of visual proof at work in Genet, since here it is the very activity by which the body is abstracted into meaning that is at stake.

It is consistent that the rose—historically an overdetermined metaphor, as already noted—would attach to such demonstrative logic and its internal tensions. Like the body, it promises fixed meaning while in the same instance exposing the production of meaning in all its arbitrariness. For the rose oversignifies in a dual sense. Its meanings, in various cultural traditions, are highly codified, thereby inevitably inspiring the kind of queer iconoclasm we will see at work in Genet's cinematic legacy—an oppositional uncoupling of this signifier from its customary signifieds. At the same time, the omnipresence of such imagery in romantic, erotic, and religious contexts means that the rose is oversignificant also in terms of its exceptional polyvalence: the figure itself appears complicit in its perpetual resignification. Ultimately, though, to borrow a phrase from Gertrude Stein, a rose is a rose is a rose. Precisely the overinsistence on *equivalence* across these iterations reveals it as an identity-in-difference, as the failed passing of a catachresis. While this will be true both for the self-alterity that obtains between the literal and figural valences of any given trope as well as for its various occurrences and accretions over time, for the queer filmic poetics under discussion here it becomes attached to the representation and legibility of gay identity as such, marking the gradual decay of formal queer decadence.

A Rose Is a Rose

Celebrated by no less than Rainer Werner Fassbinder as one of the most essential, if relatively more arcane, directors of the New German Cinema, Schroeter is perhaps best known for being the subject of a heated debate between Fassbinder and activist director Rosa von Praunheim on gay politics in filmmaking. At issue was the publicity of Schroeter's gayness: von Praunheim attacked Schroeter for his reluctance to add his name to a coming-out declaration, and Fassbinder, in turn, berated von Praunheim for his presumed monopoly on arbitrating representations of homosexuality in German film.[22] While I would hardly describe Schroeter as closeted, it is true that his work on the whole does not dwell sustainedly on depictions of male homosexuality—*Der Rosenkönig* being the most notable exception. If his films are nevertheless to be considered queer, this owes less to their content than to their style: a particularly grotesque variety of camp, as Alice Kuzniar has it, "performed in avant-garde high seriousness."[23] Put differently, Schroeter too is given to working in the mode of camp abjection outlined in the previous chapter.

Schroeter's celebration of bad taste recalls, then, the queer art of failure discussed there. As the filmmaker himself puts it: "I don't make any differences between kitsch and culture. . . . For me kitsch is camp. There are no gaps between kitsch and art."[24] For Caryl Flinn, this involves, in part, an attachment to the bad taste of the bodily as opposed to more sublimated aesthetic experiences: "Schroeter's films are filled with the sort of heavy-handed artifice, staginess, uprooted objects and quotes typical of camp. But . . . Schroeter's style goes farther . . . by appropriating particularly abject *Kulturscheisse* [*sic*, cultural shit] and historical debris."[25] Declining to delineate camp's cleverness from kitsch's seemingly duped naïveté, Schroeter indulges in a particularly off-putting and derided aesthetic—an abjected kitsch at which even camp might hold its nose.

With a welcome measure of skepticism toward Eve Kosofsky Sedgwick's distinction, alluded to earlier, between kitsch-attribution and camp-recognition, Flinn argues that "Schroeter eschews this duality by finding undesirable alterity and difference within. In the sense in which the term is usually used, his is a queerer approach. This is not to say that kitsch, or even Schroeter's brand of it, *is* queer. Rather, it is to argue that kitsch may be every bit as 'knowing' as camp and in this way can be useful to queer, lesbian, and gay constituencies."[26] Mining Schroeter's cinema for this use value, Flinn concludes that "his brand of kitsch *undoes* borders between center and margin, external and internal, oppositional and majoritarian."[27] It is less that Schroeter elevates bad taste than that he debases anything that might be taken to be good taste: his mobilization of operatic and avant-garde aesthetics emphasizes kitsch in order to reveal that it was always already at the core of high art. Leaning into this internal dissonance, he undermines the—classist, racist, homophobic—tendency to project bad taste onto others.

The consequence for Schroeter's cinema and its cultural impact is, as Flinn rightly intuits and as I intend to explore further in this chapter, a blurring of the boundaries between oppositional and mainstream aesthetics and, more surprisingly, between queer art and its heteronormative other—ultimately even between the avant-garde and (though Schroeter never was and never will be broadly popular) pop culture. Defending Schroeter against von Praunheim's rather self-contradictory indictment that he has become an elitist but pandering sellout, Fassbinder excoriates also the commodity fetishism attached to the label of underground cinema: "His films received the quite useful 'underground' pedigree [*»Underground«-Etikett*], which rendered them in a flash as beautiful, but nonetheless exotic plants, ones so far away which blossom in such a strange fashion that one in the end could not really deal with them. And precisely that is just as simple as it is wrong and stupid. Because Werner Schroeter's films are not far away; even if they are beautiful, that still does not make them exotic. On the contrary."[28] This is not, Fassbinder argues, a rare flower only relevant in the far-flung climes of a queer subculture, but rather, as he goes on to insist, the most globally insightful filmmaking there is. It is merely a necessary and misleading marketing scheme that ostracizes Schroeter and occludes his pertinence: as evident from Fassbinder's recourse to English to describe this underground label, commercialism and oppositional aesthetics have already begun to collapse one into the other.

Fassbinder may be projecting a touch. Schroeter never appeared particularly interested in marketing his films to a general public or even, for that matter, to his most adamant admirers,[29] whereas Fassbinder's explicit aim, as he phrases it in his final interview about *Querelle*, was "to create a kind of German Hollywood . . . a cinema that is as wonderful and universally understandable as Hollywood but at the same time not as hypocritical."[30] Schroeter had in fact long dreamed of adapting this Genet novel himself—a desire that was equal parts ethical, political, personal, erotic, and stylistic. To quote from his autobiography:

> Since deciding to go on developing new forms of style, I had been busy adapting *Querelle de Brest* in my own way. It would have been

> a necessary . . . and intensive look at evil and the beauty of evil. Only criminals and artists still have scope of their own in bourgeois society. . . . For me, homosexuality was and still is attractive as the design of an artist's life, if you reject the social norms of materialism and consumerism. Being gay, being an artist, opposing the system and thus, logically, heterosexuality as the prescribed form of sex have more poetic substance than doing something socially acceptable that one doesn't really understand, because the society in which you live formulates that social enforcement as a repressive claim.[31]

While *Querelle* would, of course, ultimately become Fassbinder's own final film in 1982, just a few years later, after the death of New German Cinema proper, Schroeter would complete *Der Rosenkönig*—certainly his most significant, extended and explicit treatment of gay male content and characters: Albert (Mostefa Djadjam), who seeks to cultivate the perfect rose, and a young thief, Fernando (Antonio Orlando), who becomes his willing hostage.[32]

Their first encounter occurs when Albert surprises the youth looting a local chapel and holding an exculpatory dialogue with a mute crucifix that he perceives to be giving him a recriminatory glance—a moment indicative of how Schroeter himself will pillage, demolish, and repurpose Catholic iconography: "You're always leaning on me," the youth tells the Crucified, "I'll smash your face. You'll see." This film would seem to make good, then, on the rebellious promise—a queer resistance to heteronormative mores, consumerism, and commodification—that Schroeter identified in the source material for *Querelle*.

Notably, Schroeter gives an almost identical justification with regard to his feud with Praunheim; counterintuitively, it is the inherently political nature of his homosexuality, as Schroeter sees it, that keeps him from engaging in gay politics: "I usually said I couldn't sign a protest about the oppression of gays because, personally, I didn't feel oppressed. . . . I always regard my own sexual inclinations as giving me a chance to do unconventional work. I was in more conflict with myself than with straight people and had to be prepared for more opposition, but I guess that is the case with all outsiders."[33] The queer self-dissonance I have been observing throughout this study has been reframed here as an aesthetic and, indeed, ethical imperative.

In the pages to come, though, I'll be following up on Fassbinder's misgivings about the potential commodification of this antagonistic stance, examining how even the most shocking of filmic imagery risks, even invites, being recuperated into the very clichés it attempts to disarticulate. Lambasting *Der Rosenkönig* in the *New York Times*, Vincent Canby suggests, for instance, and without mincing words, that a recognizably European art-cinema aesthetic has reached the point of ridiculousness: "Werner Schroeter's 'Rose King,' opening today at Film Forum 1, is one of those supposedly avant-garde films that aren't easy to write about without cracking up, but I'll try." Noting that "Mr. Schroeter has a formidable reputation in Europe" and that he "composes his images as deliberately as a high-fashion photographer" (surely, cinematographer Elfi Mikesch deserves much of the credit on this point), Canby bemoans the "long, static shots" and languid characters, who "like the film, aren't going anywhere."[34] While more traditional in its narrative construction than Schroeter's early underground work (on his turn to narrative cinema, the director commented that "it is much more radical to play with the content than with the aesthetics of the image"), it is true that *Der Rosenkönig* is nevertheless driven forward more by associative and repetitive editing than by its perplexing, murky dialogue and rather fragmentary plot.[35] The influence of Genet's oneirically meandering *Chant d'amour* is detectable throughout, but the floral tropes at play there take a horrifically brutal twist at the film's spectacular dramatic, narrative, and erotic climax: the scene of grafting to which I alluded by way of introduction.

The sequence begins with a bouquet of long-stemmed roses caressing the passive torso of Fernando, bound and resembling a reclining Saint Sebastian, before the flowers are brusquely tossed aside, revealing the hand of Albert holding a knife, which—with the flair and sound effect of a slasher film—he plunges into the attractive form before him. (The wound itself, like Albert's face, for the moment remains unseen.) An energetic zarzuela with a techno beat—orchestrated by Luis Cobos in an apt analog to Schroeter's own penchant for combining classical repertoire with pop kitsch—sets in, inciting a period of frantic and incoherent crosscutting, an anachronic and haphazard parallel editing among the various spaces that have constituted the film's core visual motifs: a rose-adorned journal burning in hay, Magdalena Montezuma's gaunt face smeared with black tar, Fernando's (apparently unharmed) body being tossed around by waves at the seashore. But what dominates the montage is a recurrent stomach-churning shot, lingering sadistically in extreme close-up, of Fernando's wrist being slit open and the wound being deepened with trembling effort, blood pooling as a red rose is tucked into the aperture (fig. 2). Or perhaps, rather: wrists and wounds and roses in the plural. Schroeter's montage does not distinguish sufficiently between the different iterations of this image to discern context or chronology, to make definitive narrative sense of the event(s) depicted. Instead, the whole of the film seems to condense and crystallize into this moment of cutting, superficially disregarding but thereby illustrating and instantiating its internal *différance*: a wound is a wound is a wound. By the same logic, the rose/wound turns out to be essentially self-referential. The virgule occasionally joining the two in this chapter is meant to indicate this switch point from the abject to the erotic as well as the peculiar semiotics of this pairing: the rose is a metaphor for the wound just as the wound is for the rose. Either term could be taken to signify the other.

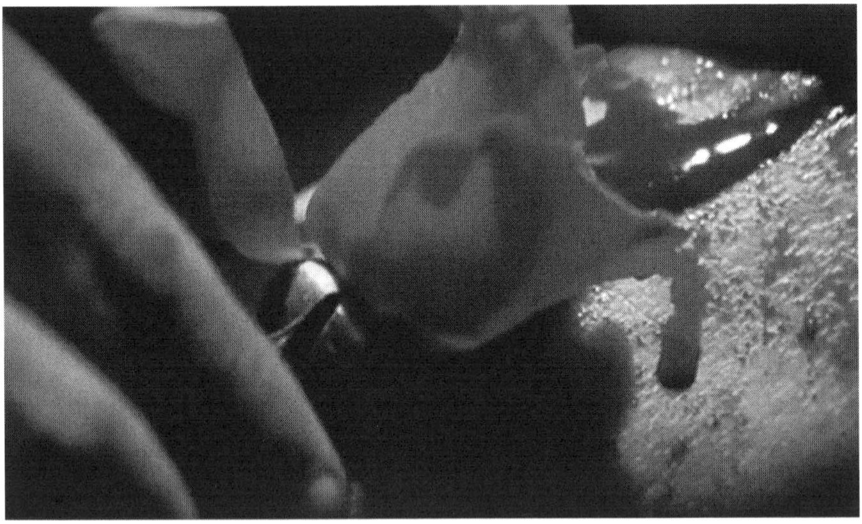

Fig. 2. A rose grafted into the beloved's body. From *Der Rosenkönig* (*The Rose King*, dir. Werner Schroeter, 1986).

As Michelle Langford affirms, with an eye to Walter Benjamin, Albert performs "a kind of allegorical montage upon the body itself, a montage that brings together his obsession with creating the perfect rose and his . . . homoerotic desires. . . . The homoerotic body in *Der Rosenkönig* is achieved through showing the processes of cutting and violating, which are usually concealed or disavowed" in narrative cinema.[36] Elsewhere, both with specific regard to Schroeter and more generally, I have theorized such narrative wounds as filmic cuts that ineluctably injure narrativity by severing and fragmenting cinematic images but at the same time do the very work of narrativizing these images by arranging them into a montage, into an overarching storyline constituted precisely *by* its fragmentation.[37] So too does this sequence, a musical interlude and ecstatic interruption of visual frenzy that would appear to suspend any narrative development, provide an orgasmic narrative culmination and one of the few legible plot points of the entire film. As Langford continues:

> The erotically disfigured body of Fernando in *Der Rosenkönig* . . . cannot be equated with just any form of cutting and framing in film. This is not the seamless linkage of fragments that we find in organic montage, but rather the kind of montage whose importance lies in the cut itself. Schroeter achieves the violation of wholeness through the destructive violence of allegorical montage, which in this case afflicts the body with its allegorical intention. The illusory wholeness of the idol is dispersed, but its erotic power remains intact.[38]

In short, the ostensibly organic editing of more seamless narrative cinema is demythologized, denaturalized, and deconstructed—but like the battered body of the beloved in this sequence, it discomfitingly retains its sex appeal. Its striptease has less to do with the depiction of the naked body itself than with the unmasking and unmaking of its figuration: the violence of dismemberment into abstraction.

The disturbing sequence continues in this fashion for several minutes, concluding only when Albert carries the now rose-covered corpse into the garden as the music transitions again into the more serenely operatic—there Elisabeth Schwarzkopf singing Gustave Charpentier: "Depuis le jour où je me suis donnée / toute fleur semble ma destinée" (Since the day I gave myself away / every flower seems to be my fate). Thus Schroeter reveals, realizes, and literalizes the inherent violence of the Genetian grafting outlined earlier: "I shall so bedeck him with flowers that . . . he will himself become a flower."[39] But as the earlier tempo accelerates, Schroeter ever more overtly and more emphatically insists on the affinity between Albert's cuts into his victim's flesh and the filmic cuts that produce this increasingly intellectual montage, as if the character were exercising extradiegetic, directorial agency: the most visceral moment of the film is also its most aestheticizing and its most self-reflective. There is a blunting, rather flattening effect to this filmic metareflection: the equivalences implied by the relentless parallel editing suggest that any of these images could substitute for any other, reminding the viewer that these gruesome incisions, like the cinematic cuts causing them to repeat, are merely visual effects. When the final shot before the credits returns to the opening image of a tightly framed red rose, it is ambiguous whether this restatement of the leitmotif is intended as a resignification or merely a reconfirmation, but, set now against a darker background and blooming to the point of wilting, it seems possible that the cliché has decayed into its own undoing.

Benjamin's view of allegory—a fragmentary, artificial mode, which he traces from the Baroque to Baudelairean modernism, heightened in its theatricality, resisting the organic wholeness of romantic symbolism—is deployed across the scholarship on Schroeter I am citing here, and rightly so. Kuzniar sees it as operative in queer representation, contending that, through the repeated linkage of roses to blood, the "conventional symbol of the rose . . . becomes macabre and mawkish, with its traditional valence further reversed through association with a male instead of a female character and with homosexual rather than heterosexual love."[40] In other words, again the kitsch overdetermination of the rose inspires the violent resignification to which it will be subjected: it is precisely because its metaphoricity is so oversaturated with semiological possibilities that it becomes a site of temptation for a denaturalization of these always-arbitrary associations.

But this is arguably less a reversal than a simple displacement: from the feminine to the masculine, from the heterosexual to the homosexual, from romance to violence, from the comfortingly knowing and condescending self-satisfaction with which any average viewer deciphers a Georgia O'Keeffe to the homophobic panic that might accompany his picking up on an insinuation of sodomy. Like the queer tendency to highlight and thus undermine successful passing that I have been observing throughout this study, Schroeter's allegorical montage delights in its own elusiveness, though here it is an elusiveness of excess. As Flinn summarizes Benjamin: "Allegory works with heightened referentiality, hyperbolized style, and theatricalized performance, as if to acknowledge its own representational inadequacies. . . . Absence becomes a psychological, erotic, stylistically charged hot spot."[41] While the mutilation of Fernando's body is preceded by some vaguely erotic fondling, the sex scene palpably anticipated from the beginning of the film is never delivered. In its place Schroeter offers only this violent dissection of the sexualized male body revealing nothing underneath.

Pushing the rose/wound motif past its breaking point, Schroeter calls into question the capacity of an avant-garde aesthetic to uncover a deeper truth beneath the patina of cliché. Outward appearances aside, this disjointed editing achieves the same seamlessness as the protocinematic dissolve Genet effectuates in transforming Harcamone's body and its accoutrements into flowers. The sequence is tied together not only by a steady tempo of the rollicking extradiegetic music but by a series of intradiegetic sound bridges uniting the various spaces as if they were, for acoustic purposes, entirely indistinguishable. At one moment, an unheard scream of Fernando's, his head thrown back and his mouth agape in an amplified imitation of the Laocoön, is ventriloquized by an unseen screech owl presumably located in the forest to which Schroeter occasionally cuts—but, tellingly, neither directly before nor after this shot.[42] If it weren't for these background noises, one could almost take this to be a music video, albeit an unusually morbid one. The dismemberment of the "cute little Neapolitan" Orlando, an off-straight twink in both Schroeter's films and in his life, somehow affords the idolized youth, paled by moonlight, an oddly aesthetic wholeness, transforming him into a writing surface—like a blank white page.[43] Although the obvious abhorrence of this scene in *Der Rosenkönig* would seem to fly in the face of camp artifice and playfulness, the result is not, as I have been insisting, the interiority such incisions into the body would appear to guarantee, but rather a celebration of surfaces. Queer content has hidden itself behind extravagantly, ostentatiously queer style.

What would seem to be the narrative climax of the film turns out to be an aesthetic aside not dissimilar to the aria with which it ends. I'll be observing the political legacy of such aestheticizing interludes throughout the rest of this chapter and also in the chapters to come: into the music video passages that punctuate the films of François Ozon and Xavier Dolan, for instance. As to Schroeter, there is a rather obvious attempt, in the minimal scholarship available on the film, to rehabilitate the ethics of this repugnant moment: Langford reads it as a kind of violent parody in the extreme of the notion of homosexuality as a perversion of nature, and Kuzniar suggests that the violence erupts in part from a closeting and repression of homosexuality enforced here by a jealous mother. Both scholars, following Schroeter's famous champion Michel Foucault, ultimately conclude, however, that any social critique in Schroeter's film draws its weight and force from the way in which, as Langford, puts it, a "desire to desire differently may be activated."[44] Contrary to intention, the obstinate abjection of Schroeter's most sustained depiction of male homosexuality is thereby—if not entirely dismissed—domesticated and reduced to a strictly formal concern.

In a sense, then, the queer subject also vanishes. As Flinn sees it: "What thus becomes important in reading this director's eloquence is not the psychology of repression (which is certainly not, as Rosa von Praunheim would read it, applied to the person of Werner Schroeter) but the enigmatic, scintillating articulation or surfacing of the symptoms of desire. . . . The issue of who is the agent or object of desire is subordinate to the very articulation of desire."[45] As in Gide's *acte gratuit*, what is represented here is erotic-libidinal action exceeding attributable agency. Implicitly, this view also establishes a relationship between the abject body (and the psychology of repression it would seem to insinuate) and camp superficies. It is not only, as Kuzniar claims, that "the violence arises in the aftermath of a closeting," but more acutely that *un*closeting occurs by means of the violence of self-abstraction. The supposed queer subject disintegrates and disappears into its self-expression.

In a recorded, and later published, conversation with Schroeter, Foucault himself suggests that the at moments eroticized relationships between women in *Der Tod von Maria Malibran* (*The Death of Maria Malibran*, 1972) and *Willow Springs* (1973) are best characterized not as love but rather as passion.[46] Examining this distinction, Keith Robinson provides a useful definition of the latter: "Foucault sees in Schroeter's work evidence of an intense passion that simultaneously erases the power to say I and desexualizes the body in the singularities of suffering-pleasure. The camera in Schroeter's films plunges the body into atrophy, breakdown and crisis, disassembling its unity in a process at once calculated and aleatory."[47] What Foucault describes as immediate, passionate evidence in Schroeter thus brings the core concerns of the present chapter together with those of this study on the whole: the ecstatic, abject corporeal assault of *Der Rosenkönig* is revealed to be of a piece with an arbitrary (in the opposing senses of willful and determined by chance) poetics of self-erasure and camp desexualization.[48]

Scars of New German Cinema

Among the vignettes of its collage-like narrative, Monika Treut's and Elfi Mikesch's collaboration *Verführung: Die grausame Frau* briefly depicts an inscription into the human body, what a published excerpt from the screenplay describes as a "Ceremony of the Bleeding Rose."[49] This tattoo by scarification—the image of a rose carved into the flesh with a knife—is said to be a sign of election bestowed by the film's central figure, the dominatrix Wanda (Mechthild Großmann), on one of her female-presenting subjects, Friedrike (Georgette Dee). I am avoiding the word *lesbian* advisedly both because Treut bristles at this label for her filmmaking (if not necessarily for herself) and because the house of fantasy where *Verführung* is set, reminiscent of the brothel in Genet's *Le balcon* (*The Balcony*, 1956), caters to a compendium of sexual persuasions, cataloguing all manner of kinks, which at once play to recognizable stereotypes and defy easy identity categorization.[50] Still, in more theoretical, quasi-sociological reflections on the lesbian S/M scene in New York, Treut insists on the necessity of an all-female environment: "Lesbian because a man, even in the role of the submissive masochistic, would always take on the role of the director."[51] This isn't entirely borne out by the blocking of the sequence, where the women perform the ceremony with Wanda at the center on a revolving stage—a direct parallel to the revolve employed for Genet's *Balcon*—while one of her female servants carves the rose into another's back. Other women, as well the few men present, including Wanda's most jealous ex, Gregor (Udo Kier), watch in silence. But the potential allusion to the Amazonian Feast of Roses from Heinrich von Kleist's romantic drama *Penthesilea* (1808) makes this ceremony and its reprisal at the end of the film legible as a sapphic affair. Nor is it insignificant that the film's reception has consistently characterized Treut as a lesbian filmmaker, her protests notwithstanding. The incision here is a superficial one, delivered solemnly, received unflinchingly. The cinematography—chiaroscuro lighting, canted angles—vaguely resembles the general expressionism of *Der Rosenkönig*, but the neat, efficient continuity editing of reaction shots does not: the moment is over in a matter of seconds.

The ecstatic frenzy of Schroeter is reserved instead for the climax of *Verführung*, where a mosh pit of leather daddies, humming and yelling, are confined to cages around the perimeter of a stage while the women again perform an erotic ceremony. The rites themselves are still relatively tame: an arm smeared with what appears to be blood and decorated with white feathers, some licking and petting, a brief moment of disciplinary but fairly gentle restraint with the handle of a whip.[52] That is, until Gregor bursts in on the scene, armed with a gun that he fires at Wanda with the self-assured but almost clumsy nonchalance of a film noir gumshoe. An instant of stunned silenced and then a reaction shot of Wanda from a slightly different angle than before, almost a jump cut or a continuity error, looking down at her cupped hand as if holding a baby bird that has fallen from its nest and then slowly sinking to the floor. The cut back to Gregor, now in the background, with the shocked performers foregrounded, noticeably violates the 180-degree rule: for a brief instant it appears that this attack has succeeded in suspending the cinematic illusion. But after just a beat, smiling in surprise, Wanda emits a gasping chuckle and general laughter at Gregor begins to resound from all corners as he retreats. After a quick cut away to some wax figures of nuns in various poses of supplication, also in the gallery, the final shot of the film is of Wanda—the stigmata of her injured hand being lovingly kissed by Justine. (Surveying Genet's flowers, Derrida reminds us that the apex of the style, the exposed tip of the pistil that becomes visible when a flower blossoms, is called the *stigma*.[53]) Laughing heartily, Wanda looks to where Gregor has departed with a mixture of pity, scorn, longing nostalgia, and, perhaps, a hint of pride.

But like the counterrevolutionary conclusion to Genet's *Balcon*, this ending casts doubt on the very possibility of transcending mere fantasy. Gregor's unanticipated violence has not penetrated through to anything more real than the scripted violence of the playacting it interrupts.[54] Wanda's emasculating laughter might be taken then as subtly directed not only toward Gregor but also toward the literary-filmic history on which the earlier rose imagery draws. This is not to say that the earlier aesthetic of injury is unequivocally derided—both Treut and Mikesch are full-throated in their admiration for Schroeter—but rather that this might be a hopeful, affirmative laughter in a Nietzschean vein: one which, in its own way, constructs by way of deconstruction, renews through critique.

What Flinn identifies as a mode of "body camp" in Treut and contemporary queer filmmakers working in Schroeter's wake finds its power and its purpose not in the supposedly irrefutable gravity of the wounded or abject body, but instead in playful resignification. "At the hands of directors like Fassbinder . . . bodies were utterly deconstructed, often torn apart limb by limb, so as to leave little possibility of recovery," Flinn argues, whereas Treut deploys "characteristics of camp" that "can help us move forward *with* the idea of role-playing, props, and absence, rather than lost imagined integrities of the body, psyche, or nation."[55] Reading Treut's work as a "textbook illustration" of Judith Butler's ideas on gender performativity, Flinn notes that "Treut relies upon conventionally coded body parts to render *absent* the same, gendered bodies from which they are derived. The material body, in other words, is thus not far behind all this role-playing, appearing in displaced bits, like so many allegorical fragments."[56] While Flinn has in mind Treut's later *Die Jungfraumaschine* (*The Virgin Machine*, 1988), this is also an apposite description of the fort-da games involving the various fetish objects—by definition fragmentary and metonymic—showcased throughout *Verführung* and the derealizing effect they have on the bodies they represent, as confirmed by the film's deflationary finale. In its potential rebuttal to the earlier iterations of the wound/flower motif, the film thus goes beyond the first-blush insistence on corporeal significance in order to ratify instead an aestheticizing impulse that I have been excavating in Genet and Schroeter.

A surprising German Studies darling, *Verführung* featured prominently in academic discussions surrounding antiporn debates and other hot topics of the late '80s and early '90s (for many feminists, Treut's praise for Camille Paglia proved particularly hard to stomach) and has been assured an association with New German Cinema both by its filmmakers' pedigrees (beyond Mikesch's work with Schroeter, both Treut and Mikesch worked early on with Rosa von Praunheim) and by its scholarly reception. Flinn, for example, as we have already seen, reads Treut's work in relation to New German Cinema and its afterlives, and Andrea Riemann understands *Verführung* specifically as an extension of the reconfiguration of power in Fassbinder's late work, with special attention to *Querelle*.[57] The nonacademic reception of *Verführung*, which remains more obscure than the earlier cult classic, seems less persuaded by this legacy. The newspaper of record, for instance, distinctly echoes its assessment of *Der Rosenkönig*, concluding that *Verführung* "meanders along the line between artiness and art, between shrewd self-consciousness of film genres and empty stylization. . . . 'Seduction,' which opens today at the Bleecker Street Cinema, degenerates into an uneasy mix of Fassbinder and 'Cabaret,' an inadvertent parody of everything that is frustrating about German cinema and the avant-garde."[58] The ambivalent exoticism Fassbinder saw as a self-defeating sales pitch for underground cinema has clearly lost its charm. And this despite the fact that Treut often films in English and often abroad, especially in the United States, with the overt aim of courting broader international audiences. Treut and Mikesch are deemed too amateurish to produce high art and insufficiently skilled to work within the tight parameters of a slickly competent genre film. Their provocative aesthetic unevenness is seen as either just a slipup or, worse, as trying too hard. In a queer context the charge of unintentional parody is especially damning: it implies an unrewarded earnestness, it revokes the right to bad taste and irony—or at the very least reserves this prerogative for a more mainstream, which is to say a straighter, style.

The situation is somewhat different on the other side of the Atlantic. One of the flagship films of what B. Ruby Rich has influentially dubbed New Queer Cinema, Todd Haynes's *Poison*, stirred up quite the controversy when it was released, becoming a prominent flash point in the culture wars of the time in part because it had received production funding from the National Endowment for the Arts.[59] But it also launched the career of one of the best-known and most broadly accessible queer filmmakers working today. Generally, *Poison* is considered to be a bit rougher around the edges and a bit more provocative in its aesthetics than Haynes's later movies, making it a good place to look for what is truly queer about New Queer Cinema, before it devolves, as Rich laments less than a decade after coining the term, into "just another niche market, another product line pitched at one type of particularly discerning consumer."[60] James Morrison, for one, judges that "of the first wave of films from New Queer Cinema, *Poison* . . . is the most challenging formally and perhaps the most sophisticated thematically, channeling the spirits of Jean Genet, Fassbinder, and Pier Paolo Pasolini while tempering its forthright avant-gardist odium with spurts of abject lyricism and brainy camp."[61] This squarely situates *Poison* in a lineage of the European avant-garde.

In the case of Haynes, this is a very specific kind of queer—or, more precisely, gay male—abjection at a particularly fraught historical juncture for the stigmatization of homosexuality. Rather surprisingly, I've almost never seen Schroeter's *Rosenkönig* discussed within the context of the AIDS crisis on the cusp of which it appeared. With his erstwhile interlocutor Foucault dying during filming, one can glean from Schroeter's own statements on the subject that he was aware of the crisis, yet he proclaims not without a note of proud satisfaction that the film "could not be used in the AIDS campaign protesting against the stigmatizing of homosexuals. It was not meant to be topical or a public service announcement."[62] This is, however, almost universally the lens through which *Poison* has been read. "The film," Haynes concedes in an interview,

> is absolutely the result of AIDS and also a result of Genet. . . . All of a sudden there was this metaphor for homosexuality lurking, this awful, horrible metaphor of AIDS that had to be continually distinguished, and I think it *should* be distinguished from homosexuality. . . . At the same time, what is so fascinating about Genet is that he was deeply interested in what was particularly transgressive, and *only* what was transgressive, about homosexuality—and what was erotic about it as well.[63]

Hearkening back to Schroeter's politicized gayness, in *Poison* Haynes is torn between two contradictory impulses: between a desire, on the one hand, to distinguish homosexuality from the stigma placed on it by the AIDS epidemic and, on the other, to retain, even at the risk of celebrating abjection, an oppositional gay aesthetic—which, as the filmmaker repeatedly insists in interviews from the time, should be more about formal provocation than about content or gay characters.

This gets a little muddled, however, by a persistent conflation of aesthetics and thematics in his statements regarding the film. Haynes repeatedly dismisses what he refers to as a "gay sensibility" as a question merely of *content*: "People define gay cinema solely by content: if there are gay characters in it, it's a gay film. It fits into the gay sensibility, we got it, it's gay. It's such a failure of the imagination, let alone the ability to look beyond content."[64] In this same interview he argues against the essentialism implied by this label, instead observing a manner of self-forgery: "I don't believe that there is an essential gay sensibility either. What is so interesting about minorities identifying themselves historically and rewriting their own history is that, in a sense, it is *an attempt to create an essential difference that isn't really true.* But it's one that they are writing as opposed to the status quo. So it's a way of disarming the conventions of difference that have been imposed on us and rewriting our differences."[65]

Taken together these assertions indicate a resistance to assimilation—which would align with his criticism of more mainstream films with gay content—and a programmatic repurposing of stigma for the production of new cultural forms that must remain perpetually attuned to their contingency and arbitrariness, to the fact that they are counterfeited.[66] Self-determination emerges again as a product of constraint and of failed passing, as the fabrication of a perceived difference where none really existed to begin with. As Morrison phrases it: "Haynes' work is less important for its representation of gay experience than for its assertions of a new kind of queer agency in cultural production."[67] If the young filmmaker (Haynes was still shy of thirty when *Poison* debuted) occasionally fails to distinguish between substance and style, between queer content and queer sensibility, this is surely because the mode of self-fashioning in question refuses to privilege any ostensible essence over its expression.

And yet *Poison* passes brilliantly as gay avant-garde. While decidedly sleeker than the works treated so far in this chapter, or in this book for that matter, *Poison* does belong to the same tradition of queer stigma(ta). "*Poison* introduces us," writes Laura Christian for *Camera Obscura*, "to a host of marginal figures who, in masochistically embracing their abjection, ascend (or perhaps one should say descend) into Genetian sainthood. . . . In *Poison*, identity is instituted through injury."[68] Haynes would appear to agree: "I think what makes *Poison* really work for some people is that it gets under your skin and makes you feel something . . . usually something very sad or disturbed."[69] But this injurious, subcutaneous aesthetic looks very different in Haynes, where the unrelentingly gloomy expressionism of *Der Rosenkönig* or *Verführung* gives way to a kaleidoscopic stylistic surfeit: garish and grainy tabloid television footage, B-movie black and white, washed out art house floral hues. Michael DeAngelis argues that Haynes's genre promiscuity is as an estrangement device—that insofar as he draws on "a variety of cinematic forms, Haynes 'queers' heterosexual, mainstream narrative cinema by making whatever might seem familiar or normal about it strange."[70] Morrison concurs that part of this queering of the mainstream, and of straight society, is achieved by means of the film's "tripartite structure that intermingles one segment of overtly queer content with two stories that simulate straight narratives from a militantly queer vantage point."[71] But it is equally significant that each of these three interwoven narratives so self-consciously adopts its own set of strict generic constraints to begin with: "Hero" is a faux-documentary, "Horror" is a sci-fi thriller and "Homo" is billed explicitly as an experimental art film.

This final portion is inspired visually and stylistically by *Chant d'amour* and based directly, if rather loosely, on Genet's *Miracle de la Rose*. Its climax depicts in flashback a recollection of the reformatory related to the narrator at the conclusion of the novel, shortly before Harcamone's own final miracles. Reimagining the experience as his own, the narrator describes being spat on by his fellow delinquents: "I received the spit in my distended mouth, which fatigue failed to close. Yet a trifle would have sufficed for the ghastly game to be transformed into a courtly one and for me to be covered not with spit but with roses that had been tossed at me. . . . I waited for roses."[72] As noted, this fantasy is recounted in the first person, although it happened not to the narrator but to a lover and fellow detainee, Bulkaen, and is related to him by yet another, Divers. At the same time, the entirety of the anecdote, going on for three pages in the *Œuvres complètes*, is set off by a column of guillemets in the left margin—an extended typographical indication of borrowing to be found nowhere else in Genet's work.

In his own iteration in this citational chain, Haynes literalizes the desire to alchemize abjection into beauty, making good on Genet's subjunctive through a series of dissolves recalling the written dissolve discussed earlier. A shot/countershot of the sky from the perspective of the persecuted boy—the heads of his tormentors bobbing in and out of the frame as they jump into the air to hock loogies at him—and of his upturned face from above are overlaid with increasingly copious flower petals in Easter egg coloring. Then, through additional dissolves, Haynes uses an image of a blooming red rose much like Schroeter's to return to the black and white of the film's "Horror" narrative (figs. 3–4).

Notably, while "Horror" does orbit around the campy, tongue-in-cheek depiction of a physical deformity allegorizing AIDS, the wound in its corporeal form is entirely absent from the portions of the film most directly dedicated to Genet and the only section explicitly dealing with homosexuality. The radicalization of Genetian abjection we find in Schroeter's *Rosenkönig* has been supplanted here by a tamer and—one might be inclined to think—all-too-pretty floral motif. In fact, culminating in this red rose, the sequence ends with precisely the kind of imagery that Schroeter's film seems to set out, as its point of departure, to dismantle. Nor is *Poison* quite as experimental or as provocative as its reception would imply: less parody than postmodern pastiche, its three plotlines hew closely to classical continuity editing and offer all of the satisfaction of genre narrative.

This is not to reproach Haynes. I am generally skeptical of aesthetic paradigms that equate violence with truth value or authenticity. *Poison* is filmed skillfully, a pleasure to watch and probably a lot more fun than *Der Rosenkönig* or *Verführung*. Despite being a work of relative juvenilia, it could hardly be accused of the clumsiness that critics discerned in these earlier films. But it seems that the avant-garde aesthetic inaugurated by Genet and pushed to its breaking point by Schroeter has itself become such an established cliché—eliciting nearly Pavlovian associations with the soi-disant homosexual style Haynes worries about—that its inherent violence has been all but entirely elided. All flower and no wound, what *Poison* retains from its predecessors

Figs. 3–4. The opening rose in *Der Rosenkönig* (*The Rose King*, dir. Werner Schroeter, 1986) and the closing rose in *Poison* (dir. Todd Haynes, 1991).

is the aesthetic of abjection on the level of plot and identity politics: the very abjection that Haynes had simultaneously hoped to demythologize (with regard to AIDS) and to embrace (in the tradition of Genet).

By which I mean that—as the structure of the film implies—Haynes's citationality treats *avant-garde*, or even *gay*, as generic categories, as if they were any other genre. The nascent commodification of the label of underground cinema suspected by Fassbinder is by now indisputable. It would seem that Genet's project to debase the most sanctified of iconographic traditions and at the same time to aestheticize abjection has, if anything, been *too* successful, has itself become a topos. The rather earnest campiness of "Homos," when compared with the other, more playful portions of *Poison*, is no longer a seriousness that fails but instead a seriousness that succeeds: camp is beginning to become more broadly marketable.

Conclusion: Coming/Out

The music video for gay pop star Troye Sivan's title track off of his second album *Bloom* (2018) borrows extensively, at moments visually verbatim, from the fetishizing close-ups of male bodies in *Chant d'amour*, the florid motifs of *Poison*, and more broadly on imagery reminiscent of a gay art house film aesthetic (figs. 5–6).[73] Such knowing cultural references are hardly surprising given that the short production was directed by videographer Bardia Zeinali, who, among his other thus far rather minimal credits, was responsible for the short horror films *Vogue* shot with the celebrities in attendance at the 2019 Met Gala on camp.

In interviews Sivan describes the song as playfully subversive, bringing queer messaging to a wider audience. He frames this as a ludic disconnect between acoustic and lyrical content, noting that the song is danceable, "consumable pop music so I can imagine the masses understanding it a little bit more, and that's funny to me." It is this dissonance, he insists, that gives the song its humor and rebellious force: "It's that light, sonically. Lyrically it's a bit more cheeky. It's just a really fun song. . . . Lyrically I think it's the most subversively queer song on the album. That's kind of what makes me like it so much—it's almost like a little inside joke."[74] But it's not a joke Sivan works very hard to keep a secret, nor is it one that has been lost on his audience. Pierre-Ange Carlotti, writing for *Dazed*, declares it a "gay anthem for bottoms," and Chris Mench, for the website *Genius*, describes it as a "metaphor-filled ode to bottoming."[75] If the lyrics—"I bloom just for you"—already rather openly, even lewdly, announce anal deflowering, the marketing around the song and videos (there is also an animated lyric video made by artist Jason Ebeyer) plays up the transparency of the song's encoded sexual metaphorics. A promotional teaser for the album depicts Sivan sitting on the edge of a bed, a lover lying in the background, tongue-in-cheekily insisting to the camera, "It's about flowers." The symbolism and secret camp argot have short-circuited: in the ironic guise of a failed passing, the album operates as a sort of coming-out for a singer who had already long since been uncloseted.

Similarly, if these hint-hint allusions lay bare what was arguably always the underlying conceit of the wound/flower coupling I've been exploring throughout this chapter—anal penetration—they also more surprisingly *re*sexualize what the song's campiness might traditionally obscure. While *blooming*, in gay parlance, refers generally to bottoming, in certain contexts (pornography,

Figs. 5–6. Roses in *Poison* (dir. Todd Haynes, 1991) and the music video for Troye Sivan's "Bloom" (dir. Bardia Zeinali, 2018).

for instance) it more specifically designates the display of a rectal prolapse resulting from anal sex or fisting—this prolapse itself is known as a *rosebud*. Obliquely alluding toward such taboos, the last look in a dazzling array of feminizing floral outfits worn by Sivan over the course of his three-minute video is a flower-patterned, skirted BDSM gimp costume, only his heavily made-up eyes and lips visible through the hood.

At the same time, in a certain sense it really *is* just about flowers; the exuberant visual energy of the music video brings to its only logical conclusion Schroeter's already postmodern proliferation of surfaces. If there is anything subversive left at all to these flowers, as Sivan claims, it is only their by-now recognizably codified betokening of queer subversion: upon the release of the track Sivan played a quick game of internet peekaboo, posting and then soon after deleting a tweet with the hashtag #bopsaboutbottoming, apparently tethering the floral signifier to its purportedly clandestine signified hieroglyphically—and in a stark reversal of their allegorical uncoupling in Schroeter's montage. But by the same gesture, this motto (or *inscriptio*, to bring the vocabulary in line with Benjamin's thinking on the Baroque) offers and immediately withdraws an explication so obvious that its redundancy-under-erasure reads as willfully enigmatic. Its disjointed relation to the titular bloom delivers all the artifice and arbitrariness of allegorical emblematicity.[76] The tweet-and-delete does a number on irony: it announces its intention to obfuscate by pointing directly to the set nature of its unambivalent symbolism; it hints at a core secret self by accidentally-on-purpose failing to conceal it.

Rather than a queering in the sense of destabilization, the emblem of the bloom might seem to entail an anchoring of identity: gay, twink, bottom. But the last of these, at least, is a designation (and one implying a rigid codification of quasi-gendered roles among gay men) that Sivan at other moments explicitly resists. To give only one telling example, asked about his preferred sexual position in an interview that has since become notorious in part for a dogged line of questioning about his celebrity crush on his straight-identifying contemporary Shawn Mendes, Sivan replied sarcastically, "Ooo . . . definitely passing." (This follows on the heels of an earlier question about whether his boyfriend would give him a "hall pass" to hook up with Mendes; a brief internet furor was stirred up this same year when Mendes was caught on camera at the camp-themed Met Gala greeting and putting his arm around a bashful-looking Sivan.) The response is surely more polyvalent than intended. Sivan presumably just means that he is taking a pass by declining to answer, but the discomfort not only with the question itself but with potentially being identified as a bottom (not to mention the faintly homophobic sports metaphorics of passing versus catching habitually applied to this scenario) seems almost to suggest that there may also be another kind of passing at stake here, even after the possibility of passing would seem to have been dismantled by the overdetermined symbolism of "Bloom."[77]

And just a few months before "Bloom" dropped, Mendes himself had revealed the cover art for his self-titled third album with a nearly nine-hour livestream of a crew reconstructing it out of wood planks, canvasses, and fresh-cut roses. The resulting image is of Mendes's face, segmented into plates, with blooming bouquets, including what appear to be blood flowers, protruding from the fissures. (The lead single from the album is the pop rock ballad "In My Blood.") While it's somewhat harder to imagine in this case that the resemblance could be intentional, the parallel to the floral grafting of Schroeter's *Rosenkönig* is notable, although the visual effect is almost entirely opposite. Despite these cracks in Mendes's classically handsome countenance, the overall aesthetic of both the album and its cover art is smooth and seamless. And while these visuals were achieved in collaboration with Brazilian digital artist Marcel Monreal, the idea was initially inspired by a piece of fan art created with the "Inner Bloom" filter of the image editing app Photo Lab, which is to say that it follows a widely available template. I think I can note without passing judgment on its aesthetic appeal that this cover—as unabashedly unoriginal as it is earnest—is the quintessence of cliché. Again, all bloom but no wound, it has the floral trappings of the camp aesthetic with none of the thorny irony.

Still, the intended implication is clearly one of vulnerability and personal authenticity: it is also a kind of coming-out album for an artist already well-known to his audience. As Oliver Skinner pointed out at the time for the public broadcasting service in Mendes's native Canada: "While the covers of his previous two records . . . maintain a distance by using homespun photos of the burgeoning pop star, the image for this self-titled work completely opens the singer up."[78] To the extent that there is anything to the evolution portrayed here, Mendes attributes his earlier emotional reserve largely to obsessive behavioral self-policing for any markers of effeminacy and an anxiety surrounding the persistent rumors of homosexuality that have inevitably accompanied his brand of soft, sensitive masculinity. A repeated childhood anecdote of having his hair braided by female cousins suggests an awareness of the dangers of camp presentation even from an early age. He also expresses anger and frustration over such stigmatizing media coverage on behalf of those who are genuinely afraid to come out.[79] At the same time, coy and flirtatious, the marketing around Mendes seems at moments almost to court such speculation, or at least to make the most of a kind of privacy striptease performed by a pop star who is shy in affect but has also been the brand ambassador for Calvin Klein underwear—a role that, from Marky Mark to David Beckham to Justin Bieber and Nick Jonas, has shrewdly made a tough, brazen, even somewhat threatening straight masculinity available as a thirst trap for homoerotic enjoyment.

Steven Maynard has observed the striking whiteness of the Bruce Weber photographs that defined the brand's aesthetic: always white men, wearing white underwear, shot exclusively in a black and white that works "to emphasize, sometimes to almost illuminate, the whiteness of the fabric" and through which "homoeroticism comes to be defined as white."[80] Describing the most recent campaign, featuring the aptly named Jeremy Allen White, Jennifer Wilson has playfully dubbed the aesthetic "fuccboi minimalism."[81] And this monochrome minimalism itself would seem to trope on the homoerotic imaginaries of Genet's filmmaking, where, as Jane Giles points out, the process of rendering beloved bodies as flowers also entails such whitening:

> Genet actually achieves the transposition of a man into a flower through the warder's fantasy in *Un Chant d'amour* . . . signaled by the image of luminous white blossom[s] swinging toward an outstretched hand, an abstraction of the sight which catches the warder's eye outside the prison at the beginning of the film and thus initiates his investigation. Stylistically the whole of the warder's fantasy is characterized by this chiaroscuro lighting, and the white bodies of the men are photographed to resemble the white blossom, making a visual match and therefore an equivalent in the mind of the viewer.[82]

Quoting Maynard, Richard Dyer situates this aesthetic within a long tradition of Christian iconography—the "whitening of Christ"—pertinent not only to the representational tradition at issue in this chapter but also to the echoes of an ambivalently unmarked whiteness we will discover again in Xavier Dolan.

Shooting Mendes for Calvin Klein, photographer Mario Sorrenti seems to trope on such whitewashing. A video promo for the campaign depicts Mendes on an empty platform that slopes seamlessly into an illuminated blank background to create the illusion of an edgeless void. This staged backstage access to the photo shoot is initially in color—or whatever minimal color Mendes's skin tone makes available, since most everything else in the image is perfectly white—but as the camera pushes in on the young man, his hands behind his head, the color fades away (see figs. 7–12). Mendes cracks a smile, looking directly into the lens, and a logo appears as the campaign's tagline is read aloud by his disembodied voice: "Iconically . . . Calvin Klein."

Troye Sivan's whiteness is in its own way ethereal: the almost otherworldliness of his platinum bottle-blond-accentuated pallor is further emphasized in "Bloom" by draping outfits falling off his slight shoulders to expose a body so smooth and white and thin it seems to risk vanishing. But, notably, his own advertisements for Calvin Klein's Feel Pride campaign (not *proud*, per se: the difference remains marked) are shot in breezy, comforting pastels.[83] There is something decidedly less campy, more insidiously normative, about how the potential for effacement is inflicted, in the more classic Calvin Klein commercial, on the body of Shawn Mendes. Leaving sexuality aside, as does the trope itself, he is every bit the off-straight twink. If the concluding close-up seems again to suggest a naked intimacy—by the time the camera movement has found its mark, the underwear being advertised is no longer in the frame—it at once insinuates, I would argue, a certain featurelessness or aesthetic-ideological neutrality. Sublimating this blank body into a literal icon, it tacitly renders its whiteness, to borrow Dyer's phrase, as "unmarked, unspecific, universal."[84] It makes visible the invisible: look, it insists, nothing to see here.

Nonetheless, the announcement of the partnership with Calvin Klein posted to the musician's Twitter account, this image at least in warmer tones,

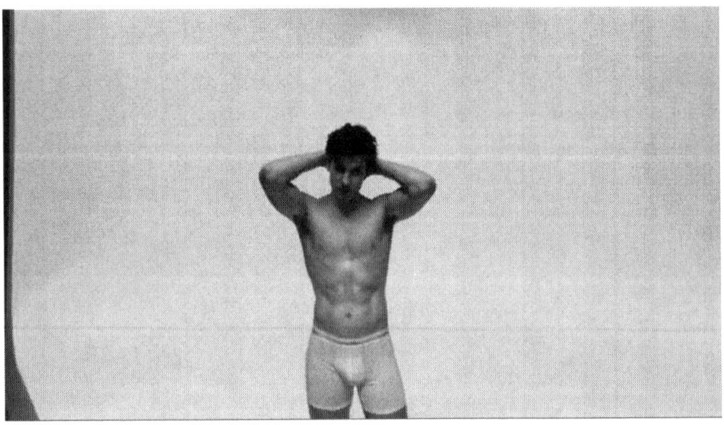

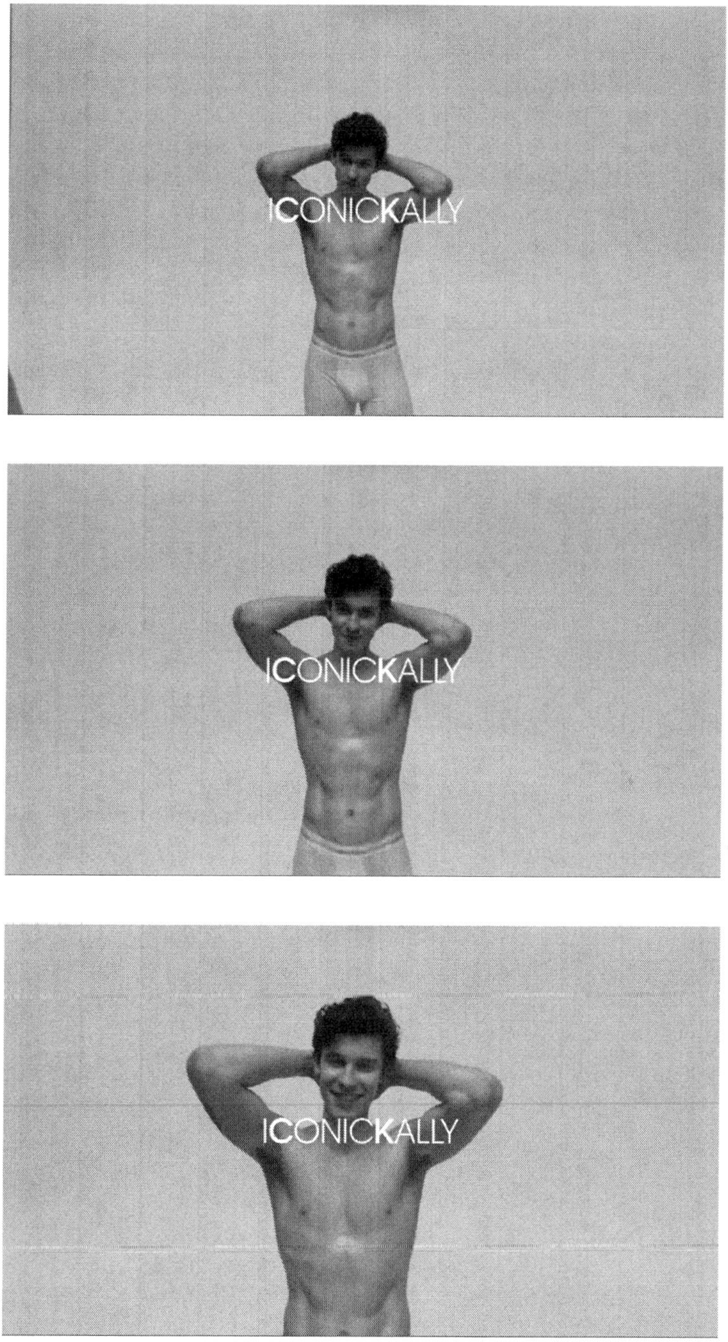

Figs. 7–12. A track in on Shawn Mendes and a simultaneous fade to black and white in Calvin Klein's Spring/Summer 2019 campaign.

features Mendes reclined in a strangely skimpy bucket armchair wearing only boxer briefs, his knees spread wide for a generous crotch shot and the admirable musculature of his torso on ample display; the text beside the requisite at signs and hashtags reads, "Campaign coming this week." In an analogous game of hide-and-state-the-obvious, the single "In My Blood" was teased on social media with cryptic floral motifs and repeated implications that this would be the singer's most intimate work yet—but also with a Times Square billboard reading, "SHAWN MENDES COMING SOON." Look: nothing to see here. Not yet at least. Is the temptation to discern the echo of an absent *out* in all of these comings (out) at all forgivable? Maybe not. But it can't be bad for business either.

The lyrics of "In My Blood" speak of Mendes's mental health struggles but are easily transposable to the experience of being closeted, including a potential allusion to the It Gets Better Project. (And it is possible that Mendes's trans producer and writing partner, Teddy Geiger, who announced that she was transitioning while working on the album, was an influence here.) The rather maudlin music video culminates with Mendes supine and sopping wet in a field of digitally rendered flowers, smoothing the rough edges of the analog(ous) beds of roses where Schroeter's film had ended.

I should be clear that I have no desire to insinuate that Mendes is in fact gay or closeted nor to accuse him of being a bad ally or a media whore. (As this book goes to print, and in anticipation of the release of another self-titled album, *Shawn*, in November 2024, the singer has again been addressing rumors about his sexuality with refreshed openness and a new sense of fluidity.) My interest lies instead in what becomes of such gay tropes of authenticity, indeed of the trope of authentic gayness itself, when read across the belated coming-out albums of Mendes and Sivan. The latter may well feel as winking as the former is self-serious, but both of their lead singles flawlessly perform an anxiety regarding a failure to pass, or to pass as oneself. If camp traditionally fobs off failed passing as willfully elected, these two recording artists inversely make a pretense of revealing the cracks in a carefully curated public face. The orgasmic grafting of Genet and Schroeter has been sutured into a self-decoding cryptogram.

This returns us, finally, to the contentious issue of Schroeter's outness and to Caryl Flinn's guiding query, cited earlier in this chapter, with regard to the relationship between camp and kitsch. To put a finer point on it, it begs the question of what becomes of the camp subversion of established clichés after this subversiveness has itself become cliché, after camp signifiers have themselves been, in a sense, codified *into* kitsch. I belabor this issue in part because it anticipates debates surrounding queer pathos and sentimentality that will be significant in the final chapters of this study. With a nod to Susan Sontag's description of camp as "a kind of love," Flinn notes that "one term of opprobrium that critics constantly evoke is kitsch's investment in sentimentality—a feeling, of course, but not one of love. For them, sentimentality can be automatically rigged and triggered; it engages exaggerated, scripted reactions to things that are vicariously experienced. It is unearned emotion in short."[85] Rosa von Praunheim's infamous attack on Werner Schroeter was occasioned by just such an accusation that the turn to linear narrative and (minimal) commercial appeal ushers in an undesirably clichéd earnestness: "His recent acclaim has paralyzed him. He takes himself seriously and unfortunately also the things he used to quite rightfully make fun of."[86] In short, by momentarily abandoning camp irony, Schroeter has sold out to kitsch. In this spat between friends and sometimes lovers the question turns largely on an aesthetic preference between Werner Schroeter's ardent roses and Rosa von Praunheim's more playfully ironic style. But to give the incomparably campy Praunheim due credit, perhaps what he has recognized here, conversely, is the danger that even an oppositionally queer aesthetic will succumb to codification and become formulaic. What might be gleaned from the debate over Schroeter's identity politics is that this is also the danger of identity itself.

Surveying Schroeter's work, Flinn concludes, against apparent scholarly consensus, that "kitsch can articulate decidedly *un*formulaic emotions."[87] But this optimism toward a reclaimed kitsch, it seems to me, is probably less rewarded by the floral formulae recycled in recent years by Mendes and Sivan, where even its most insistently *homo*sexual iterations—the formal provocation of gay avant-garde cinema flattened into the glossy pride vibe of "Bloom"—can be so readily and smoothly recuperated into the *un*marked, unspecified, vanilla, and presumptively *hetero*sexual aesthetic of "In My Blood." With regard to all these flowers, this is in part because the ubiquitous and overdetermined symbolism of the rose has, as demonstrated in the preceding, made it so attractive a target for the constant queerings and resignifications discussed throughout this chapter. But surely, if conversely, this is also to some degree a consequence of the lability of *queer* itself: an empty, floating signifier that designates a function as much as it does any identity category and over time comes to signal only identity's own function as an empty placeholder.

Part 3

Token Subversion

Chapter 5

New Camp Extremity

Adaptation and Experimentation in François Ozon

In an emotional outburst in the final act of François Ozon's *Gouttes d'eau sur pierres brûlantes* (*Water Drops on Burning Rocks*, 2000)—his adaptation of a young Rainer Werner Fassbinder's first go at playwriting—the film's protagonist, Franz (Malik Zidi), attempts to reassert himself against his domineering older lover, Léopold (Bernard Giraudeau), exclaiming: "You're all so strange, like marionettes, incapable of moving on your own, manipulated by God knows what!" Protesting, as he is scripted to do, against the very (pre)script that he obeys by doing so, Ozon's figure, like Fassbinder's before him, exposes the machinery of authorial manipulation. A moment later—in a musical number so out of place in the film's diegesis, an act so gratuitous that it feels almost metaleptic—Ozon adds another element to this mise en abyme, as an awkward Franz fails to keep step with a synchronized song and dance he performs with the other characters. The puppetry appears to have gone awry.

In this instance, as throughout the film, *Gouttes d'eau* offers an apt testing ground for an examination of queer free will and failed passing both diegetically and on an authorial level. Notably, this dance sequence was added by Ozon—whose flair for campy musical interludes was already established in the gender-bending early short "Une robe d'été" ("A Summer Dress," 1996) and would be fully consummated in the later *8 Femmes* (*8 Women*, 2002) and *Potiche* (a title translating very roughly to "trophy wife" 2010)—to the source material borrowed from Fassbinder. In this sense, Franz's paroxysm and bad dancing also elicit speculation into Ozon's own assertion of autonomy vis-à-vis the original author of the text he is adapting. This chapter will explore tactics of (film) adaptation, and adaptability as such, as they pertain to the evolution of queer identity in Ozon's reception of Fassbinder. As Pamela Demory summarizes the confluence of queer adaptation: "To adapt is to modify, to evolve, to transform, to repeat, imitate, parody, make new. To queer something is to make it strange or odd, but also to turn or transform it. To queer then, may be to adapt; to adapt is to queer."[1] If Judith Butler is correct in contending that (gender) identity is forged through imperfect repetition, then Ozon's reception of Fassbinder can be seen both as an homage and as a site of queer contestation, as the later filmmaker engenders himself both in and against the earlier auteur's image and the genre of queer filmmaking it epitomizes.

Briefly historicizing Ozon in relation to the broader context of the present project, I will first attend to the incessant accusations of copycatism that have accompanied his career: the critical anxiety that his forays into genre cinema are all-too-slick, too adeptly executed, to fulfill the queer mandate to radical aesthetics and, by presumptive extension, politics. In short, Ozon's work has often been lamented as mere simulacrum of earlier gay avant-gardes. This knee-jerk complaint may be symptomatic of what Demory identifies as an unfortunate affinity between nonheteronormative sexualities and adapted texts: "Both adaptation and queerness suffer from the stereotype of being secondary, somehow less authentic. To identify something as an adaptation is to recognize it in relation to something else—something prior, something that for at least some people is more true. Similarly, to identify something as queer is to place it in relation to something that seems to have been already established as 'normal' or 'straight.' "[2] But, while age-old anxieties regarding homosexual artificiality—discussed, for instance, in my opening chapter on André Gide—are certainly detectable in the reception of Ozon's work, more palpable still, at this historical juncture, is the concern that what is sometimes belittled as Ozon's derivativeness might be a sign that *queer* has lost its novelty, that *gay* itself has become too marketable a generic category.

Turning to the Fassbinder adaptation specifically, I will interrogate the manner in which Ozon at once courts and shirks this label: a willfully failed passing that updates the earlier director's open aversion to identity politics a quarter century on. If Ozon's detractors fault him for an overdependence on formulaic tropes, his advocates celebrate his protean approach to genre as reflective of a transgressively pansexual worldview. Fassbinder's and Ozon's resistance to being tokenized as gay filmmakers notwithstanding, a careful examination of the mutable sexualities and mix-and-match erotic couplings of *Gouttes d'eau* will reveal that it is perhaps not so much that queer fluidity has become a matter of course in Ozon's suspension of fixed identity categories as it is that cis gay male experience—historically a token of subversion—struggles against its own fungibility and its tendency to represent subversion as such. But by attempting to *subvert* such tokenism, I will argue, Ozon's project risks reinforcing, even reifying, this association and thus despite itself maintaining male homosexuality as a universalized experience of queerness.

Ozon's work can appear self-contradictory. On the one hand, it tends toward aestheticization, free self-invention, and playful queer caprice. On the other, it is prone to an evidentiary paradigm in which the body seems intended to act as a guarantor of profundity and meaning. If the first of these modes sets sexual identities in flux, suggesting their general equivalence and substitutability, the indexical logic of the latter has a rather more cementing effect. Torn between these conflicting inclinations, *Gouttes d'eau sur pierre brûlantes* ends up, I will argue, laying bare the inherently phantasmagoric quality of the filmic body itself and thus, ultimately, of the myth of (self-) identity it incorporates and sustains.

Genre Queer

François Ozon is a filmmaker of sometimes muted extremes. From his beginnings as a director of rather experimental shorts through the polished international successes for which he is best known, Ozon has displayed astonishing, even virtuosic mastery of an eclectic compass of styles, moods, and genres—vacillating, throughout his prolific career, between sexually explicit thrillers, bittersweet melodramas, wispy period pieces, and fluffy musical comedies. Such variety has made Ozon at times attractive to audiences and film scholars alike but has also elicited repeated critiques of sterility and superficial pastiche.

At least from *Gouttes d'eau* to his most recent release, *Peter von Kant* (2022), Ozon has shown himself to be an avid Fassbinder aficionado, inscribing his own work into his German predecessor's meteoric career with increasing insistence. But if the stylistic promiscuity and the breakneck speed with which Ozon works—coming out with a feature-length film nearly once a year since the turn of the millennium—make such parallels plausible, the reception of Ozon's oeuvre has proven rather hesitant to grant him unchallenged legitimacy as a pretender to the legacy of a gay avant-garde. As Andrew Asibong grumbles at the outset of the first monograph published on the filmmaker: "If Ozon's films usually lack the genuine emotional highs and lows often generated by [Pedro] Almodóvar, Fassbinder and [John] Waters . . . this is surely down to the way in which Ozon so confidently repackages their aesthetics within the ironic framework of a devastatingly knowing—and extremely French—cleverness. Even if Ozon's cinema is deeply marked by the raw influence of the Spanish, German and American sons of melodrama, his is ultimately a studied intellectual project."[3] This not uncharacteristic concern that Ozon's productions might not be rough enough around the edges to do any real emotional damage or achieve serious aesthetic or political subversion comes to inflect considerations of his status as an auteur—deliberations, as I intend to show, tightly entwined with the question of how *queer* (or not) Ozon's filmography is taken to be. This is a metric—as can be sensed in Asibong's discernment of the supposedly French flavor given to a European American homosexual aesthetic—at once historical and geographic. Ozon's queer credentials will depend on how he is to be situated with regard to the broader heritage of movements like those discussed in the previous chapter, not only New Wave European cinemas like Fassbinder's or the predominantly American influence of New Queer Cinema but now also the so-called New French Extremity that forms the immediate backdrop to Ozon's first films.[4] As a respondent to and participant in this periodization of perpetual novelty, the question, plainly put, becomes whether Ozon actually has anything new to offer. What has been frequently denigrated as Ozon's postmodern proclivity for rote citationality, blank parody, and hollow formalism suggests an attendant worry about a pedigreed queerness perceived to be increasingly devoid of dissidence, substance, and grit.

Criticism on Ozon has thus insistently related the capriciousness of his repertoire to the question of self-expression—with scholars and cinephiles wondering whether the filmmaker displays a sufficiently recognizable, individual style to warrant having the title of auteur bestowed upon him.[5] Thibaut Schilt, for instance, pointing to the generically hybrid nature of Ozon's cinema, sees it as exemplifying "the paradox of contemporary auteurism" in that it "reveals that the boundary between auteur cinema and its so-called mainstream counterpart is more porous than one might think."[6] For the present purposes, I am less invested in resuscitating any notion of directorial genius than I am in probing how the self-conscious staging of this tension between so-called art cinema and mainstream popular movies comes to embody the uneasy interplay between the modes of queer abjection and camp performativity discussed in the preceding chapters of this book.

In this sense, Ozon is also a representative case study for debates around the aesthetic merit of the New French Extremity, a term initially intended disparagingly when it was coined by James Quandt to describe the sexually vivid and often gory films of Ozon, Gaspard Noé, Catherine Breillat, and other contemporaries.[7] Scholarly treatments of what Tim Palmer describes a bit more neutrally as the "new French cinema of the body" have similarly attended to its status as "a hybrid cinema, merging high art intellectualism with low art body horror." Palmer, for one, concludes that by "exploring sexuality and physicality at fascinating extremes, this controversial strand of contemporary French cinema has a rigorous, committed intensity akin to the avant-garde at its most dynamic and compelling."[8] But, taking issue with the first decades of scholarship on this cinematic trend, Mauro Resmini persuasively deconstructs the theoretical tendency to understand the naked and, especially, injured body as proof positive of verism and to attribute an unusual degree of authenticity to these "exceptionally graphic depictions of sex and violence and . . . an aesthetic that privileges the shocking, the horrific, and the abject."[9] (I am, as the preceding chapter has hopefully made plain, far more receptive to Resmini's skepticism.[10]) As Ozon moves breathlessly from one film project to the next, he seems alternately to exploit spectatorial credence in the corporeal and more knowingly to rescind its guarantee of truthfulness by turning time and again to genres, like the movie musical, more undeniably devoted to fantasy.

In other words, Ozon's work marks another new moment in queer aesthetics' negotiation—treated in the previous chapter—between depictions of bodily abjection and its potential stylization, as reflected, for instance, in Alistair Fox's description of the filmmaker's disparate cinematic styles, "ranging from extreme camp inflected with a high degree of artifice . . . to an equally extreme and serious psychological realism."[11] What is more: in the queer case of Ozon, the critical dismay at his flirtation with the gamut of popular genres might amount to a sort of slut shaming, and the preoccupation with the potential superficiality of his mimicry of indie aesthetics might betray a longer history, dating back at least to Gide, of unwittingly homophobic discourses surrounding purported gay insincerity. Leaving aside the question of whether a heterosexual filmmaker would be held to account in this same way for a personal investment in their own work, we can observe how the issue of earnestness itself gets tied to notions of national cinema after the height of the AIDS crisis (in the United States and Europe, at least) and in a post–Cold War European context. Asibong, as we have already seen, understands Ozon to be distinctly and decidedly French and by virtue of national cliché thus also a bit aloof. But Nick Rees-Roberts—who, in his study of *French Queer Cinema*, rather neglects Ozon, providing instead a sustained discussion of his in many ways comparable contemporary Christophe Honoré—consistently disparages "the narcissism and pathos associated with much artistic production of AIDS in France," arguing instead for a popular cinema "eschewing sentimental pathos in favor of bitter-sweet camp (combining a darkness of humor with a lightness of touch)" that he advocates as more "artistically and politically viable."[12] Even for sympathetic scholarly interpreters, it seems, queer aesthetics are faced with the difficult task of navigating between what we might chart as the Scylla of paranoid parody and the Charybdis of reparative overinvestment.

Most recently, Emma Wilson has argued that, in "his challenge to the heteronormative, to binary gender and sexuality, Ozon has appropriated pathos as one means of queer contestation."[13] Ozon, as she sees it, is not so much specifically French as "aligned with the boundary-crossing, pan-European, high art aesthetic. . . . Ozon identifies as queer in his films."[14] On this reading, Ozon's queerness and aesthetic or stylistic mutability get forcefully repoliticized:

> The blurring of the contours of desire, and the crossing of ever-permeable boundaries between homosexuality and heterosexuality, are aligned with an aesthetic that looks beyond the boundaries of national cinemas and cultures. Ozon's art identifies itself with a high art tradition across Europe, thus defining a queer aesthetic markedly in contrast to Anglo-American queer representations. Permeability across sexual and national (artistic) boundaries carries particular force in Ozon's films, making them queer in a political as well as

> sexual sense. . . . The unlikely means used to achieve gender and sexual trouble, and the reinvention of the affective and erotic dynamics of European cinema, are what I describe here as queer pathos.[15]

The tightly intertwined political, sexual, and aesthetic stakes of queerness are not only emphatically reasserted here but now take on international, almost utopian dimensions: "Pathos itself may be political (for Ozon specifically, but also potentially for other European artists) . . . and open possibilities for a queer (nonnormative) sociality."[16] Recalling what Rees-Roberts identifies as bittersweet camp, Wilson posits that Ozon interrogates "the shame or otherwise of pathos . . . and envisages the possibility of tenderness and intimacy without mawkishness or sentimentality."[17] Phrased differently, what Rees-Roberts had dismissed as manipulative, "apolitical and even exploitative" kitsch is reclaimed both for its politics and its poignancy, perhaps revealing at its core the kind of earnest appropriation camp seeks out in a reparative mode.[18]

The question of prepackaged pathos and of Ozon's ostensibly unfeeling mobilization of incompatibly diverse tropes and genres is significant because it has a lot to tell us about the potential codification, over time, of a specifically gay yet broadly transatlantic aesthetic of the kind discussed in my previous chapter. Commenting on cinema's relative oversaturation (when compared to other queer communities) with male homosexuality, Rees-Roberts notes, for instance, the "wider socio-economic limits of queer representation from within independent production companies that imitate the dominant preference for explorations of gay male over lesbian sexuality, whilst promoting their products as cutting-edge art."[19] Of Ozon specifically he argues that the filmmaker "gives a normative spin to gay male sexuality": combining a portrayal of sex as "realistically raw, complete with erection shots," that at the same time "tames the action with glossy images of the lovers that resemble homoerotic advertising stills."[20] The implicit fear here, ironically enough, is that Ozon might somehow undeservedly *pass* as politically subversive or as aesthetically interesting purely because of his homosexuality: opposing substance to style, this viewpoint would appear to privilege a quasi-pornographic realism allegedly devoid of any aestheticization while also insinuating that stylization itself risks effacing the subversive force of sex by derealizing the on-screen body.

The tone for such complaints was set early on by a frequently cited review of Ozon's first full-length film, *Sitcom* (1998), which proclaimed him a "young homo spoon-fed on queerness to the extent of simply coughing it up again in his works."[21] Schilt, surveying scholarly and popular perspectives on the film I will be analyzing most closely here, revisits this description, connecting it to considerations of genre and periodization: "Given the generic instability of postmodern films, and notably Ozon's, and in light of the fact that Ozon consistently revisits genre in unpredictable ways, some critics, especially those of Gallic descent, have concluded that *Gouttes d'eau* is nothing other than a shallow pastiche devised by 'a young homo spoon-fed on queerness' or simply 'a postmodern *exercice de style.*' "[22] Such concerns over commodified queerness and postmodern play with generic templates suggest that if Ozon offends it may well be because he is not offensive enough, because he, like Todd Haynes before him, treats a gay avant-garde aesthetic just as he would any other genre in an unthinking recycling and concomitant reification of established gay tropes. In other words, he has transformed queer identity itself into a genre.

Token Subversion

In what follows I will examine this generic flattening through a reading of one of the first of two Ozon films most obviously indebted to the tradition I have been treating in this book: *Gouttes d'eau sur pierres brûlantes* (*Water Drops on Burning Rocks*, 2000)—adapted, as already noted, from an early theater script of Fassbinder's, *Tropfen auf heiße Steine* (1964), written when Fassbinder was nineteen but first unearthed and produced only posthumously. (The later Fassbinder-inspired *Peter von Kant* will be discussed, if more briefly, in due course.) Though somewhat more political in its orientation than Ozon, the subversiveness of Fassbinder's own project can also be thought of as an attempt to save genre from itself and to repurpose it to the director's own ends. A cursory glance at his filmography reveals that this is true not only of his approach to Sirkian melodrama but to genres like the gangster film, the Western, or science fiction, to name just a few. As Fiona Handyside summarizes, from his position as part of "a European art-house aesthetic tradition of a creatively powerful auteur working within a national cinema," Fassbinder attempts "to re-map the way Hollywood's genre formulae work."[23] However, one genre in which Fassbinder does *not* see himself working is that of what one might call gay cinema, and it is important to acknowledge that, for the most part, neither Fassbinder nor Ozon is in the habit of overtly problematizing sexual identity as such. If Fassbinder's earliest films featuring lesbian and gay characters—*Die bitteren Tränen der Petra von Kant* (*The Bitter Tears of Petra von Kant*, 1972) and *Faustrecht der Freiheit* (*Fox and His Friends*, 1975)—rubbed contemporary audiences the wrong way, even being denounced as homophobic, surely this is largely because their surprisingly simple taking for granted of same-sex relationships seemed so out of step with more explicitly engaged, nascent post-Stonewall identity politics.[24] In his public comments, Fassbinder frequently takes exception to gay exceptionalism and to what he sees as a performative stigma or shame politics, still reverberating in queer thought today: "This is exactly what I was trying to say in 'The Bitter Tears of Petra von Kant' or 'Fox and His Friends,' that the same mechanisms of oppression are at work in gay relationships as in other relationships. And the gays were very angry with me over this, because they always want to think of themselves as something special. . . . They want to be abnormal. That's idiotic."[25] In an interview with the gay magazine *Christopher Street*, for example, Fassbinder muses rather confusingly that "as long as one has to talk about homosexuality it is a problem. . . . *Generally everyone is a homosexual and therefore it is not a problem.* . . . You can discuss the problem of homosexuality when it is a social problem to be a homosexual, but we can't really talk about homosexuality because homosexuality is not a problem."[26] Declaring the universality of homosexuality, Fassbinder inverts the historical interdiction against gay love daring to speak its name: no longer hiding in the shadows, homosexuality now becomes ineffable—hardly worth discussing—because it has, as Fassbinder sees it, gotten so mainstream.

If this would seem to imply that homosexuality had already (the interview is from 1979) lost its provocative edge, Fassbinder seems at moments to take some credit for this development. Of *Faustrecht*, specifically, he once contended: "It is certainly the first film in which the characters are homosexuals, without homosexuality being made into a problem. In films, plays or novels, if homosexuals appear, the homosexuality was the problem, or it was a comic turn. But here, homosexuality is quite different, it's a love story, where one person exploits the love of another person, and that's the story I always tell."[27] Distinctly echoing such comments, Ozon himself seems inclined to see *Gouttes d'eau* as a universalizable drama: "It's the story of a couple and it could just as well be about a man and a woman or even two women. We dive into the anecdotal and the daily life of a couple and manage, despite it all, to give a universal vision of the couple."[28] And indeed, read structurally, *Gouttes d'eau* restages the same obviously, if unorthodox, oedipal tropes recognizable in Ozon's earliest efforts, beginning with the early *courts métrages* "Photo de Famille" ("Family Photo," 1988) and "Victor" (1993), both of which resemble dress rehearsals for the breakthrough campy family drama *Sitcom*: the domineering father, the timorous gay son violently asserting himself, incestuous siblings and parents.

Ozon often expresses mild frustration at being classed as a gay filmmaker: "I don't really give a shit about the label gay cinema, although it bores me. What bothers me is to hear people saying 'We've had it up to here with those topics', when, hey, nobody gives [heterosexual filmmakers] a hard time for making straight films."[29] (Anticipating an infamous statement made by Xavier Dolan, the subject of my next and final chapter, when refusing the Queer Palm, Asibong describes this statement as a "characteristically flippant but revealing" resistance to "ghettoization."[30]) In an interview with *The Guardian*, which pointedly describes him as resembling "an elegant tomboy," while reassuring the reader that "there is nothing remotely camp about him," which is to say that he *could* pass as straight, Ozon admits: "I've always thought my films were less about homosexuality than bisexuality."[31] As we shall see, the shifting sexualities of *Gouttes d'eau* would initially seem to confirm suppositions of a primary bi- or even pansexuality, or rather a free-floating queerness that can occupy any of these categories without settling there definitively—just as Ozon seems equally at home in the various genres he chooses for his films while remaining stylistically perpetually on the move.

Gouttes d'eau is a four-act piece for four players, taking place exclusively in the apartment of Léopold, an attractive aging bachelor, and focusing on his relationship with the twenty-year-old and hitherto predominantly heterosexual Franz, whom he has cruised and brought home just before the start of the film and whom he seduces as the first act ends. The second act depicts their later cohabitation as an unhappy but sexually satisfied couple, with Franz having assumed the role of Bavarian houseboy, decked out in lederhosen, for the frequently traveling Léopold. (This fairly pornographic costuming, I would suggest, fetishizes Malik Zidi as European despite the Algerian paternal origins attested to by the actor's name.) In the third act, Franz's former fiancée Anna (Ludivine Sagnier) intrudes on this domestic intranquility and, in Léopold's absence, spends two days in bed with her erstwhile lover. The bacchanalian final act sees Léopold's unexpected early return followed quickly by the arrival of a former lover of his own, Véra (Anna Thomson). With all the characters now accounted for, Léopold takes advantage of the situation to choreograph, rather literally, an orgy in which Franz refuses to participate, electing instead to commit suicide.

This is the first film of Ozon's to adapt a preexisting text—an interesting decision, as Asibong notes, for a director who had already, at a relatively early age, established "such a seemingly incontrovertible identity as a highly personal *auteur* working exclusively from his own scripts or original ideas."[32] Ozon makes the material his own not by shying away from his debt to Fassbinder but instead by leaning into it: "Rather than construct a slavish filmic homage to the German's play, however, with *Gouttes d'eau* Ozon boldly remolds the original narrative and emphasis in order to construct quite a different piece, as much an Ozon 'original' as anything else in his filmography, yet weirdly impregnated with a myriad of elements lifted from *other* Fassbinder films."[33] Indeed, if as a play, *Tropfen auf heiße Steine* anticipates a quartet of Fassbinder films dedicated to queer thematics, as a cinematic adaptation, *Gouttes d'eau sur pierres brûlantes* serves as a kind of viewer's digest of their core concerns and visual motifs. Setting aside *Querelle* (1983), which is not so much a queer film as a queer universe, Fassbinder's primary queer corpus—the depiction of lesbianism in *Petra von Kant* and of male same-sex relationships in *Faustrecht*, later coupled with a background bisexuality in Fassbinder's autofictional contribution to *Deutschland im Herbst* (*Germany in Autumn*, 1978) and the introduction of an ambiguously trans character with Erwin/Elvira from *In einem Jahr mit 13 Monden* (*In a Year of 13 Moons*, also 1978)—betrays perhaps a Genetian desire to taxonomize gender identities, sexual orientations, and queer milieux.[34] While Ozon's oeuvre can also seem at moments like a compendium of various sexualities, the categories are less distinctly defined and considerably more fluidly inhabited by his characters and there is on the whole no evident aspiration for any sort of comprehensiveness or systematicity.

An asterisk to this might be the castration anxiety surrounding representations of the trans feminine—a through line one might trace from Genet's Divine in *Notre-Dame-des-Fleurs* to Fassbinder's Elvira and onward to the phonetically very similarly named Véra. Seemingly unsatisfied with the permutations and possibilities for erotic combination already on offer in Fassbinder's script, Ozon borrows the guiding trope of *In einem Jahr mit 13 Monden* for his adaptation of Véra, who, as Léopold announces unceremoniously by way of introduction, had undergone a surgical sex change in an unsuccessful effort to retain his waning affection: "Allow me to introduce an old girlfriend. An old buddy, I should say. He had his dick cut off in Casablanca." Within the economy of sexualities circulating in the film (gay, straight, bisexual, trans, lesbian, perhaps, but the last of these primarily as Léopold's pornographic fantasy[35]) Véra's castration is put into an all-but-explicit parallel with Franz's descent into servitude: the trans feminine is a cautionary tale of the fate that awaits him if he fails to act of his own volition.[36]

What is more, while this introduction elicits comical surprise from Franz and Anna, and likely nervous laughter from the audience, the trans figure is explicitly intended to proffer a kind of bodily proof of the gravity of these intersecting plotlines. As Ozon explains his casting choice of the American actress Anna Thomson for this part: "I didn't want this character of the transexual, who arrives at the end, to be a gag. I wanted a suffering body."[37] Inverting Fassbinder's contention that *Faustrecht* is the first film not to give homosexuality a comic or tragic turn, Ozon claims to treat Véra not as a trope but rather as a person—or at least as a body. As if resorting to the same strategies of corporeal authentication that characterize the New French Extremity, Ozon enjoins us to imagine Thomson's spindly and at moments slightly knock-kneed, even boyish physique as the site of an engendering injury. However, in so doing, Ozon makes this body meaningful, significant, not literal but rather figurative: Verá's backstory is the return of the repressed, the abjected element against which Franz will have to form himself if he is to achieve autonomy and subjectivity.

Echoing common critical perspectives on the French cinema of the body discussed above, Victor Fan reads Fassbinder's *In einem Jahr mit 13 Monden* beside Almodóvar's *La mala educación* (*Bad Education*, 2004) to argue that "transsexual bodies allow what is being concealed to bleed through the screen as an unsanctioned reality that has yet to be organized and imaged as public discourse."[38] While never directly depicted, the sex reassignment—too ambivalent to be described as gender affirmation—through which Erwin (Volker Spengler) becomes Elvira would, on this account, perforate the text and permit the profilmic event of Fassbinder's autobiographical reality to emerge in the cinematic universe.[39] The apogee of this procedure would be an early sequence in which Elvira narrates the history of this sex change over a gruesome extended montage of cows being slaughtered in an abattoir, drawing an overly obvious and frankly distasteful parallel between the operation and the bodily dismemberment so painfully depicted both visually and acoustically: Fan notes that Spengler's lips do not move throughout much of this monologue, and Kaja Silverman points out that his "voice is so miked as to draw attention to the fact that although he appears in this scene, his voice does not derive from his body, but proceeds from some other space altogether. If anything, the corporeality which supports that voice is provided by the waiting and dying animals; Erwin's words might be said to be a prolongation of their cries."[40] Building on Silverman's influential work on dismantled masculinity and masochistic ecstasy in Fassbinder, Fan concludes that a kind of ventriloquism is at play, through which Fassbinder's film expresses unsanctioned homosexual desire. Specifically, "Erwin/Elvira's gender-reassigned body is . . . best understood as a fundamentally empty body that can be potentially appropriated by everybody around her/him as a signifier."[41] Rather than the kind of immediacy the transgendered body appears to promise, however, what results from this ventriloquy is an enhanced discursivity: "The dissociation between the voice and the body, and the discourse about the body and the body itself, is a key narrational device that opens up to the *mise-en-abyme* of the film."[42] A site of metacommentary, of spectatorial and authorial (dis)identification, the trans body at once instantiates a desire for autobiographical indexicality and denies the extratextual immediacy that incorporation appears to assure.

This insight has important repercussions for the representational schema according to which Véra is meant to incarnate a possible future for Franz in *Gouttes d'eau sur pierres brûlantes*; more largely, it calls into question the apparent exchangeability of the various positions, sexualities, and identities the film dramatizes. The gender trouble occasioned by Elvira and Véra has set critics on a kind of scavenger hunt: a game of find-the-fag not unlike the one Michael Lucey identifies in the reception of Gide's *Faux-monnayeurs*. The chase begins early enough in the Fassbinder film, as Fan reminds us, when another trans character, Soul Frieda (Walter Bockmeyer), suggests that Elvira was probably "already a woman to begin with in her soul" only to be told that, by Elvira's own account, they never felt themselves to be a woman nor identified as gay before their operation. (Taking some liberty with textual precedent and historical-linguistic context, this pronoun feels most appropriate and most efficient for both Elvira and Véra, for reasons that are hopefully becoming clear.[43]) The old sexological model of inversion—a woman trapped in a man's body—is already coming undone. That "Erwin submits to this mutilation out of desire for another man," which is to say, out of a desire for manhood, is, for Silverman, "a point whose importance cannot be overemphasized."[44] Concluding that the only homosexual subject position made available in this film is through Fassbinder's "self-immolating identification" with his protagonist, Silverman nevertheless insists that Erwin becomes a woman out of a similarly self-sacrificial desire for and (dis)identification with masculinity.[45] Thomas Elsaesser concurs that this is a process not of becoming oneself but of becoming the other's other: "What seems to be at stake is that a man becomes a lover by inverting the biological and morphological signifiers of sexual identity, though not because he 'feels' a woman, or identifies with women, but because he tries to be his beloved's love object."[46] (The notion of *feeling a woman* recalls Divine's *feeling woman* and *thinking man* from *Notre-Dame-des-Fleurs*.) Like in *Querelle*, at least as I have interpreted it in this book, male homosexual subjectivity is manifested only under erasure.

In the reception of *13 Monden* and *Gouttes d'eau* this effacement ends up dissolving both male homosexuality and trans femininity as much as it does the distinction between them. For example, in an otherwise impassioned polemic against the at times rather homophobic tendency to pigeonhole Ozon as a gay filmmaker, Adam Bingham nonetheless participates in the fag hunt, declaring a pyrrhic victory when he concludes, on the basis of Franz's and Léopold's bisexual engagements: "There is, in point of fact, only one character of the four in the film that can be seen as more or less unambiguously homosexual, and that is the transsexual who is now a woman."[47] When it comes to the adaptation of Véra in *Gouttes d'eau*, which borrows as much from Elvira as it does from the original play, this vanishing trans position troubles, as I have already suggested, the fluidity and dissolution of discrete identity categories toward which Ozon's cinema might otherwise appear to aspire. Arguing that *Gouttes d'eau* presents "homosexuality as unproblematic," Schilt takes it as a typically Ozonian exposition of the "fragility of the gay/straight border as well as the mutability of the socially constructed masculine/feminine border (and in the case of Véra, the biological male/female) delineations."[48] But, examined more carefully, feminization here turns out to be a one-way street. Exhibiting a certain degree of perceptible panic over the loosey-goosey-ness of contemporary cultural paradigms and perhaps not negligible schadenfreude at their comeuppance, Asibong concludes that while "according to the values of most postmodern cultural theory, Vera exemplifies the freedom and disconcerting hybridity of the border-crossing, 'decentered' subject, . . . as usual in Ozon's cinema, there can ultimately be no glibness for the transgressing individual, no freedom in the adoption of voluntary servitude."[49] And even Schilt has to wonder why Anna Thomson's obvious American accent would go uncharacteristically unacknowledged in the film's diegesis, attempting to explain this "deficit" by surmising that Ozon already "had to work overtime to justify the German setting and origins of [his] French-speaking, but occasionally German-reciting and lip-syncing, characters."[50] Clearly a lot is riding on what Emma Heaney identifies as the trans feminine allegory, discussed in my chapter on Genet's *Notre-Dame-des-Fleurs*: not only its fraught tendency to stand in for the gay male experience but the very alignment of trans figures with notions of transgression, transposition, transfiguration, transformation, or translation.

I will return to the question of intercultural exchange very briefly at the end of this chapter, but for the moment I merely want to note how Véra's failure to incorporate and illustrate mutability—rather lamented by Schilt but taken as a welcome cultural corrective by Asibong—relates to larger debates surrounding the universality or specificity of homosexual representation. With regard to Ozon's *Le temps qui reste* (*Time to Leave*, 2005), which ambiguously allegorizes AIDS through cancer, Wilson has adapted and defended Rees-Roberts's category of the "not-about-AIDS film" to contend that by exploring "the possibilities for affect and emotion in (queer) cinema in an era where AIDS is not the lone, or even perhaps immediate, point of reference," Ozon admirably demarginalizes and even universalizes the gay male experience in socially productive ways.[51] Positioning *Gouttes d'eau* in a somewhat longer history of what we might similarly call the not-about-trans narrative, I would posit that perhaps the reason that the obligingly or coercedly trans figure—who, like Elvira or Véra, changes sex without necessarily identifying with their acquired gender—is so tenaciously pervasive as an allegory of male homosexuality is precisely because, through disidentification with their own body, they (dis)incorporate and (dis)articulate the radical dissonance that has been resounding in counterfeited gay identities at least since Gide.

If it becomes difficult, given this semiological swap, to determine with any assurance which of these identities is meant to ventriloquize—to speak through—the other, this may have something to do with the historically privileged recognizability of cis gay male experience among the many positions adumbrated by the umbrella *queer*: any sexuality depicted in these films is perhaps tacitly assumed to refer back to the autobiographical gayness of the filmmaker in question. Ozon, for his part, seems increasingly to acknowledge this not unambivalent privilege as his career progresses but without—spoiler alert—finding the means fully to remedy it. The titular *Une nouvelle amie* (*New Girlfriend*, 2014) of one of his more recent films begins her coming-out as a resolutely heterosexual family man, David (Romain Duris), with a closeted penchant for cross-dressing.[52] Carefully working to manipulate audience expectations to rather transparently pedagogical ends, Ozon teasingly anticipates and frustrates suspicions of male homosexuality throughout the narrative buildup before drawing back the curtain by exposing his protagonists' own misguided attempts to deploy this presumedly more palatable sexual deviance as an expedient cover for what is actually at issue. As in Fassbinder, the trans feminine is made into a vehicle for a mise en abyme of the procedures of queer figuration, though here with the ultimate aim of decoupling it from male homosexuality. Indeed, the only sexual encounter between men that the film portrays (voyeuristically observed and pornologically situated in the locker room showers following a rousing game of tennis) both is and is not part of the film's diegesis: it plays as a paranoid fantasy, a kind of mental cinematic projection, of the friend through whose perspective the film is focalized. Somewhat earlier, during David's first public outing as Virginia, she enthusiastically allows herself to be groped by a man in a movie theater, leading the same companion, Claire (Anaïs Demoustier), to conclude momentarily that David/Virginia is indeed a gay man, or at least attracted to men. Scattering these red herrings, I would argue, Ozon highlights cinematic involvement, or complicity, in the screening—here in the contranymic senses of projection and concealment—of trans identities.

Inverting Silverman's reading of Elvira, Virginia speculates at one point that her desire to present as female might in essence be the extension of an erotic attraction to women; Virginia would appear to exercise precisely the volition and self-determination denied to Elvira and Véra: under the aegis of sameness, her object-choice and her identity seem in perfect consonance. Although it may feel odd to speak of fixity or stability in this instance, that David definitively becomes Virginia with a kind of dying declaration—"Je suis une femme!" (I am a woman)—and subsequent rebirth appears to affirm the variety of immutably underlying identity Ozon's earlier work so insistently resists. The film has been praised for this treatment of trans subjectivity, winning a Sebastiane Award for queer filmmaking at the San Sebastián International Film Festival with the laudation that it "moves towards a personal liberation . . . that could reaffirm the identity of every person."[53] And yet, this phoenix-like reincarnation is only one iteration of a persistent motif of necrophiliac yearning that seems to betray the fundamentally metaphorical function of the trans feminine in the film: David's identification as a woman is first rekindled when preparing the remains of the dead wife, Laura (Islid Le Besco), for her funeral, cloaking her in her wedding gown—a grotesquely melodramatic gesture later mimicked by Claire, Laura's childhood friend, as she dresses a comatose David as Virginia in order to awaken her like Sleeping Beauty. Crucially, the dream of self-identity seems dependent on an embodiment for which the corpse—"the utmost of abjection"—serves as the defining limit.[54]

But if the funeral with which the film begins brings the widower and the wife's best friend closer together, this love triangle also initiates a condensation of exchanges—with both of these figures serving for one another as an increasingly amatory ersatz for the absent Laura—reflected by the ambiguity of the title, which could refer to either Virginia or Claire. Ozon's encyclopedic approach to sexuality endures intact: by the time the credits roll, the film has repeatedly depicted steamy heterosexual intercourse between Claire and her husband Gilles (Raphaël Personnaz), an aborted hookup between David and Claire and then another between Claire and Virginia (abruptly halted by an erection shot), a sapphic dream Claire has about the deceased Laura as well as her aforementioned vision of David taking Gilles from behind in the shower. *Une nouvelle amie* is no less an open market of desire than was *Gouttes d'eau*. Sexual identity remains a liquid asset, easily converted.

That all of this, despite best intentions, still occurs under the auspices of (cis) male homosexuality becomes discernible during an undeniably utopian scene set in a night club vaguely recalling John Cameron Mitchell's *Shortbus* (2006), where a drag performer, Eva Carlton (Bruno Pérard), lip-syncs Nicole Croisille's 1975 "Une femme avec toi" (A woman with you) to the enraptured reaction shots of a coalitionally diverse and diversely coupled audience, including a tearfully captivated Virginia. (Claire will later shakily reprise this song as she dresses Virginia in her hospital bed.) But how is this empathic mirroring meant to work? Has the definitional contingency and gender performativity of drag as influentially theorized in early Butler, which "suggests a dissonance not only between sex and performance, but sex and gender, and gender and performance," given way to an expression of interiority?[55] Or has Virginia's experience been reduced by this equation to mere performativity? In other words: I wonder if the trans feminine allegory for male homosexuality has been reversed by this identification or merely resurrected.[56]

If these questions linger, what is clear is that Ozon's updating of trans material for a new cultural moment[57] appears unable to deliver quite the gay erasure that it portends. Insisting on the transition from David as a good father to Virginia as a good mother, it also arguably takes part in a respectability and identity politics the filmmaker had earlier resisted.[58] Declaring that "François Ozon and *The New Girlfriend* win the trans race," Armond White, in *Out Magazine*, notes that we have come "a long way from when gay filmmakers needed to be avant-garde to shock the middle-class (*épater le* [*sic*] *bourgeoisie*). . . . Ozon's mastery takes 'shock' for granted. Now he displays a provocateur's *noblesse oblige* through Claire's compassion and David's own open-hearted sexuality. . . . His genre-fuck is more impressive than a routine gender-fuck."[59] While this particular appraisal in *Out* is perhaps more receptive than most to what others see as Ozon's coddled or oxymoronically conventional queerness, sex and genre nevertheless converge under the crossed stars of tokenism and subversion. With its by now familiar implication that Ozon's free play with genre reflects his approach to sexuality, that filmic form and queer content are of a piece, this assessment gets to what I mean to suggest with the heading of token subversion. Like Fassbinder before him, Ozon exploits and subverts generic expectation while at the same time recoiling from the notion that his sexuality might be taken as an inherent token of subversion, and yet, as his work evolves, he does not so much succeed in subverting this tokenism as he does in naturalizing it: provocation is by now simply presupposed.

Adaptation as Sexual Experimentation

The machinic, almost computational, composition of *Gouttes d'eau sur pierres brûlantes* brings this automatism to the surface and makes the film an exceptionally compelling candidate for an evaluation of the historical evolution of (homo)sexual aesthetics. Although the dance sequence is Ozon's own addition, while writing the original play Fassbinder almost certainly had in mind Arthur Schnitzler's earlier drama *Reigen* (*La Ronde*, 1897), which, as its title implies, recalls a round dance in its staging of a cross section of Viennese society through a series of sexual couplings. Later adapted by German émigré Max Ophüls as *La Ronde* (1950)—which shares the casting of the iconic Danielle Darrieux with Ozon's own *8 Femmes*—and again with the same title (though known as *Circle of Love* in English) by Roger Vadim in 1964, this somewhat subterranean but inescapable intertext constitutes another instance of Franco-German cross-cultural borrowing. It also subtly situates *Gouttes d'eau* within a tradition of scandalous productions: accused of being pornographic, Schnitzler's play was only performed decades after its private publication; Ophüls's film was initially censored for its perceived libertinism; and Vadim's iteration was the first French movie to feature a nude scene with a well-known American actress, Jane Fonda. Given the sordid history of its underlying structural conceit, *Gouttes d'eau* risks feeling comparatively tame. Remarking that gay and lesbian productions and film festivals are by "now a vibrant part of the industry," G. Allen Johnson concludes that *Gouttes d'eau* "is no longer shocking": "In this 'enlightened' age, when homosexuality is generally accepted and (almost) tolerated . . . the prevailing emotion is, 'big deal.' We've been there, seen that. . . . Ozon's film is for Fassbinder fans only."[60] The former enfant terrible of queer French film has apparently matured into a yawningly derivative cinephile.

The dramaturgy of *Gouttes d'eau* is itself an exercise in iterability. Throughout the film, but particularly preceding the largely elliptical sex scenes that conclude each act, the characters repeat key gestures and lines of dialogue—but swap roles. During the initial seduction, Franz recounts to Léopold a recurring childhood dream of an older man joining him in bed, an imagined stepfather in an overcoat. This fetishized wardrobe item—which Ozon refers to suggestively as an *imperméable* in his interview with Coulombe—will be passed around throughout the film as if it were an illustration of early misreadings of Butler's theory of performativity, which took it to posit "that one woke in the morning, perused the closet or some more open space for the gender of choice, donned that gender for the day, and then restored the garment to its place at night."[61] At the conclusion to the first act, Léopold offers to play out this fantasy and the curtain closes, so to speak, on a supine Franz, fully undressed, hands bashfully covering his genitalia, waiting for Léopold, who is standing in the doorway in his coat, revealed in a slow upward tilt from his shoes to his face. The second act ends with the same tilt of Franz in this outfit and Léopold waiting naked and suggestively prostrate on the bed—though the lovemaking continues into the next act, with Franz being fucked from behind, as if to confirm that the assumed positions have not been reversed by this inverted roleplaying, that the vestment does not afford the impermeability its French name would imply. It is Franz in the overcoat again at the end of the third act, though a downward tilt toward his feet this time shows that he is naked underneath, with Anna lying nude on her side facing away from him, her head turned invitingly in his direction. In the film's final scenes, it is not Léopold's but rather Véra's gaudy leather coat, with a feathery faux-fur collar, that Franz wears as he expires on the floor.

But notably, these sex games, inasmuch as they bring Franz's childhood dream to life, are an imperfect realization, whereas the dream is said to have repeated without deviation: "Twice I dreamed that my mother had married a man. And both times it was the same [*le même*]." Curiously, this sameness (*le même*) could refer just as easily to the man Franz dreams of as it could to the dream itself; the undecidability of its referent already introduces self-difference into a pronominal phrase meant to indicate identity. Beyond this grammatical peculiarity, Franz's evident pleasure in this sex dream contrasts to the reality of his actual stepfather, whom Franz dislikes and who is said to have caused Franz to become estranged from his mother. Moreover, asked whether he has the same physical traits (muscular legs, ample chest hair) as the figure Franz describes, Léopold can only promise an inexact copy: "Un peu" (a little).

Such discrepancy is all the more important given that Léopold's seduction of Franz hinges on precise equivalence. Just before relating his dream, Franz had confessed to masturbatory boarding school fumblings with other boys but expressed revulsion with regard to his single same-sex kiss: "But it grossed me out, it was pretty unpleasant. . . . Because I was a boy and he was a boy too." Responding to this detail in his own account of his first homosexual experience, Léopold assures his mark that it is no different than kissing a girl: "It's true I didn't want to kiss him. At the time that felt unnatural to me. But it wasn't. Essentially it's exactly the same thing." Trite as it is (the subsequent reference to "the ancient Greeks" elicits a blasé eyebrow raise from Franz), this turns out to be a very clever ploy: insisting momentarily on the *essential* similarity of heterosexual and homosexual behavior, Léopold makes identification itself the essence of sexual attraction, thereby essentializing the sameness of same-sex activity and elevating *homo*sexuality over heterosexuality. Franz seems taken enough by this general theory of resemblance and the partial likeness of Léopold to the man of his dreams, although, inspected closely, they do not fully satisfy the oneiric logic he has elaborated, which amplifies mere similitude into the indubitably identical: "He came into my bed and I had the impression that I was getting smaller and smaller, almost like a girl. . . . Yes, he entered me like I was girl. He just lay down on me as if I were a girl and then I must have been one in the dream." Introducing an incongruity between fantasy and reality, Léopold's incapacity to pass fully for the man of Franz's dreams foreshadows the latter's own failure or refusal to become a woman like Véra.

This failed passing complicates the easy assumption of identity that might otherwise be inferred from the revolving costuming of the ritual. Criticism on the film seems more or less unanimous in its judgment that all of this roleplaying ultimately amounts to nothing. Arguing that the "line-swapping game is of no lasting consequence whatsoever" and that, in the final account, "only Leopold really gets to be the 'daddy,'" Asibong sees "their shared feminization" as the "one truly inescapable process of subjugation into which Franz, Anna, and Vera appear to be increasingly cemented."[62] The freedom and self-realization aimed at through the film's drama therapy are, in this view, only imaginary: "While the players may believe that they can manipulate and alter their roles within it to suit their needs at any given time, the non-negotiable horror at the heart of the apparently show-like situation is altogether less flexible."[63] With regard to the flexibility of sexual identity, Asibong continues, Franz's "apparently unproblematic bisexuality" may appear to offer an out, but "as the film goes on we realize that we simply cannot speak of anything like choice in the position Franz has come to occupy."[64] Anne Marie Parent and Nicolas Xanthos concur: "Individual identity escapes the control of the individual: it anchors itself in a desire that determines it independently of one's own will or action."[65] In their interpretation, this is because the film "stages a constitutive identitary dependence on the other insofar as it shows that we are not in masters of ourselves."[66] Directed by a desire for other bodies, sexual orientation is determined by alterity. I will return to this recognition later, as it casts new light on Ozon's insistence throughout his career on filmic strategies of corporeal verification.

Read in this way, *Gouttes d'eau* becomes a radical rebuttal of the whole notion of queer free will—a diagnosis from which Léopold is arguably exempt. Bingham understands Léopold to be "brash and in control, having sex with different people to show that he can and to assert dominance and independence," whereas "Franz, on the other hand, turns out ultimately to be a mass of contradictions"—implying that self-sovereignty is, as I discussed with reference to Genet's Our Lady, a function of self-identity.[67] But more or less reversing the daddy-twink dynamics of that earlier text, and most of those discussed up until this point, here it would apparently be the pederast instead of the relative ephebe who comes to represent such wholeness and autonomy.

It is true that despite an early temper tantrum over a board game and his self-description in Fassbinder's script as *eigensinnig* (stubborn, or more literally, self-minded), it is pointed out within the first ten minutes of the film that the ironically surnamed Franz Meister chews his fingernails and smokes compulsively.[68] As Parent and Xanthos see it, then, only Léopold gets to play the puppeteer and determine the roles and identities in these games, but it is worth remembering that the older man becomes *l'homme de rêve* Franz wishes for and that, while the roles of the scenario are variously occupied, it is therefore Franz's, not Léopold's, fantasy that determines the overarching choreography of the sex play punctuating each act—or at least until the orgasmic conclusion from which Franz lethally excuses himself.

That these lovers' spats stage a dispute over directorial control is further intimated by the autobiographical alignment of Franz with a young Fassbinder and the fact that Fassbinder himself plays a Franz in *Faustrecht* in an identification that carries through many of his works from *Tropfen auf heiße Steine* to the 1980 television adaptation of *Berlin Alexanderplatz*. (Not to mention that Franz is the translation into German of François Ozon's own *nom propre*.) Looking past the obvious Herr/Knecht dynamics, then, this multiplicity of possible selves and filmic doppelgänger might be taken as a hint that we have been looking in the wrong place for liberty and self-expression, that it is not to be discovered in the seemingly untroubled self-correspondence of a Léopold but rather in the self-dissonant fluctuations of someone like Franz. If agency, authorial or otherwise, is to be located in Ozon's adaptation, one should begin by searching in the spaces opened by the near misses of these synonymous or slant-rhymed counterparts: Franz for Fassbinder's other Franzes; Franz (or Léopold) for Fassbinder himself, or for Ozon himself; Léopold and his dream double; Franz and Véra and so on—as well as in whatever further queerings, alterations, or perversions the film executes on its source material, namely, in Ozon's distorted doubling of Fassbinder.

Body Language

For to whatever extent these variations on a theme *do* allow Ozon's characters to operate Butlerian catachresis on their prescribed roles, it is also true that Ozon—working with and against the script he has inherited from Fassbinder—alternates, not unlike Franz, between autonomy and obedience. In the same interview where he had averred the necessity of including the suffering trans body to give the film heft, Ozon attests to cutting these moments short, a kind of coitus interruptus, in order to frustrate the viewer and leave things open to the imagination.[69] Admittedly, the sexual rituals here are pretty vanilla: though Léopold claims that Véra likes it rough, causing them to avert their eyes abashedly, and suggests to Franz that he also gets off on bondage, the most we see in the film is a little light spanking, politely requested and given with Anna's vocal consent.

But while *Gouttes d'eau*, despite extended nudity, is admittedly not as graphic nor nearly as violent as many of Ozon's productions, nor really even any more explicit than standard French cinematic fare, these carefully choreographed scenes, with their quasi-sadomasochistic roleplaying, do deviate from Fassbinder's original script, where sex is never directly depicted. (Granted, one can only guess at Fassbinder's mise-en-scène had he ever chosen to produce the play himself.) Turning back to this interview, it is elucidating to compare its claim to the corporeal to what the filmmaker has to say about the deceptive frivolity of the dance number with which the film climaxes: "It was necessary for the bodies to let off steam before the tragic end. I wanted it to explode, for there to be a moment of release, of apotheosis, of bodily liberation for these people who never stop talking."[70] Similarly, in the protracted dialogue between Franz and Léopold, which begins to feel teasingly drawn out after the viewer has realized where it is leading, Ozon makes a point of emphasizing that neither Franz nor his partner speak in the dream: Franz watches the man in the overcoat undress in absolute silence. Repeatedly in this initial dialogue and, indeed, throughout the film, the characters thematize the comparative value of conversation (which invariably leads to conflict) versus sex (which, until the last act, at least, seems to go off without a hitch). Taken together these assertions imply that the three primary interventions Ozon makes into his source material—the insertion of the trans feminine element, the musical number, and the love scenes—all rely on physicality as a measure of the film's meaningfulness. That the fanciful dance sequence would be included in this trio of additions indicates that Ozon is reconfiguring the relationship between camp artifice and the body abject that has so confused his critics: directly preceding the largely unseen orgy, the tongue-in-cheek but not unsexy samba performed by all four characters proves a necessary supplement to the lacking obscenity that would otherwise underwrite the provocation and the purchase of Ozon's work in a smuttier mode.

Though I have never seen it remarked upon, this sequence itself borrows allusively from a moment in *13 Monden*, which in turn tropes overtly on the Jerry Lewis and Dean Martin comedy *You're Never Too Young* (1955). Attempting to reconnect with the former lover, Anton Saitz (Gottfried John), for whom they changed their sex, Elvira is, as Silverman puts it, "obliged to participate in a game of mimicry": in what is clearly a frequently rehearsed ritual, Saitz and his business associates prance and march around in imitation of the movie playing on a television set in the background.[71] As Silverman interprets it, this sequence works to dissociate Elvira—despite their "predilection for sexual masquerade"—from "the world of gay camp" and displaces it instead onto Anton, who, camping up Jerry Lewis's already campy gestures, "grossly exaggerates this . . . dimension of the performance, so that what in effect emerges is a heterosexual imitation of gay camp."[72] To my eye, though, what is amplified is not so much the effeminacy of the shenanigans as their manic, almost lurid eccentricity: what comes across as goofy in the first performance is revealed to be grotesque by its repetition. Camp, in this case, would not be a matter of lightheartedly resignifying stigma but now instead is a matter of reabjectifying the body at play. The screwball comedy, in Fassbinder's deft hands, becomes a horror show.

Silverman describes *You're Never Too Young* as if it were a cross-dressing farce, and surely, beyond even the habitually winking homoeroticism of Martin's and Lewis's onscreen coupling, there are elements of that genre in the premise of this number, where Lewis, posing as a young boy, is welcomed to a school for girls. The very structuring conceit of the film is, in fact, one of (failed) passing, with a parrotlike Lewis impersonating any number of other characters, including a(n in)credible transgender imitation over the telephone: screwing up his face to demonstrate great exertion, Lewis is dubbed in this instant by a woman's voice, itself exaggeratedly aping 1950s upper-class WASPy femininity. Sitting at a switchboard, which he makes a frantic show of not knowing how to operate, Lewis points up the felicity of this enactment as doubly reliant on technological constraint: divorcing sound from image as Fassbinder does with Elvira in the slaughterhouse, here the filmic medium briefly exploits the very disembodiment that defines the technical limitation of telephony. And yet, through the extreme and exaggeratedly effortful camp of his mannerisms in this moment, the dizzying relay of simulacra this produces—a woman speaking for a man speaking as a woman—condenses and anchors itself precisely in the performing body. It is fundamental to this gimmick that if Lewis successfully poses as a woman in the plot, he does not do so for the viewer. Through the transparency of such failed passing and the technological restrictions of this ruse, he exercises metaleptic agency and fleetingly takes control of the determinant cinematic apparatus: autonomy emerges counterintuitively as a stepping-outside-of-oneself and allowing oneself to be ventriloquized from elsewhere.

The sequence quoted in *13 Monden* is another such moment where Lewis manipulates the machinery of spectacle: he is not so much imitating the schoolgirls here, as Silverman summarizes it, but is in fact *leading* the welcoming march (over Dean Martin's initial protest and after a quick apprenticeship where he follows his straight man's footsteps) through a series of increasingly absurd improvised bourrées. Rather undercutting Anton's arbitrary and mercurial sovereignty, in *13 Monden* this ostensibly straight man is, then, only *emulating* authority—and only after his own hysteric objection, all part of the performance, that he doesn't want to play along. Intercut with close-ups on the distorted television image, the dance routine proceeds in spurts and starts, with Elvira, clearly no Ginger Rogers, smiling but struggling to keep up in heels, a feather boa trailing dangerously around their ankles, an open handbag dangling cumbersomely from a bent elbow and a photograph of their younger self as Erwin held precariously in hand. When Elvira finally tumbles to the ground, the misstep almost seems intended to play as intentional: the forward foot appears prepared to take Elvira's body weight before it is drawn back suddenly to cause a slow, rather controlled collapse. Curiously, this elicits not reprimand but praise from Anton; it also seems to jog his memory: pensively, he mutters the name Erwin and, holding their hat as if against a strong wind, Elvira nods and apologizes.

This could be interpreted as an instance of exposure, as the trappings of femininity falling apart under the strain of Elvira's effort, revealing Erwin underneath. But the true moment of recognition comes a few seconds later. Elvira in fact steps to the side, all but entirely out of the frame, and skips the finale, where Anton leaps into his chauffer's (Günther Kaufmann's) arms an instant after the television close-up showing Lewis and Martin executing the same cradle lift. Almost imperceptibly dismantling the illusion of absolute synchronicity, this parallel editing intimates its own underlying limitation: the inevitable imperfection of repetition. It is the name Elvira that Anton calls out now, snapping his fingers and pointing almost toward the viewer, since all that is visible of Elvira is an elbow and a few wisps of feather, so dark that they blend into the border of the screen. Identification, even a measure of extratextual interpellation, succeeds by breaking the fourth wall: Elvira comes back into being by sidestepping prescribed protocol, through a disappearance from the image locating their body as liminal to the film's diegesis. This moment provides concrete substantiation of the conclusion reached above that if the obligingly transgendered body does indeed provide any indexicality or referentiality, if it makes itself available to the ventriloquizing process of allegorization, it does so by absenting itself, in another sense, from the filmic imaginary.

With these cinematic precedents established, we can turn, finally, to the significance of the surprising line dance in Ozon's *Goutte d'eau*, which, in an apparent paradox, fully sublimates the film's escapades into pure fantasy precisely through its recourse to the corporeal. Richard Dyer has influentially maintained that the genre of movie musical is at base utopian—an argument adapted (and quite tellingly so for the current inquiry) by Linda Williams to apply to the "utopian 'numbers'" or sex scenes of pornographic films.[73] But if Schilt, in his monograph on Ozon, still holds out some hope for the idealistic mutability occasioned by the erotic games in *Gouttes d'eau*, the dance routine nevertheless disappoints: "It lays bare the very artifice of this entertainment piece, first, by letting the sequence 'sneak up on us' (we know we are *not* watching a musical) and, second, by exposing Franz (who dies shortly thereafter) as unable to keep up with the beat."[74] Schilt goes so far as to attribute this clumsiness to the actor, Malik Zidi, himself and takes its correspondence to the character to be a happy coincidence; similarly, he argues that "Sagnier's and Thomson's wide smiles betray the fact that the actresses, not the characters, are dancing here."[75] With a nod to Susan Sontag, Handyside agrees that there is a kind of scare-quoting at work in this performance of Tony Holiday's "Tanze Samba mit mir" (Dance the samba with me; 1977) through which the spectacle places itself under erasure, thereby allowing the actors' bodies to emerge in parallel with the characters they portray: "By setting Fassbinder's text in an imagined 1970s' West Germany, thus deliberately underlining its artifice by contrast to contemporary France, Ozon further distances the viewer. We never forget that we are watching actors performing, as well as characters suffering. This emphasis on performance underlines the film as Camp."[76] In short, despite—or perhaps rather precisely by dint of—its estranging contrivance, the dance sequence becomes so ecstatic, so beside itself, that it self-destructs and breaks through to the profilmic as would, at least ostensibly, the wounded corpus delicti in another filmic idiom.

Accordingly, as a diegetic and narrative rupture, the sequence feels almost external to the film. Although the source of the music can be intuited and will be revealed when Léopold abruptly takes the needle off the record, it begins acousmatically—and with a tinny quality that sounds extradiegetic—over a sequence of close-ups of the characters' asses, each in turn, bobbing along to the beat. The impression that this is more of a music video than a moment in the plot is heightened by the fact that the sequence is reproduced unmodified and in its entirety as the French trailer for *Gouttes d'eau.* (The American version adds some titles for context and to give a sampling of critical praise but is otherwise almost identical.) At once distinct from the film and implied, for marketing purposes at least, to be an apt synecdochic distillation, this interlude appears to make good on the promise of both flawless repeatability and perfect, unencumbered fantasy denied in the earlier sexual roleplaying and its variations on a dream.

If it weren't for Franz's slipups, that is. While he has to keep a careful eye on Léopold to remind himself of the steps, Franz only really breaks form twice: first mistakenly jumping forward as the others fall back into line and again, in the only clearly gendered moment of the choreography, when he misses his final turn and, with visible hesitation, decides to wait to pivot with the women instead—an error Parent and Xanthos take to be another sign of his gradual feminization.[77] Silverman, on the other hand, understands Elvira's blundering dancing in *13 Monden* as an indication that they "cannot be assimilated to homosexuality [nor to] heterosexuality"—an argument one might neatly apply to the bisexual Franz.[78] But to do so would ignore the fact that Franz does not manage, other than in death, to escape his homosexual subservience to Léopold nor would it account for the retransposition of this trope from the trans body back onto the off-straight male. In fact, while we are given no sense as to when or how the characters have learned this choreography, it does seem to be Véra who is the instigator of the dance—which is cut to elliptically after they ask if they can put on a record, as if permission had been granted to control the montage also. It is a subtle but significant elision that enhances the antinaturalistic effect of the musical intrusion while also revealing-by-concealing what is at stake in its filmic heritage. The original dance tutorial of *You're Never Too Young*, in turns learned and taught by Jerry, was an exercise in instruction. So too the stumbling steps haltingly copied by Elvira, thinking on their feet, as it were, in *13 Monden.* What is lacking in *Gouttes d'eau* is the leader: unlike Jerry or Anton, Léopold stands in line with the other dancers, singled out only by his self-serious charisma. The uncharacteristic elusiveness of this particular allusion in a film that otherwise foregrounds its cinephilic references suggests that the acculturation is now complete, that conformity has been internalized, and that these moves, whatever they might signify, are known in advance.

And yet Franz struggles. Given Ozon's ambivalence with regard to his status as a gay filmmaker, his habitual resistance to identity politics, it is telling that only Franz—Fassbinder's and Ozon's on-screen double and debatably the gayest character in the film—would have such difficulty toeing the line. While Léopold is the one who openly declares that he prefers sex with boys, this is not borne out by his behavior: in the final scenes he unmistakably favors Anna, his newest acquisition, over either of the others. He is further masculinized—and thus, by the law of stereotype, heterosexualized—by his patriarchal bent and his position as the film's sole sexual penetrator. Instead, narrative identification has wandered in this instance from the daddy to the otherwise off-straight twink.

Franz's gangling awkwardness in this moment perturbs the utopian illusion of the ludic camp excursus: his disobedient body renarrativizes this outwardly incidental diversion, bringing us back to the text, pointing toward the previous iterations of its missing intertexts and serving as a reminder of the processes of discipline and indoctrination the pageantry of the digression would otherwise appear to disavow. Narratologically, finally, the disruptive nature of Franz's dancing has the symbolic effect of suspending the substitution game by which queer identities take the place of or morph effortlessly into one another. Failed passing interferes with fungibility. Inadvertently stepping out of and then back into the line leading from Anna (in her early stage of sexual apprenticeship) to Véra (in their wretched existential enslavement), Franz interrupts its trajectory: situated among these alternative possibilities, cis male homosexuality, by now old hat, regains its subversive function and is, in a sense, requeered, its dissidence playfully restored.

If Franz's failed passing in this instance and his ultimate refusal to become Véra interrupt the semiological exchangeability of queer identities toward which Ozon's work so often seems to tend, this is also true of the film on the whole and its elaboration of the category of gay male identity. Flouting the internal demand of Franz's dream that it repeat without variation, *Gouttes d'eau sur pierres brûlantes* stresses the difference inherent to same-sex desire. This impossibility of self-correspondence undermines the sameness Léopold celebrates in homosexuality, with repercussions also for the comparability of this category as it congeals across film history: like Franz's faltering participation in the line dance, Ozon's participation in the tradition of gay cinema he traces back to Fassbinder at once perpetuates and perverts it.

As if responding to those who critique his contributions to queer cinema as too smoothly generic, the sharp incongruity of this intermission, embodied in Franz's endearing klutziness, undercuts its own surface escapism and utopianism. In my chapters on Genet I argued that self-erasure is a compensatory mechanism for the impossibility of complete self-abstraction or self-aestheticization—themselves seemingly intended to redress the impossibility of self-coincidence. Returning to *Gouttes d'eau*, for Asibong, the "preposterous dance sequence . . . takes the film's anti-naturalism to its climax. Ozon's predilection for the cinematic creation of a sense of life performed rather than lived can be helpfully understood as . . . a desire to create a world in which characters have immersed themselves so deeply in fantasy and ritual that, rather as in a Genet play, their very surroundings have taken on the air of overt and unashamed spectacle."[79] But if *Gouttes d'eau* evokes the bewildering, if ultimately futile, role reversals and theatrical mises en abyme of *Les bonnes* (*The Maids*, 1947) or *Le balcon* (*The Balcony*, 1956), it recalls their doomed endings as well: its final frames are of Véra pressed against a window they cannot open, trapped in this apartment with Franz's cooling body. Although shot from outside the building, the sound quality does not change: as if to make clear that this was filmed in studio, we hear Véra fumbling at the window as if we were still inside the apartment ourselves until the camera begins to dolly out and the diegetic sound gives way to Françoise Hardy's "Träume" (Dreams, 1970), which continues over the closing credits. Released by the French chanteuse only in Germany, the song speaks of the illusiveness but also of the formative nature of fantasy: it begins on a note of disenchantment but ends with the ambivalent injunction to see our dreams "With other eyes . . . As they often steer our thoughts / Onto the paths / That we then follow." Oriented as we are by the tropes of received reveries, all that can be done is to give them yet another turn.

In einem Jahr mit 13 Monden also concludes with a corpse, predictably enough Elvira's, and a song about dreams: Connie Francis's "Schöner fremder Mann" (1961), adapted from her international pop hit "Someone Else's Boy" (1961). The German title—which could be translated as *handsome stranger* or, verbatim, *handsome foreign man*—puns on the idiom *fremdgehen*, which means to cheat or to fool around on someone; if this *Schlager* (a piece of sentimental, light pop) recounts a dream of infidelity, it also hints at the deceptiveness of fantasy. With his own Genetian flair for betrayal, Fassbinder ends his film with a verse not present in the original version—"The time will come / When my dream will finally / Become reality"—but lets the record skip repeatedly over the last word, stuttering out "*Wirklichkeit*" (reality) a half a dozen times, insisting on the realization of the fantasy while at once allowing it to dissolve into a demonic echo chamber.

Ozon opts instead for a hall of mirrors. Working in Fassbinder's trademark visual idiom, the orgy is first depicted only indirectly, acousmatically, with the camera trained on Franz's countenance as he peeps through the bedroom doorway, thereby aligning the audience with his perspective. The next shot frames Franz in the trifold bathroom vanity—troping on a bit of filmic vocabulary reminiscent of a kaleidoscopic mirror scene in *13 Monden* (and countless other occasions in Fassbinder) but also, and more distinctly, on the conclusion to Werner Schroeter's *Malina* (1991), where the partitions between panes of glass cause the triplicate reflection to resemble a film strip (see figs. 13–14).[80] Emboldening the interpellative and identificatory gambit, Franz looks directly into the mirror and, through it, straight into the camera: the viewer is summoned into the film and, just as when Anton points to an offscreen Elvira, asked momentarily to inhabit this body.

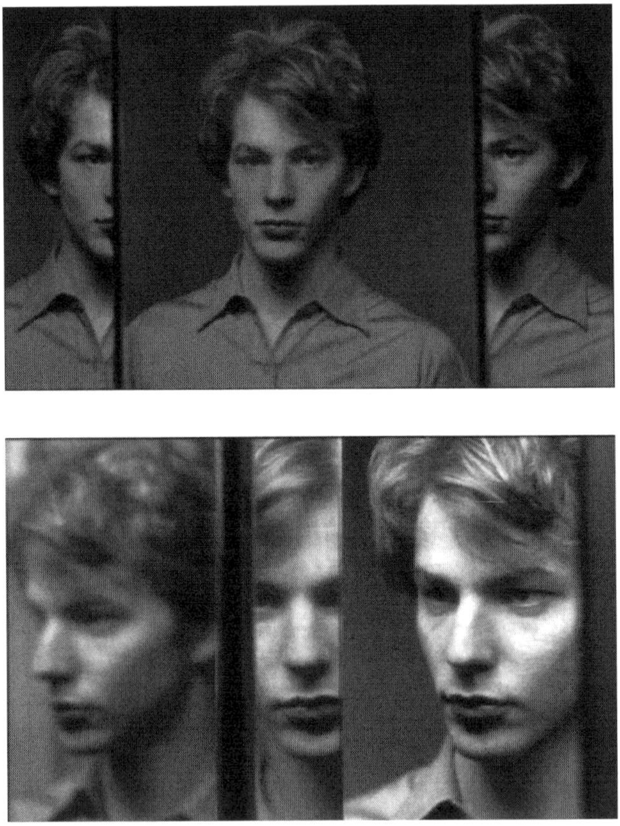

Figs. 13–14. Franz (Malik Zidi) at the mirror in *Gouttes d'eau sur pierres brûlantes* (*Water Drops on Burning Rocks*, dir. François Ozon, 2000).

The transcendence into a realm of incarnated but nonetheless chimeric cinematic make-believe thereby subtly established, Ozon proceeds to a cartoonish assassination of Léopold, shot in the forehead by Franz, whose maniacal expression, somewhere between a grin and a grimace, exchanges glances with the shocked faces of Anna and Véra, looking also directly into the camera, as if accusing the audience of murder. The subsequent cut back to the bathroom reveals this to be imaginary, though now Franz is shot from a less direct angle, rupturing his eye contact with the viewer, which is preserved only partially and only fleetingly in a sliver of mirror that seems to be casting back the reflection of another reflection. It is from this abstracted perspective that we watch him remove the bottle of poison from the medicine cabinet.

At no point do we see him swallow its contents: unlike the fantasized murder of Léopold, complete with a tidy bullet wound, the action leading up to the actual death in the film's diegesis is never visualized. As was the gay shower scene in *Une nouvelle amie*, Franz's most rebellious act is included only under erasure; even so, that shower and this bullet are given an embodiment not granted to the most important plot point of *Gouttes d'eau*: we are presented with a graphic image of a gunshot that is merely imaginary but are provided no visual evidence of the real poison being taken, although this constitutes the film's most decisive act. His suicide is the closest Franz comes to exercising metaleptic agency: what has *not* happened rhymes better with the apparatus of cinematic phantasmagoria than what has. Instead, we are obliged to take Franz's word for it when he tells Véra he has poisoned himself and to wait for his cadaver for confirmation.

When all is said and done, Véra rushes to retrieve their coat from Franz, exposing underneath a pallid physique matching their own in its frailty, before deciding to cover it again. If, by cloaking Franz in this feminine attire, Véra proleptically foreshadows Claire's role in *Une nouvelle amie*, the gesture also anticipates the same nearly necrophiliac longing (after confirming that he finds them attractive, Véra had just suggested to Franz that they attempt to build a life together) to locate stable selfhood in the body. And yet this funereal rite also suspends the principle of incorporated self-identity through a condensation of substitutions to which the body proves susceptible: Ozon intercuts Anna's and Léopold's continued lovemaking with the shots of Franz lying down on the floor to die and, a moment later, going limp, as if equating these physical acts and suggesting that Anna has fully supplanted Franz, who had himself replaced Véra, in Léopold's life.

Shrouding Franz in apparel becoming a drag queen, Véra consummates the repeated derealization into cinematic fantasy leading up to this moment: the dance routine, the mirror scene, Léopold's imagined corpse. It is ultimately unclear whether Véra—their name, like Claire's, ringing with visible truth—is a witness to physical evidence or to mere cinematic projection: despite these attempted transfers, Ozon cannot manage convincingly to collapse the dissonance of drag into the consonance of the trans identity of someone like Virginia in *Une nouvelle amie*, just as Genet's Our Lady ultimately testifies to the impossibility of fantasized ipseity he represents. Véra's frilly overcoat offers meager protection to Franz's remains, only an air of exquisite ridiculousness. And this is all there is to attest to his one act of true autonomy, his suicide, which is otherwise never imaged. Camp abjection has turned itself inside out: the mirage of self-sovereignty is no longer situated in camp performativity but instead in the abject body par excellence—the corpse.

So much for corporeal proof. As I've been arguing throughout this chapter, the evidentiary aspiration invested in the filmic body has a tendency to collapse into its opposite: moments of mise en abyme or of formal meta-awareness exposing the narratological and technological apparatus structuring the cinematic imaginary. This makes sense once we recognize that the desire for the extradiegetic (indexical, autobiographical, political, or otherwise) shares an underlying affinity with metaleptic narrative intrusion. Always on the fringes of the text, promising an extratextuality they will never deliver, Fassbinder's and Ozon's characters assert agency by giving it up: acknowledging and exploiting constraint, they escape the narrative in which they are embedded only by absenting themselves from it.

But like sexuality itself, Ozon's cinema remains governed by a desire for *other bodies*, including other bodies of work. As if in acknowledgment of his debt to the legacy in which his work is embedded, the final line Ozon gives to Léopold, repeated throughout the film to the lover thirty years his junior, reverberates across the three decades separating Fassbinder from Ozon: "Toi, tu as besoin de moi" (It's you who needs me). If indeed meant as a tribute, it's one with an oedipal, patricidal sting to it inasmuch as it is an unfaithful rendition of the original. Fassbinder's play had ended with an erotic affirmation: Véra responding to Léopold's invitation back into the bedroom with the words, "O ja" (Oh, yes).[81] That Léopold's surname is Bluhm betrays that Fassbinder is also working according to a template—and a paradigmatic one at that: James Joyce's recycling of the Ulysses myth. (This passing likeness gains the full force of identity in the film, since the sole time the name is spoken aloud it is indistinguishably homophonic with a French pronunciation of Bloom.) Echoing the amorous final words of Molly Bloom, Joyce's adulterous Penelope, Fassbinder's Véra insinuates the ecstatic self-suspension of their predecessor's jouissance.

With his fatalistic rewriting, Ozon makes this ending his own less by inserting anything original than by turning to an image, as he does in attaching the trans feminine trope to Véra, from elsewhere in Fassbinder's corpus: another jilted lover, Marlene (Irm Hermann), with her palm pressed against a window in *Petra* (figs. 15–16)—which Ozon has most recently, and very loosely, reimagined as *Peter von Kant*.[82] There's nothing new under the sun. And yet, what could be more faithful to the infidelity of a Molly Bloom than this promiscuous repurposing? There is an acceptance of fate, an amor fati again almost Nietzschean, perhaps even a sort of freedom, to this embrace of the eternal return of the not-quite-same.

Conclusion: Transacculturation

For a film set in Cologne, Ozon's more recent feature, *Peter von Kant* (2022), contains, like *Gouttes d'eau*, surprisingly little German—but its few phrases are significant. As its key acoustic leitmotif, the film repeatedly returns to a German-language rerecording, interpreted by the actor Isabelle Adjani, of *Querelle*'s ballad: "Jeder tötet, was er liebt" ("Each Man Kills the Thing He Loves"). (Dance numbers only slightly less surreal than the one in *Gouttes d'eau* punctuate *Peter von Kant* at important moments.) The appearance at the end of the film by one of Fassbinder's leading ladies, Hanna Schygulla, gives gravity to the extended homage to the earlier filmmaker but also marks

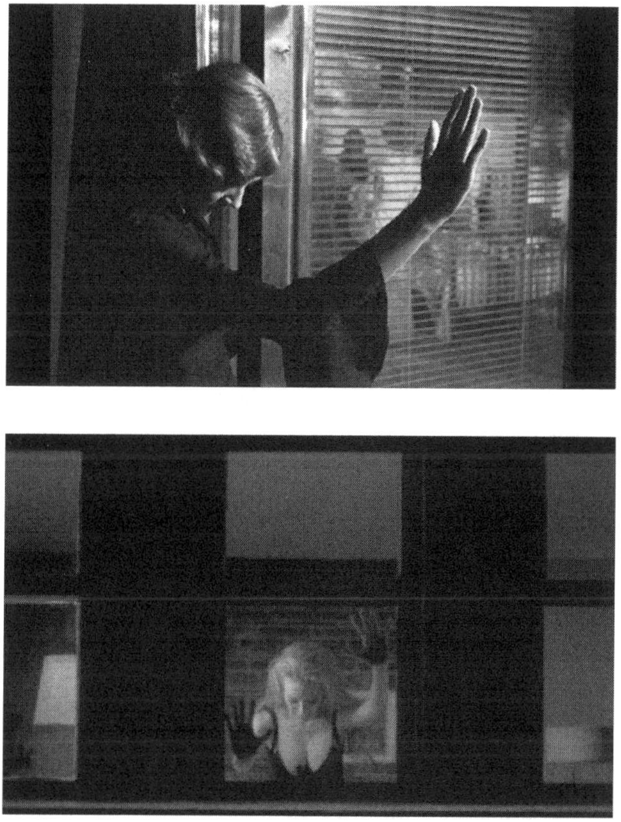

Figs. 15–16. Marlene (Irm Hermann) at the window in *Die bitteren Tränen der Petra von Kant* (*The Bitter Tears of Petra von Kant*, dir. Rainer Werner Fassbinder, 1972), and Véra (Anna Thomson) at the window in *Gouttes d'eau sur pierres brûlantes* (*Water Drops on Burning Rocks*, dir. François Ozon, 2000).

a difference: her heavily accented French (as unremarked-upon as Verá's in *Gouttes d'eau*) gives way on occasion to a native German that none of the other characters seem to notice as incongruous. A final line of German, merely the evocation of a title, is delivered early on by the Fassbinder figure himself, the titular Peter von Kant (Denis Ménochet), who laments the fate of the rejected screenplay for none other than *Tropfen auf heiße Steine*. This self-allusion by way of prolonged allusion to another auteur at once places Ozon's work into the context of Fassbinder's and appropriates Fassbinder's work into Ozon's—even his self-citation has an accent, fails to pass.

The American DVD release of *Water Drops on Burning Rocks* contains among its otherwise minimal special features a screen of "Sing-a-long Subtitles" with the lyrics to Holiday's "Tanze Samba mit mir" provided both in

German (though sloppily, without diacritics) and in English translation. The same feature provides an English version of the otherwise unsubtitled Heinrich Heine poem "The Lorelei," recited twice by Franz in the film. Both texts are about seduction and cultural borrowing: Holiday's is a German-language version of an Italian song (Raffaella Carrà's "A far l'amore comincia tu," also from 1977) popularizing a Brazilian genre, whereas Franz abandons his Heine soliloquy in both instances with its evocation of the Rhein, the emblematic border between France and Germany.

But that the DVD extra is billed as a singalong rather than as a dance tutorial (especially given the insistent imperative of the song's German title and lyrics) seems to serve as an invitation to recitation for the viewer as well, highlighting, perhaps, that this poem, too, is about the inescapability of received tropes:

> I wonder what it presages—
> I am so sad at heart;
> A legend of bygone ages
> Haunts me and will not depart.[83]

Franz's given name, after all, aligns him not only with François Ozon or with the various Franzes of Fassbinder's cinema, but with France itself: more specifically, with France in a German idiom. The relative inflections to the words *earnest* and *sincere* in English can be felt, I've long held, in their respective cognates: there is a somewhat greater gravity to the German *ernst* (serious, grave) as opposed to the French *sincère* (honest, genuine). I might submit that if Franz spoils the orgy and the dance number it is because he is given to an earnestness of this more stereotypically Teutonic variety. In French he might be described with ironic condescension as *un brave garçon*—loosely: a good boy. In German, *brav* means obedient. In any event, the solemn reprisal of this Heine text is delivered to the mirror, directly preceding the fantasized killing of Léopold, as if the frank, if momentary, suspension of the linguistic illusion (the unacknowledged incongruity of these characters speaking French in a German setting) were necessary for the escape into the visual cinematic imaginary.

Here and throughout his career Ozon raises the question of cultural translatability as a foil for the universalizable potential of his cinema, of its characters' identities and experiences. With regard to the film's title, Ozon errs on the side of evocative but somewhat unintelligible literalness: Schilt points out that Fassbinder's drama already played catachrestically on the German idiom *ein Tropfen auf den heißen Stein*: a drop of water on hot stone.[84] (Though they mean slightly different things, the English-language equivalent would be *a drop in the bucket*, the French *une goutte d'eau dans l'océan*.) Adopting and adapting an expression meant to convey something so inconsequential as to evaporate on contact, Ozon concedes, perhaps, to the futility of the sexual experimentation the film stages. But the title might also suggest, once more, that a certain measure of self-sublimation is necessary to the process of becoming significant.

For, on the whole, concerns about Ozon's genre films do not seem indicative of any illegibility but rather of a fear over the loss of cultural specificity, as if to imply that the French or more generally European appropriation of genre is not catachrestic or iconoclastic enough. Despite his complaint over icy French intellectualism, Asibong ultimately concludes that "Ozon's films and their numerous representations of sexual desire are best understood . . . neither as symptoms of specifically French *fin de millénaire* drives to shock audiences through explicitness, nor as ever-proliferating artefacts from a reassuringly established French gay male subculture. Instead, Ozon . . . persistently disrupts his audience's expectations of what could possibly be meant by coherence of either sexuality or subjectivity." For Asibong, Ozon thus belongs "less to nation-, gender- and sexuality-specific cinematic contexts than to a potentially international tendency, the legacy of intellectual and political struggles emerging from Europe and the Americas from the mid-1960s onward, toward the constant affirmation of radically unmoored, provisional, and postmodern sexual behaviors, affiliations, and identifications."[85] Blurring the borders of once-discreet sexual identities in order to access a broader audience, Ozon also calls into question the very category of French or even European art cinema vis-à-vis Hollywood studio productions and American cultural paradigms.

For Armond White, writing again for *Out Magazine*, this is precisely what gives Ozon's work its purchase. In a review of the lush period piece *Frantz* (2016), White gushes that Ozon "makes queer movie conventions a thing of the past."[86] The Franco-German coproduction is itself a remake, in nostalgic black and white, of the 1932 film *Broken Lullaby*, made by another German émigré, Ernst Lubitsch, who in turn adapts Maurice Rostand's drama about the aftermath of the First World War, *L'homme que j'ai tué* (*The Man I Killed*, as the British release of Lubitsch's film translates the title), from the year previous. Revolving around the hidden guilt of a French soldier, Adrien Rivoire (Pierre Niney, whose abs alone are worth the price of admission), for the viewer familiar with Ozon's work, the film teases a gay love story as its secret center. But in the end this subtext proves to be a diversion from what turns out to be a strictly heterosexual affair—although one orbiting, as in *Une nouvelle amie*, around a necrophiliac desire for a perished third party, the eponymous Frantz (Anton von Lucke), whom Adrien has killed in battle. As White sees it, "Frantz flips that old Hollywood irony of gay filmmakers disguising their inclinations behind the emotional and stylistic flourishes of heterosexual stories (women's pictures)."[87] Rather than heterosexual melodrama allegorizing the love that dare not speak its name, here the anticipated homoerotic subtext gradually erases itself to become more broadly meaningful.

And yet there are traces: traces of difference and of *différance*. Fan notes the "Derridaesque word game" in *13 Monden* of Anton Saitz's adamance that his name is spelled Saitz and not Seitz: an exclusively orthographic distinction, like Bluhm for Bloom or, for that matter, Frantz for Franz.[88] This added but inaudible *t* marks another iteration of an identity-in-difference, perpetually linked to the lineage from which it departs. The iconicity of Ozon's European intertexts situates him squarely within a once-dominant European-American heritage, in large part the exile tradition of filmmakers like Ophüls and Lubitsch. So far, this book has shared this leaning toward predominantly French and German source materials, but if Ozon's cinema makes good, for better or for worse, on Fassbinder's unfulfilled promise of a European Hollywood, it does so by renegotiating the minoritarian as it relates to various forms of cultural hegemony. In order to interrogate both the generational and geographic resonances of this cultural diplomacy, so to speak, this study's final chapter will turn to the young Québécois filmmaker, Xavier Dolan, who, despite his relative linguistic marginality (working in a regionally specific French), has often been read as symptomatic of a nonidentarian, postnational, and postgay sensibility.

Chapter 6

Not Nothing

Xavier Dolan's Vanishing Gay Aesthetic

Perhaps more than any other figure treated in this book, Xavier Dolan appears to embody a fantasy of self-determination: the figure of the queer prodigy who has created himself entirely ex nihilo. His directorial debut, a feature-length production written before he even came of age, won multiple awards at Cannes while Dolan was still shy of twenty. Like Rainer Werner Fassbinder, Dolan has starred in many of his own films, leading to incessant charges of narcissism now more generational in resonance than homophobic—though it is surely likely that many of the complaints about Dolan's millennial inclinations serve as a cover for closeted judgments about perceived gay vanity.[1]

It is also possible that a good deal of the irritation at the wunderkind's hubris has to do not only with his coming out of nothing but also, so to speak, out of nowhere. A Québécois director working primarily in his native joual dialect of French, Dolan has, over the past decade or so, consistently been lauded for his locally set films and panned for his attempts in more widely spoken idioms.[2] His only production to feature a cast of European French actors, *Juste la fin du monde* (*It's Only the End of the World*, 2016), was met with general critical disappointment; his more recent English-language effort, *The Life and Times of John F. Donovan* (2018), seems universally considered the worst of his career. (For what it's worth, while I personally do find the latter atrociously clumsy, I was quite taken with the former.) On the whole, critics and audiences seem to require of Dolan that he negotiate between the local and the global, the minoritarian and the mainstream, while always remembering where he comes from—or, put more bluntly: without ever daring to forget his place.

True at once of his status as a Québécois and as a young gay man, this disciplinary demand is compounded by Dolan's participation in a postidentitarian and even postnational millennial episteme that provokes, in equal measure, panic and resignation over a perceived decay of cultural specificity. Attending to the question of origins, this chapter will examine how Xavier

Dolan's repeated depiction of motherhood—specifically as it manifests in his directorial debut *J'ai tué ma mère* (*I Killed My Mother*, 2009) and in his most successful film, *Mommy* (2014)—betrays an underlying reflection on gay style. I noted in passing in chapter 3 that the repudiation of the maternal is the defining characteristic of the abject as theorized by Julia Kristeva. Marking the moment of individuation (from the mother), a certain matricidal impulse is fundamental both to abjection and to the passage into subjectivity it makes possible. For Dolan as a filmmaker, what is thematized as an ambivalent abjection of the maternal proves necessary for his aesthetic maturation, for his coming into his own as an auteur. After offering a brief initial overview of bad taste as it relates to mothers in Dolan, I will examine how the director self-consciously mobilizes maternal kitsch as part of the reputedly more specifically homosexual variety of bad taste known as camp. Finally, I will suggest that Dolan's deployment of this camp sensibility enacts an unexpected form of *closeting*: allowing queer content to vanish behind an arguably commodified queer aesthetic that neither comes from nor recedes without resistance into nothing. This dynamic is rendered all the more poignant by Dolan's recent announcement of his intention to retire from making feature films, though not necessarily from filmmaking entirely—a decision that he emphatically characterizes as an expression of personal freedom.[3]

Maternal Kitsch

Vital to my line of argumentation is the observation that filial-maternal conflicts in Dolan often center around issues of taste. As Liz Czach summarizes the mother-son duo of the first film, Chantale, the mother, played by Anne Dorval, "is tacky, or as the Québécois put it, her home, behavior, and clothing could be described as *quétaine*—an adjective [connoting] something kitsch or lacking in refinement." Hubert, on the other hand, incorporated by Dolan himself, "clearly can't abide his mother's poor taste and his inability to love her as a son is imbedded in his dislike of her lifestyle. The conflict between them [lies] principally [in] this disjuncture in taste."[4] The film begins with Hubert—his face tightly framed in black and white, interspersed with extreme close-ups of his eyelashes fluttering and of his fingers as he picks at his cuticles—briefly and elliptically recounting his mounting difficulty with his mother. In illustration of this conflict, Dolan then transitions immediately to a visual inventory, now in vividly garish color, of the various articles of kitsch (mounted butterflies and Hummel figurines) adorning Chantale's home. (This debut was actually filmed in Dolan's childhood home, although he admits to having enhanced the tasteless appearance of the set.) These objects are now intercut with a slow-motion view of Chantale's mouth, again in extreme close-up, as she sloppily consumes a slice of orange and a sesame seed bagel with cream cheese, literalizing the notion of taste and rendering it grotesque through the association. That these shots are also framed through the son's perspective is made plain by repeated cuts to his exasperated eyes. The desire to kill off the mother in this first film is depicted as a crime of self-defense against an excruciating and suffocating overabundance of brash bad taste.

Dolan has stated publicly that if a feeling of matricidal animosity toward his mother animated his first feature, *Mommy* was intended, in a way, to avenge her. It is interesting to note, then, that the first conversation in *Mommy* between mother and son—Die (Dorval again) and Steve (Antoine Olivier Pilon this time)—also revolves around an aesthetic explicitly designated kitschy. Steve has just been expelled from boarding school for violent behavior, in a sense inverting the narrative trajectory of the first film, where Hubert is sent off to boarding school at the end of what might be considered the second act. Bringing Steve home, Die asks him not to judge her for the decor of their new rental and the surfeit of patterned upholsteries and wallpapers left there by the recently deceased previous tenant, whose taste Die describes as *quétaine*. With the tacky mother thus exorcised in *Mommy*, it is instead the son, Steve, who seems to have questionable taste, later gifting his mother kitschy knickknacks like porcelain elephants and the blingy necklace from which the film takes its title. Suspecting they are stolen, Die rejects these presents, provoking an outburst of violence to which I will return, but is nonetheless seen wearing the necklace later on, including in the film's most euphoric moment. This evolution is further solidified by Dolan's most recent film, *Matthias & Maxime* (2019), where it is the chosen mother (Micheline Bernard) rather than the biological mother (Dorval at her most abject yet as an aging and abusive alcoholic incapable of caring for herself) who exemplifies *quétaine* domesticity, now portrayed as nurturing through the lens of a more reparative camp. In *Mommy* the impression of an embrace of kitsch is reinforced by the willfully schmaltzy, late-nineties-nostalgic soundtrack[5] coupled with the inevitable assumption that this son, too, is at least in part a quasi-autobiographical representative for Dolan himself.

Dolan, who handles the costuming for his films personally, has emphasized that, if anything, the mother in *Mommy* dresses too young for her age, contrasting her taste with the vintage retro styles to which his female characters are more often inclined. Fulvia Massimi has noted, for instance, the "temporal drag" of the "kitsch extravaganza of Anne Dorval's clothing in *J'ai tué ma mère*" and other wardrobe choices throughout Dolan's work,[6] but this is nowhere more apparent than in a throwaway line at the beginning of his own not-about-AIDS film *Juste la fin du monde*, where the mother, seeking to appeal to her gay son's presumedly fabulous sense of fashion, is described as a *travelo*, a derogatory French term for a transvestite, linking her look explicitly to drag. Justifying her attire, she declares that "Louis loves fashion and color! Like all gays!" As Nick Rees-Roberts has it: "The transphobic slur . . . serves to acknowledge the more intertextual drag styles of some of

Dolan's mothers, whose looks, in true serial pop fashion, tend to resemble one another."[7] The same might be said of the maternal bit part played by Dorval in *Les amours imaginaires* (*Heartbeats*, 2010), whose futuristic look (blue wig, red-sequined dress) provokes an argument on fashion within an intimate queer kinship.

The plot of *Les amours imaginaires* involves a kind of chosen family—an unconsummated love triangle between two best friends, Francis (Dolan) and Marie (Monia Chokri), who fall for the same off-straight twink, Nicolas (Niels Schneider)—and would readily lend itself to an interpretation in which the fraternal affection between the two leads is the ballast that keeps Dolan's Francis from maturing into a stable homosexual relationship. Dorval's character, Désirée, is first seen dancing rather too sexily with her son Nicolas, provoking his suitors' jealousy and further cementing his position as the erotic object around whom the film turns. Adding to the impression of a family feud, the song playing in this scene, "Pass This On" (2003), by the Swedish brother-sister electronic duo The Knife, in fact begins with the lyrics, "I'm in love with your brother." That the band is best known for their song "Heartbeats" (2009), from which Dolan's film likely takes its international English-language title, invites further consideration of this chain of associations. (The title in French is likely an allusion to the 1998 song "Imaginary Love" by Dolan's queer compatriot Rufus Wainwright.) And, sure enough, the music video for "Pass This On"—which condenses the varied senses of *passing* as exchange or contagion, on the one hand, and as persuasive imitation, on the other—depicts a drag performer (Rickard Engfors) lip-syncing to the song in front of an audience who at first appear hostile and homophobic but end up merrily dancing along.

Himself a director of music videos, Dolan's enterprise is so song driven that it sometimes feels as if visual effects were an accompaniment to the soundtrack rather than the other way around.[8] Dolan's approach to the music in his films is not to sample it as, say, Quentin Tarantino does but rather to reinterpret it, almost as would a cover band. Through the tangential intertext of this particular cover, Dolan makes the marketing of queer content to a broader audience into a family affair: recognizably familial structures or symbolic implications of incestuous desire seem to operate as a cover for (frustrated) homosexuality.

The reprisal of "Pass This On" in *Les amours imaginaires* itself turns into a highly stylized stroboscopic dance video providing a visual history of homosexual aesthetics from Michelangelo's David to Jean Cocteau's *Le livre blanc* (*The White Book*, 1928) and comparing these flashing images to Nicolas's countenance in Francis's and Marie's mind's eyes (figs. 17–19). The point of such studied iconography is surely that Nicolas—whose role itself might be read as a near reprisal of the off-straight twink played briefly by Schneider in Dolan's first film—is a blank slate for the projection of fantasy, but I will have more to say on the extreme whiteness of these references, even

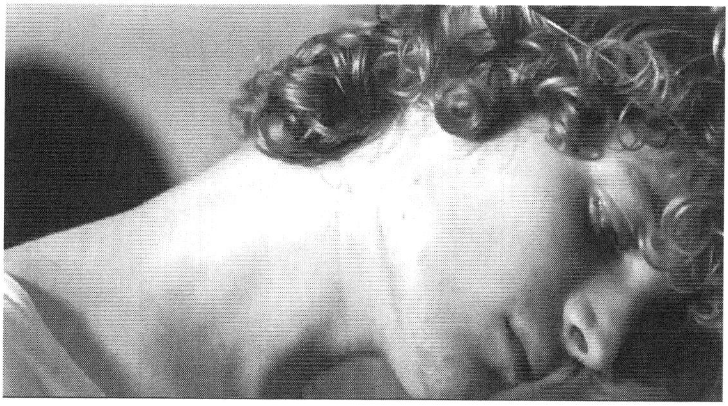

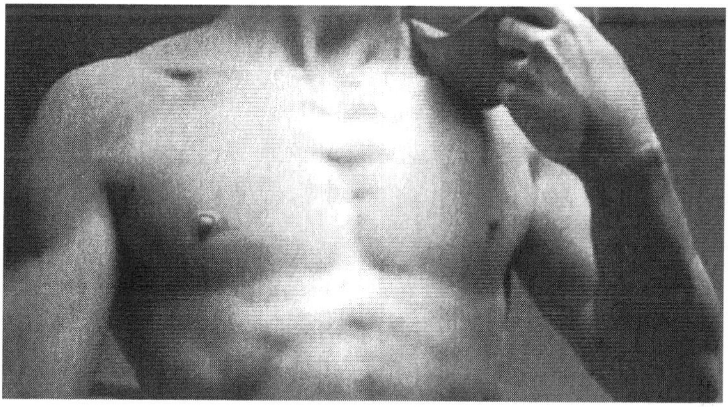

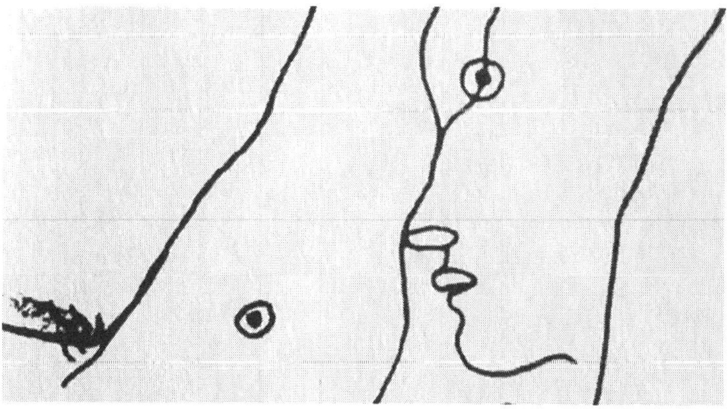

Figs. 17–19. Strobe effect as Nicolas (Niels Schneider) dances, interspersed with images of Michelangelo's David and homoerotic drawings from Jean Cocteau's *Le livre blanc* (*The White Book*, 1928). From *Les amours imaginaires* (*Heartbeats*, dir. Xavier Dolan, 2010).

when tinted blue, in the conclusion. If the transient focalization of the film through Francis's view at this and other moments perhaps emphasizes the authorial implications of a character played by the film's director, the strobe effect further recalls cinema's origins in stop-motion photography. It is as if Dolan were anxious to establish both his queer credentials and his prowess as a film geek.

The mise en abyme of this moment makes the preceding dispute over style all the more potentially metareflective, as Francis moves on from critiquing Désirée's outfit to disparaging Marie's vintage throwback wardrobe. Like Dolan's gracelessly aging mothers, Die or Désirée, Marie, whose name itself iconographically suggests motherhood, has committed the cardinal sin of camp: she is trying too hard. Overidentifying with her retro aesthetic, she forgets to signal her performance as ironic and instead becomes a sad self-parody. Ultimately, then, what I hope to have suggested through this cursory introductory survey of mothers in Dolan is that bad taste might serve in his work as a hidden index of his evolving attitude toward the representation of homosexuality and its attendant anxieties—or, to put it more pointedly: with this queer subtext brought to the surface, we might begin to recognize how these disputes over style increasingly reveal an ongoing negotiation with the codes and conventions of the quintessentially homosexual sensibility known as camp.

Notes on Camp

Judging by the rather baffling array of outfits to grace the red (or rather pink) carpet at the 2019 Met Gala, Camp: Notes on Fashion, the aesthetic remains ill understood and difficult to define. Providing a primer on the topic to accompany the event, the *New York Times* reminds us that "Susan Sontag defined camp as an aesthetic 'sensibility' that is plain to see but hard for most of us to explain: an intentional over-the-top-ness, a slightly (or extremely) 'off' quality, bad taste as a vehicle for good art."[9] The *Times* also produced a short explanatory video, more confusing than it is elucidating, featuring cultural figures ranging from performance artist Carmelita Tropicana to scholar Jack Halberstam.[10] Part of the aim of this effort is clearly to achieve an updated and more inclusive definition of camp—a mode of perpetual anachronism for an in crowd composed of social outcasts—for the present day. As playwright Charles Busch notes in the video, "It seems that camp today is not so based on white, gay male cultural references."[11]

But if there is a coherent view of camp that emerges from these interviews, it is that its heritage seems uncertain in an age when cultural borrowing or appropriation and a concomitant scare-quoting appear to have become *de règle*. As Halberstam has it: "Gay culture has penetrated mainstream culture and that means that it would be very hard to separate out camp from the mainstream."[12] Fashion designer Zaldy Goco agrees, extending the aesthetic question into epistemological territory: "We're just in a time of such artifice that it's like camp is all around us."[13] The dynamic of derealization I have been observing throughout this study is exacerbated, as many of the artists and critics in the video lament, by the always-already endlessly mediated feel of our current cultural moment. What, these figures ask, is to become of camp—succinctly defined by Richard Wollen as a "playful connoisseurship of kitsch"—in a postmodern episteme that also seems post-*taste*, in a waste heap of recycled cultural copies without originals, where no sense of style or refinement remains sacrosanct and thereby available for subversion.[14]

And although scholarship on a filmmaker as young and as recent as Dolan is, unsurprisingly, still relatively scant, limited largely to a single collection of essays edited by Andrée Lafontaine, I am already far from the first to consider Dolan's body of work within the context of a camp aesthetic and a camp ethos. Florian Grandena and Pascal Gagné have argued, for instance, that "not unlike camp," kitsch nostalgia contributes to the specifically queer (nonlinear, nonteleological) temporality of Dolan's films.[15] With direct reference to Sontag and an indirect allusion to Halberstam, Mercédès Baillargeon has spoken of Dolan's "camp aesthetics of failure" in her analysis of *Mommy*—though at times her fairly capacious understanding of camp self-consciousness and willful artifice seems to conflate it with a more universal, postmodern marriage between high taste and low, thereby divorcing the camp mode somewhat from the gay cultural milieu to which it is most endemic.[16]

Nick Rees-Roberts, on the other hand, opposes these two cultural phenomena, declaring that "in the case of Dolan, rather than adopting a glossy postmodern aesthetic to neutralize the impact of narrative by emptying it of its thematic content, his cinema of excess ambitiously deploys camp hyperbole and proliferating surfaces precisely as the formal means to embed individual stories of love, longing and desire within broader cultural questions of conflict, constraint, and power, in relation to contemporary societal issues of identity, language and location."[17] I want to highlight that an authenticating function is attributed to camp in this account, almost an indexical quality. If the postmodern, as it is described here, is all about style at the expense of substance, camp's unpolished offness is seen as an antidote to that anonymity and obscurity. I noted in chapter 4 how a young Todd Haynes occasionally conflates a gay sensibility with gay thematic content in discussing his first feature film. But camp, the gay sensibility par excellence, is understood here to serve a *renarrativizing* purpose. Its ever-imperfect fit and refusal to fade into the foreground, as it were, its peculiar form of failed passing, tells a story: one of situated identity. Recalling but also in a sense reversing the universalizing effect of François Ozon's intermittent earnestness, in the uncharted wasteland of globalized, postnational, postmodern culture, camp exaggeration and artifice, according to this perspective, act as a kind of *pharmakon*, the poison that is the cure, reasserting the queer cultural specificity of Dolan's filmmaking.[18]

But whether identity and identity politics are best understood as relating to inwardness or to outward expression is a matter of debate. Whereas Bill Marshall argues that Dolan's ostensible "eschewal of depth models in favour of a proliferation of surfaces . . . can be said even to generate a queer style,"[19] Rees-Roberts seems to hint that these deceptive surfaces betray a hidden depth, locating the "aesthetic queerness of Dolan's cinema" instead in an "overall decorative sensibility [that] is purposefully off, consciously designed to be so awful, it's good."[20] Such Genetian so-bad-it's-good-ness echoes, but with a slightly different resonance, Baillargeon's sentiment that "all of Dolan's aesthetic choices feed into a camp aesthetic based on exaggeration, over-stylization, and a self-conscious artificiality."[21] Clearly there is as of yet no consensus on the operation of camp in Dolan: it is at once understood to be an instrument of transgression and a symptom of conformity, a marker of queer cultural specificity but also of postmodern homogeneity, an obstinate aesthetic of brave, deliberate failure and a cheapening affinity for the merely cosmetic.

Perhaps the most critical stance, and also the one most pertinent to the present inquiry, is taken by Julianne Pidduck, who, in an essay titled "Queer Male Authorship and the Fabulous Leading Lady," rather faults Dolan for his "ostentatious performance of 'taste' " and for "cut[ting] a figure of queer male genius."[22] Proposing Dolan as the pinnacle of a "queer art of success" diametrically opposed to the queer art of *failure* celebrated by Halberstam, Pidduck critiques the young filmmaker's knack for self-commodification, even vilifying him for his achievements: "Dressed to the nines, basking in the limelight, releasing a new film practically every year, raking in countless awards, Dolan is the model neoliberal queer subject."[23] Dolan, on this account, is faulted for *failing to fail*, as if success were somehow a betrayal of the queer cause and of the queer community. This is a dynamic recognizable from my discussion of Ozon in the previous chapter. At issue—as is often the case in the critical reception both scholarly and more popular—is the question of whether Dolan ought to be seen as a subversive, avant-garde authorial enfant terrible or instead as a superficial, derivative, millennial cinematic sellout.

Building on Stephen Maddison's work on the films of Pedro Almodóvar to interrogate whether the "heterosocial bonds" between Dolan and his lead actresses create a space for nonheteronormative, feminist representations of female characters, Pidduck connects this judgment call to Dolan's relationship to his leading ladies: "Dolan is openly gay and makes public his passionate relationships with women, while remaining discreet about his sexual and intimate relations with men. Dolan's performances of masculinity and sexual orientation are inflected through media discourse . . . highlighting the leitmotif of emotionally charged relationships between mothers and their queer sons."[24] Leaving aside the potentially tacit implication that Dolan has some sort of public duty to open up about his sex life, Pidduck's is a point well taken. Seeming to intimate the desexualizing effect of such camp attachment to female screen icons, Pidduck appears to suggest, perhaps unwittingly, that these relationships enact a form of closeting: occluding queer provocation behind an unthreatening veneer of heterosocial adulation.

As has frequently been noted, throughout his oeuvre Dolan pays homage to camp emblems and texts ranging from Jean Cocteau to John Waters (fig. 20) but nonetheless steadfastly refuses the label of gay filmmaker, infamously refusing the Queer Palm at Cannes for his third film, *Laurence Anyways* (2012), declaring such prizes "ghettoizing" and "ostracizing" and proclaiming to *Le Monde* (though he later admits to having regretted his choice of words) that the fact that "such awards exist disgusts me."[25] As Marshall summarizes, "Dolan himself famously refuses the categorization of 'gay' or 'queer' filmmaker, while being at ease with his queer identity/identification as such."[26] Massimi thus aligns Dolan with a nonidentitarian but nevertheless transgressive "post-gay sensibility," which "champion[s] maternal and non-normative male subjects over the centrality of fatherhood and straight masculinity."[27] And Stefano Genetti argues that the filmmaker transposes the "identitary affirmation" of the source text into an "elusive, porous identity to be constantly reformulated"—ultimately concluding that this marks a shift from identitary fiction to an understanding of identity *as* a fiction.[28] Dolan's affirmation of his own homosexuality while simultaneously resisting being pigeonholed as a gay filmmaker would, on this reading, result in a more capacious and fluid concept of what it means to be *queer* as an act of becoming rather than as a stable identity category.

Fig. 20. A cheeky, blink-and-you'll-miss-it allusion to John Waters's *Pink Flamingos* (1972). From *Juste la fin du monde* (*It's Only the End of the World*, dir. Xavier Dolan, 2016).

But while Dolan bristles at his films being labeled gay, he has no qualms about calling them camp—in fact, repeatedly offering this descriptor himself. Asked in a television interview with George Stroumboulopoulos how he feels about having won the Queer Palm, the director responds: "I'm gay . . . obviously. . . . My films aren't. They're campy, they can be campy, *Heartbeats* is pretty campy, but . . . *Laurence Anyways* is a love story between a man and a woman [who] carry on with the love that they've always known, trying to forget about labels."[29] While the descriptors Dolan uses for his characters in this instance are a bit misleading, given that the film is about the gradual self-discovery and coming-out of a trans woman, his reluctance to have this feature, specifically, called queer is double-edged. His account of the film's narrative universalizes it beyond tidy identity categories, but Dolan also seems acutely aware of the potential hazards of such generalization, seething at once at the idea that his films are queer by extension of his own biographical gayness—that this trans narrative might merely allegorize his own queer experience—and, in turn, at the notion that his own cis male gayness might be broadly tokenized as representative of all queer perspectives.

The specificity of camp in Dolan's usage seems intended—and unsurprisingly so, given camp's association primarily with gay men—to call into question *queer* as an identity category lumping together all nonheteronormative sexualities but also to divorce sexuality from style. At the same time, in order to make this distinction, the director does refer back to his own homosexuality: "I'm gay . . . obviously." And the evidence Dolan flippantly presents in this broadcast of his own ostensibly obvious gayness is particularly indicative: he points at his socks. This occasions a comedic exchange, as Stroumboulopoulos—who notes with a laugh that he is not gay—is himself wearing mismatched and playfully patterned socks. (Dolan's aren't visible to the camera.) Focusing on artifice, on wardrobe, as if it were a reliable indicator of the self-expression of one's sexuality, Dolan contends that his films are not queer but rather camp. If he has escaped the constraints of the identity label it is only by distilling it into an aesthetic category—and one he would clearly like to imagine as more unambiguously legible than it actually is. This hardly feels postgay.

It is worth remembering, in this context, that camp designates not only a self-consciously homosexual style but also the unconscious, reputedly irrepressible behaviors by which gay men out themselves, willingly or not. This quality of camp as an involuntary tell is telling. One might consider, for instance, an early interview Dolan gave in the days immediately after the premiere of *J'ai tué ma mère*. Asked when he first began to identify as gay, Dolan responds primarily by speculating as to when he first became identif*iable* as gay to an outside observer: "Being camp I would always dress with my mom's clothes and, you know, have things with other guys, but I never thought back then that that meant I was homosexual, you know."[30] The development of same-sex desire, he says more or less explicitly, was not determinate of queer identification; it was recognition by alterity that was the deciding factor.

Fixating again on superficial signifiers (camp clothing and his own questionable effeminacy or, a moment later, fabulousness) but listing these alongside sexual behavior without distinction, Dolan hollows out the purported inner essence of homosexuality and reveals it as a label with which one only later learns to identify through violent interpellation: "And then in high school it became obvious. And I was really unhappy with that. The bashing scene is something inspired from reality. So . . . yeah. That was the entrance into gayness."[31] The potential for camp identification emerges even later still, as a diagnostic tool for determining the etiology of the harm done: "Apparently for them it seemed obvious. But I'm not that effeminate." (He interrupts himself here to wave his hands self-disparagingly in a parody of gay effeminacy so exaggerated that it reads almost more as motor stereotype, hand flapping, or stimming than as a stereotypical mincing.) He continues, "So I don't understand. But seriously I'm not, you know, I'm not the fabulous guy, and it's okay but it's not me. So I didn't know, was it so obvious?"[32] Dolan seems to be asking—in a querulous tone, almost as if he desires an answer to this rhetorical question—if the interviewer finds him capable of passing.

Putting this into terms that have become familiar over the course of this book, this gives a different, more introspective turn to what Eve Kosofsky Sedgwick describes as camp-recognition, since here it is a recognition of insult, as theorized for instance by Didier Eribon and discussed in chapter 2, that is at stake: the gay self is made less by elective affinity than by necessity. Put differently, camp-(self-)recognition seems a *consequence* of something akin to kitsch-attribution, here encoded as the attribution of effeminacy, as the recognition of one's own previously unnoticed abjection. If a young Dolan disavows the mannerisms and markers of bad taste—very significantly, his *mother's* clothing—he fears have gotten him into trouble, his evolving attitude toward such failed passing can perhaps also be observed over the course of his filmography, which has so frequently been qualified as camp. (And so often so in an attempt to defend his aesthetic excesses and redeem his ostensibly postidentitarian persuasions.) In the remainder of this concluding chapter, I'd like to put some pressure on the unexpected meeting point between the disavowal of camp-as-behavior and the affirmation of camp-as-aesthetic—between the repudiation of the involuntary bad taste one attributes to kitsch and the celebration of bad taste recognized in camp—as it relates to motherhood and gay identity in *J'ai tué ma mère* and *Mommy*.

The Mother in the Closet

After all, as Pidduck again notes, "publicly 'out' from the beginning of his career yet highly ambivalent about gay or queer labels, Dolan's 'self-fashioning' as a filmmaker and his public persona . . . is imbricated with his passionate attachments to his fabulous leading ladies, and with his penchant for high-octane family dramas and impossible love stories."[33] Peter Knegt reminds us that Dolan has cast both Anne Dorval and Suzanne Clément (who plays the teacher in *J'ai tué ma mère* and Kyla, the tutor, in *Mommy*) in multiple films and that Dolan "insists that he doesn't just write *parts* for the actresses, he writes *movies* for them."[34] The filmmaker's passionate adulation of aging female actresses, as Dorval often describes herself in relation to the youthful Dolan, makes it possible to recognize the degree to which such idolatry and iconicity are at once eroticizing and desexualizing. Dolan's films are perhaps the first works considered in *Flamboyant Fictions* without an easily discernible pornographic impulse: gone are the daddy-twink dynamics of André Gide's pederast and bad boy pairings; instead, the naughty boys in Dolan's films are coupled with camp mothers.

The narrative of *J'ai tué ma mère* rather reverses the course of the love story between Dolan and his screen divas, surprisingly making it possible to read its *refusal* of queer identification with Chantale's outmoded lowbrow taste as a potential form of closeting or even as an indicator of internalized homophobia. Conversely, perhaps this might also make it possible to understand *Mommy*, which at first blush might appear uncharacteristically devoid of explicit queer content, as I suggested earlier on, as a subtle reaffirmation of such affective attachments. We are now in a position to better evaluate this assessment, recognizing how the later film will resuscitate queer identifications as a matter of style.

On the whole, the reception of these two films has too often tended to polarize them, reducing *J'ai tué ma mère* to a straightforward coming-out narrative and treating *Mommy* as if it had nothing to say about homosexuality. Insightfully refocusing this discussion on the question of taste, Czach contends that, in the first film, "Hubert's teenage outbursts and aggression are not due to his mother's disapproval of his homosexuality, but rather the result of Hubert's disapproval of and shame at his mother's lower middle-class status, and the attendant assumption that she is homophobic. If Hubert feels stigmatized and humiliated it is not because he is gay but because his mother is an embarrassment."[35] Czach accordingly reads the kitsch dynamic predominantly as a question of class anxiety or class shame that gets mistaken, by the film's characters and its critics alike, for conservative values and even homophobia: "Chantale's social conservatism is . . . assumed not because of her actions, but because of the way she dresses, her home décor and her 'bad taste.'"[36] Starkly inverting early critiques of Fassbinder's *Faustrecht*, this is not an uncommon perspective on the film or on Dolan more largely, as if his early work could be salvaged from being reduced to this kind of dime-a-dozen gay coming-of-age tale only if its comings out are refigured more as a question of class politics than one of sexuality.[37]

It has also been noted that all of this focus on motherhood in Dolan's film work and self-promotion tends to obscure the influence of his father, the singer and actor Manuel Tadros, who has bit parts across Dolan's filmography and whose name is preserved in the title of his son's production company, Sons of Manuel, but elided from the professional persona. (Dolan grew up with the hyphenated surname Dolan-Tadros.) Like the absentee father of *J'ai tué ma mère* or the deceased dad in *Mommy*, this elision recalls Judith Butler's suggestion that societal heterosexism constitutes and sustains itself through an enforced refusal on the part of the gendered subject to grieve the loss of cathexis in the same-sex parent: the boy becomes a boy, and a presumably heterosexual one at that, through a disavowal of his homosexual attachment to the paternal figure.[38] It is understandable that Dolan would want to make a name for himself beyond associations with his father, who is well-known in the Montreal entertainment industry. But through this fort-da game the young filmmaker also opts for a more recognizably Québécois appellation aligned with Franco-European whiteness, whereas the Egyptian-born Tadros is of Coptic and Syro-Lebanese descent.

There is a sense in which *Mommy* responds to the demand for a cinema that might pass as straight—and that decidedly does register as white. With regard to the purportedly more mature later film, Knegt summarizes what seems to be the common consensus: "*Mommy* is the first film by the openly gay Dolan not to offer an LGBT character as a main subject. All four of his previous films had a central LGBT character, with Dolan himself playing the gay men on three of those occasions. . . . But *Mommy*'s main trio are all heterosexual."[39] Squarely situating queerness exclusively as a matter of content considered independently from questions of form, not only does this perspective rather dismissively gloss over suggestions of intimacy between the two female leads and the literal ménage à trois of the establishment of a nonheteronormative, nonpatriarchal household, it also seems to take at face value Steve's exaggerated misogynist bravado as an indication of his presumed heterosexuality. Which is not even to mention his nearly drag turn as Céline Dion (fig. 21) or the homophobia he endures when performing karaoke—both deftly analyzed by Jason R. D'Aoust in what is surely the most sensitive reading of the film to date.[40] Arguing that "Steve's vocal identifications [with Dion or with the absent father] are queer even though the film is unclear about Steve's sexual orientation," D'Aoust is the first to insist on *Mommy*'s queerness independently from the autobiographical angle—without taking recourse to the ostensible evidence of Dolan's own sexuality.

In this same spirit, and in an attempted corrective to the misguided critical either/or that would make the one film gay and the other not by divorcing queer subject matter and queer aesthetics, I would like to propose that the entire oedipal drama of both films reflects a love-hate relationship with queer and quirky taste, which is to say, as I have been suggesting, that Hubert's and Steve's at moments matricidal impulses reflect an evolving attitude toward camp interpellation (to being recognized as gay) and camp performativity (to consenting to play up this role). As Karen Redrobe outlines in her book on *Vanishing Women: Magic, Film, and Feminism*, Sigmund Freud

Fig. 21. Steve (Antoine Olivier Pilon) lip-syncing to Céline Dion's "On ne change pas" (1998) and re-creating the iconic look from *Let's Talk about Love* (1997). From *Mommy* (dir. Xavier Dolan, 2014).

argued as early as 1921 that "a boy who identifies with his mother risks homosexuality," prompting later feminist thinkers not only to excavate, as Butler does, the presupposition of heterosexuality embedded in the theorization of the Oedipus complex but even to insist, as does Julia Kristeva, that "the (symbolic) murder of the mother constitutes an absolute requirement" for healthy maturation and adult autonomy.[41] Even D. W. Winnicott—for whom a form of maternal "failure"[42] is required for the healthy maturation and individuation of the child—pathologizes mama's boys, suggesting that a risk of homosexuality is attendant, as Carol Mavor summarizes it, to the "*mother's failure to fail* her child at the right time, with just the right amount of pulling back."[43] This is, as Mavor recognizes, symptomatic of what Eve Kosofsky Sedgwick diagnoses as a broader cultural "effeminiphobia" surely still lingering in mental health discourses surrounding young men's sexuality and behavior.[44] Dolan subtly but significantly turns such psychoanalytic trajectories on their heads, seeming to suggest that vestigial, heterosexualizing, imagined erotic attachments to the mother are precisely what prevents these boys from fully growing up and becoming healthy, adult *homo*sexual men.

While I have no wish to contradict Sedgwick's central claim in *Epistemology of the Closet* (1990) about the constitutive necessity of homosexuality to the emergence and maintenance of heterosexuality, I have so far been opting for the term off-straight, rather than off-*gay*, for better or worse, to recognize the sameness of same-sex attraction—in a paradigm of anxiously, if often exuberantly, failed passing—as disidentificatory to and derivative of its difference from its heterosexual opposite. But the onus probandi of this operation has by now shifted: the knee-jerk presumption is that if Steve is indeed straight, this would make him exceptional within Dolan's oeuvre—a kind of near miss for most of his other central protagonists, and most notably for the auteur himself as incarnated in the quasi-autobiographical Hubert. At turns intimating and disavowing the easy assumption of what would then be Steve's now unmarked *homo*sexuality, Dolan marks him instead as *off-gay*. Rather than the filmmaker himself in a cameo, it is, perhaps, the public personae of the maternal Dorval and Clément, within Dolan's self-mythology, that underpin ontological authentication: the reality fetish traditionally attached to the off-straight twink, loses (or at the very least now more convincingly conceals) its pornographic appeal. With Steve's off-straightness, or rather off-gayness, serving now more as an identification than as a sexual ideal, the erotics of the film turn instead on an ambivalent oedipal attachment to the mother.

An innocent enough anxiety about incest is introduced early in *Mommy*. When Steve asks in the first minutes of the film if he will have his own bedroom, his mother informs him that she has no intention of spooning with him at the age of forty. (With characteristic sass, he reminds her that she is forty-six.) Still during this opening sequence, as Steve and Die walk down the street toward their new home, a cherubic boy playing street hockey lifts his facemask to get a better look, prompting Steve silently to snarl and to put his arm protectively around his mother (figs. 22–24). What might have, given the context of Dolan's oeuvre, been interpreted as a homoerotic exchange of glances has been reinterpreted and resignified as heterosexual desire, with Steve encouraging, or enabling, his mother's desire to feel youthful—though she is oblivious to the other boy and visibly misinterprets this gesture merely as filial affection.

Or is Steve turning to his mother as a beard? In *J'ai tué ma mère*, Chantale seems to intuit this dynamic when, learning of her son's homosexuality, she expresses a feeling of being effaced: "It's as if . . . as if everything, every little thing, were being erased. As if . . . I donno . . . It feels like none of it's there anymore, our special moments, our trips. It's as if it all disappeared." With regard to her gay son, however, as if describing the obverse to her own fear of vanishing, she remarks, "C'est pas rien, être . . . un homosexuel. C'est quelque chose" (It's not nothing being . . . a homosexual. It's something). One might also translate this last line as, "It's a thing." The film's English-language subtitles decidedly overstate what Chantale is saying, rendering these lines as "It's a big deal . . ." and "Big stuff." But, for reasons I hope will become clear, I'll be insisting here on a verbatim translation as *not nothing*.

Figs. 22–24. Steve clinging a bit too closely to his mother (Anne Dorval). From *Mommy* (dir. Xavier Dolan, 2014).

Read against the grain, we might take this to imply that becoming *something*, being sturdily taxonomized as homosexual, saves Hubert from the disappearance to which his mother will be subjected: Hubert only gains this sexual identity, and subjectivity tout court, it seems, at his mother's expense. Die gives a similar speech at a pivotal moment of *Mommy*, confiding in her son that he will learn to love her less and less in time. But these comments stand in stark contrast to Steve's arrested development and the self-erasure of his repeated suicide attempts as well as to the conclusion to the film where it is not the mother who has vanished but the son. Especially considering Steve's ambiguous, if not stunted, sexuality, it is possible to see *Mommy* as undoing a process of gay individuation that had unsteadily been accomplished by *J'ai tué ma mère*: Die is resurrected as her child's chief emotional and at moments even erotic attachment. During the Céline Dion routine, for instance, he dances fairly salaciously with her, at one point cupping her breasts, eliciting an eyeroll and a slap on the wrist.

We see the difficulty of moving past the mother already in the first film. Chantale has a habit of showing up where and when she is least wanted, bursting in on Hubert in school after he has fictively and unceremoniously done away with her in a writing assignment. Later, Hubert fantasizes about smashing Chantale's gaudy plates in a twenty-second slow-motion montage but resolves instead simply to tell her that he hates her: go ahead and hate me, she responds, but I'm still here. She then resumes humming Edith Piaf's "La Vie en rose," a tic that her son has identified as one of his pet peeves as early as the opening sequence. It is significant that his own fantasy of violent destruction is set to the film's same recurring retro-kitsch theme music as the opening, composed for strings but otherwise reminiscent of Eric Satie's *musique d'ameublement* or Yann Tiersen's score for Jean-Pierre Jeunet's *Le destin fabuleux d'Amélie Poulain* (*Amélie*, 2001): if the slow-motion interlude confers on Hubert a certain degree of metaleptic agency, the ability not only to imagine but to *image* and in so doing to *realize* alternatives to the film's actual plot, it also aligns him with the same kitschy and vaguely French musical taste.

And indeed, half-buried in the basement, the garish patterns of the previous tenant—which I am playfully suggesting as a hypotextual holdover from Dorval's earlier role as Chantale—haunt the mise-en-scène of *Mommy*, crowding its otherwise unembellished sets with drabber, faded versions of the same floral motifs. The kitsch, it seems, is inescapable. As is the queer baggage that is schlepped from one film to the next—and not only by dint of the filmmaker's sexuality, or even by association with Pilon's earlier role as an implied queer kid and stigmatized bullying victim in Dolan's music video for the song "College Boy" by the band Indochine, but indeed by virtue of the filmmaker's evolving camp aesthetic. Even the home videos with which *J'ai tué ma mère* concludes, signifying a desired reconciliation, might also hint at a regression: a nostalgic 1:1 aspect ratio anticipating its hipsteresque revision in *Mommy*, from analogue to Instagram filter.[45] Here Hubert meets his mother halfway between the bare black-and-white art house–style footage of his autobiographical video essay, which punctuates the plot, and the vibrant claustrophobia of the film's diegesis.[46] In true camp fashion, the mother's kitschy proclivities have been reappropriated and resignified as queer style. In *Mommy* they will persist *primarily* as stylistic choices, with the potential queer content of the film often drowned out by its aesthetic excesses.

This is most apparent in the film's most famous montage—set gratuitously, if seemingly unironically, to "Wonderwall" by Oasis—where Steve, skateboarding with his arms outstretched as if in flight, reaches out and expands the edges of the frame, widening it to fuller and more customary dimensions. Tossing his head back slightly in a triumphant sigh, Steve breathes deeply as if tasting fresh air for the first time in forever. Like the Britpop playing in the background, this gesture and the metaleptic manipulation it exercises are in questionable taste, heavy-handed but undeniably affective. Dolan is daring his spectator not to be moved by it despite their better judgment and reassuringly superior sense of taste. An instant later Steve is shown defiantly running down the middle of a highway with a grocery cart (recalling and recasting the shopping run where he procured the white porcelain knickknacks and gawdy word charm necklace) shouting *liberté* in a send-up of Mel Gibson's already over-the-top *Braveheart* (1995). Modeling the audience reaction Dolan aspires to elicit, Die and Kyla, by this point dual mother figures and elective coparents, laugh along in exasperated but cathartic resignation.

This epiphanic sequence is cast into relief as a kind of coming-out if one takes into account the concatenation of queer associations habitually attached to similar music video moments across Dolan's oeuvre: the gay history embedded in the strobe scene of *Les amours imaginaires*, for instance, or the visual allusion to the falling cereal in gay auteur Gregg Araki's *Mysterious Skin* (2004, itself likely a reference to the flower petals of Todd Haynes's *Poison*) in the magic realist touch of slowly descending clothing at a pivotal moment of *Laurence Anyways*. (A single shot of marshmallows falling around Nicolas's face in *Les amours imaginaires* solidifies this association.) But the studied, highbrow cinephilia and cultural showmanship of a film like *Les amours imaginaires*, in many ways as eager to prove itself as are its insecure central characters, has by this point in Dolan's career given way to unapologetic self-indulgence. Momentarily controlling the narrative framing and tenor, Steve has consummated what might be understood as a shift across Dolan's filmography from paranoid to more reparative camp.

But the wider screen lasts only as long as the song itself before bad news returns the film to its tighter framing, refocusing it on Die's perspective. In his own comparison of these two films, Loïc Bourdeau sees Die, whose name is a diminutive for Diane, as a feminist success story: "Her nickname, which she signs with a heart in place of the dot, even strengthens her image as an independent woman, one who has actually killed the mother—the one normative model offered to women—to become two distinguishable and self-chosen identities: a woman *and* a mother."[47] But, beyond the reminder of Die's own less than sophisticated taste inscribed into her signature itself, this summary seems to betray some confusion as to whom it is Die kills. Or rather, in an inverse of the dynamic described before, Die's highly questionable flourishing would occur at the expense of the possibly queer son, perhaps even only by foreclosure of his queerness, taken in the broader sense of the word. This may be what is at stake during the tensest minute in the film, when, enraging Steve by refusing his tacky gifts, Die is forced by an explosion of violence exceeding anything in *J'ai tué ma mère* to lock herself away in the same basement where the nostalgic kitsch is kept, tellingly hiding in the *closet*.

Noting Dolan's tendency to literalize this metaphor ("[a distinct epistemology] of the closet that Dolan takes verbatim"), Genetti describes Dolan's vision of closeting as "less hermetic, more elastic, with cracks allowing glimpses of the contradictions of desire."[48] During the excruciating duration of Die's retreat to the closet we see only a sliver of light on her face as she gaspingly peers through a crack in the door waiting for her son to calm down (figs. 25–26). Notably, when Die opens the closet door, subtly anticipating Steve's expanding of the frame, and reemerges into the light of day, it is Kyla she discovers: another mother, a glimmer of hope.

Straight out of a horror film, this closeting is in stark contrast to the kind manifested in Die's later, glossy, soft-lit, shallow-focus fantasy of her son's picture-perfect wedding—one of the few moments of the film that would explicitly imply at least her perception of (or hopes for) Steve's heterosexuality. The later daydream sequence enacts a kind of revenge for the fantasies of broken tchotchkes and a murdered mother at the core of the first film. Occurring just before Die has Steve committed, this is the only other time in *Mommy* that the aspect ratio expands, suggesting that a struggle over metaleptic agency is also at stake in these maternal-filial conflicts. Here Die pictures the good life as a heteronormative one with the cloying mawkishness of a Christmastime television commercial. Outfitting Steve with a counterfeit identity of her own design, Die can only imagine her son happy by literally imagining him as someone else: Steve here is played by another actor, noticeably at least a head taller than Pilon. (Highlighting this incongruity, earlier in the film Diane had teased her son about his height, asking if he intended to remain five foot seven for the rest of his life.) There may be a measure of metareflective cinematic self-critique embedded in this fantasy and highlighted by its parallel with the earlier expansion of the borders of the image. If camp is, per Sontag, characterized by a seriousness that fails, what is both appealing and oddly off-putting about the affective excesses of *Mommy* is the self-serious seamlessness with which they succeed in moments like this—despite the undeniable strangeness of the film's underlying but wholly superfluous and rarely evoked conceit (a dystopian Canada where unruly

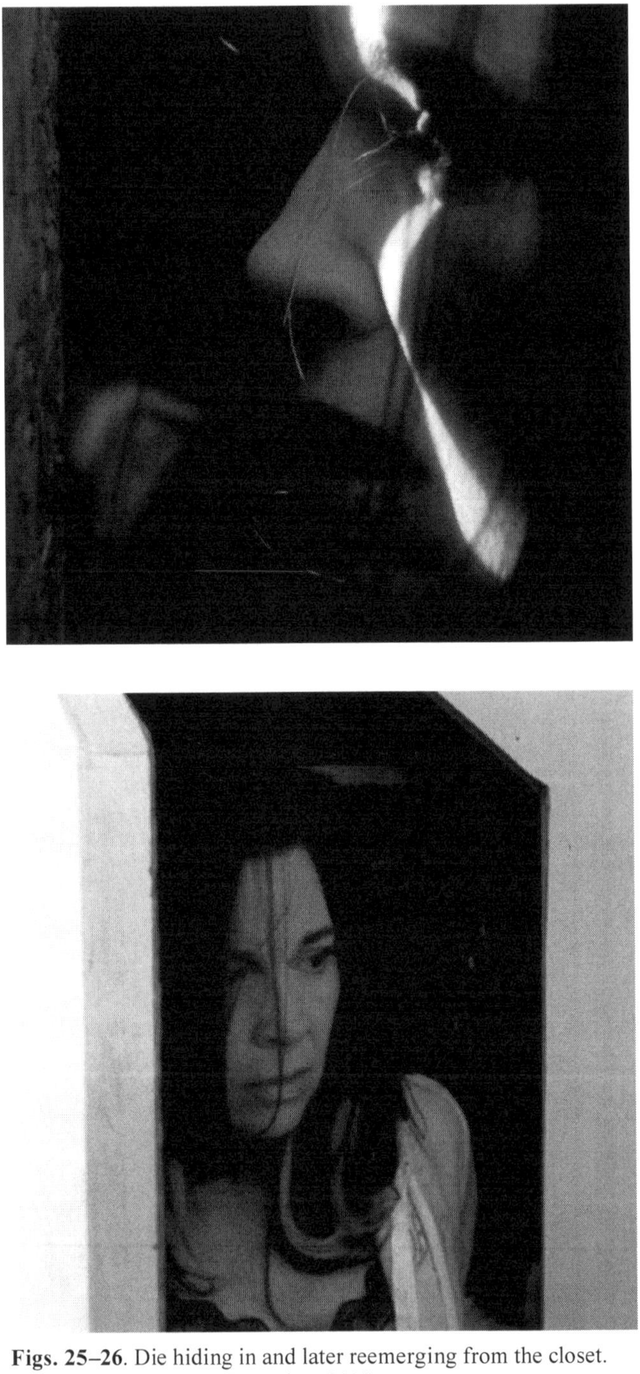

Figs. 25–26. Die hiding in and later reemerging from the closet. From *Mommy* (dir. Xavier Dolan, 2014).

children can be institutionalized more or less at whim) and the sometimes vulgar sentimentality of its approach.

But whereas Dolan's characters occasionally take control, as I've been observing, of his films' montage, cinematography, and music, they seldom seem to have such autonomy when it comes to their own voices. This is particularly true of *Mommy*'s queerest moments, the Céline Dion lip sync and Steve's abominable singing at the karaoke bar, but is also thematized by Kyla's debilitating stutter—the traumatic result of having lost a son of her own. Like the Visconti I evoked at the outset of this book, Dolan's films are themselves lip-synced, dubbed only afterward, since most of the live sound is corrupted by the director's habit of playing music on set to keep the actor's movements more harmonious.[49] But here this acoustic dissonance is one that Dolan is at great pains to conceal and that ends up being all but indiscernible in the final cut: the sound production of his films is as polished and immersive as the visual concord achieved by this process. Still, certain thematic traces do persist of the acousmatic stepping-out-of-character I have highlighted in Fassbinder, Schroeter, and Ozon. Steve's final lines in *Mommy* are delivered to a telephone held to his ear (he is in a straitjacket) by an arm extending offscreen to an undepicted body, as if he were a marionette. Fully restrained and, as he laughingly points out, heavily sedated, Steve also appears to be ventriloquized. He acts, as Claudia Kotte notes, "merely [as] the medium through which his therapists speak."[50] This is reflected by his insistently inquiring afterward whether his apology was satisfactory, which is to ask, in other words, whether the performance was convincing. It is not that Steve's contrition is disingenuous but rather that he is unsure whether its expression has been persuasive. I might even suggest that this plaintively repeated query reverberates with Dolan's not entirely rhetorical question, in the early interview I cited above, about whether he is capable of passing.

Ending at once in repression and revolt, *Mommy* gives another turn to the agential trope of failed passing I have been theorizing throughout this book. Parting ways with Kyla, and having unconvincingly played it off as a happy event, the last image of Die is her holding in a scream—a visual echo of the facial tics accompanying Kyla's stammer. It is at this moment of mirroring that the romantic potential of this coupling is most palpable and most perceptibly impossible. The optimistic face that Die had put on during their final conversation—the façade is broken only momentarily for an impassioned soliloquy on the subject of hope—is unpersuasive. It is through the cracks and contradictions of this failed performance that love comes into view.

Dolan then cuts to Steve, still straitjacketed, apparently still chemically subdued, with his head lolling slightly. But as an inattentive orderly temporarily removes his constraints, Steve suddenly comes to life and breaks free, casting off the restrictive garment with an outstretched arm recalling the earlier flight simulation on his longboard. And here again Steve attains a certain measure of metaleptic control: an extreme close-up of his receding hand depicts an

Figs. 27–29. Steve's escape. *Mommy* (dir. Xavier Dolan, 2014).

outstretched index finger (fig. 27), blurrily reminiscent of the Sistine Chapel, and triumphant orchestral music blossoms out of nowhere as if it had just been cued by this gesture. As he sprints headlong toward a floor-to-ceiling window, tinted crepuscular, a drum beat sets in and then the screen goes black. The credits begin to roll over the first lines of Lana Del Rey's "Born to Die" (2011): "Feet don't fail me now . . ." At once conducting this course of events and faithfully following an unfortunate trope this study has traced from gay French modernism through the present day, suicide seems the only escape from the confines of a restrictive text. But although it seems that Steve will reach the window before he is caught, the ending remains open. The final shots are of his defiant face (fig. 28), looking almost directly into the camera, and a canted low angle from behind of his feet, midstride. The cut to black occurs before his toes touch the ground. He is literally in flight (fig. 29).

Conclusion: Post(er)-Gay

Maybe I am reminded of Michelangelo because the uniform whiteness of the wardrobe in this moment, matching the complexion and general coloring of the strikingly blond actor wearing it, inscribes this ending into the history of gay aesthetics documented by the early music video montage of *Les amours imaginaires* and adds Dolan to its lineage of white gay aesthetes. This is yet another iteration, the filmmaker seems to suggest, of a tradition extending forward from these marble male nudes and Cocteau's white paper on homosexuality. Informing my earlier examinations of the sublimated blank white body, Richard Dyer has exposed how visual culture hypocritically demands at once that whiteness be perceived and acknowledged while also remaining unobserved: "Whites must be seen to be white, yet whiteness as race resides in invisible properties and whiteness as power is maintained by being unseen. To be seen as white is to have one's corporeality registered, yet true whiteness resides in the non-corporeal."[51] Or more pithily, as Dyer phrases it in a concluding chapter on the whiteness of death, "to be white is to be nothing."[52] This paradoxically embodied transcendence of the corporeal is, for the representational tradition excavated by Dyer, epitomized by the stigmatized body of Christ—an observation that invites a reconsideration of the ending of *Mommy* not only in the context of the iconography addressed especially in chapter 4 but also with an eye to Antoine Olivier Pilon's prior role in the music video for Indochine's "College Boy," where Dolan, with an uncharacteristically graphic violence, has him beaten, pissed on, tased, riddled with bullet holes, and brutally crucified in pristine black and white. Nailed to the cross in front of a crowd of blindfolded onlookers, many filming the spectacle on their cellphones, Pilon concludes this video too with a drooping nod of the head, looking directly into the camera and whispering, "Merci." It is as if he is taking a bow.

If this grotesquely overstated imagery, from a filmmaker sometimes denigrated as overly sleek and shallow, revels in an eroticized abjection, it also raises the question of queer visibility. Notably, as in *Mommy*, it is only an inference that Pilon's character is gay: the video itself provides no hints beyond his being bullied. That this video is widely understood to be a commentary on homophobia—and it unquestionably is—is an assumption made largely on the basis of Dolan's biography. Controversially, the video was banned from television in France, where it was taken to be an unsubtle and unwelcome intrusion into debates over gay marriage and an attack on the Catholic right.[53] Dolan's open letter in response focuses on the aesthetics of violence and only evokes homophobia in passing as one entry in a longer list of cultural ills.[54] Even at his most polemical, Dolan is playing hide-and-seek. Or rather: he is hiding in plain sight. Writing from Quebec to a French politician, all of Dolan's other examples of social issues—American gun violence, a school shooting in Connecticut, youth suicides in Texas—are drawn from the political context of the United States. Triangulating the transnational expression of his personal experience through this culturally more hegemonic position, Dolan appears to be appropriating for himself, and for his sexual and geographic marginality, an unmarked, unspecified, universal applicability—the same kind of self-ascribed (in)visible global universality by which whiteness defines itself in Western society.

Courting the same queer associations he rebuffs, Dolan is exerting a prerogative to be seen while remaining unseen. As he points out, the scandal occasioned by the censorship guaranteed that the video would be viewed online millions of times in a matter of days. To the degree that the ending of *Mommy*—where Steve's exquisite corpse is never offered up for view—rewrites the Indochine clip in a less explicit idiom, it attends to the contradictory requirements for visibility already evident, as Dyer continues, in the very naming of the attribute *white*: "White is both a color and, at once, not a color and the sign of that which is colorless because it cannot be seen: the soul, the mind, and also emptiness, non-existence and death, all of which form part of what makes white people socially white. Whiteness is the sign that makes white people visible as white, while simultaneously signifying the true character of white people, which is invisible."[55] Almost as if through osmosis, Dolan borrows this impossible demand of whiteness for his (non-)depiction of homosexuality in *Mommy*, a homosexuality that, if presumed to present itself, does so with a tacit self-assertion habitually reserved for heterosexuality and similarly hegemonic positions. Nothing to see here. No coming-out is necessary. This is an awkward transposition and mainstreaming that never quite succeeds—and in that failed passing perhaps retains something of the countercultural. By the same token, turning toward the dying sunlight and absenting himself from his own narrative at the end, as have so many of his literary and cinematic predecessors, Steve makes manifest the very self-erasure that might (un)mark him as potentially queer.

This, then, might also indicate an oedipal attitude toward Dolan's queer forefathers in the tradition inaugurated by Gide and codified by the Genet-Fassbinder nexus at the heart of this study. After all, as Butler concludes in the essay on gender melancholia, such refused identifications also govern the relationship between homosexuality and heterosexuality more globally. On the one hand, heterosexist "renunciation requires the very homosexuality that it condemns, not as its external object, but as its own most treasured source of sustenance. The act of renouncing homosexuality thus paradoxically strengthens homosexuality, but it strengthens homosexuality precisely *as* the power of renunciation."[56] But if gayness persists, in this way, by the operation of its very prohibition, this also means, conversely, that "within the formation of gay and lesbian identity, there may be an effort to disavow a constitutive relationship to heterosexuality," since such "disavowal is understood as a political necessity in order to *specify* gay and lesbian identity over and against its ostensible opposite, heterosexuality."[57] Butler further understands this, then, as "a rejection of heterosexuality that is to some degree an identification *with* a rejected heterosexuality."[58] And it is perhaps this unsteady identification with the majoritarian that informs Dolan's project in a moment that feels postgay precisely because its gayness is so neatly defined.[59]

As *Mommy*'s predictable and ambivalent ending—at once commonplace and rebellious—indicates, it is hard to say that there is anything particularly oppositional about Dolan's aesthetic on the whole, although he certainly merits the title of auteur. (His carefully curated image is in fact a textbook illustration of auteurism.) As gay fades away to white, so to speak, his work, at least in its more indulgently millennial moments, seems to embrace all of the earnestness of kitsch with none of the cutting irony of camp. Apparently responding to such unambiguous emotional appeal, and fulfilling a long-standing dream, *Mommy* was the first of Dolan's films to be accepted into the official competition at Cannes, five years after *J'ai tué ma mère* premiered there, catapulting its director overnight to worldwide recognition. Although a fêted darling of the film festival, Dolan's relationship to Cannes has, as I have already mentioned, not been without conflict, specifically with regard to the question of labeling his films as queer. One might then revealingly transpose the oedipal drama evolving from *J'ai tué ma mère* into *Mommy* onto this scenario: what is being closeted in the later film is explicit queer content, which seemingly goes subterranean in an attempt by Dolan to be taken seriously as an auteur and not just as a precocious gay parvenu. This is, again, the universalizing flipside to François Ozon's inadvertent reassertion of camp tokenism, but now Ozon's protean panqueerness has been flattened into a rather homogenizing style. As it is impossible for Dolan's films to pass completely unmarked-as-queer or for Dolan himself entirely to avoid tokenization as a poster boy for the contemporary state of queerness, he instead ostentatiously emphasizes the easy palatability of his camp aesthetic—failed passing made fun—almost as a spectacular distraction from queer interpretations: camp as a form of closeting. On the one hand, Dolan takes advantage of the superficial markers of a purportedly camp affect—an aesthetic that already connotes homosexuality only by desexualizing it—in order to queer even his straightest-seeming film. On the other, camp on this occasion has been so thoroughly diluted as to render it essentially indistinguishable from any other lustrous music video aesthetic.[60]

Perhaps the repeated absences and erasures documented by this book respond to an unfulfilled desire for self-transcendence, the yearning to exist beyond one's inherent, embodied contradictions. When the fantasy of a unified self proves unattainable, the closest anyone can come appears to be to vanish. (Nothing to see here.) And this insistence becomes all the more pronounced as the identity in question is made at once increasingly visible and also, through this ubiquitous visibility, increasingly *in*visible. At the end of his work on whiteness, Dyer suggests that the panicked "suspicion of nothingness and the death of whiteness is, as far as white identity goes, the cultural dominant of our times, that we really do feel we're played out."[61] But, although Dolan for the most part seems unconcerned with preserving anything queer or subversive about his gay identity, his films after *Mommy* nonetheless flirt with gay themes in interesting ways, further developing his filmic poetics of failed passing. The European *Juste la fin du monde*, as I have already mentioned, obliquely allegorizes AIDS while removing the more overt references of the source text.[62] And the plot of his English-language foray, *The Life and Times of John F. Donovan*, orbits around closetedness, suspicion, and celebrity. But the most recent feature, *Matthias & Maxime*, a return to local Québécois settings and the joual dialect, is, perhaps tellingly, Dolan's first film about the *emergence* of gay desire: the closest thing to a coming-out narrative he has produced, it reads as a reintroduction of sorts to a queer francophone filmmaker in all of his situated particularity.

If it is indeed to be his final film, this might suggest a consummation of the tendency to self-erasure chronicled by this book, a self-sublation more than a century in the making. If, in the end, there is anything postgay about Dolan, it may well be that he has thus far persisted in making gay movies long after this tradition, written in invisible ink, seemed entirely assured, taken for granted. Dolan's vanishing gay aesthetic is continuous with an established queer aesthetic of vanishing—a failed passing now verging on passing away entirely, making a spectacle of its own disappearance. His public statements on the subject frame this decision not only as a matter of feeling ever smaller, more insignificant, given the state of the world, as a retreat from the world itself,[63] but also as the assertion of a prerogative to *non*-self-expression, to silence, as the necessary precondition for any artistic vocation.[64] Refusing to choose between camp and commercial appeal, between stylized failure as queer success and stylistic passing as queer failure, Dolan has aestheticized gay identity into something that isn't really anything at all. But that's not nothing.

Coda

✦

Flamboyant Failures

My childhood misrecognition of Luchino Visconti's *Morte a Venezia* (1971) as having nothing to do with desire turns out to be an impression inscribed in the work itself—indeed in the long narrative tradition of failed passings to which it belongs. "It's a love story," Visconti insists in footage from a recent Swedish documentary, but "a very pure love, a love that is not at all sexual nor erotic. But a superior love, a love, let's say . . . the perfection of love."[1] Directed by Kristina Lindström and Kristian Petri, *Världens vackraste pojke* (*The Most Beautiful Boy in the World*, 2021) had its debut at Sundance fifty years after the premiere of Visconti's own film in London and subsequent screening at Cannes and takes its title from a remark the Italian director made on the earlier occasion about his youthful star, Björn Andrésen, apparently intended to embody this chaste ideal of love.

The insistent interdiction against the erotic is perhaps necessary as a social safety mechanism given the plot of the film: the aging composer Aschenbach's obsession with a teenage boy named Tadzio, an attraction consummated only through ponderous glances, lascivious ogling, and tedious diatribes on the ethics of art. As Visconti later notes of the younger actor: "He had to be truly cold, like a statue. He understood the role exactly, he is perfect. There is no danger of slipping into sexuality. Which would be a serious mistake." False on its face, the claim that sexuality has been sublimated from the film into an unsensual, even unsensuous, sculptural aestheticism not only evokes the Michelangelo motif extending from Jean Genet to Xavier Dolan, it further correlates to the deployment of Platonic dialogues in the Thomas Mann novella being adapted. Just as *Morte a Venezia* depends on its cultural pedigree—Visconti's noble birth, his work with Jean Renoir, his early association with Italian neorealism—as a cover for its more prurient concerns, so too does *Tod in Venedig* (1911) couch its erotic content in classical erudition and intertextuality. References to Greek pederasty abound, highlighting the selfsame intergenerational sexual attachment that they euphemize.

What Dorrit Cohn recognizes as narrative indirection in *Tod in Venedig* is a form of willfully failed passing that would be at home in André Gide: taking the opposite course of a bildungsroman, the narrator gradually distances himself from the strict focalization on Aschenbach's perspective, drifting into a sententiousness that reads, to the attentive interpreter, as a contrasting foil for Mann's more sympathetic, ambivalently complicit attitude toward his protagonist's homoerotic bent.[2] That Thomas Mann's own obvious homosexual inclinations remained rather an open secret until the release of his journals, two decades following his decease, is testimony to the persistence and persuasiveness of an epistemology of passing despite and by dint of such flamboyance.[3]

This is, as Robert Tobin demonstrates, itself the result of a prohibition: "Because such love is not capable of realization, Mann sees homosexual desire as an aesthetic and nonphysical phenomenon. As far as Mann is concerned, male homosexual desire is primarily satisfied through visual observation. . . . The aestheticism of homosexuality explains for Mann its connection to form and formalism."[4] Queerness has been sublimated into style. Tobin maps the course Mann charts between competing contemporary views of male homosexuality, some conservative and masculinist, others more progressive but pathologizing. Mann, Tobin reveals, takes a dialectical approach to these opposing views, ultimately "accepting the existence of sexual identity but then arguing that in the modern world this specific homosexual identity has universal relevance and societally structuring power."[5] This expands on Eve Sedgwick's reading of the text, where the Platonic-Socratic allusions demonstrate that "Western thought is importantly constituted and motivated by a priceless history of male-male pedagogic or pederastic relations."[6] It is, as we've observed, precisely such a universal relevance that is inflatedly aspired to and at the same time unsteadily taken for granted by the whiteness of off-straight twinks like Tadzio.

This elision of difference is, in other words, itself a gesture of failed passing. Marie-Louise James has situated *Tod in Venedig* within an exoticizing, even orientalist tradition within German culture, extending from the neoclassicism of Johann Joachim Winckelmann to Johann Wolfgang von Goethe's *Italienische Reise* (*Italian Journey*, 1816) to the Prussian photographer Wilhelm von Gloeden—who, as Jennifer Evans notes, catered to "closeted fin-de-siècle aristocratic patrons [with] his mail-order trade in images of Sicilian youths."[7] Werner Schroeter—whose films and infatuation with Antonio Orlando betray an unmistakable fetish for Italy and its boys—hearkens back to this tradition.[8] Evans, citing Roland Barthes and relying on work by Javier Samper Vendrell, notes that von Gloeden's youths at once fail to uphold the racist standards of male beauty they invoke—"too swarthy was their skin, too dark their complexions"—while also serving "as visual reenactments of a vision of the Greek homoerotic past captured within a European imperial gaze accustomed to looking at and fantasizing about its Others."[9] The scope of Visconti's casting tour across Scandinavia and Central and Eastern Europe lays bare how both the literary and film versions of *Death in Venice* participate in a whitewashing of the same exoticized and racialized erotics on which they fundamentally depend.[10]

It is important to remember that in C. Riley Snorton's critique of Sedgwick, too, "her closet still relies on a theory of embodiment that disavows how racialization" conditions "the phenomenological experience of pornotropic exploitation that gives rise to the glass closet as a collective rather than an individual concern."[11] Whereas pornotroping, as coined by Hortense Spillers, originally refers to the sexualized suffering of black women's bodies, a related, if rather inverted, phenomenon can be discerned, I would argue, in the erotic violence repeatedly inflicted on the corpus of off-white twinks discussed here—from Antonio Orlando to Malik Zidi—and in the racial fetishization of Björn Andrésen's celebrity image in Japan during his time there as an actor and pop singer.[12] (In the documentary his manager from this period calls him "the perfect idol" and refers to him as a *bischōnen*, which he defines as "the ideal young man," noting that the word "has a homosexual aspect.") Pornotroping, as summarized by Michael A. Chaney, "transforms a person into flesh. It involves putting flesh on display and thereby satisfying voyeuristic desire by reinforcing the viewer's perception of bodily integrity in contrast to the view of objectified flesh."[13] But in the case of the off-straight twink, it is the objectified body itself that is granted an illusory wholeness—while nonetheless retaining a pornographic insistence on corporeal ontology. Even in its most visceral iterations, the body of the off-straight twink is less flesh than projection surface.

Visconti only directly addresses Andrésen a few times in the footage included from the initial casting interview in the biographical documentary. Early on, with a wave of his fingers, the filmmaker instructs the young man to turn his head, though we are shown no sign of the actor complying even after the request has been translated. Instead, with a cut back to Andrésen, from the now off-screen dialogue between Visconti and an assistant, we hear the latter comment over the image of this youthful countenance that "Il est très beau dans les photos, j'ai vu" (I noticed that he is very handsome in the photos). Visconti then asks the fifteen-year-old directly, still in French, if he has brought these images with him. Andrésen shakes his head.

By the end of the casting session, as it is spliced together in the documentary, he will have been very much photographed. We are even treated to a moment of mise en abyme anticipating the unmanned camera observing Tadzio at the conclusion of Visconti's film, with the film camera capturing this archival footage positioned behind another photographer snapping headshots. The boy will also have been stripped down to a conspicuously modish bathing suit: if the resemblance to Greek statuary is indeed undeniable, as the camera tilts slowly down this lanky body leaned against a wall, such classical timelessness will still have to be fully refurbished from this retrofitted 1970s teen-idol aesthetic.

Before being undressed, Andrésen is asked to pace around a few steps. The request to disrobe is then directed not toward him but instead to the interpreter: "Dis-lui d'enlever son pullover" (Tell him to take off his sweater).

It is difficult to discern whether Andrésen has some sense of what is being asked of him before the subsequent translation; he seems almost to slow his gait in anticipation. Nor is his response to the direction entirely unambiguous. Seeming at first surprised but not particularly scandalized, he asks the translator to repeat the instruction and then signals his understanding with a bashful sigh and a brief turn away. But before he can fully untuck his shirt, Visconti interrupts with an additional order: to look into the camera. To which the casting assistant adds, in Swedish, that he should smile. He does so subtly at first, then more broadly, flashing his eyebrows in a silent chuckle upon hearing the director's approving response: "Molto bello."

We do not watch him strip. The film cuts to Andrésen pacing again, suddenly shirtless, as an ominous extradiegetic music sets in. There is a long beat the next time he is told to smile, which now feels more sinister given the scoring and the increasing nudity. He glances on this occasion toward Visconti, off camera, with a gaze as inscrutable as a fashion model's smirk: something between cheek, defiance, and compliance. But the last of these is definitively delivered in this instance solely by a jump cut to a slightly different angle, picking up again a brief moment before a beaming, laughing, boyish grin forms charmingly across Andrésen's face. Even in this critical retelling, Visconti has clearly found his icon. And so be it if a little editing is required.

Asked in a later moment from the documentary, in an on-camera interview at the Piazza San Marco, what he had been looking for in his Tadzio, Visconti replies, pointing toward Andrésen by way of illustration: "Exactement ce qu'il est. Exactement ça" (Exactly as he is. Exactly that). As if, the interviewer offers, he had been comparing auditioning hopefuls to a picture he already possessed: "Comme si vous aviez eu une photo de lui." Visconti agrees.

In the narrative established by the documentary's editing and editorializing, this imagined image takes on a function not incomparable to the counterfeit coin at the heart of chapter 1: it stands in for the lacking photographs from the initial casting, betraying a desire to start from concrete facts rather than from abstract thoughts. *Exactement ce qu'il est.* Andrésen is precisely that which he already is and always was, which is to say, he is Tadzio, the embodied abstraction of beauty, of eros, itself. He transcends the contradiction between the universal and the particular, between an idea and its instantiation, between the trope and its turning, between a fantasy and its filmic realization. But in this case the phantasmal promise can only be fulfilled by the ontological sorcery of cinema—with Björn Andrésen's bodily presence supplanting the immateriality of the merely ideational. Waving a lit cigarette with the flair of a conductor's baton, the auteur proceeds to describe the physique in front of him, fastidiously demonstrating its specifications with precise, quickly rhythmic gestures toward his own face and the young man's: "He is blond, he has this perfect profile and he has gray eyes. You see, he has . . . perfectly gray." At this point Visconti touches Andrésen's shoulder briefly, then gestures sharply toward his left eye, as if he had, with a

Fig. 30. Tadzio (Björn Andersen) vanishing into the skyline. From *Morte a Venezia* (*Death in Venice*, dir. Luchino Visconti, 1971).

magician's misdirection, another *tour de passe-passe*, just pulled a coin from behind the boy's ear.

The framing pans left to the model, who is caught gazing confidently at someone or something off camera and who now turns back to Visconti curiously, with an intensity suggesting he might be trying to read the director's lips. Visconti continues: "The color of water, Monsieur Mann says. In fact, it's this color we have today." The young man now lifts his gaze to the sky with a glance that reads less as if he were evaluating the weather than as though he were taking a direction. Or perhaps an instruction. Especially with the potential parallel to André Gide in mind, the moment comes across as almost pedagogical in tone. As in the initial audition Andrésen demonstrates through a sort of mimed comprehension that he cannot quite follow the conversation, fails to pass persuasively by doing so so very visibly. We never, to my knowledge, hear Björn Andrésen speak undubbed in Visconti's film, and in Benjamin Britten's operatic adaptation Tadzio is a ballet dancer with no singing part. Andrésen conveys in a later voice-over that Visconti only ever gave him four directions: go, stop, turn around, and smile. He is not only an idol but an ideal, perfection itself in a cameo. No acting is required.

He is, after all, pure image—having evaporated into the atmosphere surrounding him, just gray on gray, off-white. This grayness recalls the cloudy final view of Tadzio in *Morte a Venezia*: vanishingly small in an extreme long shot, difficult to distinguish against a murky background, an abandoned camera pointing at him from afar, emphasizing the scopophilic desire of this filmic fantasy (fig. 30). If Visconti's anatomy lesson in the Piazza San Marco insists on the material substantiation of the off-straight twink idol, this disappearance at the beach is its ethereal obverse: the dissolution into absolute iconicity. In a sense, then, Tadzio expires along with Aschenbach, passing away at the same moment.

For this is an essence forged of error and of failure. The documentary ends with a now elderly Andrésen reciting a soliloquy excerpted from a letter written by his mother: "There is not much left of me. . . . I have no feeling left for what I am and what I'm not. I look around. Am I this or that, here or there? I'm becoming invisible. I've given everything I had away. But I will not die." Evaporating into the ether, he himself becomes atmospheric: accident dissolved into a universal essence.[14] If the trope of the off-straight, off-white twink has staying power, perhaps it is because it so obstinately fails to recognize its own passing. Unlike the starts and stops, the lateral jumps and alternate genealogies of Svetlana Boym's *off-modern*, this is an arrested development. Its pretense to timelessness suggests an immutable ideal. Purely imaginary, the figure manages to remain perfectly self-identical. It is constant. The off-straight twink is ever youthful, for he does not age. His histories do not move forward.

✦

Nor does gay history, it seems, move on without him. If *Flamboyant Fictions* has traced a cultural narrative from its off-straight origins to its off-gay present, this is less because of a rejection of this figure and what it represents than because of an increasing identification with its universalizing tendencies. As sexuality is sidelined as a marker of subversion, the younger auteurs treated here can seem too seamless, appear inadequately queer, alongside the more outrageous provocations of an earlier avant-garde. In Jean Genet's reception by Rainer Werner Fassbinder, or Fassbinder's own perpetual revisions by François Ozon, gayness may be perceived to persist only as an apparently empty token of earlier innovation.

Similarly, some audiences may feel, as David Glassco writes, that the adaptation into art cinema "has travestied Mann" and that "we must reject the kind of trite thoughts and obvious emotions provided by Visconti."[15] This anticipates the charges of sentimentality frequently leveled against François Ozon or Xavier Dolan and my own gut feeling that Todd Haynes is occasionally inclined toward uncritical pastiche, taking the edge off the more off-putting homosexual aesthetic on which he draws. With the growing dissociation of camp self-invention from its abject origins, yet without ever fully sublimating an insistence on corporeal ontologies, an earlier essentialism appears and disappears as increasingly one-dimensional.

But bad taste has, as we have seen, long been a defining trait of this aesthetic. And so has its essentializing, universalizing impulse. It is incumbent upon us then to continue to discover hidden depths in what might appear too sleek and shallow. Stewart Burrows argues that at the basis of the "accusation that Visconti 'fail[ed] Thomas Mann' is a belief in the existence of a necessarily single, authoritative reading of Mann's text."[16] It is, at least in the case of the unquestionably queer Visconti, a refusal of ambivalence and a failure to read for form. And if the younger generations of auteur treated here seem indeed more reparative in their approach to queer history, it might be taken less as a sign that this history itself has decayed as an aesthetic paradigm than that it has once again achieved its aims. Aschenbach, a *stream of ashes*, as it would be translated: the very name suggests a current that has consumed itself and been exhausted. Its guiding stars are *out*: shining in continued testimony to lights long ago extinguished. Ever unable to pass, this narrative tradition passes away into its failures.

The widespread impression that contemporary queer cinema now feels less distinctly homosexual than its modernist influences—but instead loosely bisexual or generally pan-trans or emptily postgay—might seem to indicate an erasure and derealization, a loss of cultural specificity that perhaps regrettably accompanies gradual destigmatization, thereby lessening the urgency and relevance of a paradigm of passing. But where such queer mainstreaming historically attaches specifically to gay men, it may in small part reflect the tacitly interpellative quality of what is colloquially referred to as *flamboyance*. As queer cant, even in an off-gay idiom, camp appears exclusionary, but it's a weak password—not because it is too easily imitated but rather because it is so easily understood. It is what Philip Core, in one of the earliest studies of the sensibility, calls "a lie that tells the truth": it wantonly broadcasts its intention to subvert, it flaunts the secret that it refuses to keep.[17] It indoctrinates its audience in advance.

That any form of passing or its failure continues to arouse such vehement reaction—as is evident in the flaring culture wars over drag queens and trans bathroom rights and the terrifying recent wave of overtly antiqueer legislation—betrays the violence necessary to sustain mythologies of stable subjectivity unthreatened by alterity. The particular homophobia that flamboyance inspires is arguably less about the intolerability of effeminacy than about the power of its universalizing implication: you've cracked the code without even trying, it whispers, you understand this argot, this may indeed be meant for *you*. This inculcative queering, feminization, or homosexualization threateningly and presumptively reverses the directionality of what Sedgwick sees as a potentially reparative camp recognition.

Perhaps, then, ultimately, this demonstrates the continued need for paranoid interpretation. It strikes me, for example, as surprising, in retrospect, that as a child I would have empathized with Aschenbach and not with his beloved boy, especially given the relatively more robust psychology the latter character is granted in Visconti vis-à-vis his source text. Not everyone, after all, was oblivious to the sexuality of the film. Some contemporary critics complained that Tadzio had become not only a "beautiful youth" but a "pretty little tease"—seducing an Aschenbach reduced to "a foolish dirty old man" or "a fussy old man," as he is variously described, "an absent-minded professor who is in reality a lecherous fag."[18] And even Aschenbach, after all, seemingly models his abject attempt at feigned youthfulness not after his idol, but instead after the made-up fop or the repugnant street singer (played in Britten's opera by the same baritone) who fill him with a nauseating loathing.

Identities forged, as all are, through such catachresis must remain perpetually provisional, contingent upon the possible distortion of future iterations and citations. This openness to eventuality, it occurs to me, is surprisingly very much in keeping with Sedgwick's aspiration for a reparative reading that might register the could-be-otherwise of accident, exhibiting all the "features of a queer reading that can attune it exquisitely to a heartbeat of contingency."[19] What has emerged from the various discourses—literary, cinematic, theoretical—discussed throughout this book is an understanding of queer agency not as subjective intention manifested in action but rather as an activity whose intention and the subject to whom that intention will later be attributed materialize only afterward, through self-interpretative reflection. From Nietzsche to neuroscience we struggle with the notion that the self could in the end be nothing more than a post facto fiction, mere narrative invention. But that our selves may not exist does not make the experience of them any less real; it implies instead that selfhood is constituted first by its expression.[20] This is not an argument against narrativity but rather for the forms of storytelling that help us recognize how we instantiate and at once exceed ourselves.[21] It requires an attentiveness not only to aesthetic acceptance and stylistic passing but also to their hidden failures, to the whispered wish to vanish that has always lingered in flamboyance.

NOTES

Introduction

1. On the contribution that French literary modernism and its narratological innovations made to the articulation and encoding of gay male identity, and hence to the kind of eventual codification that will be examined here, see Lawrence R. Schehr, *French Gay Modernism* (Urbana: University of Illinois Press, 2004).

2. See José Esteban Muñoz, *Disidentifications: Queers of Color and the Performance of Politics* (Minneapolis: University of Minnesota Press, 1999), 5–6.

3. I am drawing here, as I will explore especially in chapters 4 and 6, on Richard Dyer's excavation of the contradictory demand of whiteness to (in)visibility. See Richard Dyer, *White* (London: Routledge, 1997).

4. See Eve Kosofsky Sedgwick, *The Epistemology of the Closet* (Berkeley: University of California Press, 1990).

5. For another use of this slogan and an examination of its implications, see Ivan Raykoff, "Queer Patriotism in the Eurovision Song Contest," in *The Oxford Handbook of Music and Queerness*, ed. Fred Everett Maus and Sheila Whiteley (Oxford: Oxford University Press, 2022), 503.

6. Linda Schlossberg, "Introduction: Rites of Passing," in *Passing: Identity and Interpretation in Sexuality, Race, and Religion*, ed. María Carla Sánchez and Linda Schlossberg (New York: New York University Press, 2001), 3.

7. Schlossberg phrases this thought rather pithily: "Passing becomes a form of passive resistance, one that protects the gay subject from hostile interpretations." Schlossberg, "Rites of Passing," 3.

8. Elaine K. Ginsberg, "Introduction: The Politics of Passing," in *Passing and the Fictions of Identity*, ed. Elaine K. Ginsberg (Durham, NC: Duke University Press, 1996), 4.

9. Pamela Caughie, *Passing and Pedagogy: The Dynamics of Responsibility* (Urbana: University of Illinois Press, 1999), 2, 22. Indeed, one of the explicit aims of Caughie's book "is to move 'passing' from its negative associations with disguise, impersonation, appropriation, and fraudulence and to refigure it as a potentially ethical practice." Caughie, *Passing*, 48.

10. Anna Camaiti Hostert would presumably concur: "I propose to treat passing as a metaphor for identity formation, as well as a metaphor for transgression—for the practice of violating boundaries that masquerade as absolute and universal when they are, in fact, contingent, historical and local." Anna Camaiti Hostert, *Passing: A Strategy to Dissolve Identities and Remap Differences*, trans. Christine Marciasini (Madison, NJ: Farleigh Dickinson University Press, 2007), 15.

11. Jessa Lingel, "Adjusting the Borders: Bisexual Passing and Queer Theory," *Journal of Bisexuality* 9, no. 3–4 (2009): 396, 389.

12. C. Riley Snorton, "'A New Hope': The Psychic Life of Passing," *Hypatia* 24, no. 3 (Summer 2009): 80, 79.

13. See Sandy Stone, "The Empire Strikes Back: A Posttransexual Manifesto," *Camera Obscura* 10, no. 2 (1992).

14. Snorton, "Psychic Life of Passing," 87. The term "fragile fiction" is borrowed from E. Patrick Johnson, whose work argues against discourses of authenticity, endorsing instead an inherently appropriative blackness, in part as a means of subverting received prescriptions for black masculinity: "Because the concept of blackness has no essence, 'black authenticity' is overdetermined—contingent on the historical, social, and political terms of its production. . . . The key here is to be cognizant of the arbitrariness of authenticity, the ways in which it carries with it the dangers of foreclosing the possibilities of cultural exchange and understanding." E. Patrick Johnson, *Appropriating Blackness: Performance and the Politics of Authenticity* (Durham, NC: Duke University Press, 2003), 3. Johnson himself adapts the term from Clifford Geertz, "Thinking as a Moral Act: Anthropological Fieldwork in the New States," *Antioch Review* 28, no. 2 (Summer 1968): 142.

15. Snorton, "Psychic Life of Passing," 87.

16. Snorton, "Psychic Life of Passing," 86.

17. Snorton, "Psychic Life of Passing," 88.

18. As Snorton clarifies: "*Misrecognition* . . . is as important as recognition in the production of the self, as the quality of feeling misrecognized/unseen/wrongly viewed serves as a context for the emergence of selfhood. The sense of feeling misrecognized also serves as a site of resistance in forms of identification governed by the politics of recognition, as the possibility of misrecognition carries with it the opportunity for deliberation and the potential rejection of social scripts, which get mapped onto one's body." Snorton, "Psychic Life of Passing," 88, original emphasis.

19. Judith Butler, *Bodies That Matter: On the Discursive Limits of Sex* (New York: Routledge, 1993), 173–74, original emphasis. An original version of this chapter first appeared under the same title, "Critically Queer" in *GLQ* 1 (1993): 20.

20. Butler's newest work on the subject, which appeared while the present book was already in production, is explicitly not an attempt to defend or reevaluate the thinker's earlier gender theory in light of more recent trans and material criticism but rather an excavation of the catch-all phantasmatic specter constituted by what is understood as *gender* by all manner of contemporary rightwing ideology. See Judith Butler, Who's Afraid of Gender (New York: Farrar, Straus and Giroux, 2024).

21. Butler, *Bodies That Matter*, 184, original emphasis.

22. The German cognate *fehlen*—a verb denoting lack, absence, error, something missing or something that misses its mark, without necessarily connoting failure in any charged or normative sense—might give a better feel for what I am trying to express. This phenomenon could be playfully described, adapting a Jack Halberstam title important to chapter 3, as the queer art of *Fehl*-ure. See Jack Halberstam, *The Queer Art of Failure* (Durham, NC: Duke University Press, 2011).

23. Or as *the* matter of identity, as Butler's title punningly implies. With this work in mind, Snorton makes the case for an account of passing that occasions reconceptualization of corporeal materiality itself: "Paying attention to the psychic dimensions of passing opens up new modes of thinking about the materiality of transsexual bodies." Snorton, "Psychic Life of Passing," 78, original emphasis.

24. Eve Kosofsky Sedgwick, *Touching Feeling: Affect, Pedagogy, Performativity* (Durham, NC: Duke University Press, 2002), 13.

25. Ellen Samuels, "My Body, My Closet: Invisible Disability and the Limits of Coming-Out Discourse." *GLQ* 9, no. 1 (2003): 240. See also John Swain and Colin Cameron, "Unless Otherwise Stated: Discourses of Labelling and Identity in Coming Out," in *Disability Discourse*, ed. Marian Corker and Sally French (Philadelphia: Open University Press, 1999).

26. Caughie, *Passing*, 22.

27. Caughie, *Passing*, 28.

28. I agree here with Butler's view of agency as inescapably mimetic: "'Agency' would . . . be the double-movement of being constituted in and by a signifier [like queer], where 'to be constituted' means 'to be compelled to cite or repeat or mime' the signifier itself." Butler, *Bodies That Matter*, 167.

29. Schlossberg, "Rites of Passing," 2.

30. Dennis R. Cooley and Kelby Harrison, introduction to *Passing/Out: Sexual Identity Veiled and Revealed*, ed. Dennis R. Cooley and Kelby Harrison (Lanham, MD: Lexington Books, 2012), 5. Such discomfort over the denial or repudiation of authentic selfhood is also readily discernible across many of the contributions to this series of printed exchanges and debates. Lamenting queer studies ostensible abandonment of ethics and contending that a Butlerian model of performativity "overlooks the role of biological bodies," Harrison's later monograph on passing is also fundamentally reliant on the notion of an unchanging underlying self, of an established agency fixed in place prior to the activity of passing. See Kelby Harrison, *Sexual Deceit: The Ethics of Passing* (Lanham, MD: Lexington Books, 2013).

31. Camaiti Hostert, *Passing*, 12, my emphasis. See also Cheryl A. Wall, "Passing for What? Aspects of Identity in Nella Larsen's Novels," *Black American Literature Forum* 20, no. 1–2 (Spring–Summer 1986): 97–111.

32. Camaiti Hostert, *Passing*, 12.

33. As Nicholas de Villiers writes of passing's inverse, namely, *coming out*: "The metaphor of 'coming out of the closet' is . . . propounded not just as a manner of being truthful but also as the quintessential gesture of acknowledging who one is. To 'come out' is first and foremost to locate an identity not just in a speech act but in a speech act by which one presumably discloses a previously closeted 'secret.' 'Coming out of the closet' is thus the seemingly ubiquitous metaphor for understanding the connection between homosexuality, identity, and speech (usually conceived as authentic, true, and free expression of a formerly repressed sexuality)." Nicholas de Villiers, *Opacity and the Closet: Queer Tactics in Foucault, Barthes and Warhol* (Minneapolis: University of Minnesota Press, 2012), 1–2.S

34. Lingel, "Bisexual Passing," 396.

35. Ginsberg, "Politics of Passing," 4.

36. Heather Love, "Beginning with *Stigma*," *GLQ* 25, no. 1 (2019): 34, my emphasis.

37. Sedgwick, *Touching Feeling*, 6.

38. My own undertaking in these pages resonates to an extent with recent attempts to reconcile deconstructive reading strategies trained on rhetoric and tropology with those focusing on professedly extralinguistic affective states grounded in the materiality of the body. See, e.g., Rei Terada's influential *Feeling in Theory: Emotion after the "Death of the Subject"* (Cambridge, MA: Harvard University Press, 2003) or, more recently and perhaps more pertinently, Eszter Timár's article, "The Body of Shame in Affect Theory and Deconstruction," *Parallax* 25, no. 2 (2019). Such studies might be seen as a renewal (although perhaps now more cooperative in spirit) of the debate inaugurated by Ruth Leys's critique of affect studies and the responses by William E. Connolly and later Adam Frank and Elizabeth A. Wilson, among others, in the pages of *Critical Inquiry* in 2011 and 2012.

39. Sedgwick, *Touching Feeling*, 6.

40. Sedgwick, *Touching Feeling*, 61.

41. Sedgwick, *Touching Feeling*, 61, 62.

42. Heather Love, "Doing Being Deviant: Deviance Studies, Description, and the Queer Ordinary," Special issue on "Queer Theory without Antinormativity," *differences* 26, no. 1 (2015): 74, original emphasis. See also Heather Love, "Doing Being Deviant," in *Underdogs: Social Deviance and Queer Theory* (Chicago: University of Chicago Press, 2021), 136–60.

43. Sedgwick, *Touching Feeling*, 13.

44. See Susan Sontag, "Notes on 'Camp,'" *Against Interpretation and Other Essays* (New York: Picador, 1966), 275–92.

45. Sedgwick, *Touching Feeling*, 64

46. Sedgwick, *Touching Feeling*, 139.

47. Sedgwick, *Touching Feeling*, 149. It is at the conclusion to the initial publication of the essay that Sedgwick first puts into print her concerns about "the uses scholars are trying to make of performativity as they think they are understanding it from Judith Butler's and other related recent work: straining eyes to ascertain whether particular performances (e.g. of drag) are really *parodic and subversive* (e.g. of gender essentialism) or *just uphold the status quo*. The bottom line is generally the same: kinda subversive, kinda hegemonic. I see this as a sadly premature domestication of a conceptual tool whose powers we really have barely yet begun to explore." Sedgwick, "Queer Performativity: Henry James's Art of the Novel" in *GLQ* 1 (1993): 15.

48. Sedgwick, *Touching Feeling*, 63.

49. We might think of this bracketing (*Einklammerung*) as a phenomenological *epochē*, of course, suspending judgment on a supposed reality to which one has no direct access. But the origin of the English term in the Middle French *braguette*, meaning codpiece, perhaps more playfully suggests the contours of a sexuality made visible through transparently disguised abstraction.

50. C. Riley Snorton, *Nobody Is Supposed to Know: Black Sexuality on the Down Low* (Minneapolis: University of Minnesota Press, 2014), 21. See also Marlon Ross, "Beyond the Closet as Raceless Paradigm," in *Black Queer Studies: A Critical Anthology*, ed. Patrick E. Johnson and Mae G. Henderson (Durham, NC: Duke University Press, 2005).

51. See Sedgwick, *Epistemology of the Closet*, 75. Discussed by Snorton, *Nobody Is Supposed to Know*, 21.

52. Ginsberg, "Politics of Passing," 2.

53. Amy Robinson, "It Takes One to Know One: Passing and Communities of Common Interest," *Critical Inquiry* 20, no. 4 (Summer 2009): 716. Quoted in Ginsberg, "Politics of Passing," 4.

54. Snorton, *Nobody Is Supposed to Know*, 4; de Villiers, *Opacity and the Closet*, 6.

55. Svetlana Boym, *The Off-Modern* (New York: Bloomsbury Academic, 2017), 130, 6. Boym's mention of an aesthetics of failure follows immediately on the heels of a citation of Susan Sontag's essay on the camp sensibility. Boym, *The Off-Modern*, 129.

56. Sedgwick, *Touching Feeling*, 138.

57. This insight echoes Sedgwick's earlier allusion to the "glass closet" upon which Snorton's terminology is troping: "Coming out is a matter of crystallizing intuitions or convictions that had been in the air for a while already and had already established their own power-circuits of silent contempt, silent blackmail, silent glamorization, silent complicity. After all, the position of those who think they know something about one that one may not know oneself is an excited and empowered one—whether what they think one doesn't know is that one somehow is homosexual, or merely that one's supposed secret is known to them." Sedgwick, *Epistemology of the Closet*, 79–80.

58. Sontag, "Notes on 'Camp,'" 283.

59. Pamela Caughie, "Passing as Modernism," *Modernism/Modernity* 12, no. 3 (2005): 401.

60. Caughie, "Passing as Modernism," 404.

61. Camaiti Hostert, *Passing*, 15.

62. Lisa Walker, *Looking Like What You Are: Sexual Style, Race and Lesbian Identity* (New York: New York University Press, 2001), 10, 1.

63. Caughie elaborates this thought specifically in the context of North American academia: "When various postmodern theories that deconstruct the 'self' converge with various studies programs that revive it, anxiety arises over the positions we find ourselves in as professors and learners in the newly configured university." Caughie, *Passing*, 13.

64. Caughie, *Passing*, 13.

65. I draw here again on the work of Snorton, who highlights this capacity of passing in work on cross-gendered fugitive narratives, examining "how fungibility became critical practice-cum-performance for blacks in the antebellum period" and ultimately proposing that "fungibility and fugitivity figured two sides of a Janus-faced coin, in which the same logic that figured blackness as immanently interchangeable would also engender its flow." C. Riley Snorton, *Black on Both Sides: A Racial History of Trans Identity* (Minneapolis: University of Minnesota Press, 2017): 57, 84.

66. I am thinking specifically of Vivaldo's lament over the cock-teasing opacity of his own characters in *Another Country* (1962): "He did not seem to know enough about the people in his novel. . . . He could move them about but they themselves did not move. He put words in their mouths which they uttered sullenly, unconvinced. With the same agony, or greater, with which he attempted to

seduce a woman, he was trying to seduce his people: he begged them to surrender up to him their privacy. And they refused—without, for all their ugly intransigence, showing the faintest desire to leave him. They were waiting for him to find the key, to press the nerve, tell the truth. *Then* they seemed to be complaining, they would give him all he wished for and much more than he was now willing to imagine." James Baldwin, *Another Country* (London: Penguin Classics, 2001), 130.

67. A passing sailor in *Giovanni's Room* (1956) distills and embodies the trope of the off-straight twink, with whom the narrator at once identifies and disidentifies: "There was a sailor, dressed all in white, coming across the boulevard, walking with that funny roll sailors have and with that aura, hopeful and hard, of having to make a great deal happen in a hurry. I was staring at him, though I did not know it, and wishing I were he. He seemed—somehow—younger than I had ever been, and blonder and more beautiful, and he wore his masculinity as unequivocally as he wore his skin." James Baldwin, *Giovanni's Room* (New York: Vintage International, 2013), 91–92. Speaking of sailors, Jean Genet, who makes a sort of unnamed but undisguised cameo at a house party in this novel, is also potentially an influence on the crime at its core: Giovanni's strangulation of the predatory queen Guillaume, itself reluctantly imagined by a narrator unable to control his own tortured fantasy, echoes the unthinking murder of Joachim in Genet's maritime *Querelle de Brest* (1947), discussed in chapter 3. Baldwin, *Giovanni's Room*, 112, 154–57.

68. Valerie Rohy, "Displacing Desire: Passing, Nostalgia and *Giovanni's Room*," in Ginsberg, *Passing and the Fictions of Identity*, 231, 219.

69. See André Gide, *Journal*, vol. 1, ed. Eric Marty (Paris: Gallimard 1996), 671; *Journals: 1914–1927* (Urbana: University of Illinois Press, 2000), 246. For a more careful and more thorough account of the emergent terminology in French, see the first chapter of Michael Lucey, *Never Say I: Sexuality in the First Person in Colette, Gide, and Proust* (Durham, NC: Duke University Press, 2006), 29–56. For the German-language context, see Robert Deam Tobin's introduction to *Peripheral Desires: The German Discovery of Sex* (Philadelphia: University of Pennsylvania Press, 2015), 1–26.

70. Michael Lucey expresses a reasonable hesitation, for instance, about the notion of modern pederasty discussed in chapter 1: "Amin's suggestion that 'we have misread [Genet] as a gay man rather than a pederast' . . . implies a shared set of cultural concepts and maybe a shared historical and geopolitical point of view in which 'gay man' and 'pederast' can be held each to be conceptually coherent in its own right, and the opposition between them to be durably meaningful." Michael Lucey, *Someone: The Pragmatics of Misfit Sexualities from Colette to Hervé Guibert* (Chicago: University of Chicago Press, 2019), 266n27. See Kadji Amin, *Disturbing Attachments: Genet, Modern Pederasty, and Queer History* (Durham, NC: Duke University Press, 2017), 28.

71. I borrow the phrasing *subversive edge* from Phillip Bryan Harper's critique of the same locution in an early reading of Jenny Livingston's *Paris Is Burning* (1990). See Phillip Bryan Harper, "'The Subversive Edge': *Paris Is Burning*, Social Critique and the Limits of Subjective Agency," *diacritics* 24, no. 2–3 (Summer-Autumn, 1994): 90–103.

72. Leo Bersani, *Homos* (Cambridge, MA: Harvard University Press, 1995).

Chapter 1

1. Kadji Amin, *Disturbing Attachments: Genet, Modern Pederasty, and Queer History* (Durham, NC: Duke University Press, 2017), 185.

2. Amin, *Disturbing Attachments*, 188.

3. Amin, *Disturbing Attachments*, 14.

4. Amin, *Disturbing Attachments*, 41.

5. Amin, *Disturbing Attachments*, 41, my emphasis.

6. Amin, *Disturbing Attachments*, 41.

7. Amin is not unaware of this issue, speaking of "the worrisome harmony between queer's much trumpeted mobility, flexibility, adaptability, and portability and the demands for accelerated obsolescence and flexible and mobile labor that characterize late capitalism." *Disturbing Attachments*, 182. This is, moreover, a process in which my own monograph, which is not without its own coinages and redefinitions, cannot help but performatively participate.

8. Naomi Segal, for instance, already in 1998, considers it "well established that the main model for Robert de Passavant is Cocteau." Naomi Segal, *André Gide: Pederasty and Pedagogy* (Oxford: Clarendon Press, 1998), 264.

9. André Gide, *Romans et récits: Œuvres lyriques et dramatiques* (Paris: Gallimard, 2009), 2:339; *The Counterfeiters with Journal of "The Counterfeiters,"* trans. Dorothy Bussy and Justin O'Brien (New York: Alfred A. Knopf, 1972), 204.

10. Namely, Gide's dialogues on homosexuality and pederasty, *Corydon* (first privately published in 1911 and 1920, but not with Gide's name until 1924) and his autobiographical *Si le grain ne meurt* (*If It Die . . .* , also 1924), where he shockingly recounts his discovery of his homosexuality during a trip to Algeria with Oscar Wilde. For more on Gide's insistence, at this moment in his career, on "the publicness of his homosexuality," see Michael Lucey, *Gide's Bent: Sexuality, Politics, Writing* (Oxford: Oxford University Press, 1995), 108–9.

11. See also Emily Apter's *André Gide and the Codes of Homotextuality* (Saratoga, CA: Anma Libri 1987), which, as its title implies, probes the connections between textuality and sexuality in the author, but surprisingly does not deal with *Les faux-monnayeurs*.

12. Lucey, *Gide's Bent*, 109.

13. Lucey, *Gide's Bent*, 110.

14. Lucey, *Gide's Bent*, 110.

15. Segal, *Pederasty and Pedagogy*, 264.

16. Segal, *Pederasty and Pedagogy*, 172.

17. Gide, *Romans*, 2:237; *Counterfeiters*, 80.

18. Jean Genet, *Our Lady of the Flowers*, trans. Bernard Frechtman (New York: Grove Press, 1963), 207.

19. As David LaGuardia helpfully traces this etymology: "'Desrober' originally meant 'to relieve one of one's clothes,' as in the English 'to disrobe.' In [another] context, however, it signifies specifically to rob, and by a familiar reversal remarked by Freud . . . 'dérober' in modern French means 'prendre furtivement' [take furtively], and, by extension, 'masquer, cacher, dissumuler' [mask, hide, dissimulate], and, even, when speaking of things, 'empêcher de voir, masquer à la vue' [to keep from seeing, to mask from sight]. In other words, this term, which is derived from the Old German *rauben*, translated by the editors of the *Petit Robert* as 'dépouiller,' 'to skin,' includes a spectrum of meanings ranging from revelation

to hiding, from uncovering to concealing from view." David LaGuardia, *Intertextual Masculinity in French Renaissance Literature: Rabelais, Brantôme and the "Cent Nouvelles Nouvelles"* (Aldershot, UK: Ashgate, 2008), 139.

20. Gide, *Counterfeiters*, 410.

21. Lucey, *Gide's Bent*, 142.

22. Lucey, *Gide's Bent*, 142.

23. Gide, *Romans*, 2:215; *Counterfeiters*, 51.

24. Gide, *Romans*, 2:333; *Counterfeiters*, 197, translation modified.

25. In his introduction to *Sexual Dissidence*, Dollimore contrasts what he understands as Gide's essentialism to Wilde's antiessentialism, with a clear preference for the latter. Jonathan Dollimore, *Sexual Dissidence: Augustine to Wilde, Freud to Foucault* (Oxford: Oxford University Press, 1991). Lucey also takes issue with this rigid paradigm. Lucey, *Gide's Bent*, 11–12n17. Personally, as my introduction to this book perhaps suggests, I subscribe to José Esteban Muñoz's by now no longer novel "belief that the use-value of any narrative of identity that reduces subjectivity to either a social constructivist model or what has been called an essentialist understanding of the self is especially exhausted. Clearly, neither story is complete, but the way in which these understandings of the self have come to be aligned with each other as counternarratives is now a standard protocol of theory-making processes that are no longer of much use." José Esteban Muñoz, *Disidentifications: Queers of Color and the Performance of Politics* (Minneapolis: University of Minnesota Press, 1999), 5–6.

26. Gide, *Counterfeiters*, 186, translation modified, ellipsis in the original.

27. Scott Branson notes how Wilde and Gide also "undermine the codification of homosexual desire as a love of self in their retelling of the Narcissus myth" by figuring Narcissus himself as mere reflection. Scott Branson, "Gide, Wilde and the Death of the Novel," *MLN* 127, no. 5 (December 2012): 1237.

28. André Gide, *Journal*, vol. 1 (Paris: Gallimard 1996), 1171, my translation.

29. Gide, *Counterfeiters*, 171. The word is in English in the original. Gide, *Romans*, 2:311.

30. Gide, *Counterfeiters*, 172, original emphasis.

31. Gide, *Counterfeiters*, 189.

32. Gide, *Counterfeiters*, 189.

33. Gide, *Counterfeiters*, 173.

34. Gide, *Counterfeiters*, 173.

35. As Kirk Wetters notes: "Gide's novel is, however, not identical with Édouard's; it cannot be the case that *The Counterfeiters* of the diegesis literally is Gide's novel—at least not without producing an infinite regress and subordinating external reality to the reality of the novel and thereby reversing their hierarchy. The most that can be said is that Gide's novel is about Édouard's novel (of the same title) and perhaps that 'counterfeiting' defines both novels' form and content." Kirk Wetters, *Demonic History: From Goethe to the Present* (Evanston, IL: Northwestern University Press, 2014), 164–65.

36. Gide, *Counterfeiters*, 170–71.

37. Gide, *Counterfeiters*, 176, translation modified.

38. Gide, *Counterfeiters*, 176, ellipsis in the original.

39. Gide, *Romans*, 2:317; *Counterfeiters*, 176, translation modified, second ellipsis in the original.

40. I use *metalepsis* here in the sense employed by Gérard Genette to designate an intrusion of the extradiegetic narrator into the diegetic universe of the novel. Gérard Genette, *Narrative Discourse: An Essay in Method*, trans. Jane Lewin (Ithaca, NY: Cornell University Press, 1980). For a useful gloss of Genette and an expert treatment of *Les faux-monnayeurs*, see also Dorrit Cohn, "Metalepsis and Mise en Abyme," trans. Lewis S. Gleich, *Narrative* 20, no. 1 (January 2012): 105–14.

41. Gide, *Counterfeiters*, 51.

42. Gide, *Romans*, 2:233; *Counterfeiters*, 74.

43. Gide, *Romans*, 2:175; *Counterfeiters*, 3.

44. Susan J. Ringler, who describes *le démon* as the novel's "most irritating and least understood character," documents its five intrusions as well as the various references to *le diable* in the novel. Susan J. Ringler, "Gide's 'Les Faux-monnayeurs': Demons and Present Tense Verbs," *Romance Notes* 20, no. 1 (Fall 1979): 29.

45. Ringler, "Demons," 29.

46. Gide, *Counterfeiters*, 204; *Romans*, 2:339.

47. Henri Massis, "L'influence de M. André Gide," *La revue universelle*, November 15, 1921, my translation.

48. Catharine Savage Brosman, "Gide et le démon," *Claudel Studies* 13, no. 2 (January 1986): 46, my translation.

49. André Gide, *Essais critiques* (Paris: Gallimard, 1999), 637, my translation, original emphasis.

50. On Gide's demon as Socratic daimon, see Claudia Bouliane, "Le démonisme d'André Gide: Le pouvoir de l'induction." *Fabula / Les colloques, Les écrivains théoriciens de la littérature (1920–1945)*, May 9, 2013, http://atelier.fabula.org/colloques/document1841.php. See also Wetters, *Demonic History*, 12.

51. Gide, *The Counterfeiters*, 384.

52. Segal, *Pederasty and Pedagogy*, 248, 333. Adapting the precedent of Leslie Fiedler, Segal works out a more complicated but perhaps slightly confused taxonomy of good bad boys and bad bad boys that need not concern us here. Segal, *Pederasty and Pedagogy*, 239–52. See also Fiedler, *Love and Death in the American Novel* (New York: Criterion Books, 1960). On the alabaster blondness of Lafcadio, see Segal's chapter on "Gide's Skin" in her *Consensuality: Didiez Anzieu, Gender, and the Sense of Touch* (Amsterdam: Rodopi, 2009), 85.

53. Segal, *Pederasty and Pedagogy*, 239.

54. Gide, *Counterfeiters*, 204; *Romans*, 2:339.

55. Gide, *Counterfeiters*, 204.

56. Gide, *Counterfeiters*, 204.

57. Gide, *Counterfeiters*, 204.

58. Gide, *Romans*, 2:456, my emphasis; *The Counterfeiters*, 382, my emphasis.

59. Gide, *Romans*, 2:465; *Counterfeiters*, 394, original emphasis.

60. André Gide, *La nouvelle revue française* 158 (November 1, 1926): 610–11. Gide's two letters on the subject and a published selection of *fait divers* are also contained as "News Items" in *Judge Not* (Urbana: University of Illinois, 2003), 89–128; from which edition I will cite.

61. Emily Apter, "Allegories of Reading / Allegories of Justice: The Gidean *Fait Divers*," *Romanic Review* 80, no. 4 (1989): 561, 569. As Apter has it, "Gide's *faits divers*, both published and unpublished, illustrate the cliché that life imitates

and even outstrips art in its configurations of the grotesque and bizarre. In this respect they form a perfect counterpart to novels such as *Les caves du Vatican* or *Les faux-monnayeurs*, the plots of which are stamped with the imprint of deviant narrative strategies typically found in the *fait divers*." Apter, "The Gidean *Fait Divers*," 564.

62. André Gide, *Ne jugez pas* (Paris: Gallimard, 1969), 145; *Judge Not*, 93, translation modified.

63. Gide, *Judge Not*, 92. See also Gide's nearly identical avowal in his introduction to his piece on the Redureau Affair: "Surely no human act is entirely unmotivated; no act is gratuitous, except in appearance. But we must agree here that current psychological expertise doesn't allow us to understand everything and that there are many unexplored regions, or *terrae incognitae*, on the map of the human soul." Gide, *Judge Not*, 59.

64. See Victoria Reid, *Gide and Curiosity* (Amsterdam: Rodolpi, 2009), 191–201. Alain Goulet speculates that Gide's guilt results from his having rebuffed his friend's advances. Goulet, "Sur une figure obsédante—vers l'origine de la création littéraire," *La revue des lettres modernes*, no. 1033 (1991): 47–60.

65. As Scott Branson, in a recent article on Gide and Wilde, has commented on the inclusion of the touched-up *fait divers* at the end of *Les faux-monnayeurs*, "for Gide the motiveless act—or *acte gratuit*—signifies the ultimate pleasure fiction offers, since it couples the desire for representation with the resistance to explanation, the very limits of the literary. The ambivalence resides in the act itself, a forced suicide, which Gide registers doubly by countering his narration of Boris's death with Édouard's theoretical refusal. . . . By placing this 'outrageously real' event in his own novel, Gide tries to have it both ways: he simultaneously represents and refuses to represent reality in the form of Boris's death." Branson, "Death of the Novel," 1236.

66. Gide, *Counterfeiters*, 396.

67. Gide, *Romans*, 2:359; *Counterfeiters*, 250.

68. Gide, *Counterfeiters*, 396.

69. Gide, *Counterfeiters*, 246.

70. Gide, *Romans*, 2:356–57; *Counterfeiters*, 246–47.

71. Gide, *Counterfeiters*, 247.

72. Gide, *Romans*, 2:463–4; *Counterfeiters*, 391, my emphasis.

73. Gide, *Counterfeiters*, 391, both ellipses in the original.

74. Gide, *Romans*, 2:461; *Counterfeiters*, 388.

75. Judith Butler, *Bodies That Matter: On the Discursive Limits of Sex* (New York: Routledge, 1993), 167.

76. Lafcadio, the character whose voice we hear in this passage, goes on to speculate that existence itself is governed by the imperative "'Let all that can be, be!' That's my explanation of Creation . . . In love with what might be." André Gide, *Les caves du Vatican* (Paris: Gallimard, 1996), 191, ellipsis in the original; *Lafcadio's Adventures*, trans. Dorothy Bussy (New York: Vintage Books, 2003), 207, original emphasis, both ellipses in the original.

77. Leonid Livak, *How It Was Done in Paris: Russian Émigré Literature and French Modernism* (Madison, WI: University of Wisconsin Press, 2003), 197. Also quoted in Reid, *Gide and Curiosity*, 240n93.

78. Gide, *Counterfeiters*, 386–87.

79. Reid, *Gide and Curiosity*, 239.

80. Gide, *Romans*, 2:458; *Counterfeiters*, 384.

81. Anna-Louise Milne, "Gide's Polymorphous Perversity, or French Modernism's Arrested Development," *Romanic Review* 99, nos. 1–2 (2008): 110.

82. Sontag, "Notes on 'Camp,' " 287.

83. Milne, "Gide's Polymorphous Perversity," 110, 117.

84. Milne, "Gide's Polymorphous Perversity," 108.

85. Milne, "Gide's Polymorphous Perversity," 107.

86. Milne, "Gide's Polymorphous Perversity," 107. For another take on such queer world making as autofabulation, see Tavia Nyong'o, who similarly describes a suspension of binaries of true and false resulting from a "*drive for the virtual* . . . on the part of black subjects." Tavia Nyong'o, *Afro-Fabulations: The Queer Drama of Black Life* (New York: New York University Press, 2019), 14.

87. Recalling Lucey's considerations of the question of sincerity and authenticity in homophobic readings of *Les faux-monnayeurs*, Alison James has helpfully distinguished between the two, demonstrating that while the former (*sincérité*) may be the operative principle in Gide's autobiographical writing, what concerns him when it comes to the *fait divers* is the latter (*authenticité*). But this is not, as might be expected, a question of facticity: "The authenticity of a document has less to do with any intention of veridicality than it does with the indexical character of the document itself, its attachment by a link of causality to a given context or site of enunciation." Alison James, "Le fait divers aux frontières de la fiction: la rhétorique documentaire d'André Gide," *Bulletin des Amis d'André Gide* 46, no. 177/178 (January–April 2013): 79.

88. Walt Whitman, *Song of Myself and Other Poems by Walt Whitman* (Berkeley, CA: Counterpoint, 2010), 69.

89. Paul de Man, "Whatever Happened to André Gide? (1965)," in *Critical Writings, 1953–1978* (Minneapolis: University of Minnesota Press, 1989), 135.

90. De Man, "Whatever Happened to André Gide?," 131.

91. Milne has also noted that queer readings of Gide in the wake of de Man have "thus dismantled part of the very epistemological frame [of] the dichotomy between sincerity and inauthenticity, or the inner truth of the subject versus the various external guises, or 'inauthentic' masks, in de Man's final conclusion." Milne, "Gide's Polymorphous Perversity, 106.

92. Branson, "Death of the Novel," 1236.

93. Michael Lucey, *Never Say I: Sexuality in the First Person in Colette, Gide, and Proust* (Durham, NC: Duke University Press, 2006), 23.

94. Lucey, *Never Say I*, 23.

95. Branson, "Death of the Novel," 1236.

96. Milne reminds us that this "sense of growing into youth, with the concomitant notion that naturalness or harmonious existence is the result of creation and effort, finds an echo in the numerous occasions in Gide's autobiographical work where he liked to claim that he grew younger as he got older." Milne, "Gide's Polymorphous Perversity," 116. Beyond the Peter Pan trope highlighted here, the formal play of J. M. Barrie's novel *Peter and Wendy* (1911) emphasizes narratological arbitrariness in a manner that would situate it in the tradition of counterfeiting excavated here. Segal also picks up on the affinity with Barrie. See Segal, *Pederasty and Pedagogy*, 349.

97. Jean Cocteau, *Poésie critique*, vol. 1 (Paris: Gallimard, 1959), 220–21, my translation.

98. Lee Edelman, *Homographesis: Essays in Gay Literary and Cultural Theory* (New York: Routledge, 1994), 114. Also quoted by David Halperin, *Saint Foucault: Towards a Gay Hagiography* (Oxford: Oxford University Press, 1995), 67.

99. David Halperin, "The Normalization of Queer Theory," *Journal of Homosexuality* 24, nos. 2–4 (2003): 342.

100. Friedrich Nietzsche, "On Truth and Lying in an Extramoral Sense," in *Friedrich Nietzsche on Rhetoric and Language*, ed. Sander L. Gilman, Carole Blair, and David J. Parent (Oxford: Oxford University Press, 1989), 250.

101. Robyn Wiegman and Elizabeth A. Wilson, "Introduction: Antinormativity's Queer Conventions," *differences* 26, no. 1 (2015): 4, 11. Wiegman and Wilson are quoting from Halperin, "Normalization of Queer Theory," 341.

Chapter 2

1. Jean Genet, *Our Lady of the Flowers*, trans. Bernard Frechtman (New York: Grove Press, 1963), 82.

2. Genet, *Our Lady of the Flowers*, 170.

3. Jean Genet, *Notre-Dame-des-Fleurs* (Paris: Gallimard, 2000), 20; *Our Lady of the Flowers*, 69.

4. Genet, *Notre-Dame-des-Fleurs* 31; *Our Lady of the Flowers*, 76–77, translation modified.

5. Judith Butler, *Bodies That Matter: On the Discursive Limits of Sex* (New York: Routledge, 1993), 4.

6. For the continuation of Butler's inquiry into the tropology of subjecthood, mediating between Jacques Lacan, Louis Althusser, and Michel Foucault, see, especially, Judith Butler, *The Psychic Life of Power: Theories in Subjection* (Stanford, CA: Stanford University Press, 1997).

7. José Esteban Muñoz, *Disidentifications: Queers of Color and the Performance of Politics* (Minneapolis: University of Minnesota Press, 1999), 9, 31.

8. Muñoz, *Disidentifications*, 6.

9. Genet, *Our Lady of the Flowers*, 83, translation modified.

10. I am grateful to Jonas Rosenbrück for bringing this association to my attention.

11. Didier Eribon, *Insult and the Making of the Gay Self*, trans. Michael Lucey (Durham, NC: Duke University Press, 2004), 7.

12. Eribon, *Insult*, 111.

13. While *différance* is, of course, rightly understood to be a central concept in Derridean thought on the whole, here I refer specifically to its earliest elaboration in his discussion of Edmund Husserl's phenomenology, especially in chapters 5 and 6 of *La Voix et le phénomène* (*Voice and Phenomenon*, 1967), where it is perhaps most rigorously connected to questions of subjectivity. See Jacques Derrida, *Voice and Phenomenon: Introduction to the Problem of the Sign in Husserl's Phenomenology*, trans. Leonard Lawlor (Evanston, IL: Northwestern University Press, 2011), esp. 51–74.

14. Leo Bersani, *Homos* (Cambridge, MA: Harvard University Press, 1995).

15. James Creech, "Outing Jean Genet," *Yale French Studies* 91 (1997): 117–40.

16. To cite just one formulation of this argument, "'Shameful' individuals reinvent themselves out of the exclusion that makes them such, and become, by an affirmation of what they are, producers of new forms of individually or collectively constructed subjectivity." Didier Eribon, *Une morale du minoritaire: Variations sur un thème de Jean Genet* (Paris: Fayard, 2001), 294, my translation.

17. Michael Lucey, *Someone: The Pragmatics of Misfit Sexualities from Colette to Hervé Guibert* (Chicago: University of Chicago Press, 2019), esp. 58–84.

18. Claire Boyle, "Friend or Foe? Misidentification, Abject Selfhood and Genet's Queer Reception," in *Soi-Disant: Life-Writing in French*, ed. Juliana de Nooy, Joe Hardwick, and Barbara E. Hannah (Newark: University of Delaware Press, 2005), 18. Creech similarly contends that "Genet inscribes us as a vous he presumes to be—whom he parasitically needs to be—hypocritical, censorious, scandalized." Creech, "Outing Jean Genet," 123. See also Colin Davis, "Genet's *Journal du voleur* and the Ethics of Reading," *French Studies* 48 (1994) and *Ethical Issues in Twentieth-Century French Fiction: Killing the Other* (New York: St. Martin's Press, 2000).

19. Genet, *Notre-Dame-des-Fleurs*, 93; *Our Lady of the Flowers*, 120.

20. Genet, *Notre-Dame-des-Fleurs*, 54; *Our Lady of the Flowers*, 66.

21. Jerry Aline Flieger, "Dream, Humor and Power in Genet's *Notre-Dame-des-Fleurs*," *French Forum* 9, no. 1 (January 1984): 72.

22. Flieger, "Dream, Humor and Power," 73.

23. As Pierre Laforgue puts it, "The novelistic space is in an undecidable interval between fiction and reality. This is how we see the narrator moving endlessly between the one and the other, if not even giving himself over to an absolute conflation of the one and the other." Pierre Laforgue, *Notre-Dame-des-Fleurs où La Symphonie carcérale* (Toulouse: Presses Universitaires du Mirail, 2002), 22, my translation.

24. Nadia Louar, "Notre dame du queer ou du mauvais genre en traduction," *Palimpsestes* 21 (2008): 15, my translation.

25. In an enchanting, if admittedly dated, reading of the animation of key objects in the author, John Plotz builds on Jacques Derrida's study of Genet in *Glas* (*Clang*, 1974) to demonstrate that "the embrace of abjection—humiliation that is also attachment to the power that spurns one—is the site of both escape from and reunion with the language game." Meaning that if a certain number of Genet's privileged objects (Plotz's example are the penis, the rose, and the tube of Vaseline) might seem to manage momentarily to escape mere discursivity and transcend to an unmediated "thing-in-itselfness," they do so through the same gesture of expenditure and self-emptying (in all three cases a kind of cumming) that ultimately returns them to the system of textual play determined by difference (from other signifiers). John Plotz, "Objects of Abjection: The Animation of Difference in Jean Genet's Novels," *Twentieth-Century Literature* 44, no. 1 (Spring 1998): 109, 110. It is worth noting, in order to avoid unnecessary confusion, that the text of this article was later plagiarized in *Orbis Litterarum* under the title "Of Hermeneutics and Difference: Genet's (Dys)functional Objects." See also Jacques Derrida, *Glas* (Paris: Éditions Galilée, 1974); *Clang*, trans. Geoffrey Bennington and David Wills (Minneapolis: University of Minnesota Press, 2021).

26. Boyle, "Friend or Foe," 26.

27. Jean-Paul Sartre, introduction to Genet, *Our Lady of the Flowers*, 17.

28. Michael Lucey, "Genet's *Notre-Dame-des-Fleurs*: Fantasy and Sexual Identity," *Yale French Studies* 91 (1997): 85–86.

29. Lucey, "Fantasy and Sexual Identity," 102.

30. Genet, *Our Lady of the Flowers*, 209.

31. Genet, *Our Lady of the Flowers*, 209–10.

32. "He was very much afraid of being discovered." Genet, *Our Lady of the Flowers*, 173. Peter Stonely demonstrates that Culafroy "values ballet as self consciously artificial, fanciful and escapist, and as a form that is oriented toward expressiveness and pleasure. . . . Culafroy grabs onto ballet as something that gives a justification to his outsider status." Peter Stonely, *A Queer History of the Ballet* (London: Routledge, 2007), 145.

33. For an enviably, splendidly lucid exegesis of Jacques Derrida's deconstruction of the philosophical notion of auto-affection, see Leonard Lawlor, "Auto-Affection," in *Jacques Derrida: Key Concepts*, ed. Claire Colebrook (London: Routledge, 2014), 103–38. In Edmund Husserl's idealized usage, as Derrida explains, auto-affection means self-experience, the experience of "selfness," or, rather, more precisely, if more difficultly, the experience of the self experienced as identical to the self experiencing that self. A critique of this view, Lawlor rightly contends, forms the conceptual core of Derridean deconstruction: "It is possible to say without exaggeration that every deconstruction Derrida has ever written targets auto-affection. Deconstruction aims to show that all auto-affection, however it is conceived, is really and fundamentally hetero-affection. All the neologisms or redefined terms that Derrida developed throughout his life (from 'différance' to 'anachronism') attempt to name this aporetical relation between sameness and otherness to which the deconstruction of auto-affection leads us." Lawlor, "Auto-Affection," 130.

34. Eve Kosofsky Sedgwick, *Touching Feeling: Affect, Pedagogy, Performativity* (Durham, NC: Duke University Press, 2002), 63.

35. Genet, *Our Lady of the Flowers*, 210–11, ellipses in the original.

36. Muñoz, *Disidentifications*, 3.

37. Judith Butler, *Gender Trouble: Feminism and Identity* (London: Routledge, 1991), 135.

38. Genet, *Notre-Dame-des-Fleurs*, 37; *Our Lady of the Flowers*, 81.

39. Emma Heaney demonstrates how early sexological discourses from the beginning of the twentieth century had affirmed certain feminine aspects for homosexual men, while renouncing male effeminacy. For instance, of Edward Carpenter's *Intermediate Sex* (1908) she writes: "His text betrays his belief that the viability of a gay male political future is tied to the promotion of a Uranian who expresses a limited number of qualities that Carpenter identifies as traditionally feminine (among these intuition and gentleness) but does not flaunt other feminine qualities (among these shrillness and jealousy). These latter qualities constitute what I call the feminine remainder." Emma Heaney, *The New Woman: Literary Modernism, Queer Theory and the Trans Feminine Allegory* (Evanston, IL: Northwestern University Press, 2017), 6. Carpenter's own description of the extreme case of the effeminate male recalls the maligned attributes and behaviors one might class under the rubric of *camp*: "A distinctly effeminate type, sentimental, lackadaisical, mincing in gait and manners, something of a chatterbox, skillful at the needle and in woman's work, sometimes taking pleasure in dressing

in woman's clothes; his figure not unfrequently betraying a tendency towards the feminine, large at the hips, supple, not muscular, the face wanting in hair, the voice inclining to be high-pitched, etc.; while his dwelling-room is orderly in the extreme, even natty, and choice of decoration and perfume. His affection, too, is often feminine in character, clinging, dependent and jealous, as of one desiring to be loved almost more than to love." Quoted in Heaney, *New Woman*, 7.

40. Genet, *Notre-Dame-des-Fleurs*, 258; *Our Lady of the Flowers*, 81.

41. Genet, *Notre-Dame-des-Fleurs*, 258; *Our Lady of the Flowers*, 235.

42. Genet, *Notre-Dame-des-Fleurs*, 258; *Our Lady of the Flowers*, 235.

43. Genet, *Our Lady of the Flowers*, 235.

44. Genet, *Notre-Dame-des-Fleurs*, 258; *Our Lady of the Flowers*, 235.

45. Genet, *Notre-Dame-des-Fleurs*, 258; *Our Lady of the Flowers*, 235.

46. Genet, *Our Lady of the Flowers*, 235.

47. Genet, *Notre-Dame-des-Fleurs*, 258; *Our Lady of the Flowers*, 235.

48. Butler, *Gender Trouble*, 136.

49. Heaney, *The New Woman*, 195.

50. Genet, *Notre-Dame-des-Fleurs*, 100; *Our Lady of the Flowers*, 124.

51. Genet, *Our Lady of the Flowers*, 142–43.

52. Genet, *Our Lady of the Flowers*, 143.

53. While perhaps now culturally dated, some studies of perceived gender have apparently demonstrated, as Aaron Devor has summarized, that "maleness is readily seen whenever there are indicators of it, whereas femaleness is only seen when there are compelling female cues and an absence of male cues." Aaron H. Devor, *Gender Blending: Confronting the Limits of Duality* (Bloomington: Indiana University Press, 1989), 49. In a study of theatrical cross-dressing, Alisa Solomon also paraphrases these findings: "As the presumed universal, maleness is more invisible in its artificiality. Sociological studies have demonstrated that maleness is assumed unless proven otherwise. Shown photographs of people with characteristics of both sexes, participants tend to see a man if there is any male signifier. . . . Femininity, on the other hand, is always already associated with spectacle, masquerade and illusion." Alisa Solomon, "It's Never Too Late to Switch," in *Crossing the Stage: Controversies on Cross-Dressing*, ed. Leslie Ferris (London: Routledge, 1993), 145.

54. Genet, *Our Lady of the Flowers*, 181.

55. Genet, *Notre-Dame-des-Fleurs*, 126; *Our Lady of the Flowers*, 142.

56. Genet, *Our Lady of the Flowers*, 143–44.

57. Genet, *Our Lady of the Flowers*, 268.

58. In his monograph on the novel, Pierre Laforgue makes a similar observation: "According to the Latin etymology, a personage, is a mask (*persona*) through which a voice speaks. This corresponds perfectly to what *Notre-Dame-des-Fleurs* does with the literary character in a novel. The personage is literally a trick by which someone other than itself passes and makes of it precisely a personage." Pierre Laforgue, *La symphonie carcérale*, 19, my translation.

59. Genet, *Our Lady of the Flowers*, 144.

60. As Lucey summarizes: "Marchetti starts out as an invention of Divine, her buddy, and one who will top Notre-Dame for her, providing a fantasmatic pivot around which she, as Marchetti's buddy, might participate in this 'topness' in order to be able to have a sexual relation with Notre-Dame. . . . Her sexual gambit doesn't work. But her creation of Marchetti does. The novel takes him

up and uses him as a character on more or less the same plane as Notre-Dame or Mignon." Lucey, "Fantasy and Sexual Identity," 96.

61. Genet, *Our Lady of the Flowers*, 273.

62. Genet, *Our Lady of the Flowers*, 266.

63. Genet, *Our Lady of the Flowers*, 85. At one point Divine gains a decade over the course of a single chapter: "Since I wish to show the reader a few candid shots of her, it is up to him to provide the sense of duration, of passing time, and to assume that during this first chapter she will be between twenty and thirty years of age." (This instruction to the reader is rendered all the more aleatoric by the fact that there are no clear chapter breaks in the novel.) At another moment, Divine's arbitrary age is revealed to be a function of narratorial identification: "How are we to explain that Divine is now thirty and more? For she really must be my age so that I can appease my need to talk about myself, simply. I feel such a need to complain and to try to win a reader's love." Genet, *Our Lady of the Flowers*, 109, 212.

64. Genet, *Our Lady of the Flowers*, 266–67.

65. Genet, *Our Lady of the Flowers*, 266.

66. Genet, *Our Lady of the Flowers*, 266.

67. Genet, *Our Lady of the Flowers*, 198, translation modified.

68. Genet, *Our Lady of the Flowers*, 259, translation modified.

69. Genet, *Our Lady of the Flowers*, 267.

70. Genet, *Our Lady of the Flowers*, 269.

71. Genet, *Œuvres complètes*, 3:22, left column; "What Remains of a Rembrandt Torn into Little Squares All the Same Size and Shot down the Toilet," in *Fragments of the Artwork*, trans. Charlotte Mandell (Stanford, CA: Stanford University Press, 2003), 91–92.

72. Genet, *Our Lady of the Flowers*, 267–68.

73. Genet, *Our Lady of the Flowers*, 92.

74. Butler, *Gender Trouble*, 136.

75. Genet, *Our Lady of the Flowers*, 261.

76. Genet, *Our Lady of the Flowers*, 261.

77. Genet, *Our Lady of the Flowers*, 162; *Notre-Dame-des-Fleurs*, 153.

78. Genet, *Our Lady of the Flowers*, 127.

79. Genet, *Our Lady of the Flowers*, 241.

80. Genet, *Notre-Dame-des-Fleurs*, 250; *Our Lady of the Flowers*, 230.

81. Genet, *Our Lady of the Flowers*, 231–32.

82. Genet, *Our Lady of the Flowers*, 272–73.

83. Genet, *Our Lady of the Flowers*, 138.

84. Genet, *Our Lady of the Flowers*, 272–73.

85. Genet, *Our Lady of the Flowers*, 135; *Notre-Dame-des-Fleurs*, 114, ellipsis in the original.

86. Genet, *Our Lady of the Flowers*, 138.

87. Genet, *Notre-Dame-des-Fleurs*, 244; *Our Lady of the Flowers*, 225, my emphasis, translation modified.

88. Genet, *Our Lady of the Flowers*, 296.

89. Genet, *Our Lady of the Flowers*, 294, 295.

90. Genet, *Our Lady of the Flowers*, 294.

91. Genet, *Our Lady of the Flowers*, 52.

Chapter 3

1. *Die Zeit*, "Garten der Lüste: Jean Genets Schattenwelt," review of *Querelle*, by Rainer Werner Fassbinder, no. 38, September 17, 1982, https://www.zeit.de/1982/38/garten-der-lueste/, my translation.

2. Edmund White, *Genet: A Biography* (New York: Alfred A. Knopf, 1993), 615; Werner Schroeter, *Tage im Dämmer, Nächte im Rausch: Autobiographie* (Berlin: Aufbau Verlag, 2011), 213–20; Werner Schroeter with Claudia Lenssen, *Days of Twilight, Nights of Frenzy: A Memoir*, trans. Anthea Bell (Chicago: University of Chicago Press, 2017), 143–48.

3. Thomas Waugh, *Fruit Machine: Twenty Years of Writings on Queer Cinema* (Durham, NC: Duke University Press, 2000), 135, 136.

4. On the question of camp in Fassbinder, Schroeter, and Rosa von Praunheim, see Randall Halle, "Rainer, Rosa and Werner: New Gay Film as a Counter-Public," in *A Companion to Rainer Werner Fassbinder*, ed. Brigitte Peucker (Chichester, UK: Wiley-Blackwell, 2012), 542–63; and Johannes von Moltke, "Camping in the Art Closet: The Politics of Camp and Nation in German Film," *New German Critique* 63 (Autumn 1994): 76–106.

5. Jack Halberstam, *The Queer Art of Failure* (Durham, NC: Duke University Press, 2011), 186–87.

6. Halberstam, *The Queer Art of Failure*, 109, my emphasis.

7. Halberstam, *The Queer Art of Failure*, 109.

8. Halberstam, *The Queer Art of Failure*, 110, original emphasis.

9. Amin, *Disturbing Attachments*, 28.

10. Halberstam, *The Queer Art of Failure*, 2, 109.

11. Jack Halberstam, *Female Masculinity* (Durham, NC: Duke University Press, 2018), 238.

12. Halberstam, *Female Masculinity*, 238.

13. Halberstam, *Female Masculinity*, 9.

14. Halberstam, *Female Masculinity*, 239.

15. Among others to address the issue, Pamela Robertson Wojcik has perspicaciously highlighted how "the use of blackness as an authenticating discourse has become part of a transnational camp aesthetic" and argued elsewhere, more provocatively, that, in certain contexts, "camp may be, after all, a kind of blackface." Pamela Robertson Wojcik, *Guilty Pleasures: Feminist Camp from Mae West to Madonna* (Durham, NC: Duke University Press, 1996), 21; "Mae West's Maids: Race, Authenticity, and the Discourse of Camp," in *Hop on Pop: The Politics and Pleasures of Popular Culture*, ed. Henry Jenkins, Jane Shattuc, and Tara McPherson (Durham, NC: Duke University Press, 2003), 298.

16. As Tobias Nagl and Janelle Blankenship point out, "In all of the films Kaufmann made with Fassbinder, Nono is certainly the most sexually fetishized of Kaufmann's roles, resonating with images of the hypersexual 'black stud' popular in 1970s gay leather culture from the Village People to Tom of Finland's erotic drawings." Tobias Nagl and Janelle Blankenship, "'So Much Tenderness': Günther Kaufmann and the Ambivalences of Interracial Desire," in *A Companion to Rainer Werner Fassbinder*, 535.

17. Eve Kosofsky Sedgwick, *Touching Feeling: Affect, Pedagogy, Performativity* (Durham, NC: Duke University Press, 2002), 149.

18. I take the phrase "politically ambivalent" from Sianne Ngai's description of ugly feelings in her book of the same name. Sianne Ngai, *Ugly Feelings* (Cambridge, MA: Harvard University Press, 2005), 26.

19. Karen Van Godtsenhoven, "WorldPride at the Met: The Otherness of Camp," Metropolitan Museum of Art, June 24, 2019, https://www.metmuseum.org/blogs/now-at-the-met/2019/worldpride-met-otherness-camp.

20. Van Godtsenhoven, "The Otherness of Camp." While the attempt to overcome the perceived whiteness of camp attested to by the various materials surrounding this exhibition—to be discussed in greater detail in my final chapter—is laudable, it perhaps itself risks underplaying the defining significance of elements of, for instance, black culture to both popular and, perhaps especially, scholarly understandings of the term. On the latter point I am thinking in particular of the ball scene documented in Jennie Livingston's *Paris Is Burning* and filtered through Butler's *Gender Trouble*, both of which appeared in 1990.

21. Eve Kosofsky Sedgwick, *The Epistemology of the Closet* (Berkeley: University of California Press, 1990), esp. 155–57. If habitus, as theorized by Pierre Bourdieu, refers to ingrained behaviors and habits, hexis designates their physical embodiment in posture, bearing, accent, and so on. See, especially, the second chapter of Pierre Bourdieu, *Le Sens pratique* (Paris: Éditions de Minuit, 1980); *The Logic of Practice*, trans. Richard Nice (Stanford, CA: Stanford University Press, 1990).

22. Kathryn Bond Stockton, *Beautiful Bottom, Beautiful Shame: Where "Black" Meets "Queer"* (Durham, NC: Duke University Press, 2006), 213. Stockton's call for a history of dark camp grows out of a monograph attuned specifically to the surprising imbrications of queerness and blackness as signifiers of cultural abjection—associations that when overlooked make camp seem superficial and obsolete, despite its obvious staying power in the critical and cultural vocabulary. See especially Stockton, "Dark Camp: Behind and Ahead," in *Beautiful Bottom*, 205–21.

23. Ingrid Hotz-Davies, "The Jewel in the Gutter: Camp and the Incorporation of Dirt," in *The Dark Side of Camp: Queer Economies of Dirt, Dust, and Patina*, ed. Ingrid Hotz-Davies, Georg Vogt, and Franziska Bergmann (New York: Routledge, 2018), 22, original emphasis.

24. Susan Sontag, "Notes on 'Camp,'" *Against Interpretation and Other Essays* (New York: Picador, 1966), 275.

25. Sontag, "Notes on 'Camp,'" 275, my emphasis.

26. Sontag, "Notes on 'Camp,'" 280.

27. Mark Booth, *Camp* (London: Quartet Books, 1983), 179.

28. Sontag, "Notes on 'Camp,'" 282. Harald Galef and David Galef, "What Was Camp," *Studies in Popular Culture* 13, no. 2 (1991): 12.

29. Sontag, "Notes on 'Camp,'" 280.

30. Sontag, "Notes on 'Camp,'" 280.

31. Sedgwick, *Touching Feeling*, 63.

32. Sedgwick rather celebrates this aspect, which also accounts for the capaciousness of what counts for her as queer: "The shame-delineated place of identity doesn't determine the consistency or meaning of that identity, and race, gender, class, sexuality, appearance, and abledness are only a few of the defining social constructions that will crystallize there, developing from this originary

affect their particular structures of expression, creativity, pleasure, and struggle." Sedgwick, *Touching Feeling*, 63.

33. Galef and Galef describe this similarly: "At base, camp is an aesthetic joke, a satire at the expense of others. One compensates for feelings of inferiority, or simply alienation from mainstream society, by becoming part of a cognoscenti, an out-group that announces its status as an in-group." Galef and Galef, "What Was Camp," 16.

34. Philip Core, *Camp: The Lie That Tells the Truth* (New York: Delilah Books, 1984), 1.

35. I quote here from Heather Love's excavation of disavowed historical backwardness in queer modernist literature in *Feeling Backward: Loss and the Politics of Queer History* (Cambridge, MA: Harvard University Press, 2007), 4, but this position, mutatis mutandis, can be traced back, perhaps, as far as Bersani and Edelman's antisocial thesis. As David Halperin summarizes: "Gay subjectivity is divided against itself, formed in stigma, in rejection by others—especially by those whom one desires—and by oneself. Our very loves and pleasures are constituted in relation to parts of ourselves that are causes of irredeemable shame in our social experience of them. In the era of gay pride, moreover, such shame is the occasion for further shame." David Halperin, *What Do Gay Men Want? An Essay on Sex, Risk and Subjectivity* (Ann Arbor: University of Michigan Press, 2007), 70. See also Robert L. Caserio, Lee Edelman, Judith Halberstam, José Esteban Muñoz, and Tim Dean, "The Antisocial Thesis in Queer Theory," *PMLA* 121, no. 3 (May 2006): 819–28.

36. For Ingrid Hotz-Davies, for instance, "camp tends to debunk psychoanalysis," which she takes to be too absolutizing: "Clearly in such a version . . . the abject can certainly beckon desire, but . . . there can never be any friendly co-existence of the abject and the non-abject—after all, nothing less than the existence of the psyche is at stake!" Hotz-Davies, "The Jewel in the Gutter," 22.

37. Eribon has taken credit for this archeology and accused Halperin of intellectual dishonesty for echoing certain arguments from his untranslated *Une morale du minoritaire: Variations sur un thème de Jean Genet* (Paris: Fayard, 2001) in *What Do Gay Men Want?*, which was published a half decade later.

38. Jean Genet, *Our Lady of the Flowers*, trans. Bernard Frechtman (New York: Grove Press, 1963), 126.

39. "Kristeva never mentions homosexuality; she virtually never even alludes to it." Halperin, *What Do Gay Men Want?*, 70.

40. Julia Kristeva, *Powers of Horror: An Essay on Abjection*, trans. Leon S. Roudiez (New York: Columbia University Press, 1982), 45.

41. Halperin, *What Do Gay Men Want?*, 78.

42. Insisting on the subversive potential of camp and trying to reclaim camp politics and poetics in the 1990s, Meyer influentially takes issue with Sontag's privileging of style over content, but camp's encounter with abjection, as I've been arguing, tends to reveal, in Wildean fashion, that style *is* substance, even if camp, as I am recasting it here, lacks the sovereign self-determination often ascribed to it. See especially Moe Meyer, "Introduction: Reclaiming the Discourse of Camp," in Moe Meyer, ed., *The Politics and Poetics of Camp* (London: Routledge, 1994), 1–22.

43. Andrew Britton, "For Interpretation: Notes against Camp," in *Britton on Film: The Complete Film Criticism of Andrew Britton*, ed. Barry Grant (Detroit:

Wayne State University Press, 2009), 389. Britton further concludes that "the ideological place of any individual at any given time is the site of intersection of any number of determining forces, and one's sense of oneself as 'gay' is a determinate product of that intersection—not a determinant of it." Britton, "Notes against Camp," 390.

44. Halperin, *What Do Gay Men Want?*, 70.

45. Stockton, *Beautiful Shame*, 205.

46. Roy Grundmann, "*Querelle*'s Finality," in *A Companion to Rainer Werner Fassbinder*, 598, 599.

47. Grundmann, "*Querelle*'s Finality," 599.

48. Steven Shaviro, "Masculinity, Spectacle and the Body of *Querelle*," in *The Cinematic Body* (Minneapolis: University of Minnesota Press, 1989), 164.

49. In her thirty-sixth note she describes camp as "the sensibility of failed seriousness, of the theatricalization of experience. Camp refuses both the harmonies of traditional seriousness, and the risks of identifying with extreme states of feeling." Just two notes later, however, she concedes: "There is a seriousness in Camp (seriousness in the degree of the artist's involvement) and, often, pathos." Sontag, "Notes on 'Camp,' " 287.

50. Rainer Werner Fassbinder, *Querelle Filmbuch* (Munich: Schirmer/Mosel, 1982), 11, my translation.

51. Fassbinder, *Querelle Filmbuch*, 11, my translation.

52. Fassbinder, *Querelle Filmbuch*, 11, my translation.

53. Jean Genet, *Œuvres complètes* (Paris: Gallimard, 1952–1979) 3:173; *Querelle*, trans. Anselm Hollo (New York: Grove Press, 1974), 4.

54. Caryl Flinn, "Declined Invitations: Repetition in Fassbinder's Queer 'Monomusical,' " in *A Companion to Rainer Werner Fassbinder*, 326. See also White, *Genet*, 615.

55. Fassbinder, *Querelle Filmbuch*, 11, my translation.

56. Stephen Luttmann, for instance, rightly suggests that this "claim to have abandoned the novel in an imperfect or incomplete state can be read as an integral part of the novel itself." Stephen Luttmann, "Narrators, Narrated Realities and the Nature of Artwork in Jean Genet's *Querelle de Brest* and Rainer Werner Fassbinder's Film *Querelle*," *Kodikas/Code/Ars semeiotica* 14, no. 1–2 (1991): 9. The Genet passage is quoted from the same page in Luttman. My translation.

57. Genet, *Querelle*, 255.

58. Genet, *Querelle*, 18.

59. Genet, *Querelle*, 251, my emphasis.

60. As in the German *Willkür*: literally, *choice* or *decision of the will*, but today used in the contradictory senses of pure randomness and absolute despotism. I am grateful to Kristina Mendicino for pointing me in this direction.

61. Flinn, "Monomusical," 327. For more on Fassbinder's anti-identitarian positions, discussed more thoroughly in the next chapter, see Volker Woltersdorff, " 'Grundsätzlich ist jeder homosexuell und deshalb ist es kein Problem': Homosexuelle Minderheiten und Fassbinders Filme," in *Rainer Werner Fassbinder*, ed. Michael Töteberg (Munich: edition text+kritik, 2015), 108–20.

62. Jean Genet, *Querelle de Brest* (Paris: Gallimard Imaginaire, 2010), 239, my translation. Not present in the translated Grove edition nor in the *Œuvres complètes*.

63. Ingrid Hotz-Davies, Georg Vogt, and Franziska Bergmann, "Introduction: 'The Dirt Doesn't Get Any Worse': The Alliance of Camp and Dirt," in *The Dark Side of Camp*, 2.

64. Hotz-Davies, "The Jewel in the Gutter," 20. For Britton, this is precisely why camp fails to critique the norms of masculinity, which always remains its reference point, albeit reflected through a distorted mirror: "Camp always connotes 'effeminacy' not 'femininity.'" Andrew Britton, "Notes against Camp," 137.

65. Quoted in Michael Lucey, *Someone: The Pragmatics of Misfit Sexualities from Colette to Hervé Guibert* (Chicago: University of Chicago Press, 2019), 90, Lucey's translations, slightly modified. I retain Lucey's rendering of *pédé* as *faggot*, which I find appropriate here, though I would submit that it does not express the same violence of that word in all contexts, which is why I choose to shorten it to the slightly gentler *fag* in the second iteration. Delightfully, Lucey translates *enculé* with the neologism *buttfuckee*.

66. Lucey, *Someone*, 88.

67. Genet, *Querelle de Brest*, 238, my translation; this passage is not present in the Grove edition, and I cannot locate it in the *Œuvres complètes*.

68. On the subversive politics of bottoming in Genet and elsewhere, see, among many others, Guy Hocquenghem, *Homosexual Desire* (Durham, NC: Duke University Press, 1993); Leo Bersani, *Homos* (Cambridge, MA: Harvard University Press, 1996); and, more recently, Tan Hong Nyungen, *A View from the Bottom: Asian American Masculinity and Sexual Representation* (Durham, NC: Duke University Press, 2014).

69. White, *Genet*, 290.

70. Genet, *Querelle*, 79.

71. Genet, *Œuvres complètes*, 223.

72. Hector Kollias contends that Seblon "is best understood as the fantasmatic presence of Genet as an implied reader," but I would insist that he is an implied reader in Wolfgang Iser's sense as well. Hector Kollias, "Jean Genet's Queer Origins: A Reading of *Querelle de Brest*," *French Studies* 60, no. 4 (2006): 481. See Wolfgang Iser, *The Implied Reader: Patterns of Communication in Prose Fiction from Bunyan to Beckett* (Baltimore: Johns Hopkins University Press, 1974).

73. I have extensively consulted the version of the script held at the music library of the Zentralbibliothek Zürich (Standort, Signatur: Musik, Magazin Chor MFSD 170; Strichcode: ZD3253514) as well as the ten different drafts contained in the materials left to the Deutsche Kinemathek—Museum für Film und Fernsehen by Kurt Raab and in the collections on Harry Baer and Michael Fengler.

74. From an interview with Kurt Raab in Kurt Raab and Karsten Peters, *Die Sehnsucht des Rainer Werner Fassbinder* (Munich: Bertelsmann Verlag, 1982), 340, my translation.

75. As Luttmann points out in a painstakingly thorough comparison of the film, novel, and published screenplay, "Genet's refusal was of course perfectly consistent with the narrator who, while telling his story, relinquished control over it, and with an author whose 'revision' of his novel demonstrated his subsequent lack of interest in it. . . . In the case of *Querelle*, this ending points beyond itself to the novel in the form of Jean Genet, the man who created it, but in so doing abandoned it to itself. This is . . . what *Querelle de Brest* is ultimately about; and

this title demonstrates one last time the film's reason for being: to be *about* a work of literature." Luttmann, "Narrated Realities," 32.

76. Mary M. Wiles, "A Double Voice: The Dual Paternity of *Querelle*," in *Postmodernism in the Cinema*, ed. Cristina Degli-Esposti (Providence: Berghain Books, 1998), 239.

77. Halberstam, *The Queer Art of Failure*, 110.

78. Halberstam, *The Queer Art of Failure*, 110.

79. Kollias sees the play of identities in *Querelle de Brest* similarly: "Genet's queer (non-)subjects can only be located at a pre-subjective site of undifferentiated narcissism which is the very origin of subjectivity." While I disagree, perhaps merely semantically, with Kollias's assumption that Genet locates homosexuality in the sex acts themselves, I largely agree with the conclusions he draws: "Genet's notion of homosexuality, founded on the event of the act of anal sex rather than the self-understanding of a subject, as well as his notion of origin as that which both founds and deconstructs what springs forth from it, as at the same time its condition of possibility *and* impossibility turn out to be, or perhaps rather fall back to being, notions that radically *disavow* the logic of identity and of origins." Kollias, "Jean Genet's Queer Origins," 487, 488.

80. Genet, *Querelle de Brest*, 217, my translation.

Chapter 4

1. Jean Genet, *Journal du Voleur* (Paris: Gallimard, 1963), 9; *The Thief's Journal*, trans. Bernard Frechtman (New York: Grove Press, 1964), 3.

2. Jean Genet, *Fragments*, trans. Charlotte Mandell (Stanford, CA: Stanford University Press, 2003), 42, translation modified.

3. Jean Genet, *Miracle of the Rose*, trans. Bernard Frechtman (New York: Grove Press, 1994), 264.

4. Charles Baudelaire, *Intimate Journals*, trans. Christopher Isherwood (London: Black Spring, 1989), 64.

5. Genet, *Miracle of the Rose*, 264.

6. Genet, *Miracle of the Rose*, 164.

7. Richard Dyer, *Now You See It* (London: Routledge, 2003), 131.

8. Genet, *Miracle of the Rose*, 16.

9. Genet, *Miracle of the Rose*, 16, translation modified.

10. Genet, *Miracle of the Rose*, 17.

11. Genet, *Miracle of the Rose*, 210.

12. Genet, *Miracle of the Rose*, 286.

13. Genet, *Miracle of the Rose*, 17.

14. Edmund White, preface to *The Cinema of Jean Genet: Un chant d'amour*, by Jane Giles (London: BFI, 1991), 3.

15. Michael Hardt, "Prison Time," *Yale French Studies* 91 (1997): 69.

16. Plotz, "Objects of Abjection," 108.

17. See Walter Benjamin, *Origin of German Tragic Drama*, trans. John Osborne (London: Verso, 1998).

18. White, preface, 3.

19. Although a laboratory for his most experimental work and a locus of his literary evolution, Genet's shorter verse is exceedingly cryptic and receives little scholarly attention. Élise Nottet-Chedeville, particularly, has been most

recently attempting to correct for this oversight. See Élise Nottet-Chedeville, "Les évolutions poétiques de Genet: Expérimentations stylistiques et opportunisme littéraire," in *Écritures évolutives aux XXe et XXIe siècles, ed.* Sophie Jollin-Bertocchi (Leiden: Brill-Rodolpi, 2019), 108–25; and "Genet et la rhapsodie poétique," *Genesis* 47 (2018): 141–54. Even the author distanced himself from the original publication of much of his poetry alongside a series of homoerotic lithographs by Roland Caillaux, claiming that he found the rather pornographic images too vulgar. On the publication history of these poems and Caillaux's *Vingt lithographies pour un livre que j'ai lu* (1945), see Nottet-Chedeville, "Les évolutions poétiques de Genet," 109n3.

20. Pascale Caron, "Pour quelques paillettes en plus . . . Le funambule de Jean Genet et l'image poétique du movement," *Littérature* 139 (2005): 24–43.

21. White, preface, 2.

22. For an overview of this debate, see Alice Kuzniar, *The Queer German Cinema* (Stanford, CA: Stanford University Press, 2000), 113–15.

23. Kuzniar, *Queer German Cinema*, 123.

24. Quoted in Kuzniar, *Queer German Cinema*, 123.

25. Caryl Flinn, *The New German Cinema: Music, History, and the Matter of Style* (Berkeley: University of California Press, 2004), 233. With regard to taste and its relationship to the corporeal, the reference is to Pierre Bourdieu, whom Flinn discusses briefly in this context. Flinn, *New German Cinema*, 236–37.

26. Flinn, *New German Cinema*, 240. See also Eve Kosofsky Sedgwick, *The Epistemology of the Closet* (Berkeley: University of California Press, 1990), esp. 155–57.

27. Flinn, *New German Cinema*, 233.

28. Rainer Werner Fassbinder, "Homage to Werner Schroeter," in *West German Filmmakers on Film: Visions and Voices*, ed. Eric Rentschler (New York: Holmes & Meier, 1988), 197.

29. On Schroeter's disinterest in making his films available for viewing, see the anecdote that begins James Quandt's review of Schroeter's autobiography and the very welcome recent volume edited by Roy Grundmann, which sadly does not contain a chapter on *Der Rosenkönig*. James Quandt, "Ecstatically Florid Farragoes," *New York Review of Books* 66, no. 11 (June 2019): 61–62; see also Roy Grundmann, ed., *Werner Schroeter* (Vienna: Österreiches Filmmuseum and the SYNEMA-Gesellschaft für Film und Medien, 2018), esp. 44–46. Schroeter does admit to putting a bit more effort into marketing the specific film in question in the debate with von Praunheim: "So we were able to come up with the right ads and special press issues, in which I gave a serious account of my film. In the past, I had always talked ironically about the films I directed, as if they were pulp fiction." Schroeter with Lenssen, *Days of Twilight*, 122.

30. Rainer Werner Fassbinder with Dieter Schidor, "'Ich mußte mein Leben gelebt haben, um diesen Film machen zu können': Rainer Werner Fassbinder über QUERELLE," in *Fassbinder über Fassbinder: Die ungekürtzten Interviews*, ed. Robert Fischer (Frankfurt am Main: Verlag der Autoren, 2004), 622, my translation.

31. Schroeter with Lenssen, *Days of Twilight*, 144–45.

32. As Roy Grundmann puts it: "When Schroeter in the late 1970s and early 1980s won wider acclaim with four feature films . . . the New German Cinema was in its final phase. By the time he returned to feature filmmaking with *Der*

Rosenkönig (*The Rose King*), released in 1986, it was history." Roy Grundman, "The Passions of Werner Schroeter: An Introduction," in *Werner Schroeter*, 7–56.

33. Schroeter with Lenssen, *Days of Twilight*, 126.

34. Vincent Canby, "Film: 'The Rose King,' by Werner Schroeter," *New York Times* (December 30, 1970), C10.

35. Quoted in Ulrike Sieglohr, "Divine Rapture: The Films of Werner Schroeter," *Film Comment* 48, no. 3 (May/June 2012): 53. As Kuzniar notes, "*Der Rosenkönig* has a more realistic setting and clearly delineated plot, while still relying on long, photographic takes that suspend the narrative." Kuzniar, *Queer German Cinema*, 132.

36. Michelle Langford, *Allegorical Images: Tableau, Time and Gesture in the Cinema of Werner Schroeter* (Bristol, UK: Intellect Books, 2006), 158. For an admirably accessible overview of Benjamin's career-long exploration of the allegorical, see Bainard Cowan, "Walter Benjamin's Theory of Allegory," *New German Critique* 22 (Winter 1981): 109–22.

37. See Ian Fleishman, *An Aesthetics of Injury: The Narrative Wound from Baudelaire to Tarantino* (Evanston, IL: Northwestern University Press, 2018), esp. 166–88 and 195–214.

38. Langford, *Allegorical Images*, 160.

39. There is a not insignificant (queer) theoretical history to the consideration of grafting in Genet as a textual strategy, including in Derrida's study of Genet, where he notes of the author's literary montage: "Keep count of the crosscutting effects and you will see that the tissue keeps reforming over the gash." Jacques Derrida, *Clang*, trans. Geoffrey Bennington and David Wills (Minneapolis: University of Minnesota Press, 2021), 33, right-hand column. Derrida emphasizes that Genet's flowers are, strictly speaking, neither natural nor artificial—an observation that Katrin Pahl, in ongoing work, is expanding into an inquiry into the possibilities of not entirely metaphorical queer procreation: "Quite in keeping with queer theory, [the graft] troubles the distinction between nature and culture or between the naturally given and the artificially produced." Katrin Pahl, "Queer Procreation: Reading Kleist Plantwise," *Qui Parle* 28, no. 1 (2019): 137–66. See also Fleishman, *An Aesthetics of Injury*, esp. 130–35.

40. Kuzniar, *Queer German Cinema*, 131–32.

41. Flinn, *New German Cinema*, 180.

42. Kuzniar notes a similar kind of ventriloquism at work in the film on the whole: "In the gender reversals of *Der Rosenkönig*, Albert's sublimated passion is communicated as through ventriloquism, via the female operatic voice singing the aria 'Vissi d'arte' from Puccini's *Tosca*, 'I have lived for art and love.'" Kuzniar, *Queer German Cinema*, 137.'

43. Schroeter, *Days of Twilight*, 152. On Schroeter's relationship to the predominantly heterosexual Orlando, see Schroeter with Lenssen, *Days of Twilight*, 161–69.

44. Langford, *Allegorical Images*, 160.

45. Flinn, *New German Cinema*, 137.

46. Werner Schroeter and Michel Foucault, "Passion According to Werner Schroeter," trans. John Jonston, in Grundmann, *Werner Schroeter*, 206–14.

47. Keith Robinson, "The Passion and the Pleasure: Foucault's Art of Not Being Oneself," *Theory, Culture and Society* 20, no. 2 (2003): 127.

48. Gérard Courant, *Werner Schroeter* (Paris: Goethe-Institut/Cinémathèque Française, 1982), 44; Schroeter and Foucault, "Passion According to Werner Schroeter," 210.

49. Monika Treut, "Die Zeremonie der blutenden Rose: Vorüberlegungen zu einem Filmprojekt," *Frauen und Film* 36 (February 1984): 35, my translation.

50. On Treut's aversion to identity politics, see Gerd Gemünden, Alice Kuzniar, and Klaus Phillips, "From Taboo Parlor to Porn and Passing: An Interview with Monika Treut," *Film Quarterly* 50, no. 3 (1997): 4–5. This was Treut's first feature; Mikesch was, as I have already mentioned, Schroeter's favored cinematographer for *Der Rosenkönig* and other projects. The script builds on perspectives on sadomasochism elaborated in Treut's scholarly dissertation, as acknowledged by the film's subtitle.

51. Treut, "Die Zeremonie der blutenden Rose," 35–42, my translation.

52. On the whole, Treut's films aren't nearly as pornographic as the scholarly discourse and their marketing might lead one to believe. On Treut's flirtation with pornography and her contentious relationship to antiporn feminism, see Muriel Cormican, "Pro-Porn rhetoric and the Cinema of Monika Treut," *Women in German Yearbook* 19 (2003): 179–99.

53. Derrida, *Clang*, 29, right-hand column.

54. Barbara Mennel points out that Wanda is a voyeur and video artist, combining elements of Mikesch (as cinematographer) and Treut (as director) and collapsing the body of the artist-practitioner and audience into one in a kind of closed-circuit synchronous feedback loop. Barbara Mennel, "Wanda's Whip: Recasting Masochism's Fantasy—Monika Treut's *Seduction: The Cruel Woman*," in *Triangulated Visions: Women in Recent German Cinema* (Albany: State University of New York Press, 1998), 160.

55. Flinn, *New German Cinema*, 181–82.

56. Flinn, *New German Cinema*, 188.

57. Andrea Riemann, "Subjection and Power in Monika Treut and Elfi Mikesch's *Seduction*—the Cruel Woman: An Extension of the Configuration of Power in Rainer Werner Fassbinder's Late Oeuvre," in Robin Griffiths, ed., *Queer Cinema in Europe*, 181–93 (Bristol: Intellect Books, 2008). Riemann builds on slightly later work by Judith Butler than what is predominantly discussed in the present study—particularly *The Psychic Life of Power* (1997)—to examine how the masochistic figures of *Verführung* derive agency from their subjection and subjectivation.

58. Caryn James, "Review/Film; 'Seduction: The Cruel Woman,' a Study in Power," *New York Times*, November 3, 1989, C17.

59. See B. Ruby Rich, *New Queer Cinema: The Director's Cut* (Durham, NC: Duke University Press, 2013), xvii.

60. B. Ruby Rich, "Queer and Present Danger," *Sight and Sound* 10, no. 3 (March 2000): 24. Also cited in Michael DeAngelis, "Authorship and New Queer Cinema: The Case of Todd Haynes," *Auteurs and Authorship: A Film Reader*, ed. Barry Keith (Oxford: Blackwell, 2008), 292.

61. James Morrison, "Still New, Still Queer, Still Cinema?" *GLQ* 12, no. 1 (2006): 141–42.

62. Schroeter with Lenssen, *Days of Twilight*, 165, translation modified.

63. Quoted in Justin Wyatt, "Cinematic/Sexual: An Interview with Todd Haynes," in *Todd Haynes: Interviews*, ed. Julia Leyda (Jackson: University Press of Mississippi, 2014), 26–30.

64. Quoted in Wyatt, "Cinematic/Sexual," 32.

65. Quoted in Wyatt, "Cinematic/Sexual," 30, my emphasis.

66. See, e.g., his comments on the camp sensibility after Stonewall and what he fears will become of it after the success of the Frank Oz comedy *In & Out* (1996), starring Kevin Kline, in Keith Phipps, "Interview with Todd Haynes," in *Todd Haynes: Interviews*, 93–100.

67. Morrison, "Still New, Still Queer," 143.

68. Laura Christian, "Of Housewives and Saints: Abjection, Transgression and Impossible Mourning in *Poison* and *Safe*," *Camera Obscura* 19, no. 3 (2004): 94.

69. Quoted in Wyatt, "Cinematic/Sexual," 29, ellipsis in the original.

70. DeAngelis, "Authorship and New Queer Cinema," 293. Also quoted in Morrison, "Still New, Still Queer," 139–40.

71. Morrison, "Still New, Still Queer," 143.

72. Genet, *Miracle of the Rose*, 267.

73. My thanks to Iggy Cortez and Gary Kafer for pointing me in this direction and to the former for his fruitful insights on this constellation over the course of many conversations. In addition to those mentioned, Kafer has identified specific shots from the music video that would appear to be modeled on moments from Jean Cocteau's *Le Sang d'un poète* (1930), Kenneth Anger's *Fireworks* (1947), and James Bigwood's *Pink Narcissus* (1971), as well as Derek Jarman's *Edward II* (1991) and *Wittgenstein* (1993). Personal conversation.

74. Peter Robinson, "Interview with Troye Sivan: 'I Feel so Much More Fully Realized as a Person," *Pop Justice*, March 1, 2018, https://www.popjustice.com/articles/troye-sivan-interview-i-feel-more-fully-realised-as-a-person/.

75. Pierre-Ange Carlotti, "Troye Sivan: Atomic Blonde," *Dazed*, March 14, 2018, https://www.dazeddigital.com/music/article/39346/1/troye-sivan-boy-erased-new-album-interview; Chris Mench, "Troye Sivan's 'Bloom' Is a Metaphor-Filled Ode to Bottoming," *Genius*, May 4, 2018, https://genius.com/a/troye-sivan-s-bloom-is-a-metaphor-filled-ode-to-bottoming.

76. On Benjamin's understanding of the allegorical emblem, specifically, see Karoline Kirst, "Walter Benjamin's 'Denkbild': Emblematic Historiography of the Recent Past," *Monatshefte* 86, no. 4 (Winter 1994): 514–24.

77. All references to this interview with Matt Fistonich for the September 2019 issue of New Zealand's *express Magazine* are quoted from Roisin O'Connor, "Troye Sivan Criticizes Interviewer for Asking If He's a 'Top or Bottom,' " *The Independent*, August 29, 2019, https://www.independent.co.uk/arts-entertainment/music/news/troye-sivan-interview-top-bottom-question-boyfriend-shawn-mendes-a9083106.html.

78. Oliver Skinner, "Shawn Mendes's Revelatory New Album Art Shows in a Single Glance That the Pop Star Is Growing Up," *CBC Arts*, May 23, 2018, https://www.cbc.ca/arts/shawn-mendes-s-relevatory-new-album-art-shows-in-a-single-glance-that-the-pop-star-is-growing-up-1.4678074.

79. See Patrick Doyle, "Confessions of a Neurotic Pop Idol," *Rolling Stone* 1332 (December 2018): 59–60; and Dax Shepard, "Shawn Mendes,"

Armchair Expert with Dax Shepard, podcast audio, December 15, 2020, https://armchairexpertpod.com/pods/shawn-mendes.

80. Steven Maynard, "What Color Is Your Underwear? Class, Whiteness, and Homoerotic Advertising." *Border/Lines* 32 (1994): 8; quoted in Richard Dyer, *White* (London: Routledge, 1997), 76.

81. Jennifer Wilson, "The Shareable Feast of Jeremy Allen White's Calvin Klein Ad," *New Yorker*, January 10, 2024, https://www.newyorker.com/culture/annals-of-appearances/the-shareable-feast-of-jeremy-allen-whites-calvin-klein-ad.

82. Jane Giles, *The Cinema of Jean Genet: Un chant d'amour* (London: BFI, 1991), 62.

83. Conversely, and curiously, Bardia Zeinali's music video for Mendes's "If I Can't Have You," one of the final singles off the same self-titled album as "In My Blood," shares the sparse, stripped-back studio setting and black-and-white aesthetic of his Calvin Klein promo.

84. Dyer, *White*, 45.

85. Flinn, *New German Cinema*, 239; Susan Sontag, "Notes on 'Camp,'" *Against Interpretation and Other Essays* (New York: Picador, 1966), 291.

86. Rosa von Praunheim, "With Fond Greetings to Champagne-Schroeter," in *West German Filmmakers*, 195.

87. Flinn, *New German Cinema*, 265.

Chapter 5

1. Pamela Demory, "Queer/Adaptation: An Introduction," in *Queer/Adaptation*, ed. Pamela Demory (Cham, Switzerland: Palgrave Macmillan, 2019), 1. Inquiry into queer adaptation is only recently emerging as a distinct field but owes an often-acknowledged debt to Fiona Handyside's study of the film in question in this chapter. See Fiona Handyside, "Melodrama and Ethics in François Ozon's *Gouttes d'eau sur pierres brûlantes/Water Drops on Burning Rocks* (2000)," *Studies in French Cinema* 7, no. 3 (2007): 207–18.

2. Demory, "Queer/Adaptation," 1. Demory concludes, quite rightly, that "foundational to both disciplines—queer studies and adaptation studies—is a critical challenge to those assumptions about originality, authenticity and value." Demory, "Queer/Adaptation," 1–2.

3. Andrew Asibong, *François Ozon* (Manchester: Manchester University Press, 2008), 57.

4. For Adam Bingham, Ozon is "particularly problematic and to some extent marginal because it is impossible to put any kind of label on him or to place him with any confidence in any aspect of French filmmaking. He has self-consciously flirted around certain genres and trends (the extreme element of French cinema, exemplified by, say, Gaspard Noé), but only to compound and provoke, shock and surprise." Bingham also discusses Ozon with reference to what he calls "New Gay Cinema" (which, as Mark Hain notes, is "a classification [Bingham] doesn't define, but one which presumably removes Ozon entirely from the confines of French cinema and posits him instead as a member of an international trend"), although with the parenthetical caveat: "(though now this is as much a problematic category in which to put Ozon as any other)." Adam Bingham, "Identity and Love: The Not-So Discreet Charm of François Ozon," *Kinoeye* 3, no. 13 (November 10, 2003), https://www.kinoeye.org/03/13/bingham13.php; Mark

Hain, "Explicit Ambiguity: Sexual Identity, Hitchcockian Criticism and the Films of François Ozon," *Quarterly Review of Film and Video* 24, no. 3 (2007): 278. On Ozon's uneasy association with New Queer Cinema, specifically, see B. Ruby Rich, "Queer *Nouveau*: From Morality Tales to Mortality Tales in Ozon, Téchiné, Collard," in *New Queer Cinema*, 214–35.

5. This is the opening question of one of the earliest scholarly studies of Ozon, when Mark Hain asks: "Can a filmmaker whose work is so disparate in style and tone really be called an auteur? And furthermore, does the grandiose and rather nostalgic term carry much meaning for a filmmaker like Ozon?" Mark Hain, "Explicit Ambiguity," 277.

6. Thibaut Schilt, *François Ozon* (Urbana: University of Illinois Press, 2011), 30; also quoted by Alistair Fox, "Auteurism, Personal Cinema and the Fémis Generation: The Case of François Ozon," in *A Companion to Contemporary French Cinema*, ed. Alistair Fox, Michel Marie, Raphaëlle Moine, and Hilary Radner (Chicester, UK: John Wiley & Sons, 2015), 533.

7. James Quandt, "Flesh and Blood: Sex and Violence in Recent French Cinema," *Artforum* 42, no. 6 (2004): 24–27.

8. Tim Palmer, "Style and Sensation in the Contemporary French Cinema of the Body," *Journal of Film and Video* 58, no. 3 (2006): 23, 32.

9. Mauro Resmini, "Reframing the New French Extremity: Cinema, Theory, Mediation," *Camera Obscura* 30, no. 3 (2015): 162.

10. For my own demythologization of the association between filmic violence and extratextual authenticity, see Ian Fleishman, *An Aesthetics of Injury: The Narrative Wound from Baudelaire to Tarantino* (Evanston, IL: Northwestern University Press, 2018), esp. 166–88 and 195–214.

11. Fox, "The Case of François Ozon," 535.

12. Nick Rees-Roberts, *French Queer Cinema* (Edinburgh: Edinburgh University Press, 2008), 112.

13. Emma Wilson, "Pathos as Queer Sociality in Contemporary European Visual Culture: François Ozon's Time to Leave," in *What's Queer about Europe?: Productive Encounters and Re-Enchanting Paradigms*, ed. Mireille Rosello and Sudeep Dasgupta (New York: Fordham University Press, 2013), 151. Somewhat differently, Rees-Roberts sees Honoré as "working within a Euro-American queer aesthetic tradition." Rees-Roberts, *French Queer Cinema*, 101.

14. Wilson, "Pathos as Queer Sociality," 151.

15. Wilson, "Pathos as Queer Sociality," 151.

16. Wilson, "Pathos as Queer Sociality," 152.

17. Wilson, "Pathos as Queer Sociality," 162.

18. Wilson, "Pathos as Queer Sociality," 152.

19. Rees-Roberts, *French Queer Cinema*, 111–12.

20. Rees-Roberts, *French Queer Cinema*, 116.

21. See Bingham, who quotes this dismissive assessment from "the influential Queer View website." Bingham, "The Not-So Discreet Charm of François Ozon."

22. Schilt, *François Ozon*, 118. The second quotation is taken from Handyside, "Melodrama and Ethics," 207.

23. Handyside, "Melodrama and Ethics," 208.

24. See Ronald Gregg, "Fassbinder's *Fox and His Friends* and Gay Politics in the 1970s," in *A Companion to Rainer Werner Fassbinder*, ed. Brigitte Peucker

(Chichester, UK: Wiley-Blackwell, 2012). Correcting for the early reactions against these films, Gregg praises Fassbinder for the manner in which he "bridges gay, art, and mainstream cinema." Gregg, "Fassbinder's *Fox and His Friends*," 564.

25. Rainer Werner Fassbinder, "Egal was ich mache, die Leute regen sich auf. Ein Gespräch mit Bodo Fründt und Michael Jürgs über 'Berlin Alexanderplatz' und 'Lili Marleen'," in *Rainer Werner Fassbinder: Die Anarchie der Phantasie: Gespräche und Interviews*, ed. Leo A. Lensing and Michael Töteberg (Frankfurt am Main: Fischer, 1986), 173. Also quoted in Woltersdorff, "'Grundsätzlich ist jeder homosexuell," 110. This interview is unfortunately not included in the English translation of this collection of Fassbinder materials. See Rainer Werner Fassbinder, *The Anarchy of Imagination: Interviews, Essays, Notes*, ed. Michael Töteberg and Leo Lensing (Baltimore: Johns Hopkins, 1992).

26. Will Aitken, "An Encounter with Rainer Werner Fassbinder," *Christopher Street* 4, no. 2 (September 1979): 66, my emphasis. Also quoted by Woltersdorff, who translates the sentence I have highlighted as his title, "Sexuelle Minderheiten," 110.

27. Quoted, in English translation, in Christian Braad Thomsen, *Fassbinder: Life and Work of a Provocative Genius* (Minneapolis: University of Minnesota Press, 2004), 181. Also quoted by Gregg, "Fassbinder's *Fox and His Friends*," 571.

28. Michel Coulombe, "Entretien avec François Ozon," *Ciné-Bulles: Le Cinéma d'auteur avant tout* 9, no. 1 (2000): 32, my translation.

29. Quoted in Asibong, *François Ozon*, 11n3, translation modified.

30. Asibong, *François Ozon*, 11n3.

31. Liz Hoggard, "Vampire of the Senses," *The Guardian*, August 10, 2003, https://www.theguardian.com/film/2003/aug/10/edinburghfilmfestival2003.edinburghfilmfestival.

32. Asibong, *François Ozon*, 64.

33. Asibong, *François Ozon*, 64–65.

34. In describing *Querelle* as universalizing, I am following the example, if not necessarily the categorization, provided by Woltersdorff, who classifies this same filmography according to what he understands to be three distinct anti-identarian strategies: a universalization of homosexuality in *Faustrecht* and *Deutschland im Herbst*; the totalization of the minoritarian perspective (in part through the use of camp posing, which Woltersdorff describes as "flirtation or love-hate relationship between queer subculture and the aesthetic mainstream") in *Petra* and *Querelle;* and, finally, the deconstruction of identity in *13 Monden*. Woltersdorff, "Sexuelle Minderheiten," 112, my translation. While I will be focusing on *13 Monden* here, *Gouttes d'eau* is closest thematically, perhaps, to *Faustrecht* and most visually aligned with the stage-like *huis clos* of *Petra*.

35. Ozon himself notes that his source script does not treat female same-sex relationships with the same sensitivity as Fassbinder's later work. Coulombe, "Entretien avec François Ozon," 32.

36. Anne Martine Parent and Nicolas Xanthos also read Franz's suicide in this light: "Preferring suicide to the life led by Véra and which awaits him since they are both Léopold's 'creatures.'" Anne Martine Parent and Nicolas Xanthos, "Être de langage, être de désir: Fantasme, parole et identité dans *Gouttes d'eau*

sur pierres brûlantes de François Ozon," *Australian Journal of French Studies* 43, no. 2 (2006): 195.

37. Coulombe, "Entretien avec François Ozon," 34, my translation.

38. Victor Fan, "Redressing the Inaccessible through the Re-Inscribed Body: *In a Year with 13 Moons* and Almodóvar's *Bad Education*," in *A Companion to Rainer Werner Fassbinder*, 118.

39. Fan, "Redressing the Inaccessible," 119, 120.

40. Kaja Silverman, *Male Subjectivity at the Margins* (New York: Routledge, 1992), 258.

41. Fan, "Redressing the Inaccessible," 127.

42. Fan, "Redressing the Inaccessible," 126.

43. At the very least, it strikes me as preferable to the cloven virgule of he/she and his/her generally employed by commentators on *13 Monden*.

44. Silverman, *Male Subjectivity at the Margins*, 218.

45. Silverman, *Male Subjectivity at the Margins*, 214.

46. Thomas Elsaesser, *Fassbinder's Germany: History, Identity, Subject* (Amsterdam: Amsterdam University Press, 1996), 202.

47. Bingham, "Identity and Love."

48. Schilt, *François Ozon*, 122.

49. Asibong, *François Ozon*, 70. That he sees this as symptomatic of Ozon's cultural epoch is a point Asibong makes plain: "Vera is one of many recent cinematic transsexuals whom theorists often, perhaps admirably, try to turn into heroines of postmodern reversibility, but who may, upon closer analysis, embody a horrifyingly static lack of agency." Asibong, *François Ozon*, 70n25.

50. Schilt, *François Ozon*, 127.

51. Wilson, "Pathos as Queer Sociality," 152. Rich similarly sees *Le temps qui reste* as exemplary of "a contemporary French queer cinema open to flexible gender and genre choices, with latitude to confront or displace the centrality of AIDS as a marker of the time." B. Ruby Rich, *New Queer Cinema*, 223.

52. While I have no wish to fault the film for the impossibility of adequately addressing all perspectives at once, one of the elisions operative here is of the rather undertheorized and arguably underrepresented (or most often at best inaccurately represented) phenomenon of heterosexual male-to-female transvestitism, which, as Samantha Allen shows, alternately occupies heteronormative and nonheteronormative positions and thus poses particular difficulties for queer thought. See Samantha Allen, "Whither the Transvestite?: Theorizing Male-to-Female Transvestitism in Feminist and Queer Theory," *Feminist Theory* 15, no. 1 (2014): 51–72. Taking a different view, Levilson C. Reis praises Ozon's film for its turn away from the "temporary transvestite" narrative to a depathologized view of transgender identity, which he sees as correcting the heternormativity of earlier films, including *Gouttes d'eau*. Levilson C. Reis, "Goodbye, 'Temporary' Transvestites—Hello, New Girlfriend! Ozon's Transgenre and Transgender Crossovers in *Une nouvelle amie* (2014)," *French Screen Studies* 20, no. 1 (2021): 44–45.

53. GEHITU, "Une nouvelle amie / The New Girlfriend: Sebastiane 2014 Award," laudatory text, September 26, 2014, https://www.sansebastianfestival.com/2014/related_news/1/4843/in.

54. Julia Kristeva, *Powers of Horror: An Essay on Abjection*, trans. Leon S. Roudiez (New York: Columbia University Press, 1982), 4. Walter Benjamin, whom I evoked in passing in the previous chapter, sees the corpse as emblematic of the function of allegory, which, put in bodily terms, makes meaning through dismemberment: "Allegorization . . . can only be carried through in all its vigor in respect of the corpse." Walter Benjamin, *Origin of German Tragic Drama*, trans. John Osborne (London: Verso, 1998), 217.

55. Judith Butler, *Gender Trouble: Feminism and Identity* (London: Routledge, 1991), 187.

56. Reis provides a more detailed reading of this club scene and its reprisal, although—conflating drag queens and transvestites—he speciously assumes the heterosexuality of the *transformiste* on the basis of a passing assertion of Ozon's with regard to the prevalence of straight cross-dressers. Reis, "Ozon's Transgenre and Transgender Crossovers," 54–59. See also Mariama Balde, "Interview de François Ozon pour *Une nouvelle amie*," *Daily Movies*, December 1, 2014, http://www.daily-movies.ch/interview-de-francois-ozon-pour-unenouvelle-amie. Bruno Pérard—whose actual stage name is Eva Carlton, making this role a cameo and thereby implying that this body too is intended to have an indexical function—also features in Christiane Spièro's documentary *Les reines de la nuit* (The Queens of the Night, 2019).

57. A comparison to other contemporary films focusing on trans feminine figures would be interesting but, sadly, beyond the scope of this analysis. Both Tom Hooper's commercially successful *The Danish Girl* and, more pertinently for the present project, Xavier Dolan's *Laurence Anyways* were released just a year before *Une nouvelle amie*.

58. This is not an uncommon complaint about some of Ozon's more recent productions. In its review of *Le temps qui reste*, for instance, the *Village Voice* laments: "A onetime enfant terrible, Ozon has been moving toward more conventional material. . . . *Time to Leave* winds up a tiresome affirmation of man's biological duty to procreate; the position is simplistic verging on obnoxious, especially after [earlier] attack[s] on the hetero family model." Dennis Lim, "The Dying Gaul." *Village Voice*, July 4, 2006, https://www.villagevoice.com/2006/07/04/the-dying-gaul/.

59. Armond White, "Some Like It Trans," *Out*, September 18, 2015, https://www.out.com/armond-white/2015/9/18/francois-ozon-and-new-girlfriend-win-trans-race.

60. G. Allen Johnson, "Fassbinder Revisited, Ozon's 'Water Drops on Burning Rocks,'" *IndieWire*, July 14, 2000, https://www.indiewire.com/2000/07/reviews-fassbinder-revisited-ozons-water-drops-on-burning-rocks-81534/.

61. Coulombe, "Entretien avec François Ozon," 35; Butler, *Bodies That Matter*, x.

62. Asibong, *François Ozon*, 67, 69.

63. Asibong, *François Ozon*, 67.

64. Asibong, *François Ozon*, 67.

65. Parent and Xanthos, "Fantasme, parole et identité," 196, my translation.

66. Parent and Xanthos, "Fantasme, parole et identité," 196, my translation.

67. Bingham, "Identity and Love."

68. Rainer Werner Fassbinder, *Anarchie in Bayern und andere Stücke* (Frankfurt am Main: Verlag der Autoren, 1985), 14.
69. Coulombe, "Entretien avec François Ozon," 34, my translation.
70. Coulombe, "Entretien avec François Ozon," 34, my translation.
71. Silverman, *Male Subjectivity at the Margins*, 221.
72. Silverman, *Male Subjectivity at the Margins*, 221.
73. Richard Dyer, *Only Entertainment* (London: Routledge, 2002); Linda Williams, *Hard Core: Power, Pleasure, and the Frenzy of the Visible* (Berkeley: University of California Press, 1999), 270.
74. Schilt, *François Ozon*, 126.
75. Schilt, *François Ozon*, 126.
76. Handyside, "Melodrama and Ethics," 212.
77. Parent and Xanthos, "Fantasme, parole et identité," 202–3.
78. Silverman, *Male Subjectivity at the Margins*, 222.
79. Asibong, *François Ozon*, 66–67.
80. See my chapter "The Woman on the Wall: Ingeborg Bachmann's *Malina* (1971)—Elfriede Jelinek's and Werner Schroeter's *Malina* (1991)," in *An Aesthetics of Injury*, 139–65, esp. 161–64. I have also discussed this moment in "Alter/Ego: Isabelle Huppert as Werner Schroeter's Double," in *Performative Opacity in the Work of Isabelle Huppert*, ed. Iggy Cortez and Ian Fleishman (Edinburgh: Edinburgh University Press, 2023), 55.
81. Fassbinder, *Anarchie in Bayern*, 62.
82. In a reading of Petra as a puppet master, Brigitte Peucker traces the chain a link further, uncovering in this shot a "determining cinematic allusion" to Ingmar Bergman's *Persona* (1966). Brigitte Peucker, *Aesthetic Spaces: The Place of Art in Film* (Evanston, IL: Northwestern University Press, 2019), 80.
83. Heinrich Heine, *Songs of Love and Grief: A Bilingual Anthology in the Verse Forms of the Originals*, trans. Walter W. Arndt (Evanston, IL: Northwestern University Press, 1995), 40–41. Notably, Ozon opts for a variant, reproduced here, emphasizing the primordial quality of this cultural transmission: ur*alten Zeiten* as opposed to the *alten Zeiten* of the original.
84. Schilt, *François Ozon*, 119.
85. Asibong, *François Ozon*, 13.
86. Armond White, "Ozon Elevates Gay Sensibility," *Out*, March 17, 2017, https://www.out.com/armond-white/2017/3/17/ozon-elevates-gay-sensibility.
87. White, "Ozon Elevates Gay Sensibility."
88. Fan, "Redressing the Inaccessible," 130.

Chapter 6

1. David Rooney, chief film critic for the *Hollywood Reporter*, flips this script, accusing Dolan of perpetuating such stereotypes by "fetishizing his own image." Of Dolan's fourth film, the homoerotic thriller *Tom à la ferme* (*Tom at the Farm*, 2013), he writes that "Dolan is an accomplished enough actor to withstand the attention, but he inadvertently makes this sinister quasi-thriller—which is as much about gay self-loathing as homophobia—also about auteurial self-adulation." David Rooney, "Tom at the Farm: Venice Review," *Hollywood Reporter*, September 2, 2013, https://www.hollywoodreporter.com/news/general-news/tom-at-farm-venice-review-619296/. Ever the diplomat, Dolan's tweeted

response was: "@THRmovies you can kiss my narcissistic ass." Cited in Vanessa Schneider, "Xavier Dolan. Cinémaniaque," *Le Monde*, May 25, 2016, https://www.lemonde.fr/m-gens-portrait/article/2016/05/27/xavier-dolan-cine-maniaque_4927720_4497229.html.

2. With suspiciously anthropological phrasing, Andrée Lafontaine notes in the introduction to the first scholarly volume on Dolan to appear how French audiences of Dolan's *Mommy* (2014) were charmed by the dialect's "musicality and authenticity." Andrée Lafontaine, introduction to *ReFocus: The Films of Xavier Dolan* (Edinburgh: Edinburgh University Press, 2022), 18. Tellingly, the same foul-mouthed cacophony in *Juste la fin du monde* (*It's Only the End of the World*, 2016), when shouted with a more Parisian pronunciation, was generally deemed shrill and hysterical. See Lafontaine, introduction, 19–21.

3. See, e.g., Xavier Dolan (@xavierdolan), "In light of recent articles . . ." *Instagram*, July 7, 2023, https://www.instagram.com/p/CuaTw4fu1kl/?hl=it&img_index=1.

4. Liz Czach, "Xavier Dolan's *J'ai tué ma mère* and Québec's New Cinema of Mise-en-scène," in *The Films of Xavier Dolan*, 126–27.

5. As Lafontaine has it: "once in their new context, these 'tacky,' 'unrefined' songs take on a new life outside of social judgements of taste (Céline Dion's 'On ne change pas' being the best example for most Québécois viewers, but Dido's 'White Flag' also being a good example). In his own way, Dolan . . . embraces a camp aesthetic by recovering the pleasure of these 'tacky,' popular objects. Defying commonly accepted hierarchies of taste, Dolan's music-driven cinema uses all elements of mise-en-scène to intensify emotion and create in viewers a visceral, cathartic experience." Lafontaine, introduction, 6. The Céline Dion allusion will be important later on; the Dido song mentioned here is in fact playing during the initial discussion of the former tenant's *quétaine* sensibility.

6. Fulvia Massimi, "The Transgressive Cinema of Xavier Dolan," in *The Films of Xavier Dolan*, 39.

7. Nick Rees-Roberts, "Fade to Gray: Dolan's Pop Fashion and Surface Style," in *The Films of Xavier Dolan*, 212.

8. See Claudia Kotte, "Fast and Furious. The Sound and the Fury in Xavier Dolan's *Mommy*," *French Forum* 44, no. 2 (Fall 2019): 321.

9. Bonnie Wertheim, "What Is Camp? The Met Gala 2019 Theme Explained," *New York Times*, May 4, 2019, https://www.nytimes.com/2019/05/04/style/met-gala-what-is-camp.html.

10. Shane O'Neill and Matthew Schneier, "What Is Camp (Now)?" *New York Times*, May 4, 2019, https://www.nytimes.com/video/style/100000006484770/met-gala-camp.html.

11. O'Neill and Schneier, "What Is Camp (Now)?"

12. O'Neill and Schneier, "What Is Camp (Now)?"

13. O'Neill and Schneier, "What Is Camp (Now)?"

14. Peter Wollen, *Raiding the Icebox: Reflections on Twentieth-Century Culture* (London: Verso, 1993), 161. Also quoted in Rees-Roberts, "Fade to Gray," 212.

15. Florian Grandena and Pascal Gagné, "Xavier Dolan's Backward Cinema: Straight Spaces, Queer Temporality, and Genealogical Interruptions in *Tom at the Farm* and *It's Only the End of the World*," *The Films of Xavier Dolan*, 93.

16. Mercédès Baillargeon, "Joy, Melancholy, and the Promise of Happiness in Xavier Dolan's *Mommy*," In *The Films of Xavier Dolan*, 178.

17. Rees-Roberts, "Fade to Gray," 212.

18. See Jacques Derrida, "Plato's Pharmacy," in *Dissemination*, trans. Barbara Johnson (Chicago: University of Chicago Press, 1981), 63–171.

19. Bill Marshall, "Spaces and Times of Québec in Films by Xavier Dolan," in *The Films of Xavier Dolan*, 105. Previously published as "Spaces and Times of Québec in Two Films by Xavier Dolan," *Nottingham French Studies* 55, no. 2 (2016): 189–208.

20. Rees-Roberts, "Fade to Gray," 211.

21. Baillargeon, "Promise of Happiness," 179. Baillargeon even suggests that the seemingly rather superfluous dystopian conceit of *Mommy* is a "kitsch (or even camp) . . . addition." Baillargeon, "Promise of Happiness," 179.

22. Julianne Pidduck, "The Dolandrama: Queer Male Authorship and the Fabulous Leading Lady," in *The Films of Xavier Dolan*, 58, 60. See Stephen Maddison, "All About Women: Pedro Almodóvar and the Heterosocial Dynamic," *Textual Practice* 14, no. 2 (2000): 269.

23. Pidduck, "The Dolandrama," 60. Christian Rioux has also accused Dolan of a kind of queer branding. Christian Rioux, "Méfions-nous des rebelles," *Le Devoir*, October 17, 2014, http://www.ledevoir.com/societe/actualites-en-societe/421369/mefions-nous-des-rebelles. Summarized in Jason R. D'Aoust, "The Queer Voices of Xavier Dolan's *Mommy*," *European Journal of American Studies* 11, no. 3 (2017): 4.

24. Pidduck, "The Dolandrama," 58.

25. Quoted in Sandrine Marques, "Xavier Dolan 'dégoûté' par les prix récompensant les films gays," *Le Monde*, September 20, 2014, http://www.lemonde.fr/culture/article/2014/09/20/xavier-dolan-degoute-par-les-prix-recompensant-lesfilms-gays_4490979_3246.html, my translation.

26. Bill Marshall, "Spaces and Times," 105.

27. Massimi, "Transgressive Cinema," 33.

28. Stefano Genetti, "La scène, l'écran: Questionnements identitaires et tensions du désir dans *Tom à la ferme* de Michel Marc Bouchard et de Xavier Dolan," *Itinéraires: Littérature, textes, cultures* 2019, nos. 2–3 (2019): 9, my translation.

29. Xavier Dolan, interviewed by George Stroumboulopoulos on *George Tonight*, *CBC*, October 4, 2012, https://www.youtube.com/watch?v=8dA47t0psWI&ab_channel=CBC.

30. Xavier Dolan, interviewed by Michael Glitz for *The Advocate* and *Huffington Post*, May 24, 2009, https://www.youtube.com/watch?v=N_7BtJfU6Xw&ab_channel=MIchaelGiltz.

31. Dolan, interviewed by Michael Glitz.

32. Dolan, interviewed by Michael Glitz.

33. Pidduck, "The Dolandrama," 52.

34. Peter Knegt, "Xavier Dolan Gets Respect," *Film Quarterly* 68, no. 2 (Winter 2014): 34.

35. Czach, "Québec's New Cinema of Mise-en-scène," 122.

36. Czach, "Québec's New Cinema of Mise-en-scène," 123.

37. Indeed, Pierre Bourdieu's reflections on taste and class figure chiefly in the scholarly apparatus used to approach Dolan.

38. See Judith Butler, "Melancholy Gender—Refused Identification," *Psychoanalytic Dialogues* 5, no. 2 (1995): 165–80.

39. Peter Knegt, "Xavier Dolan Gets Respect," *Film Quarterly* 68, no. 2 (Winter 2014): 35.

40. D'Aoust, "Queer Voices," 10–13.

41. Karen Redrobe, *Vanishing Women: Magic, Film, and Feminism* (Durham, NC: Duke University Press, 2003), 117, 103, 100.

42. D. W. Winnicott, "Transitional Objects and Transitional Phenomena," in *Playing and Reality* (New York: Routledge, 1996), 10.

43. Carol Mavor, *Reading Boyishly: Roland Barthes, J. M. Barrie, Jacques Henri Lartigue, Marcel Proust, and D. W. Winnicott* (Durham, NC: Duke University Press, 2007), 70, original emphasis.

44. See Eve Kosofsky Sedgwick, "How to Bring Your Kids Up Gay: The War on Effeminate Boys," in *Tendencies*, 154–64 (Durham, NC: Duke University Press, 1999). Mavor, *Reading Boyishly*, 72. While this is not to accuse her of perpetuating such effeminiphobia, notably, a similar "failure" on the part of the caregiver also informs Sedgwick's understanding of *shame*—itself a stand-in for an understanding of queerness based in sexuality. Theorizing shame through the work of Silvan Tomkins, Sedgwick locates "the protoform (eyes down, head averted) of this powerful affect—which appears in infants very early, between the third and seventh month of life, just after the infant has become able to distinguish and recognize the face of its caregiver—at a particular moment in a particular repeated narrative. That is the moment when the circuit of mirroring expressions between the child's face and the caregiver's recognized face . . . is broken: the moment when the adult face *fails* or refuses to play its part in the continuation of mutual gaze." Eve Kosofsky Sedgwick, *Touching Feeling: Affect, Pedagogy, Performativity* (Durham, NC: Duke University Press, 2002), 36, my emphasis.

45. Dolan repudiates the Instagram association and insists instead that this is a cinephilic allusion to one of the medium's original aspect ratios. See Mark Olsen, "Indie Focus: In 'Mommy,' Xavier Dolan Looks Things in the Eye," *Los Angeles Times*, January 17, 2015, https://www.latimes.com/entertainment/movies/la-et-mn-ca-xavier-dolan-20150118-story.html.

46. Perpetuating the association between nonheteronormative content and provocative aesthetics, Hannah Vaughn rather mischaracterizes the overall editing of *J'ai tué ma mère* as an avant-garde style connecting "relatively radical content to similarly radical form." Hannah Vaughn, "Filming Fracture in Xavier Dolan's *J'ai tué ma mère*," *Québec Studies* (Winter 2013): 109. Czach specifies that the film is not so much anti-Hollywood as it is of a piece with contemporary European art cinema. Czach, "Québec's New Cinema of Mise-en-scène," 123.

47. Loïc Bourdeau, "Politics and Motherhood in Xavier Dolan's *J'ai tué ma mère* and *Mommy*," in *Horrible Mothers: Representations across Francophone North America*, ed. Loic Bourdeau (Lincoln: University of Nebraska Press: 2019), 180. Elsewhere, Bourdeau makes similar claims about Dorval's character in *Les amours imaginaires* embodying "a new and more independent form of motherhood." Loïc Bourdeau, "Queering Up the Mother with Michel Tremblay and Xavier Dolan," *Contemporary French Civilization* 43, nos. 3–4 (2018): 367.

48. Genetti, "Questionnements identitaires," 9, my translation. Genetti's focus here is on the water closet in *Tom à la ferme*, of which Marshall also notes, "The

film is dominated by the space that the household . . . demand[s], namely the closet, that is a massive re-calculation of where it is safe to be 'out' or not." Marshall, "Spaces and Times," 114.

49. See Kotte, "Fast and Furious," 327.

50. Kotte, "Fast and Furious," 329.

51. Richard Dyer, *White* (London: Routledge, 1997), 45.

52. Dyer, *White*, 213.

53. See Lafontaine, introduction, 14–15.

54. See Xavier Dolan, "L'esthétisme de la controverse: lettre ouverte à propos de mon clip pour Indochine," *Huffpost Québec*, December 29, 2013, https://quebec.huffingtonpost.ca/xavier-dolan/clip-indochine-lettre-ouverte-francoise-laborde_b_3226995.html.

55. Dyer, *White*, 45.

56. Butler, "Melancholy Gender," 174.

57. Butler, "Melancholy Gender," 178–79.

58. Butler, "Melancholy Gender," 179, original emphasis.

59. As Butler continues: "For a gay or lesbian identity-position to sustain its appearance as coherent, heterosexuality must remain in that rejected and repudiated place. Paradoxically, its heterosexual *remains* must be *sustained* precisely through the insistence on the seamless coherence of a specifically gay identity." Butler, "Melancholy Gender," 179.

60. Dolan's wildly successful, sepia-toned video for Adele's 2015 hit "Hello" might be a case in point.

61. Dyer, *White*, 217.

62. In my previous chapter I discuss debates around the not-about-AIDS film. See Nick Rees-Roberts, "Queer Sexuality, AIDS and Loss," in Nick Rees-Roberts, *French Queer Cinema* (Edinburgh: Edinburgh University Press, 2008), 89–128; and Emma Wilson, "Pathos as Queer Sociality in Contemporary European Visual Culture: François Ozon's Time to Leave," in *What's Queer about Europe?: Productive Encounters and Re-Enchanting Paradigms*, ed. Mireille Rosello and Sudeep Dasgupta (New York: Fordham University Press, 2013). With regard to this film specifically, Pidduck seems to suggest that the erasure of explicit references to HIV is a form of closeting. Pidduck, "The Dolandrama," 57.

63. "I think there is a correlation between my abandonment of cinema and my abandonment of the world in general." In Lucas Bravo and Adam Sanchez, "Xavier Dolan: 'On cherche la validation des gens qui nous rejettent, pas celle de ceux qui nous acceptent et célèbrent,' " *GQ France*, September 27, 2023, https://www.gqmagazine.fr/article/xavier-dolan-lucas-bravo-interview-gq, my translation.

64. "I don't want to deal with the anxiety of performing, being successful, being loved. I don't want to depend on other people's reaction. I want to be free. . . . I'll be, always, free in how I create, and free to create when I choose to, or choose not to." Dolan (@xavierdolan), "In light of recent articles . . ."

Coda

1. All translations from the film are mine, either from the original footage, often in French, or from the voice-overs, which have been dubbed into German.

2. Dorrit Cohn, "The 'Second Author' of *Death in Venice*," in *The Distinction of Fiction* (Baltimore: Johns Hopkins University Press, 1999), 132–49.

3. See James P. Wilper, who writes, in a phrasing recalling Sedgwick's sidestepping of sexuality: "For so long, many critics and readers were able to sidestep the fact that the love felt by a man for a youth was at the heart of the novella. Only with the publication of Mann's diaries, which began in 1977, did homosexuality in the author's work and life become a central area of investigation in Mann scholarship." James P. Wilper, "Rewritings, Adaptations, and Gay Literary Criticism: Thomas Mann's *Death in Venice*," *Adaptation* 8, no. 1 (2014): 1.

4. Robert Deam Tobin, *Peripheral Desires: The German Discovery of Sex* (Philadelphia: University of Pennsylvania Press, 2015), 189.

5. Tobin, *Peripheral Desires*, 185.

6. See Eve Kosofsky Sedgwick, *The Epistemology of the Closet* (Berkeley: University of California Press, 1990), 55; quoted in Tobin, *Peripheral Desires*, 192.

7. Jennifer Evans, *The Queer Art of History: Queer Kinship after Fascism* (Durham, NC: Duke University Press, 2023), 61.

8. Specifically *Nel regno di Napoli* (*Kingdom of Naples*, 1978) and *Palermo oder Wolfsburg* (*Palermo or Wolfsburg*, 1980). That Italian, and most particularly Neapolitan, exoticism is meant to serve an authenticating function is palpable throughout Schroeter's published memoirs. See Werner Schroeter with Claudia Lenssen, *Days of Twilight, Nights of Frenzy: A Memoir*, trans. Anthea Bell (Chicago: University of Chicago Press, 2017).

9. Evans, *Queer Art of History*, 63. See also Roland Barthes's preface to *Taormina: Wilhelm von Gloeden*, ed James Woody, i–iii (Altadena, CA: Twelvetree Press, 1986); Javier Samper Vendrell, *Seduction of Youth: Homosexual Rights in the Weimar Republic* (Toronto: University of Toronto Press, 2020), esp. 77–89; and Javier Samper Vendrell, "Von Gloeden's Dog: Methodological Notes on Photography and the History of Intergenerational Intimacy," *Journal of the History of Sexuality* 33, no. 3 (September 2024): 418–37.

10. This geography—Hungary, Poland (both the fictive Tadzio and his inspiration in Mann's life are Polish), Russia, Finland, and, ultimately, Sweden—brings to light how what I elsewhere identify as an erotic impulse toward ethnological sameness can be at once specifically Nordic while at the same time masquerading as generally pan-European. See Ian Fleishman, "Rolf Hammerschmidt's *Boytropolis* and the Ethno-Ecological Imaginary," *Environmental Humanities* 14, no. 3 (2022): 680–98.

11. C. Riley Snorton, *Nobody Is Supposed to Know: Black Sexuality on the Down Low* (Minneapolis: University of Minnesota Press, 2014), 21.

12. Hortense Spillers, "Mama's Baby, Papa's Maybe: An American Grammar Book," *Diacritics* 17, no. 2 (Summer 1987): 64–81. See also Alexander Weheliye, "Depravation: Pornotropes," in *Habeus Viscus: Racializing Assemblages, Biopolitics, and Black Feminist Theories of the Human*, 89–112 (Durham, NC: Duke University Press, 2014). I am grateful to Mimi Hacking for pointing me in the direction of these discourses.

13. Michael A. Chaney, *Fugitive Vision: Slave Image and Black Identity in Antebellum Narrative* (Bloomington: Indiana University Press, 2008), 63.

14. I am inspired here by Lutz Koepnick's reading of actor Isabelle Huppert alongside photographer Roni Horn and his idea that "in our contemporary world we need to think of both mass media and artistic mediums not as mere objects, but as elemental forces, as curious hybrids of the natural and the cultural

that shape the very way in which we perceive the world in the first place." Lutz Koepnick, "Horn | Huppert | Horn," *Performative Opacity in the Work of Isabelle Huppert*, 128.

15. Quoted in Stewart Burrows, "'Desire Projected Itself Visually': Watching *Death in Venice*," in *Classics in Film and Fiction*, ed. Deborah Cartmell, Heidi Kaye, I. Q. Hunter, and Imelda Whelehan (London: Pluto Press, 2000), 137. See David Glassco, "Films Out of Books: Bergman, Visconti, Mann," *Mosaic* 16, no. 1–2 (Winter–Spring 1983): 173.

16. Burrows, "Watching *Death in Venice*," 138.

17. Philip Core, *Camp: The Lie That Tells the Truth* (New York: Delilah Books, 1984), 7.

18. Quoted in Wilper, "Rewritings, Adaptations," 6; and Burrows, "Watching *Death in Venice*," 137.

19. Eve Kosofsky Sedgwick, *Touching Feeling: Affect, Pedagogy, Performativity* (Durham, NC: Duke University Press, 2002), 147. I would even argue that, by recognizing the arbitrariness of the injunctions it reveals, paranoid exposition can regard the past as anything *but* inevitable and open up the same hopeful possibilities that Sedgwick reserves for the purview of reparative approaches to "entertain such profoundly painful, profoundly relieving, ethically crucial possibilities as that the past . . . could have happened differently from the way it actually did." Sedgwick, *Touching Feeling*, 147.

20. One of the guiding arguments of Rei Terada's *Feeling in Theory* is a comparable deconstruction of what she calls the "expressive hypothesis": "Expression is the dominant trope of thought about emotion. The ideology of emotion diagrams emotion as something lifted from a depth to a surface. . . . The claim that emotion requires a subject—thus we can see we're subjects since we have emotions—creates the illusion of subjectivity rather than showing evidence of it. This sleight of mind, in which 'expression' serves as the distracting handkerchief, strikes me as self-serving. It is this relatively large complex of circularity, naturalization, and inversion to which I refer as the *expressive hypothesis*. To object to the expressive hypothesis or any other mechanism of the ideology of emotion is not to discredit emotion, but to extricate it from expedient mythologies." Rei Terada, *Feeling in Theory: Emotion after the "Death of the Subject."* (Cambridge, MA: Harvard University Press, 2003), 11. The mythology Terada has in mind here is the credence in the subject as stable and self-identical, which she tends to abbreviate by referring simply to *subjectivity* tout court.

21. Tobin comes to a similar conclusion about Thomas Mann, who is redeemed despite himself: "Mann allows the novella, the literary work itself, to go beyond both the author and the narrator in developing an understanding of sexuality. Literature does not merely cloak the ideas of the author in a more or less accessible form—it can at times allow ideas and concepts to develop in ways that go beyond the rational thought processes of the author." Tobin, *Peripheral Desires*, 210.

BIBLIOGRAPHY

Aitken, Will. "An Encounter with Rainer Werner Fassbinder." *Christopher Street* 4, no. 2 (September 1979): 65–67.

Allen, Samantha. "Whither the Transvestite?: Theorizing Male-to-Female Transvestitism in Feminist and Queer Theory." *Feminist Theory* 15, no. 1 (2014): 51–72.

Altieri, Charles. "Affect, Intentionality and Cognition: A Response to Ruth Leys." *Critical Inquiry* 38, no. 4 (Summer 2012): 878–81.

Amin, Kadji. *Disturbing Attachments: Genet, Modern Pederasty, and Queer History*. Durham, NC: Duke University Press, 2017.

Apter, Emily. "Allegories of Reading / Allegories of Justice: The Gidean *Fait Divers*." *Romanic Review* 80, no. 4 (1989): 560–70.

Apter, Emily. *André Gide and the Codes of Homotextuality*. Saratoga, CA: Anma Libri 1987.

Asibong, Andrew. *François Ozon*. Manchester: Manchester University Press, 2008.

Baillargeon, Mercédès. "Joy, Melancholy, and the Promise of Happiness in Xavier Dolan's *Mommy*." In *The Films of Xavier Dolan*, edited by Andrée Lafontaine, 177–90. Edinburgh: Edinburgh University Press, 2019.

Balde, Mariama. "Interview de François Ozon pour *Une nouvelle amie*." *Daily Movies*, December 1, 2014. http://www.daily-movies.ch/interview-de-francois-ozon-pour-unenouvelle-amie.

Baldwin, James. *Another Country*. London: Penguin Classics, 2001.

Baldwin, James. *Giovanni's Room*. New York: Vintage International, 2013.

Barthes, Roland. Preface to *Taormina: Wilhelm von Gloeden*. Edited by James Woody, i–iii. Altadena, CA: Twelvetree Press, 1986.

Baudelaire, Charles. *Intimate Journals*. Translated by Christopher Isherwood. London: Black Spring, 1989.

Benjamin, Walter. *Origin of German Tragic Drama*. Translated by John Osborne. London: Verso, 1998.

Bersani, Leo. *Homos*. Cambridge, MA: Harvard University Press, 1995.

Bingham, Adam. "Identity and Love: The Not-So Discreet Charm of François Ozon." *Kinoeye* 3, no. 13 (November 10, 2003). https://www.kinoeye.org/03/13/bingham13.php.

Booth, Mark. *Camp*. London: Quartet Books, 1983.

Bouliane, Claudia. "Le démonisme d'André Gide: le pouvoir de l'induction." *Fabula / Les colloques, Les écrivains théoriciens de la littérature (1920–1945)*, May 9, 2013. http://atelier.fabula.org/colloques/document1841.php.

Bourdeau, Loïc. "Politics and Motherhood in Xavier Dolan's *J'ai tué ma mère* and *Mommy*." In *Horrible Mothers: Representations across Francophone North*

America, edited by Loïc Bourdeau, 169–94. Lincoln: University of Nebraska Press, 2019.

Bourdeau, Loïc. "Queering Up the Mother with Michel Tremblay and Xavier Dolan." *Contemporary French Civilization* 43, nos. 3–4 (2018): 353–72.

Bourdieu, Pierre. *The Logic of Practice*. Translated by Richard Nice. Stanford, CA: Stanford University Press, 1990.

Bourdieu, Pierre. *Le sens pratique*. Paris. Éditions de Minuit, 1980.

Boyle, Claire. "Friend or Foe? Misidentification, Abject Selfhood and Genet's Queer Reception." In *Soi-Disant: Life-Writing in French*, edited by Juliana de Nooy, Joe Hardwick, and Barbara E. Hannah, 26–40. Newark: University of Delaware Press, 2005.

Boym, Svetlana. *The Off-Modern*. New York: Bloomsbury Academic, 2017.

Branson, Scott. "Gide, Wilde and the Death of the Novel." *MLN* 127, no. 5 (December 2012): 1226–48.

Bravo, Luca, and Adam Sanchez. "Xavier Dolan: 'On cherche la validation des gens qui nous rejettent, pas celle de ceux qui nous acceptent et célèbrent.' " *GQ France*, September 27, 2023. https://www.gqmagazine.fr/article/xavier-dolan-lucas-bravo-interview-gq.

Britton, Andrew. "For Interpretation: Notes against Camp." In *Britton on Film: The Complete Film Criticism of Andrew Britton*. Edited by Barry Grant, 388–93. Detroit: Wayne State University Press, 2009.

Burrows, Stewart. "'Desire Projected Itself Visually': Watching *Death in Venice*." In *Classics in Film and Fiction*, ed. Deborah Cartmell, Heidi Kaye, I. Q. Hunter, and Imelda Whelehan, 137–56. London: Pluto Press, 2000.

Butler, Judith. *Bodies That Matter: On the Discursive Limits of Sex*. New York: Routledge, 1993.

Butler, Judith. "Critically Queer." *GLQ* 1 (1993): 17–32.

Butler, Judith. *Gender Trouble: Feminism and Identity*. London: Routledge, 1991.

Butler, Judith. "Melancholy Gender—Refused Identification." *Psychoanalytic Dialogues* 5, no. 2 (1995): 165–80.

Butler, Judith. *The Psychic Life of Power: Theories in Subjection*. Stanford, CA: Stanford University Press, 1997.

Butler, Judith. *Who's Afraid of Gender*. New York: Farrar, Straus and Giroux, 2024.

Camaiti Hostert, Anna. *Passing: A Strategy to Dissolve Identities and Remap Differences*. Translated by Christine Marciasini. Madison, NJ: Farleigh Dickinson University Press, 2007.

Canby, Vincent. "Film: 'The Rose King,' by Werner Schroeter." *New York Times*, December 30, 1970, C10.

Carlotti, Pierre-Ange. "Troye Sivan: Atomic Blonde." *Dazed*, March 14, 2018. https://www.dazeddigital.com/music/article/39346/1/troye-sivan-boy-erased-new-album-interview.

Caron, Pascale. "Pour quelques paillettes en plus . . . Le funambule de Jean Genet et l'image poétique du movement." *Littérature* 139 (2005): 24–43.

Caserio, Robert L., Lee Edelman, Judith Halberstam, José Esteban Muñoz, and Tim Dean. "The Antisocial Thesis in Queer Theory," *PMLA* 121, no. 3 (May 2006): 819–28.

Caughie, Pamela. *Passing and Pedagogy: The Dynamics of Responsibility*. Urbana: University of Illinois Press, 1999.

Caughie, Pamela. "Passing as Modernism." *Modernism/Modernity* 12, no. 3 (2005): 385–406.

Chaney, Michael A. *Fugitive Vision: Slave Image and Black Identity in Antebellum Narrative*. Bloomington: Indiana University Press, 2008.

Christian, Laura. "Of Housewives and Saints: Abjection, Transgression and Impossible Mourning in *Poison* and *Safe*." *Camera Obscura* 19, no. 3 (2004): 93–124.

Cocteau, Jean. *Poésie critique*. 2 vols. Paris: Gallimard, 1959.

Cohn, Dorrit. "The 'Second Author' of *Death in Venice*." In *The Distinction of Fiction*. Baltimore: Johns Hopkins University Press, 1999.

Cohn, Dorrit. "Metalepsis and Mise en Abyme." Translated by Lewis S. Gleich. *Narrative* 20, no. 1 (January 2012): 105–14.

Connolly, William E. "The Complexity of Intention." *Critical Inquiry* 37, no. 4 (Summer 2011): 791–98.

Cooley, Dennis R., and Kelby Harrison. Introduction to *Passing/Out: Sexual Identity Veiled and Revealed*, edited by Dennis R. Cooley and Kelby Harrison, 1–12. Lanham, MD: Lexington Books, 2012.

Core, Philip. *Camp: The Lie That Tells the Truth*. New York: Delilah Books, 1984.

Cormican, Muriel. "Pro-Porn Rhetoric and the Cinema of Monika Treut." *Women in German Yearbook* 19 (2003): 179–99.

Coulombe, Michel. "Entretien avec François Ozon." *Ciné-Bulles: Le Cinéma d'auteur avant tout* 9, no. 1 (2000): 32–36.

Cowan, Bainard. "Walter Benjamin's Theory of Allegory." *New German Critique* 22 (Winter 1981): 109–22.

Creech, John. "Outing Jean Genet." *Yale French Studies* 91 (1997): 117–40.

Czach, Liz. "Xavier Dolan's *J'ai tué ma mère* and Québec's New Cinema of Mise-en-scène." In *The Films of Xavier Dolan*, edited by Andrée Lafontaine, 119–35. Edinburgh: Edinburgh University Press, 2019.

D'Aoust, Jason R. "The Queer Voices of Xavier Dolan's *Mommy*." *European Journal of American Studies* 11, no. 3 (2017): 1–17.

Davis, Colin. *Ethical Issues in Twentieth-Century French Fiction: Killing the Other*. New York: St. Martin's Press, 2000.

Davis, Colin. "Genet's *Journal du voleur* and the Ethics of Reading." *French Studies* 48 (1994): 50–62.

DeAngelis, Michael. "Authorship and New Queer Cinema: The Case of Todd Haynes." In *Auteurs and Authorship: A Film Reader*, edited by Barry Keith, 292–303. Oxford: Blackwell, 2008.

de Man, Paul. "Whatever Happened to André Gide? (1965)." In *Critical Writings, 1953–1978*, 130–35. Minneapolis: University of Minnesota Press, 1989.

Demory, Pamela. "Queer/Adaptation: An Introduction." In *Queer/Adaptation*, edited by Pamela Demory, 1–13. Cham, Switzerland: Palgrave Macmillan, 2019.

Derrida, Jacques. *Clang*. Translated by Geoffrey Bennington and David Wills. Minneapolis: University of Minnesota Press, 2021.

Derrida, Jacques. *Glas*. Paris: Éditions Galilée, 1974.

Derrida, Jacques. "Plato's Pharmacy." In *Dissemination*. Translated by Barbara Johnson, 63–171. Chicago: University of Chicago Press, 1981.

Derrida, Jacques. *Voice and Phenomenon: Introduction to the Problem of the Sign in Husserl's Phenomenology*. Translated by Leonard Lawlor. Evanston, IL: Northwestern University Press, 2011.

de Villiers, Nicholas. *Opacity and the Closet: Queer Tactics in Foucault, Barthes, and Warhol*. Minneapolis: University of Minnesota Press, 2012.

Devor, Aaron H. *Gender Blending: Confronting the Limits of Duality*. Bloomington: Indiana University Press, 1989.

Dolan, Xavier (@xavierdolan). "In light of recent articles . . ." *Instagram*, July 7, 2023. https://www.instagram.com/p/CuaTw4fu1kl/?hl=it&img_index=1.

Dolan, Xavier. Interviewed by George Stroumboulopoulos. *George Tonight, CBC*, October 4, 2012. https://www.youtube.com/watch?v=8dA47t0psWI&ab_channel=CBC.

Dolan, Xavier. Interviewed by Michael Glitz for *The Advocate* and *Huffington Post*, May 24, 2009. https://www.youtube.com/watch?v=N_7BtJfU6Xw&ab_channel=MIchaelGiltz.

Dolan, Xavier. "L'esthétisme de la controverse: lettre ouverte à propos de mon clip pour Indochine." *Huffpost Québec*, December 29, 2013. https://quebec.huffingtonpost.ca/xavier-dolan/clip-indochine-lettre-ouverte-francoise-laborde_b_3226995.html.

Dollimore, Jonathan. *Sexual Dissidence: Augustine to Wilde, Freud to Foucault*. Oxford: Oxford University Press, 1991.

Doyle, Patrick. "Confessions of a Neurotic Pop Idol." *Rolling Stone* 1332 (December 2018): 57–61.

Dyer, Richard. *Now You See It*. London: Routledge, 2003.

Dyer, Richard. *Only Entertainment*. London: Routledge, 2002.

Dyer, Richard. *White*. London: Routledge, 1997.

Edelman, Lee. *Homographesis: Essays in Gay Literary and Cultural Theory*. New York: Routledge, 1994.

Elsaesser, Thomas. *Fassbinder's Germany: History, Identity, Subject*. Amsterdam: Amsterdam University Press, 1996.

Eribon, Didier. *Insult and the Making of the Gay Self*. Translated by Michael Lucey. Durham, NC: Duke University Press, 2004.

Eribon, Didier. *Une morale du minoritaire: Variations sur un thème de Jean Genet*. Paris: Fayard, 2001.

Evans, Jennifer. *The Queer Art of History: Queer Kinship after Fascism*. Durham, NC: Duke University Press, 2023.

Fan, Victor. "Redressing the Inaccessible through the Re-Inscribed Body: *In a Year with 13 Moons* and Almodóvar's *Bad Education*." In *A Companion to Rainer Werner Fassbinder*, edited by Brigitte Peucker, 118–41. Chichester, UK: Wiley-Blackwell, 2012.

Fassbinder, Rainer Werner. *Anarchie in Bayern und andere Stücke*. Frankfurt am Main: Verlag der Autoren, 1985.

Fassbinder, Rainer Werner. *The Anarchy of Imagination: Interviews, Essays, Notes*. Edited by Michael Töteberg and Leo Lensing. Baltimore: Johns Hopkins University Press, 1992.

Fassbinder, Rainer Werner. "Egal was ich mache, die Leute regen sich auf. Ein Gespräch mit Bodo Fründt und Michael Jürgs über 'Berlin Alexanderplatz' und 'Lili Marleen.'" In *Rainer Werner Fassbinder: Die Anarchie der Phantasie: Gespräche und Interviews*. Edited by Leo A. Lensing and Michael Töteberg, 167–80. Frankfurt am Main: Fischer, 1986.

Fassbinder, Rainer Werner. Interview with Kurt Raab. In *Die Sehnsucht des Rainer Werner Fassbinder*, edited by Kurt Raab and Karsten Peters, 333–46. Munich: Bertelsmann Verlag, 1982.

Fassbinder, Rainer Werner. "Homage to Werner Schroeter." In *West German Filmmakers on Film: Visions and Voices*, ed. Eric Rentschler, 196–99. New York: Holmes & Meier, 1988.

Fassbinder, Rainer Werner. *Querelle Filmbuch*. Munich: Schirmer/Mosel, 1982.

Fassbinder, Rainer Werner with Dieter Schidor. "'Ich mußte mein Leben gelebt haben, um diesen Film machen zu können': Rainer Werner Fassbinder über Querelle." In *Fassbinder über Fassbinder: Die ungekürtzten Interviews*. Edited by Robert Fischer, 617–24. Frankfurt am Main: Verlag der Autoren, 2004.

Fleishman, Ian. *An Aesthetics of Injury: The Narrative Wound from Baudelaire to Tarantino*. Evanston, IL: Northwestern University Press, 2018.

Fleishman, Ian. "Alter/Ego: Isabelle Huppert as Werner Schroeter's Double." In *Performative Opacity in the Work of Isabelle Huppert*, edited by Iggy Cortez and Ian Fleishman, 48–69. Edinburgh: Edinburgh University Press, 2023.

Fleishman, Ian. "Rolf Hammerschmidt's *Boytropolis* and the Ethno-Ecological Imaginary." *Environmental Humanities* 14, no. 3 (2022): 680–98.

Flieger, Jerry Aline. "Dream, Humor and Power in Genet's *Notre-Dame-des-Fleurs*." *French Forum* 9, no. 1 (January 1984): 69–83.

Flinn, Caryl. "Declined Invitations: Repetition in Fassbinder's Queer 'Mono-musical.'" In *A Companion to Rainer Werner Fassbinder*. Edited by Brigitte Peucker, 313–32. Chichester, UK: Wiley-Blackwell, 2012.

Flinn, Caryl. *The New German Cinema: Music, History, and the Matter of Style*. Berkeley: University of California Press, 2004.

Fox, Alistair. "Auteurism, Personal Cinema and the Fémis Generation: The Case of François Ozon." In *A Companion to Contemporary French Cinema*. Edited by Alistair Fox, Michel Marie, Raphaëlle Moine, and Hilary Radner, 508–65. Chichester, UK: John Wiley & Sons, 2015.

Frank, Adam, and Elizabeth A. Wilson. "Like-Minded." *Critical Inquiry* 38, no. 4 (Summer 2012): 870–77.

Galef, Harald, and David Galef. "What Was Camp." *Studies in Popular Culture* 13, no. 2 (1991): 11–25.

Geertz, Clifford. "Thinking as a Moral Act: Anthropological Fieldwork in the New States." *Antioch Review* 28, no. 2 (Summer 1968): 139–58.

GEHITU. "Une nouvelle amie / The New Girlfriend: Sebastiane 2014 Award." Laudatory text, September 26, 2014. https://www.sansebastianfestival.com/2014/related_news/1/4843/in.

Gemünden, Gerd, Alice Kuzniar, and Klaus Phillips. "From Taboo Parlor to Porn and Passing: An Interview with Monika Treut." *Film Quarterly* 50, no. 3 (1997): 2–12.

Genet, Jean. *Fragments*. Translated by Charlotte Mandell. Stanford, CA: Stanford University Press, 2003.

Genet, Jean. *Journal du Voleur*. Paris: Gallimard, 1963.

Genet, Jean. *Miracle of the Rose*. Translated by Bernard Frechtman. New York: Grove Press, 1994.

Genet, Jean. *Notre-Dame-des-Fleurs*. Paris: Gallimard, 2000.

Genet, Jean. *Œuvres complètes*. 6 vols. Paris: Gallimard, 1952–79.

Genet, Jean. *Our Lady of the Flowers*. Translated by Bernard Frechtman. New York: Grove Press, 1963.

Genet, Jean. *Querelle*. Translated by Anselm Hollo. New York: Grove Press, 1974.

Genet, Jean. *Querelle de Brest*. Paris: Gallimard Imaginaire, 2010.

Genet, Jean. *The Thief's Journal*. Translated by Bernard Frechtman. New York: Grove Press, 1964.

Genet, Jean. "What Remains of a Rembrandt Torn into Little Squares All the Same Size and Shot down the Toilet." In *Fragments of the Artwork*. Translated by Charlotte Mandell, 91–102. Stanford, CA: Stanford University Press, 2003.

Genette, Gérard. *Narrative Discourse: An Essay in Method*. Translated by Jane Lewin. Ithaca, NY: Cornell University Press, 1980.

Genetti, Stefano. "La scene, l'écran: questionnements identitaires et tensions du désir dans *Tom à la ferme* de Michel Marc Bouchard et de Xavier Dolan." *Itinéraires: Littérature, textes, cultures* 2019, nos. 2–3 (2019): 1–13.

Gide, André. *Les caves du Vatican*. Paris: Gallimard, 1996.

Gide, André. *The Counterfeiters with Journal of "The Counterfeiters."* Translated by Dorothy Bussy and Justin O'Brien. New York: Alfred A. Knopf, 1972.

Gide, André. *Essais critiques*. Paris: Gallimard, 1999.

Gide, André. *Journal*. Edited by Eric Marty. 2 vols. Paris: Gallimard, 1996.

Gide, André. *Journals: 1914–1927*. Urbana: University of Illinois Press, 2000.

Gide, André. *Judge Not*. Urbana: University of Illinois, 2003.

Gide, André. *Lafcadio's Adventures*. Translated by Dorothy Bussy. New York: Vintage Books, 2003.

Gide, André. *Ne jugez pas*. Paris: Gallimard, 1969.

Gide, André. *Romans et récits: Œuvres lyriques et dramatiques*. 2 vols. Paris: Gallimard, 2009.

Giles, Jane. *The Cinema of Jean Genet: Un chant d'amour*. London: BFI, 1991.

Ginsberg, Elaine K. "Introduction: The Politics of Passing." In *Passing and the Fictions of Identity*, edited by Elaine K. Ginsberg, 1–18. Durham, NC: Duke University Press, 1996.

Glassco, David. "Films Out of Books: Bergman, Visconti, Mann." *Mosaic* 16, nos. 1–2 (Winter-Spring 1983): 165–73.

Goulet, Alain. "Sur une figure obsédante—vers l'origine de la création littéraire." *La revue des lettres modernes*, no. 1033 (1991): 47–60.

Grandena, Florian, and Pascal Gagné. "Xavier Dolan's Backward Cinema: Straight Spaces, Queer Temporality, and Genealogical Interruptions in *Tom at the Farm* and *It's Only the End of the World*." In *The Films of Xavier Dolan*, edited by Andrée Lafontaine, 80–97. Edinburgh: Edinburgh University Press, 2019.

Gregg, Ronald. "Fassbinder's *Fox and His Friends* and Gay Politics in the 1970s." In *A Companion to Rainer Werner Fassbinder*, edited by Brigitte Peucker, 564–78. Chichester, UK: Wiley-Blackwell, 2012.

Grundmann, Roy. "*Querelle*'s Finality." In *A Companion to Rainer Werner Fassbinder*, edited by Brigitte Peucker, 579–603. Chichester, UK: Wiley-Blackwell, 2012.

Grundman, Roy. "The Passions of Werner Schroeter: An Introduction." In *Werner Schroeter*. Edited by Roy Grundmann, 7–56. Vienna: Österreiches Filmmuseum and the SYNEMA-Gesellschaft für Film und Medien, 2018.

Hain, Mark. "Explicit Ambiguity: Sexual Identity, Hitchcockian Criticism and the Films of François Ozon." *Quarterly Review of Film and Video* 24, no. 3 (2007): 277–88.

Halberstam, Jack. *Female Masculinity*. Durham, NC: Duke University Press, 2018.

Halberstam, Jack. *The Queer Art of Failure*. Durham, NC: Duke University Press, 2011.

Halle, Randall. "Rainer, Rosa and Werner: New Gay Film as a Counter-Public." In *A Companion to Rainer Werner Fassbinder*, edited by Brigitte Peucker, 542–63. Chichester, UK: Wiley-Blackwell, 2012.

Halperin, David. "The Normalization of Queer Theory." *Journal of Homosexuality* 24, nos. 2–4 (2003): 339–43.

Halperin, David. *Saint Foucault: Towards a Gay Hagiography*. Oxford: Oxford University Press, 1995.

Halperin, David. *What Do Gay Men Want? An Essay on Sex, Risk and Subjectivity*. Ann Arbor: University of Michigan Press, 2007.

Halperin, David, and Valerie Traub, eds. *Gay Shame*. Chicago: University of Chicago Press, 2009.

Handyside, Fiona. "Melodrama and Ethics in François Ozon's *Gouttes d'eau sur pierres brûlantes/Water Drops on Burning Rocks* (2000)." *Studies in French Cinema* 7, no. 3 (2007): 207–18.

Hardt, Michael. "Prison Time." *Yale French Studies* 91 (1997): 64–69.

Harper, Phillip Bryan. "'The Subversive Edge': *Paris Is Burning*, Social Critique and the Limits of Subjective Agency." *diacritics* 24, nos. 2–3 (Summer–Autumn 1994): 90–103.

Harrison, Kelby. *Sexual Deceit: The Ethics of Passing*. Lanham, MD: Lexington Books, 2013.

Heaney, Emma. *The New Woman: Literary Modernism, Queer Theory, and the Trans Feminine Allegory*. Evanston, IL: Northwestern University Press, 2017.

Heine, Heinrich. *Songs of Love and Grief: A Bilingual Anthology in the Verse Forms of the Originals*. Translated by Walter W. Arndt. Evanston, IL: Northwestern University Press, 1995.

Hocquenghem, Guy. *Homosexual Desire*. Durham, NC: Duke University Press, 1993.

Hoggard, Liz. "Vampire of the Senses." *The Guardian*, August 10, 2003. https://www.theguardian.com/film/2003/aug/10/edinburghfilmfestival2003.edinburghfilmfestival.

Hotz-Davies, Ingrid. "The Jewel in the Gutter: Camp and the Incorporation of Dirt." In *The Dark Side of Camp: Queer Economies of Dirt, Dust and Patina*, edited by Ingrid Hotz-Davies, Georg Vogt, and Franziska Bergmann, 6–25. New York: Routledge, 2018.

Hotz-Davies, Ingrid, Georg Vogt, and Franziska Bergmann. "Introduction: 'The Dirt Doesn't Get Any Worse': The Alliance of Camp and Dirt." In *The Dark Side of Camp: Queer Economies of Dirt, Dust and Patina*, edited by Ingrid Hotz-Davies, Georg Vogt, and Franziska Bergmann, 1–11. New York: Routledge, 2018.

Iser, Wolfgang. *The Implied Reader: Patterns of Communication in Prose Fiction from Bunyan to Beckett*. Baltimore: Johns Hopkins University Press, 1974.

James, Alison. "Le fait divers aux frontières de la fiction: la rhétorique documentaire d'André Gide." *Bulletin des Amis d'André Gide* 46, no. 177/178 (January-April 2013): 75–86.

James, Caryn. "Review/Film; 'Seduction: The Cruel Woman,' a Study in Power." *New York Times*, November 3, 1989, C17.

Johnson, E. Patrick. *Appropriating Blackness: Performance and the Politics of Authenticity*. Durham, NC: Duke University Press, 2003.

Johnson, G. Allen. "Fassbinder Revisited, Ozon's 'Water Drops on Burning Rocks.'" IndieWire, July 14, 2000. https://www.indiewire.com/2000/07/reviews-fassbinder-revisited-ozons-water-drops-on-burning-rocks-81534/.

Kirst, Karoline. "Walter Benjamin's 'Denkbild': Emblematic Historiography of the Recent Past." *Monatshefte* 86, no. 4 (Winter 1994): 514–24.

Knegt, Peter. "Xavier Dolan Gets Respect." *Film Quarterly* 68, no. 2 (Winter 2014): 31–36.

Koepnick, Lutz. "Horn | Huppert | Horn." In *Performative Opacity in the Work of Isabelle Huppert*, edited by Iggy Cortez and Ian Fleishman, 123–38. Edinburgh: Edinburgh University Press, 2023.

Kollias, Hector. "Jean Genet's Queer Origins: A Reading of *Querelle de Brest*." *French Studies* 60, no. 4 (2006): 479–88.

Kotte, Claudia. "Fast and Furious: The Sound and the Fury in Xavier Dolan's *Mommy*." *French Forum* 44, no. 2 (Fall 2019): 321–32.

Kristeva, Julia. *Powers of Horror: An Essay on Abjection*. Translated by Leon S. Roudiez. New York: Columbia University Press, 1982.

Kuzniar, Alice. *The Queer German Cinema*. Stanford, CA: Stanford University Press, 2000.

Lafontaine, Andrée. Introduction to *ReFocus: The Films of Xavier Dolan*. Edinburgh: Edinburgh University Press, 2022.

Laforgue, Pierre. *"Notre-Dame-des-Fleurs" où La Symphonie carcérale*. Toulouse: Presses Universitaires du Mirail, 2002.

LaGuardia, David. *Intertextual Masculinity in French Renaissance Literature: Rabelais, Brantôme and the "Cent nouvelles nouvelles."* Aldershot, UK: Ashgate, 2008.

Langford, Michelle. *Allegorical Images: Tableau, Time and Gesture in the Cinema of Werner Schroeter*. Bristol, UK: Intellect Books, 2006.

Lawlor, Leonard. "Auto-Affection." In *Jacques Derrida: Key Concepts*, edited by Claire Colebrook, 130–38. London: Routledge, 2014.

Leys, Ruth. "Affect and Intention: A Reply to William E. Connolly." *Critical Inquiry* 37, no. 4 (Summer 2011): 799–805.

Leys, Ruth. "Facts and Mood: A Reply to My Critics." *Critical Inquiry* 37, no. 4 (Summer 2011): 882–91.

Leys, Ruth. "The Turn to Affect: A Critique." *Critical Inquiry* 37, no. 3 (Spring 2011): 434–62.

Lingel, Jessa. "Adjusting the Borders: Bisexual Passing and Queer Theory." *Journal of Bisexuality* 9, nos. 3–4 (2009): 381–405.

Livak, Leonid. *How It Was Done in Paris: Russian Émigré Literature and French Modernism*. Madison: University of Wisconsin Press, 2003.

Louar, Nadia. "Notre dame du queer ou du mauvais genre en traduction." *Palimpsestes* 21 (2008): 121–34.

Love, Heather. "Beginning with *Stigma*." *GLQ* 25, no. 1 (2019): 33–38.

Love, Heather. "Doing Being Deviant: Deviance Studies, Description and the Queer Ordinary," Special issue on "Queer Theory without Antinormativity," *differences* 26, no. 1 (2015): 74–95.

Love, Heather. *Feeling Backward: Loss and the Politics of Queer History*. Cambridge, MA: Harvard University Press, 2007.

Love, Heather. *Underdogs: Social Deviance and Queer Theory*. Chicago: University of Chicago Press, 2021.

Lucey, Michael. "Genet's *Notre-Dame-des-Fleurs*: Fantasy and Sexual Identity." *Yale French Studies* 91 (1997): 80–102.

Lucey, Michael. *Gide's Bent: Sexuality, Politics, Writing*. Oxford: Oxford University Press, 1995.

Lucey, Michael. *Never Say I: Sexuality in the First Person in Colette, Gide, and Proust*. Durham, NC: Duke University Press, 2006.

Lucey, Michael. *Someone: The Pragmatics of Misfit Sexualities from Colette to Hervé Guibert*. Chicago: University of Chicago Press, 2019.

Luttmann, Stephen. "Narrators, Narrated Realities and the Nature of Artwork in Jean Genet's *Querelle de Brest* and Rainer Werner Fassbinder's Film *Querelle*." *Kodikas/Code/Ars semeiotica* 14, nos. 1–2 (1991): 9–34.

Maddison, Stephen. "All about Women: Pedro Almodóvar and the Heterosocial Dynamic." *Textual Practice* 14, no. 2 (2000): 265–84.

Marques, Sandrine. "Xavier Dolan 'dégoûté' par les prix récompensant les films gays." *Le Monde*, September 20, 2014. http://www.lemonde.fr/culture/article/2014/09/20/xavier-dolan-degoute-par-les-prix-recompensant-les-films-gays_4490979_3246.html.

Marshall, Bill. "Spaces and Times of Québec in Films by Xavier Dolan." In *The Films of Xavier Dolan*, edited by Andrée Lafontaine, 101–18. Edinburgh: Edinburgh University Press, 2019.

Marshall, Bill. "Spaces and Times of Québec in Two Films by Xavier Dolan." *Nottingham French Studies* 55, no. 2 (2016): 189–208.

Massimi, Fulvia. "The Transgressive Cinema of Xavier Dolan." In *The Films of Xavier Dolan*, edited by Andrée Lafontaine, 31–51. Edinburgh: Edinburgh University Press, 2019.

Massis, Henri. "L'influence de M. André Gide." *La revue universelle*, November 15, 1921.

Mavor, Carol. *Reading Boyishly: Roland Barthes, J. M. Barrie, Jacques Henri Lartigue, Marcel Proust, and D. W. Winnicott*. Durham, NC: Duke University Press, 2007.

Maynard, Steven. "What Color Is Your Underwear? Class, Whiteness and Homoerotic Advertising." *Border/Lines* 32 (1994): 4–9.

Mench, Chris. "Troye Sivan's 'Bloom' Is a Metaphor-Filled Ode to Bottoming." *Genius*, May 4, 2018. https://genius.com/a/troye-sivan-s-bloom-is-a-metaphor-filled-ode-to-bottoming.

Mennel, Barbara. "Wanda's Whip: Recasting Masochism's Fantasy—Monika Treut's *Seduction: The Cruel Woman*." In *Triangulated Visions: Women in Recent German Cinema*, 153–62. Albany: State University of New York Press, 1998.

Meyer, Moe, ed. *The Politics and Poetics of Camp*. London: Routledge, 1994.

Milne, Anna-Louise. "Gide's Polymorphous Perversity, or French Modernism's Arrested Development." *Romanic Review* 99, nos. 1–2 (2008): 103–18.

Morrison, James. "Still New, Still Queer, Still Cinema?" *GLQ* 12, no. 1 (2006): 135–46.

Muñoz, José Esteban. *Disidentifications: Queers of Color and the Performance of Politics*. Minneapolis: University of Minnesota Press, 1999.

Nagl, Tobias, and Janelle Blankenship. "'So Much Tenderness': Günther Kaufmann and the Ambivalences of Interracial Desire." In *A Companion to Rainer Werner Fassbinder*, edited by Brigitte Peucker, 516–41. Chichester, UK: Wiley-Blackwell, 2012.

Newton, Esther. *Mother Camp: Female Impersonators in America*. Chicago: University of Chicago Press, 1979.

Nietzsche, Friedrich. "On Truth and Lying in an Extramoral Sense." In *Friedrich Nietzsche on Rhetoric and Language*, edited by Sander L. Gilman, Carole Blair, and David J. Parent, 246–57. Oxford: Oxford University Press, 1989.

Ngai, Sianne. *Ugly Feelings*. Cambridge, MA: Harvard University Press, 2005.

Nottet-Chedeville, Élise. "Les évolutions poétiques de Genet: Expérimentations stylistiques et opportunisme littéraire." In *Écritures évolutives aux XXe et XXIe siècles*. edited by Sophie Jollin-Bertocchi, 108–25. Leiden: Brill-Rodolpi, 2019.

Nottet-Chedeville, Élise. "Genet et la rhapsodie poétique." *Genesis* 47 (2018): 141–54.

Nyong'o, Tavia. *Afro-Fabulations: The Queer Drama of Black Life*. New York: New York University Press, 2019.

Nyungen, Tan Hong. *A View from the Bottom: Asian American Masculinity and Sexual Representation*. Durham, NC: Duke University Press, 2014.

O'Connor, Roisin. "Troye Sivan Criticizes Interviewer for Asking If He's a 'Top or Bottom.'" *The Independent*, August 29, 2019. https://www.independent.co.uk/arts-entertainment/music/news/troye-sivan-interview-top-bottom-question-boyfriend-shawn-mendes-a9083106.html.

Olsen, Mark. "Indie Focus: In 'Mommy,' Xavier Dolan Looks Things in the Eye." *Los Angeles Times*, January 17, 2015. https://www.latimes.com/entertainment/movies/la-et-mn-ca-xavier-dolan-20150118-story.html.

O'Neill, Shane, and Matthew Schneier. "What Is Camp (Now)?" *New York Times*, May 4, 2019. https://www.nytimes.com/video/style/100000006484770/met-gala-camp.html.

Pahl, Katrin. "Queer Procreation: Reading Kleist Plantwise." *Qui Parle* 28, no. 1 (2019): 137–66.

Palmer, Tim. "Style and Sensation in the Contemporary French Cinema of the Body." *Journal of Film and Video* 58, no. 3 (2006): 22–32.

Parent, Anne Martine, and Nicolas Xanthos. "Être de langage, être de désir: Fantasme, parole et identité dans *Gouttes d'eau sur pierres brûlantes* de François Ozon." *Australian Journal of French Studies* 43, no. 2 (2006): 195–209.

Peucker, Brigitte. *Aesthetic Spaces: The Place of Art in Film*. Evanston, IL: Northwestern University Press, 2019.

Phipps, Keith. "Interview with Todd Haynes." In *Todd Haynes: Interviews*, edited by Julia Leyda, 93–100. Jackson: University Press of Mississippi, 2014.

Pidduck, Julianne. "The Dolandrama: Queer Male Authorship and the Fabulous Leading Lady." In *The Films of Xavier Dolan*, edited by Andrée Lafontaine, 52–79. Edinburgh: Edinburgh University Press, 2019.

Plotz, John. "Objects of Abjection: The Animation of Difference in Jean Genet's Novels," *Twentieth-Century Literature* 44, no. 1 (Spring 1998): 100–118.

Quandt, James. "Ecstatically Florid Farragoes." *New York Review of Books* 66, no. 11 (June 2019): 61–62.

Quandt, James. "Flesh and Blood: Sex and Violence in Recent French Cinema." *Artforum* 42, no. 6 (2004): 24–27.

Raykoff, Ivan. "Queer Patriotism in the Eurovision Song Contest." In *The Oxford Handbook of Music and Queerness*, edited by Fred Everett Maus and Sheila Whiteley, 503–21. Oxford: Oxford University Press, 2022.

Redrobe, Karen. *Vanishing Women: Magic, Film, and Feminism*. Durham, NC: Duke University Press, 2003.

Rees-Roberts, Nick. "Fade to Gray: Dolan's Pop Fashion and Surface Style." In *The Films of Xavier Dolan*, edited by Andrée Lafontaine, 209–27. Edinburgh: Edinburgh University Press, 2019.

Rees-Roberts, Nick. *French Queer Cinema*. Edinburgh: Edinburgh University Press, 2008.

Reid, Victoria. *Gide and Curiosity*. Amsterdam: Rodolpi, 2009.

Reis, Levilson C. "Goodbye, 'Temporary' Transvestites—Hello, New Girlfriend! Ozon's Transgenre and Transgender Crossovers in *Une nouvelle amie* (2014)." *French Screen Studies* 20, no. 1 (2021): 42–66.

Resmini, Mauro. "Reframing the New French Extremity: Cinema, Theory, Mediation." *Camera Obscura* 30, no. 3 (2015): 161–87.

Rich, B. Ruby. *New Queer Cinema: The Director's Cut*. Durham, NC: Duke University Press, 2013.

Rich, B. Ruby. "Queer and Present Danger." *Sight and Sound* 10, no. 3 (March 2000): 22–25.

Riemann, Andrea. "Subjection and Power in Monika Treut and Elfi Mikesch's *Seduction*—the Cruel Woman: An Extension of the Configuration of Power in Rainer Werner Fassbinder's Late Oeuvre." In *Queer Cinema in Europe*, edited by Robin Griffiths, 181–93. Bristol: Intellect Books, 2008.

Ringler, Susan J. "Gide's 'Les Faux-monnayeurs': Demons and Present Tense Verbs." *Romance Notes* 20, no. 1 (Fall 1979): 29–34.

Rioux, Christian. "Méfions-nous des rebelles." *Le Devoir*, October 17, 2014. http://www.ledevoir.com/societe/actualites-en-societe/421369/mefions-nous-des-rebelles.

Robinson, Amy. "It Takes One to Know One: Passing and Communities of Common Interest." *Critical Inquiry* 20, no. 4 (Summer 2009): 715–36.

Robinson, Keith. "The Passion and the Pleasure: Foucault's Art of Not Being Oneself." *Theory, Culture and Society* 20, no. 2 (2003): 119–44.

Robinson, Peter. "Interview with Troye Sivan: 'I Feel So Much More Fully Realized as a Person.'" *Pop Justice*, March 1, 2018. https://www.popjustice.com/articles/troye-sivan-interview-i-feel-more-fully-realised-as-a-person/.

Rohy, Valerie. "Displacing Desire: Passing, Nostalgia and *Giovanni's Room*." In *Passing and the Fictions of Identity*, edited by Elaine K. Ginsberg, 218–33. Durham, NC: Duke University Press, 1996.

Rooney, David. "Tom at the Farm: Venice Review." In *Hollywood Reporter*, September 2, 2013. https://www.hollywoodreporter.com/news/general-news/tom-at-farm-venice-review-619296/.

Ross, Marlon. "Beyond the Closet as Raceless Paradigm." In *Black Queer Studies: A Critical Anthology*, edited by Patrick E. Johnson and Mae G. Henderson, 161–89. Durham, NC: Duke University Press, 2005.

Samper Vendrell, Javier. *Seduction of Youth: Homosexual Rights in the Weimar Republic*. Toronto: University of Toronto Press, 2020.

Samper Vendrell, Javier. "Van Gloeden's Dog: Methodological Notes on Photography and the History of Intergenerational Intimacy." *Journal of the History of Sexuality* 33, no. 3 (September 2024): 41–37.

Samuels, Ellen. "My Body, My Closet: Invisible Disability and the Limits of Coming-Out Discourse." *GLQ* 9, no. 1 (2003): 223–55.

Sartre, Jean-Paul. Introduction to Jean Genet, *Our Lady of the Flowers*. Translated by Bernard Frechtman, 9–57. New York: Grove Press, 1963.

Savage Brosman, Catharine. "Gide et le démon." *Claudel Studies* 13, no. 2 (January 1986): 46–57.

Schehr, Lawrence R. *French Gay Modernism*. Urbana: University of Illinois Press, 2004.

Schilt, Thibaut. *François Ozon*. Urbana: University of Illinois Press, 2011.

Schlossberg, Linda. "Introduction: Rites of Passing," in *Passing: Identity and Interpretation in Sexuality, Race and Religion*, edited by María Carla Sánchez and Linda Schlossberg, 1–12. New York: New York University Press, 2001.

Schneider, Vanessa. "Xavier Dolan, cinémaniaque." *Le Monde*, May 25, 2016. https://www.lemonde.fr/m-gens-portrait/article/2016/05/27/xavier-dolan-cine-maniaque_4927720_4497229.html.

Schroeter, Werner, and Michel Foucault. "Passion according to Werner Schroeter." Translated by John Jonston. In *Werner Schroeter*. Edited by Roy Grundmann, 206–14. Vienna: Österreiches Filmmuseum and the SYNEMA-Gesellschaft für Film und Medien, 2018.

Schroeter, Werner with Claudia Lenssen. *Days of Twilight, Nights of Frenzy: A Memoir*. Translated by Anthea Bell. Chicago: University of Chicago Press, 2017.

Schroeter, Werner with Claudia Lenssen. *Tage im Dämmer, Nächte im Rausch: Autobiographie*. Berlin: Aufbau Verlag, 2011.

Sedgwick, Eve Kosofsky. *The Epistemology of the Closet*. Berkeley: University of California Press, 1990.

Sedgwick, Eve Kosofsky. "How to Bring Your Kids Up Gay: The War on Effeminate Boys." In *Tendencies*, 154–64. Durham, NC: Duke University Press, 1999.

Sedgwick, Eve Kosofsky. *Touching Feeling: Affect, Pedagogy, Performativity*. Durham, NC: Duke University Press, 2002.

Segal, Naomi. *André Gide: Pederasty and Pedagogy*. Oxford: Clarendon Press, 1998.

Segal, Naomi. "Gide's Skin." In *Consensuality: Didiez Anzieu, Gender, and the Sense of Touch*, 79–100. Amsterdam: Rodopi, 2009.

Shepard, Dax. "Shawn Mendes." *Armchair Expert with Dax Shepard*. Podcast audio. December 15, 2020. https://armchairexpertpod.com/pods/shawn-mendes.

Shaviro, Steven. "Masculinity, Spectacle and the Body of *Querelle*." In *The Cinematic Body*, 158–99. Minneapolis: University of Minnesota Press, 1989.

Skinner, Oliver. "Shawn Mendes's Revelatory New Album Art Shows in a Single Glance That the Pop Star Is Growing Up." *CBC Arts*, May 23, 2018. https://www.cbc.ca/arts/shawn-mendes-s-relevatory-new-album-art-shows-in-a-single-glance-that-the-pop-star-is-growing-up-1.4678074.

Sieglohr, Ulirke. "Divine Rapture: The Films of Werner Schroeter." *Film Comment* 48, no. 3 (May/June 2012): 50–55.

Silverman, Kaja. *Male Subjectivity at the Margins*. New York: Routledge, 1992.

Snorton, C. Riley. *Black on Both Sides: A Racial History of Trans Identity*. Minneapolis: University of Minnesota Press, 2017.

Snorton, C. Riley. "'A New Hope': The Psychic Life of Passing." *Hypatia* 24, no. 3 (Summer 2009): 77–92.

Snorton, C. Riley. *Nobody Is Supposed to Know: Black Sexuality on the Down Low*. Minneapolis: University of Minnesota Press, 2014.

Solomon, Alisa. "It's Never Too Late to Switch." In *Crossing the Stage: Controversies on Cross-Dressing*, edited by Leslie Ferris, 144–54. London: Routledge, 1993.

Sontag, Susan. "Notes on 'Camp.'" In *Against Interpretation and Other Essays*, 275–92. New York: Picador, 1966.

Spillers, Hortense. "Mama's Baby, Papa's Maybe: An American Grammar Book." *Diacritics* 17, no. 2 (Summer 1987): 64–81.

Stockton, Kathryn Bond. *Beautiful Bottom, Beautiful Shame: Where "Black" Meets "Queer."* Durham, NC: Duke University Press, 2006.

Stone, Sandy. "The Empire Strikes Back: A Posttransexual Manifesto." *Camera Obscura* 10, no. 2 (1992): 150–76.

Stonely, Peter. *A Queer History of the Ballet*. London: Routledge, 2007.

Swain, John, and Colin Cameron. "Unless Otherwise Stated: Discourses of Labelling and Identity in Coming Out." In *Disability Discourse*, edited by Marian Corker and Sally French, 68–78. Philadelphia: Open University Press, 1999.

Terada, Rei. *Feeling in Theory: Emotion after the "Death of the Subject."* Cambridge, MA: Harvard University Press, 2003.

Timár, Eszter. "The Body of Shame in Affect Theory and Deconstruction." *Parallax* 25, no. 2 (2019): 197–212.

Tobin, Robert Deam. *Peripheral Desires: The German Discovery of Sex*. Philadelphia: University of Pennsylvania Press, 2015.

Treut, Monika. "Die Zeremonie der blutenden Rose: Vorüberlegungen zu einem Filmprojekt." *Frauen und Film* 36 (February 1984): 35–43.

Van Godtsenhoven, Karen. "WorldPride at the Met: The Otherness of Camp." Metropolitan Museum of Art. June 24, 2019. https://www.metmuseum.org/blogs/now-at-the-met/2019/worldpride-met-otherness-camp.

Vaughn, Hannah. "Filming Fracture in Xavier Dolan's *J'ai tué ma mère*." *Québec Studies* (Winter 2013): 107–15.

von Moltke, Johannes. "Camping in the Art Closet: The Politics of Camp and Nation in German Film." *New German Critique* 63 (Autumn 1994): 76–106.

von Praunheim, Rosa. "With Fond Greetings to Champagne-Schroeter." In *West German Filmmakers on Film: Visions and Voices*, edited by Eric Rentschler, 191–96. New York: Holmes & Meier, 1988.

Walker, Lisa. *Looking Like What You Are: Sexual Style, Race and Lesbian Identity*. New York: New York University Press, 2001.

Wall, Cheryl A. "Passing for What? Aspects of Identity in Nella Larsen's Novels." *Black American Literature Forum* 20, no. 1–2 (Spring-Summer 1986): 97–111.

Waugh, Thomas. *Fruit Machine: Twenty Years of Writings on Queer Cinema*. Durham, NC: Duke University Press, 2000.

Weheliye, Alexander. *Habeus Viscus: Racializing Assemblages, Biopolitics, and Black Feminist Theories of the Human*. Durham, NC: Duke University Press, 2014.

Wertheim, Bonnie. "What Is Camp? The Met Gala 2019 Theme Explained." *New York Times*, May 4, 2019. https://www.nytimes.com/2019/05/04/style/met-gala-what-is-camp.html.

Wetters, Kirk. *Demonic History: From Goethe to the Present*. Evanston, IL: Northwestern University Press, 2014.

White, Armond. "Ozon Elevates Gay Sensibility." *Out*, March 17, 2017. https://www.out.com/armond-white/2017/3/17/ozon-elevates-gay-sensibility.

White, Armond. "Some Like It Trans." *Out*, September 18, 2015. https://www.out.com/armond-white/2015/9/18/francois-ozon-and-new-girlfriend-win-trans-race.

White, Edmund. Preface to *The Cinema of Jean Genet: Un chant d'amour*. By Jane Giles, 1–4. London: BFI, 1991.

White, Edmund. *Genet: A Biography*. New York: Alfred A. Knopf, 1993.

Whitman, Walt. *Song of Myself and Other Poems by Walt Whitman*. Berkeley, CA: Counterpoint, 2010.

Wiegman, Robyn, and Elizabeth A. Wilson. "Introduction: Antinormativity's Queer Conventions." *differences* 26, no. 1 (2015): 1–25.

Wiles, Mary M. "A Double Voice: The Dual Paternity of *Querelle*." In *Postmodernism in the Cinema*, edited by Cristina Degli-Esposti, 231–59. Providence: Berghain Books, 1998.

Williams, Linda. *Hard Core: Power, Pleasure, and the Frenzy of the Visible*. Berkeley: University of California Press, 1999.

Wilper, James P. "Rewritings, Adaptations, and Gay Literary Criticism: Thomas Mann's *Death in Venice*." *Adaptation* 8, no. 1 (2014): 1–15.

Wilson, Emma. "Pathos as Queer Sociality in Contemporary European Visual Culture: François Ozon's Time to Leave." In *What's Queer about Europe?: Productive Encounters and Re-Enchanting Paradigms*, edited by Mireille Rosello and Sudeep Dasgupta, 148–70. New York: Fordham University Press, 2013.

Wilson, Jennifer. "The Shareable Feast of Jeremy Allen White's Calvin Klein Ad." *New Yorker*. January 10, 2024. https://www.newyorker.com/culture/annals-of-appearances/the-shareable-feast-of-jeremy-allen-whites-calvin-klein-ad.

Winnicott, D. W. "Transitional Objects and Transitional Phenomena." In *Playing and Reality*, 15–20. New York and London: Routledge, 1996.

Wojcik, Pamela Robertson. *Guilty Pleasures: Feminist Camp from Mae West to Madonna*. Durham, NC: Duke University Press, 1996.

Wojcik, Pamela Robertson. "Mae West's Maids: Race, Authenticity, and the Discourse of Camp." In *Hop on Pop: The Politics and Pleasures of Popular Culture*, edited by Henry Jenkins, Jane Shattuc, and Tara McPherson, 287–99. Durham, NC: Duke University Press, 2003.

Wollen, Peter. *Raiding the Icebox: Reflections on Twentieth-Century Culture*. London: Verso, 1993.

Woltersdorff, Volker. "'Grundsätzlich ist jeder homosexuell und deshalb ist es kein Problem': Homosexuelle Minderheiten und Fassbinders Filme." In *Rainer Werner Fassbinder*, edited by Michael Töteberg, 108–20. Munich: edition text+kritik, 2015.

Wyatt, Justin. "Cinematic/Sexual: An Interview with Todd Haynes." In *Todd Haynes: Interviews*, edited by Julia Leyda, 26–32. Jackson: University Press of Mississippi, 2014.

Die Zeit. "Garten der Lüste: Jean Genets Schattenwelt." Review of *Querelle*, by Rainer Werner Fassbinder. No. 38 (September 17, 1982). https://www.zeit.de/1982/38/garten-der-lueste/.

INDEX